OVER 375 OF OUR FAVORITE RECIPES FOR THE HOME CHEF, ALONG WITH TIPS AND

PREPARATION TECHNIQUES FROM THE CLASSROOMS OF THE WORLD'S PREMIER CULINARY COLLEGE

THE CULINARY INSTITUTE OF AMERICA

COOKBOOK

The Culinary Institute of America

HYDE PARK, NEW YORK • ST. HELENA, CALIFORNIA

Photography by Ben Fink

LEBHAR-FRIEDMAN BOOKS

NEW YORK • CHICAGO • LOS ANGELES • LONDON • PARIS • TOKYO

LIBRARY OF CONGRESS CATALOGING-IN-PUBLICATION DATA

Cataloging-in-publication data for this title is on file with the Library of Congress.

ISBN 978-0-86730-931-7

THE CULINARY INSTITUTE OF AMERICA

President: Dr. Tim Ryan

Vice-President, Continuing Education: Mark Erickson

Director of Intellectual Property: Nathalie Fischer

Editorial Project Manager: Mary Donovan

Recipe Testing Manager: Maggie Wheeler

LEBHAR-FRIEDMAN BOOKS

A company of Lebhar-Friedman, Inc., 425 Park Avenue, New York, New York 10022

Publisher: Maria Tufts

Art Director: Kevin Hanek

Manufactured in Malaysia on acid-free paper

CONTENTS

CHAPTER 3: Broths and Soups

CHAPTER 4: Pastas, Casseroles, and Light Fare

CHAPTER 5: Main Dishes

THE CULINARY INSTITUTE OF AMERICA:
A Sixty-Year Tradition of Excellence in Culinary Education

FROM THE PUBLISHER

Lebhar-Friedman Books is proud to have published *The Culinary Institute of America Cookbook* as well as several other cookbook titles for the home cook authored by the talented chef-instructors of the CIA. Our goal is to provide you with high-quality cookbooks from respected and authoritative sources, and we hope you enjoy this collection of favorite and most-requested recipes from the world's premier culinary college.

THE CULINARY INSTITUTE OF AMERICA

THE CULINARY INSTITUTE OF AMERICA (CIA) is a private, not-for-profit college dedicated to providing the world's best professional culinary education to aspiring culinarians, industry professionals, and food enthusiasts.

A Sixty-Year Tradition of Excellence

The Culinary Institute of America opened in 1946 as the New Haven Restaurant Institute, a small cooking school in downtown New Haven, CT, with an enrollment of 50 students and a faculty consisting of a chef, a baker, and a dietitian.

The Institute, at that time a vocational training school for World War II veterans, offered a 16-week program featuring instruction in 78 popular menus of the day. Members of the New Haven Restaurant Association sponsored the original school, whose founders, Frances Roth and Katharine Angell, served as its first director and chair of the board, respectively.

As the foodservice industry grew, so did enrollment, necessitating a move in 1947 to larger quarters: a 40-room mansion adjacent to Yale University. The school's name was changed to the Restaurant Institute of Connecticut, and in 1951 it became known as The Culinary Institute of America, reflecting the diversity of the student population.

The educational program was expanded to two years, and continuing education courses for industry professionals were introduced. By the time of Mrs. Roth's retirement in 1965, the school had increased its enrollment to 400 students.

In 1969, double-class sessions were initiated to accommodate a backlog of applications, and an auxiliary campus was leased. But with more than 1,000 students and with facilities strained to the maximum, the school's administrators launched a search for a new home. They found it in St. Andrew-on-Hudson, a former Jesuit novitiate in Hyde Park, New York.

A year later, the college purchased the five-story, 150-room building situated on 80 acres of land overlooking the Hudson River. The new school opened two years later after major renovations to the facility, and its main building was renamed Roth Hall.

The expanding curriculum and the additional space available in Roth Hall enabled the CIA to establish the Epicurean Room in 1973. The public restaurant provided a realistic, hands-on setting for students. Later renamed the Escoffier Restaurant, it was awarded a three-star rating by *The New York Times* and four stars by the *Mobil Travel Guide.* The

ABOVE: An instructor gives a demonstration in one of the classrooms of the Culinary Institute of America's Hyde Park campus, circa 1977. The CIA has graduated over 37,000 students with degrees in Culinary Arts and Baking and Pastry Arts, and its graduates are among the most sought after culinary professionals in the country.

restaurant has also won *Restaurants & Institutions* magazine's Ivy Award. Its menu highlights modern interpretations of classic French cuisine.

Today, students also gain experience in our other on-campus restaurants: the Ristorante Caterina de' Medici, St. Andrew's Café, the American Bounty Restaurant, and the Apple Pie Bakery Café Sponsored by Rich Products Corporation. CIA students also prepare and serve meals for catered functions and student and employee dining.

In 1981, the CIA became the only school authorized to administer the American Culinary Federa-

tion's (ACF) master chef certification exam. The CIA employs the largest concentration of master chefs certified through the 10-day ACF-sponsored exam.

In 1993, the college was approved by the New York Board of Regents to offer two Bachelor of Professional Studies (B.P.S.) degrees—one in culinary arts management, the other in baking and pastry arts management.

The Culinary Institute of America at Greystone, a branch campus located in California's Napa Valley, opened its doors in 1995. The CIA continued to grow and in 2008 established a second branch campus, this time in San Antonio, Texas. That same year, the CIA at Astor Center opened in New York City.

Today the college enrolls more than 2,800 students in its degree programs. The CIA also offers a variety of one- to five-day Culinary Boot Camp courses for home cooks and food enthusiasts who want to expand their culinary skills and knowledge through professional instruction. To date, more than 4,500 individuals have participated in these popular programs.

Leading the Way

Throughout its history, The Culinary Institute of America has played a pivotal role in shaping the future of foodservice and hospitality. This is due in large part to the caliber of people who make up the CIA community—its faculty, staff, students, and alumni—and their passion for the culinary arts and dedication to the advancement of the profession.

Headed by the visionary leadership of President Tim Ryan '77, the CIA education team is more than 135 members strong. These talented professionals who hail from 16 countries bring a vast breadth and depth of foodservice industry experience and insight to the CIA kitchens, classrooms, and research facilities. They've worked in some of the world's finest establishments, earned industry awards and professional certifications, and emerged victorious from countless international culinary competitions. And they continue to make their mark on the industry, through the students they teach, books they author, and leadership initiatives they champion.

The influence of the CIA in the food world can also be attributed to the efforts and achievements of its more than 37,000 successful alumni. CIA graduates are leaders in virtually every segment of the industry and bring the professionalism and commitment to excellence they learned at their alma mater to everything they do.

PRIOR TO COOKING

Mise en place (Fr.): Literally, "put in place." The preparation and assembly of ingredients, pans, utensils, and plates or serving pieces needed for a particular dish or service period.

Preparation prior to the ultimate stage of cooking is the most important step that any home cook must embrace, especially when you are trying to put a meal on the table within an allotted amount of time.

Good cooking is the result of carefully developing the best possible flavor and most perfect texture in any dish. Basic flavoring and aromatic combinations constitute the flavor base, and effective preparation prior to cooking is essential whether you are an aspiring home cook or a seasoned professional.

With some advance planning, smart shopping, an organized kitchen and time-saving techniques, healthy, exciting meals can become the norm rather than the exception in your household. You may also grow to enjoy the creative outlet it provides as well as the satisfaction of a delicious, home-cooked meal spent with your family.

To expedite your cooking time, build up a supply of products that are easy to access and easy to use. Quick meals generally have fewer ingredients; for this reason, you should use quality products that will most efficiently enhance meal flavor. Using inexpensive components of lesser quality in a meal inevitably leads to unsatisfactory results. A well-stocked pantry also provides a springboard to go beyond a given recipe, substituting ingredients and creating exciting variations.

ETHNIC PANTRIES

With the availability of international ingredients, it is easy to create meal variations with a particular ethnic flavor. Use some of the items on page xx as recipe substitutions.

EQUIPMENT

The right cooking equipment simplifies and speeds up meal preparation. Setting up a kitchen, however, reflects personal preference and depends on the amount of people typically fed as well as the types of food prepared. Expensive or fancy equipment is not essential, however, quality equipment will last a lifetime and is worth the investment.

TIME-SAVING TIPS

Efficiently using the little time you have for cooking is essential. The following suggestions will hopefully become second nature and your meal preparation a pleasurable experience.

SHOPPING

- Become familiar with a favorite market or two. Try to do all the shopping for staples only once a month or every few weeks, with fresh items purchased as needed.

- List some meals you will prepare, in advance. Use this to help plan your shopping trips.

- Keep a running shopping list in your kitchen, jotting down items when you are low. A list of essential pantry items follows.

- Freeze what you can so items are readily available, using the microwave to defrost items or thaw them in the refrigerator overnight.

- Make extra servings of meals and freeze for a later date. Freeze in usable sizes and in appropriate storage containers (rigid plastic with tight lids or heavy zip-close bags). Label and date the items.

- Freeze small amounts of broth or stock in non-stick muffin tins. Once frozen, twist as you would an ice cube tray, then place in a plastic bag. Or freeze directly in quart-sized, zip-close bags. Place in a mug for support as you fill the bags.

- Fresh herbs can be chopped, placed in ice cube trays with a bit of water, then frozen. Once frozen, the cubes can be placed in freezer bags, then easily added as you cook.

- Fresh herbs, garlic or shallots can also be pureed, mixed with some vegetable or olive oil and refrigerated or frozen in small portions.

BASIC PANTRY ITEMS

- All-purpose unbleached flour
- Cornstarch
- Baking powder
- Baking soda
- Sugar
- Confectioners' sugar
- Brown sugar
- Salt
- Black peppercorns

PASTA, GRAINS, AND LEGUMES

- Capellini (angel hair pasta)
- Egg noodles, medium
- Fettuccine
- Linguine
- Penne
- Basmati/Texmati rice
- Arborio rice (risotto)
- Couscous
- Lentils

OILS AND DRESSINGS

- Extra-virgin olive oil
- Vegetable oil
- Nonstick cooking spray
- Mayonnaise

VINEGARS

- Balsamic vinegar
- Red wine vinegar
- White wine vinegar

HERBS AND SPICES

- Bay leaf
- Basil
- Chili powder
- Dill
- Oregano
- Rosemary
- Sage
- Thyme

BROTHS AND STOCKS

Beef broth or stock

Chicken broth or stock

Vegetable broth or stock

CONDIMENTS AND SEASONINGS

Mustard (Dijon, whole-grain, honey)

Hot pepper sauce

Soy sauce

Worcestershire sauce

Wine (sherry, dry red/white)

DRIED FRUITS AND VEGETABLES

Raisins

Dried mushrooms

CANNED AND BOTTLED ITEMS

Tuna (chunk light/white, in water)

Peanut butter

Tomatoes, crushed

Tomato paste

Beans, black and red kidney

Artichoke hearts

- Freeze a stick of butter and use a vegetable peeler to shave bits onto food or grate the butter to mix in for baked items or mashed potatoes.

- If you don't use a pound of bacon quickly, roll the bacon up in groups of 2 to 4 slices. Store flat in the freezer in a zip-close bag. Once frozen, store as preferred.

- Partially frozen meat or poultry is easier to cut for sauces, soups, stir-fries and scaloppine.

- To save overripe fruit, such as bananas for using in bread, freeze in zip-close bags and thaw when needed.

- Peel raw ginger with a teaspoon. Freeze in a plastic bag, grating as needed.

- Open both ends of a tomato paste can, pushing one end with the lid to remove the paste onto some plastic wrap. Wrap and freeze. Slice off pieces as needed.

FRESH AND REFRIGERATED GOODS

- Store fresh asparagus upright in an inch or so of water and cover loosely with plastic.

- Avocados and pears will ripen more quickly in a brown paper bag.

- To use avocados, slice around the pit through both ends. Twist and separate the two halves. Using the blade of a chef's knife, lodge the knife into the pit, twist slightly and lift the pit out with the knife. Pry the pit off with another utensil. Use a paring knife to make slices inside the avocado, but not through the skin. With a spoon or spatula, loosen the slices just inside the skin and pop out.

- Blueberries can be refrigerated longer than strawberries or raspberries. Do not wash berries until just before needed, although raspberries should not be washed at all. Any berry can be easily frozen and used as needed.

DAIRY PANTRY

- Butter
- Eggs
- Milk
- Sour cream
- Parmesan cheese
- Ricotta cheese
- Variety of cheeses, shredded or whole

FRESH HERBS/VEGETABLES/FRUITS

- Chives, scallions
- Parsley
- Basil
- Ginger
- Broccoli florets
- Cabbage
- Carrots, peeled, baby
- Celery
- Onions, yellow
- Potatoes, Red Bliss
- Salad greens
- Tomatoes
- Yellow squash or zucchini
- White mushrooms
- Apples
- Pears
- Lemons, limes
- Tropical fruit (mangoes, papayas, etc.)

MEAT/POULTRY/SEAFOOD PANTRY

- Beef chuck, lean, or turkey, ground
- Chicken breasts, boneless, skinless
- Italian sausage, Bratwurst/Kielbasa
- White fish fillets
- Frozen shrimp, shelled, deveined

FROZEN VEGETABLES/FRUITS

- Bell peppers
- Green beans
- Corn kernels
- Green peas, petite
- Blueberries, strawberries
- Orange juice concentrate
- Spinach
- Vegetable blends
- French fries, hash browns

OTHER PANTRY ITEMS

- Frozen pie crusts
- Frozen pizza dough or base
- Frozen puff pastry

- To seed a cucumber or zucchini, slice it in half lengthwise, then slide a small spoon down the centers to scoop out the seeds. Use an ice cream scoop to remove seeds from winter squashes.

- If cheese sticks to your grater or dried fruit sticks to your knife, spray the grater or knife first with nonstick vegetable spray. Cleanly slice goat cheese or other soft cheeses with dental floss.

- To more quickly peel hard-boiled eggs, tap and roll the eggs until cracked all over. Peel from the flatter end with the air pocket, moving around the eggs in a spiral. To crumble the eggs for a salad or garnish, press the eggs through a mesh sieve or grate on a box grater.

- Keep fresh herbs stored in a tall container of water in the refrigerator. Trim the ends as you would flowers and add about 1 inch of water to the bottoms of the stems.

- Lemons or limes are more easily juiced by first rolling them firmly on a hard surface, which loosens the membranes inside. The spent lemons and limes can be kept frozen in a zip-close bag to use later for flavoring dishes, or to add to water to prevent the browning of cut apples, potatoes or artichokes.

- When selecting melons, check for a sweet aroma at the stem end. It should yield slightly to pressure. Honeydews are more difficult to assess. The rind should be creamy white without any green. Avoid any fruit with bruises or soft spots. To remove rinds quickly, slice off the ends, then place on end, slicing strips of rind off with a serrated knife. Cut the melon in half, remove seeds, then cut as desired.

- Store fresh mushrooms in a paper bag, so they can breathe.

- Besides slicing hard-boiled eggs, an egg slicer quickly cuts mushrooms and mozzarella cheese.

- Buy partially prepared fresh items such as shredded carrots or cheese, florets of broccoli and cauliflower, pre-sliced mushrooms, washed spinach and salad mixes.

- To chop a bell pepper quickly, slice the top off first, then stand the pepper up, slicing down the sides. This easily separates the core and seeds from the sides.

- When selecting chili peppers, generally red ones are sweeter than green as they are more ripe. Usually, the larger the chili, the less hot it is.

- If needing a certain weight of potatoes to peel or cut, get the largest size you can so there are less potatoes to prepare.

- Scissors are an easy way to cut scallions or chives into precise pieces.

- To easily shock blanched vegetables, fill a bowl with ice water, drain the vegetables through a strainer, then place the strainer into the ice water. The vegetables can easily be retrieved out of the strainer.

DRY GOODS

- Storing flour, sugar, grains, legumes and pasta in capped, half-gallon, wide-mouth preserving jars allows you to easily reach a measuring cup inside the opening.

- Starting with hot tap water quickens boiling time for pasta water. Using two pots initially,

Ethnic Pantry Items

MEXICAN

Barbecue sauce

Cilantro

Cumin

Jalapeño or chipotle peppers

Monterey Jack cheese

Refried beans

Salsa

Tortillas

CARIBBEAN/SOUTH AMERICAN

Avocados

Bananas

Coconuts

Collard greens

Hearts of palm

ASIAN

Coconut milk

Green and red curry pastes

Hoisin sauce

Mirin

Nori

Oyster sauce

Rice and soba noodles

Rice vinegar

Sesame oil

Soy sauce

Wasabi

MEDITERRANEAN/MIDDLE EASTERN

Anchovy paste

Chickpeas

Cornmeal

Dried apricots and dates

Eggplant

Goat cheese

Mint

Olives

Pesto

Pine nuts

Sun-dried tomatoes

Yogurt

FRENCH

Brie

Capers

Green peppercorns

Herbes de Provençe

Tarragon

INDIAN

Cardamom

Chutney

Curry paste/powder

Fennel seeds

Turmeric

Yogurt

then combining into one of them also hastens boiling time. Use thin dried pasta, such as angel hair, for quicker cooking. Fresh pasta cooks very quickly but the consistency is quite different from dried. Drain the pasta in a colander, holding it in the sink while you use the pasta pot to make the sauce.

- When using herbs and spices which are to be removed before serving, put them in a mesh tea ball. Close the ball and hang by the chain over the pot's side into the cooked item.

- Apply barbecue or other sauces to grilled items with a squeeze bottle.

SEASONINGS

Adding seasonings at the proper point in the cooking process is one of the keys to giving a finished dish the fullest possible flavor.

The array of seasonings added to a dish can run from the ordinary salt and pepper, to the more complex array of herb and spice blends, or marinades with oils, acids, or other aromatics. In every case, though, seasonings are meant to enhance flavor, not to detract from or overwhelm the dish.

Experimenting with different flavors allows for creativity, but don't forget the basics. With the abundance of fresh herbs, spices, and aromatics now available to the home cook, salt and pepper have been somewhat forgotten. Many beginning cooks sometimes fail to use these two essential seasonings early enough during cooking, or in a quantity large enough, to bring out the best flavor of the food.

DRY RUBS

Fresh herbs and other ingredients such as garlic, fresh or dry breadcrumbs, or grated cheeses can be blended into a paste or coating to add additional flavor to dishes. The ingredients can be moistened with oil, prepared mustard, or similar ingredients to create a texture than can easily adhere to a food, or make it easier to blend it into a dish as a final seasoning.

When a spice blend is used as a dry rub to coat food, the food is left to stand after application, under refrigeration, to absorb the flavors. Very often, these rubs contain some salt to help intensify the flavors in the dish.

Dry rubs may be left on the food during cooking or they may be scraped away first. Barbecued beef and Jamaican jerked pork are examples of dishes that may be prepared using a dry rub.

MARINADES

Marinades generally contain one or more of the following: oil, acid, and aromatics (spices, herbs, and vegetables).

Oils protect food from intense heat during cooking and help hold other flavorful ingredients in contact with the food.

Acids, such as vinegar, wine, yogurt, and citrus juices, flavor the food and change its texture. In some cases, acids firm or stiffen foods; in others, it breaks down connective fibers to make tough cuts of meat more tender while aromatics provide specific flavors.

Marinades can be used to flavor other items or as a dipping sauce. Any marinade which has held raw meat or poultry and is to be used as a dipping sauce must be cooked first. Marinating times vary according to the food's texture. Tender or delicate foods such as fish or poultry breast require less time, while a tougher cut of meat may be marinated for days.

KNIVES/CUTTING BOARDS

8-inch chef's knife

Paring knife

Serrated knife

Knife sharpener

2–3 wood or plastic cutting boards, different sizes

POTS/PANS

Made of hard anodized aluminum, enameled cast-iron or heavy stainless steel with copper or aluminum-enforced bottoms and tight-fitting lids.

1–2-quart saucepan

3–4-quart saucepan

6–8-quart saucepan

5–7-inch skillet (nonstick is helpful)

9–12-inch skillet (nonstick is helpful)

Wok

OVENPROOF BAKING DISHES

If pots and pans are not ovenproof, use glass, stainless steel or enamel-lined baking dishes with reinforced bottoms.

UTENSILS

Wire whisk

Wooden spoons

Metal and rubber spatulas

Tongs

Vegetable peeler

Measuring spoons

OTHER

Bowls

Colander, strainers

Measuring cups

Pepper mill

Hand grater

Salad spinner

Food processor

Can opener

Timer

Electric mixer

Microwave oven

Toaster oven

Blender, handheld

- Keep often-used utensils such as whisks, wooden spoons and spatulas in open containers that are easy to reach.

- Use the same cutting board for different ingredients, especially if used in the same recipe (this is not safe, however, with raw meat, poultry, fish or seafood). Place a damp paper towel under the cutting board to keep it secure, then use the paper towel to clean up scraps when done.

- A bench scraper or Chinese cleaver easily removes cut items from a cutting board.

- To spray pans or tins with nonstick spray and avoid covering your workspace as well, spray the item on the flat, open door of the dishwasher. The excess spray will be washed off when the dishwasher is run again.

- When using a standing mixer, place ingredients in the mixing bowl, then cover the front of the mixer and around the bowl with a piece of plastic or a damp towel. This will prevent ingredients from splattering out.

- Measure all dry ingredients with the same utensil first, then measure the liquid ingredients so you can avoid washing between measurements. Follow the same procedure with your food processor as well.

- Use pans with ovenproof handles so the same pan may be used for sautéing on the stove and finishing in the oven.

- Clean hands are often the quickest and most thorough tool for mixing some foods such as salads or other cold preparations.

- Anticipate cleanup while preparing and cooking items. Use as few dishes as possible, line pans with foil or use nonstick sprays and soak baked-on dishes as soon as possible. Paper towels or wax paper can be used instead of dishes to hold recipe ingredients such as grated cheese or minced garlic.

- Prepare food, as much as possible, in the same dish that it will be served in. For example, blend salad dressings in the bottom of the bowl before adding the rest of the ingredients.

- Remove meats and vegetables from the refrigerator as you begin preparation. Room temperature food cooks faster than cold.

- Begin boiling water for pasta as soon as possible. The pot can be kept covered at a simmer and brought back up to a boil when needed.

- Read through the entire recipe first before beginning preparation, then assemble all the ingredients needed. For soups or stews, layer ingredients in a bowl divided by plastic wrap or wax paper, based on the cooking times. For stir-frying, ingredients may be placed on a cutting board or plate, in order of use.

Beverages and Snacks

MIMOSA

MIMOSAS ARE enduringly popular champagne cocktails that have become a brunch classic. Use freshly squeezed orange juice and good-quality champagne. If blood oranges are in season and available, try them for a dramatic twist.

MAKES 7 SERVINGS

One 750-ml bottle champagne or sparkling wine

2¼ cups fresh orange juice

Fill your glasses one-quarter of the way with champagne, allow the bubbles to settle, then fill glasses half full. After the bubbles have settled, add 2½ ounces of orange juice to each glass of champagne, or until glasses are three-quarters full.

KIR ROYALE

KIR ROYALE is made by combining champagne with crème de cassis, a deep-red liqueur made from black currants, first made by French monks in the 16th century as a cure for snakebites and jaundice. Try substituting other fruit-flavored liqueurs (peach, orange, or raspberry) for the cassis.

MAKES 5 SERVINGS

5 oz (10 tbsp) crème de cassis

One 750-ml bottle champagne or sparkling wine

10 blackberries

Add 2 tablespoons of crème de cassis to each glass. Pour in enough champagne to fill the glasses one-quarter of the way with champagne; allow the bubbles to settle. Add more champagne to fill the glasses three-quarters full. Garnish each glass with two blackberries. Serve at once.

LEMONADE

WHEN YOU buy lemons, select fruit that is heavy for its size with relatively thin skin. They will have the most juice. Let the lemons warm to room temperature, then roll them under your palm before juicing them to get even more juice from them.

LEFT TO RIGHT When making kir royale, add the crème de cassis to the glass after measuring it or add it directly from the bottle after you have practiced making the drink a few times. Prime the glass with champagne by filling the glass one-quarter full. Finish by adding champagne until the glasses are three-quarters full.

Pouring Champagne and Other Sparkling Beverages

Champagne is sold in a number of different-sized bottles from the diminutive quarter-bottle or "split" (6.3 fluid ounces) to half-bottles (12.7 fluid ounces) to 750-milliliter bottles (the standard size, which supplies 25.4 fluid ounces) to the magnum (50.8 fluid ounces and equal to 2 standard bottles). Even bigger bottles are sold, though they are difficult to find and unwieldy to pour from: the Jeroboam (equal to 4 bottles), Rehoboam (equal to 6 bottles), Methuselah (equal to 8 bottles), Salmanazar (equal to 12 bottles), the Balthazar (equal to 16 bottles), and the Nebuchadnezzar (equal to 20 bottles). When you buy champagne, get the right sized bottle for your party. Unpoured champagne doesn't hold all that well, though you can carefully stopper it and keep it refrigerated for up to 12 hours. There will be some loss of carbonation, however.

A standard 750-milliliter bottle yields five 5-ounce glasses, assuming you are using a standard champagne flute. Of course, your glass may be larger or smaller. There are some tricks for pouring champagne whether you plan to serve it on its own or in a cocktail such as a mimosa or kir.

OPEN CHAMPAGNE BOTTLES CAREFULLY

Loosen and remove the foil wrapper around the cork. Then, untwist the wire "cage" that holds the cork in place. Keep your finger on top of the cork so that it doesn't fly out when you aren't ready.

Wrap a clean napkin around the bottle and the cork to get a secure grip. Be sure you aren't aiming the bottle in anyone's direction and keep the bottle at a 45 degree angle as you open it. Twist the cork in one direction and the bottle in the other and gently ease the cork out. If you've done this properly, there may be a small pop, but there shouldn't be a big bang or an eruption of champagne. The point, after all, is to keep the bubbles in the champagne and to get the champagne into your glass.

PRIME THE GLASS

Champagne and other sparkling beverages won't run over the top of your glass if you use a two-stage approach to pouring. The first pour, sometimes referred to as "priming" the glass, doesn't fill the glass. Carefully pour in enough champagne to fill the glass only one-half to one-quarter full.

THE SECOND POUR

When you prime the glass with a little champagne, the bubbles may rise almost to the top of the glass. When they settle down, you can finish filling the glass without overflows. If you are filling a lot of glasses, prime them all first, then make a second pass to fill them all.

6⅔ cups cold water, divided use

½ cup sugar

1 cup lemon juice

8 lemon slices for garnish

1. Combine ⅔ cup water with the sugar in a small saucepan and bring to a boil. Stir to dissolve the sugar.

2. Combine the sugar-water with the lemon juice and add 6 cups cold water. Stir to combine.

3. Serve over ice garnished with a lemon slice, or store in the refrigerator until ready to use.

GINGER LEMONADE

SIMMERING THE ginger along with the sugar and water infuses its flavor throughout the lemonade. Try adding the stems of fresh herbs such as mint, lavender, or lemon balm, or pieces of orange or lime zest for even more flavor.

MAKES 8 SERVINGS

6⅔ cups cold water, divided use

½ cup sugar

¾ inch piece ginger, sliced

1 cup lemon juice

8 thin slices ginger for garnish

1. Combine ⅔ cup water with the sugar and ginger in a small saucepan and bring to a boil. Stir to dissolve the sugar. Remove the pan from the heat and allow the ginger to steep in the sugar-water for 10 minutes. Strain the mixture, pressing the ginger to extract all its juices.

2. Combine the ginger sugar-water with the lemon juice and add 6 cups cold water. Stir to combine.

3. Serve immediately over ice garnished with a ginger slice or store refrigerated until ready to use.

RASPBERRY LEMONADE

TO MAKE the raspberry puree for this lemonade, push fresh or thawed frozen raspberries through a wire-mesh sieve into a small bowl. You'll need about 1 cup berries to make ⅓ cup puree.

MAKES 8 SERVINGS

6⅔ cups cold water, divided use

½ cup sugar

1 cup lemon juice

⅓ cup raspberry puree

24 raspberries for garnish

1. Combine ⅔ cup water with the sugar in a small saucepan and bring to a boil. Stir to dissolve the sugar.

2. Combine the sugar-water with the lemon juice and add 6 cups cold water and the raspberry puree. Stir to combine.

3. Serve over ice garnished with 3 raspberries, or store in the refrigerator until ready to use.

AGUA DE JAMAICA
Hibiscus Cooler

AGUA DE JAMAICA is a delicious herbal tea from Mexico with a refreshing taste and a beautiful ruby-red color that comes from hibiscus flowers, known as *jamaica* in Spanish (pronounced *ha-MIKE-ah*). Although it does take some looking to find hibiscus flowers, you may be able to find them in natural foods stores that sell bulk herbs and spices. The flowers can leave stains, so use stainless steel or glass containers instead of plastic, aluminum, or ceramic.

MAKES 8 SERVINGS

2 quarts water, or as needed

2 cups jamaica flowers (hibiscus)

1¼ cups sugar, plus as needed

3 medium oranges, cut in half

1. Bring the water to a boil. Add the hibiscus and sugar; stir while the mixture boils for 1 minute.

2. Squeeze the juice from the oranges into a non-corrosive bowl and place the orange halves in the bowl as well. Pour the hibiscus mixture into the bowl and steep for 1 hour.

3. Strain through a sieve, pressing on the hibiscus and oranges to extract as much liquid as possible. Taste the liquid for strength and sweetness. If it is too pungent, add water. If it is too tart, add sugar. Cover and refrigerate in a pitcher until you are ready to serve.

SANGRIA

As an alternative to the recipe that follows, try serving a white sangria instead, made from a fresh, fruity white wine mixed with a combination of stone fruits: plums, peaches, apricots, nectarines, and cherries. Instead of Grand Marnier, try a nut-flavored liqueur like Amaretto.

MAKES 8 SERVINGS

3 tbsp water

3 tbsp sugar

4 strawberries, quartered

½ cup raspberries

½ cup blueberries

½ cup blackberries

8 slices peeled orange

2½ cups dry red wine

¾ cup orange juice

⅓ cup Grand Marnier

¾ cup sparkling water

1. Combine the water and sugar in a small saucepan and bring to a boil, stirring to dissolve the sugar. Remove from heat and let cool.

2. Combine the fruit in a bowl. In a large pitcher, combine the sugar-water, wine, orange juice, and Grand Marnier. Add the fruit and stir gently to combine. (The sangria can be prepared ahead to this point and held in the refrigerator for up to 12 hours before serving.)

3. Just before serving, add the sparkling water to the pitcher. Serve the sangria in wineglasses.

Breakfast Beverages

Steaming mugs of coffee, tea, and hot chocolate are the fuel for many Americans in the morning and throughout the day. Taking the time to find the best coffee, tea, and drinking chocolate means that you can make your own hot breakfast drinks, ones that equal or better the quality you are likely to find at coffee shops, delis, and drive-throughs on the way to work. We've included several recipes for spiced coffees and teas, as well as a great repertoire of cold drinks that can be served as "breakfast in a glass" or can add sparkle and elegance to a wonderful brunch.

BREWING COFFEE

The definition of a great cup of coffee is a personal thing, but to be sure that you get the coffee you like, keep three things in mind: the coffee itself, the water, and your pot.

THE COFFEE

Good-quality coffee is more widely available today than ever before. You have the choice of a wide variety of coffees, both whole bean and preground. If possible, sample a variety of beans. There are two types of coffee beans, Arabica and Robusta. Arabica is widely considered far superior to Robusta. If you buy you coffee from bulk dispensers, that is usually the type of bean you are getting. Blends incorporate a number of different varieties and even different roasts to give the coffee a specific aroma and flavor.

Another important element in a coffee's flavor is the roasting process. The darker the roast, the more pronounced and complex the flavor will be. Lighter roasts have a more delicate flavor. Espresso, French, and Italian roasts are the darkest. The beans will have a very dark color with a pronounced sheen since the oils in the beans are driven to the surface as they roast. American roasts are lighter in color and tend to look matte rather than shiny.

Whole beans maintain their quality longer than pre-ground coffee. You can store whole beans in a dark, covered container at room temperature for several days. For longer storage, keep the beans in the freezer.

Grind coffee yourself using a coffee grinder or a coffee mill. It is best to do this right before brewing the coffee. Each type of coffeemaker calls for a specific degree of grind. Drip-style coffeemakers use a fine grind. Express or plunger-style pots call for a slightly coarser grind. If you aren't certain, be sure to look at the instructions that come with your coffeepot.

The standard ratio for coffee calls for one *measure* of coffee, which translates as 1½ to 2 tablespoons of ground coffee for every 6 ounces of water you use. The more coffee you use in relationship to the water, the stronger the brewed coffee will be.

THE POT OR COFFEEMAKER

Most dedicated coffee drinkers have a favorite pot they use. Drip-style coffeemakers hold the coffee in a basket lined with a disposable paper filter, or a reusable gold mesh or nylon filter. Some baskets are cone-shaped, and others have a flat bottom.

Espresso machines are used to brew coffee with pressure. The finely ground, dark-roasted coffee is packed into a basket, and water is forced through the coffee. The result is a thick, intensely flavored little cup of coffee topped with a bit of creamy foam. Espresso is often consumed as "shots." A single shot of espresso is about 1½ ounces. Double espresso is two "shots" and so on. If you love espresso but don't have a pot, simply use triple the amount of coffee you would to make a standard brew.

Clean your pot and the basket well after each use. If you use an electric coffeemaker that holds the water in a reservoir, be sure to clean it with a vinegar-and-water mixture to remove any mineral deposits that the water can leave behind. This will keep your coffeepot functioning properly. It also improves the flavor of your coffee. Follow the instructions that came with your coffeemaker for cleaning.

THE WATER

Most coffeemakers call for cold water. Use bottled or filtered water if your tap water has an unpleasant odor or taste. Your coffeemaker should bring the water to around 190°F for the best extraction. If the water is colder than that, the coffee may taste weak. If it is too hot, the volatile oils that give coffee its rich aroma may be lost.

If you brew coffee with a non-electric coffeemaker, fill your kettle with cold fresh water and bring it to a boil. Turn off the heat and let the water rest for a minute or two so that it can cool from 212°F (the boiling point of water) down to 190°F. Clean your kettle with vinegar and water periodically to remove any buildups left behind by the water.

Lighten your coffee with milk, cream, or half-and-half. If you like sweet coffee, use granulated or raw sugar. For a different flavor, try maple syrup or molasses.

BREWING TEA

Dedicated tea drinkers know that your water should be at the boil, your pot preheated, and your tea selected carefully.

Teas can be black or green. Green tea has a mild flavor and lighter color. Black tea is fermented; the leaves and the brew are darker in color and more intensely flavored. Some teas are flavored with herbs, spices, or citrus. Herbal teas are made from herbs such as mint, chamomile, or ginger.

While some tea drinkers prefer loose teas, others find the convenience of tea bags appealing. Whether you use bags or loose tea, be sure to observe some basic guidelines.

Fill your kettle with fresh, cold water. Use bottled or filtered water if your tap water has an unpleasant odor, or if you have a water softener.

Bring the water to a full boil and then pour some into your pot to preheat it. Once the pot is hot, pour out the water and add the tea. Loose tea is added directly to the pot, but if you prefer, use either tea bags or a tea ball. A tea cozy keeps the pot hot while the tea brews.

Most teas require at least two or three minutes for a proper infusion. Remove tea bags or tea balls once the tea is the strength you like. If you like loose tea, then the leaves will stay in the pot. In that case, you should have a second pot filled with hot water so you can adjust the intensity of your own cup.

Milk, honey, sugar, and lemon wedges are common accompaniments to tea.

BLENDER DRINKS

Blender drinks, often referred to as smoothies, are increasingly popular breakfast options. They are a quick and easy way to incorporate a serving of dairy and some fresh fruit into your day. You can use any fresh fruits you like, including berries, tropical fruits like mango and papaya, peaches, pineapple, or melon. If fresh fruits aren't at their peak, frozen fruits or fruit juices are another option.

Most smoothies include yogurt as their base; choose a good-quality unflavored yogurt. It is up to you whether you prefer to use whole milk, reduced-fat, or soy yogurts. Experiment with goat or sheep's milk yogurt if they are available in your market.

MULLED AND SPICED DRINKS

Hot, steaming cups of mulled cider or wine chase the chill on cold mornings and make a perfect accompaniment to a fall or winter brunch menu. We've included a few different recipes, including cardamom-spiced coffee and mulled cider.

If you don't want to go to the bother of making a spice sachet, simply strain the mulled or spiced drink through a fine-mesh strainer to remove the herbs before you serve the drinks.

BUBBLE TEA

If you don't have a cocktail shaker, you can shake up the drink in a covered jar instead. It is important to use double-strength tea for this recipe because the flavor of the tea is diluted when you shake it up with the milk and ice. You can replace the brown sugar with honey for a slightly different flavor.

MAKES 8 SERVINGS

3 quarts plus 2 cups water, divided use

¾ cup granulated sugar

⅓ cup packed light brown sugar

1 cup small tapioca pearls

12 bags black tea

1 quart whole milk

1. Combine 1 cup water with the sugars and bring to a boil, stirring constantly to dissolve the sugar. Reduce the heat to medium and simmer 2 or 3 minutes to make a syrup. Set aside.

2. To prepare the tapioca, bring 7 cups of water to a boil in a large saucepot and add the tapioca pearls. Simmer uncovered, stirring frequently, until they are mostly transparent and slightly gummy, about 30 minutes. Remove the tapioca from the heat and cover the pan. Cool for 30 minutes, then drain through a wire-mesh sieve and rinse with cool water.

3. Add the cooked tapioca pearls to the sugar syrup and stir to coat the pearls with the syrup. Store in the refrigerator until ready to make the bubble tea.

4. Place the tea bags in a teapot or a pitcher. Bring the remaining 6 cups of water to a full boil and pour over the tea bags. Brew until you have a double-strength tea, 5 to 6 minutes. Discard the tea bags and allow the tea to cool to room temperature.

5. For each serving of bubble tea, put ⅓ cup cooked tapioca pearls into a large glass. Combine ¾ cup tea, ½ cup milk, 3 tablespoons sugar syrup, and a few cubes of ice in a cocktail shaker. Shake thoroughly and pour over the tapioca pearls. Serve immediately with a wide straw.

CHAI

Chai is a popular Indian beverage made from black tea, milk, a sweetener, and spices. Mixtures known as chai masala may include cardamom, cinnamon, ginger, and peppercorns to give the drink its heady aroma. Some sugar or honey is essential to bring out all the flavors.

MAKES 8 SERVINGS

1½ quarts cool water

12 bags Darjeeling tea

3 cinnamon sticks, 1½ inches each

4 tsp sliced ginger

1 tbsp cardamom pods

1½ tsp fennel seeds

¼ tsp cloves

⅛ tsp black peppercorns

1 vanilla bean, split

¼ cup honey, or as needed

3 cups milk

1. Bring the water to a boil in a medium saucepan. Add the tea bags, cinnamon, ginger, cardamom, fennel, cloves, peppercorns, and vanilla bean. Reduce the heat and simmer the mixture for 10 minutes, stirring occasionally, until aromatic and the mixture is a medium brown. Add the honey and milk and stir to dissolve the honey. Bring to a boil and remove from the heat.

Making Bubble Tea

Bubble tea got its start in Taiwan and has become popular throughout the world under several names: boba drink, pearl tea drink, boba ice tea, boba, boba nai cha, zhen zhou nai cha, pearl milk tea, pearl ice tea, black pearl tea, tapioca ball drink, BBT, PT, pearl shake, and QQ (which means chewy in Chinese).

MAKE A SUGAR SYRUP

Simmering sugar and water together makes a simple syrup. This syrup is blended with the softened tapioca pearls to give them some flavor, as well as to sweeten the tea and milk mixture. Sugar dissolves more readily in hot water and helps avoid having the sugar drop to the bottom of the glass.

SOFTEN THE TAPIOCA PEARLS

There are large and small tapioca pearls, as well as white and black tapioca pearls. We've used small pearls since they fit more easily through a straw. If you can find black pearls, they give the drink an interesting appearance. Large pearls call for very fat straws. You may even find that one of the straw/spoon combi-nations that you get with a root beer float at your favorite soft-serve ice cream store makes it easier to drink the bubble tea, as well as scoop up the pearls.

As the tapioca simmers, it will become translucent. The texture changes too, becoming gummy and slippery. When the softened and sweetened tapioca pearls are combined with the tea, they give the drink the appearance of big bub-bles (hence the name).

BREW AND FLAVOR THE TEA

We've used a black tea for this drink, but some bubble teas call for adding herbs and spices to the tea as it brews. Cardamom, clove, or cinnamon are all good choices. Be sure to strain them out of the tea before serving. Let the tea steep a little longer than you would if you were drinking it plain so that the fin-ished drink has a definite taste of tea.

Shake the tea and milk together with ice until it is frothy, so that you get a layer of bubbles on top of the bubble tea, as well as the tapioca "bubbles" at the bottom of the glass.

LEFT TO RIGHT Add the tapioca pearls to plenty of water. As the tapioca cooks, it will be necessary to stir more often so that the tapioca doesn't stick to the bottom of the pan. The tapioca has swelled considerably after cooking and is slightly translucent. It should be slightly gummy and a little slippery. Before mixing the tea in the shaker, have the glasses set up with the tapioca mixture in the bottom.

2. Strain the liquid through a sieve, pressing on the tea bags and spices to extract as much liquid and flavor as possible. Taste the liquid for sweetness and add more honey if desired.

3. Serve the chai immediately as a hot drink or chill and serve over ice.

CAFÉ AU LAIT

THE FRENCH have given us this wonderful steamy coffee drink, perfect to enjoy with a buttery brioche for breakfast. Serve in heated café au lait cups.

MAKES 8 SERVINGS

4 cups brewed coffee, hot

4 cups milk

Ground cinnamon for garnish, optional

1. Keep the coffee hot while you steam or froth the milk. Steam the milk using a milk steamer or bring it to a simmer in a small pan over low heat. If simmered on the stove, use an immersion or countertop blender to whip the hot milk until frothy.

2. Combine equal parts of coffee and hot milk in heated cups. Garnish with cinnamon if desired.

HOT CHOCOLATE

FOR BEST results, place the chocolate mixture in the refrigerator overnight. The mixture develops a smoother texture and richer flavor as it rests. If you are a serious hot chocolate fan, you can make a double or triple batch and then hold it in the refrigerator for up to 5 days.

MAKES 8 SERVINGS

24 oz dark chocolate, finely chopped

1 cup heavy cream

2 quarts whole milk

1. Place chocolate in a heatproof bowl. Bring the cream to a boil and pour over the chocolate. Cover and let rest for 5 minutes. Stir the mixture until completely smooth.

2. Bring the milk to a simmer. Gradually whisk the milk into the chocolate mixture. Cool completely and refrigerate until ready to use.

3. When ready to serve, slowly heat the chocolate mixture over medium-low heat. Serve hot.

HOT MULLED CIDER

YOU MAY be able to find pear cider to use instead of the more widely available apple cider. If possible, buy cider that has not been pasteurized for the freshest, fullest apple or pear flavor.

MAKES 8 SERVINGS

2 quarts cider (unfiltered)

1 cinnamon stick

3 or 4 whole cloves

3 or 4 allspice berries

Zest of 1 orange

8 thin orange slices for garnish

1. Combine all the ingredients except the orange slices in a saucepan. Simmer until the flavor of the spices and orange zest are infused into the cider, about 20 minutes.

2. Strain the cider and serve in heated mugs or glasses. Garnish each portion with an orange slice.

CARDAMOM-SPICED COFFEE

To make a sachet, cut a 7-inch square of cheesecloth. Place the cinnamon sticks, cardamom pods, and allspice berries in the center of the cheesecloth. Gather the cloth around the spices and tie closed with cotton string to make a little package. It makes removing the spices from the milk easier. Another option is to place the spices in a tea ball, breaking the cinnamon sticks into pieces to fit.

MAKES 8 SERVINGS

One 13½-oz can sweetened condensed milk

½ cup whole milk

1 spice sachet of 2 tsp cardamom pods, 2 cinnamon sticks, and 4 allspice berries

1⅔ cups ground French roast coffee

1½ quarts water

1. Warm the sweetened condensed milk, milk, and spice sachet over medium-low heat for 10 minutes. Remove the pan from heat and cover. Allow the mixture to steep for 30 minutes. Remove the sachet.

2. Brew the coffee using the 1½ quarts water to make a slightly stronger coffee. Add 2 tablespoons of the spiced milk to each cup of coffee or to taste. Serve hot.

EGGNOG

Add a shot of brandy, bourbon, or rum to each portion of eggnog before serving it to the adults, if you wish.

MAKES 8 SERVINGS

2 cups milk

2 cups heavy cream, divided use

¾ cup sugar, divided use

2 large eggs

½ tsp vanilla extract

⅛ tsp salt

Ground cinnamon or nutmeg for garnish

1. Heat the milk, 1 cup of the heavy cream, and ½ cup of the sugar in a heavy-gauge saucepan until simmering.

2. While the milk-cream mixture heats, blend the eggs with the remaining ¼ cup sugar, the vanilla, and salt. Gradually add about half of the hot milk-cream mixture to the eggs and then return the egg mixture to the saucepan.

3. Simmer the eggnog over very low heat until heated to 165°F. Continue to simmer, stirring constantly, for 3 minutes.

4. Strain the eggnog through a wire-mesh sieve into a bowl and cool rapidly in an ice bath. Transfer to a pitcher or jar, cover well, and chill for at least 2 hours and up to 24 hours before serving.

5. When you are ready to serve the eggnog, whip the remaining cup of heavy cream and fold it into the eggnog. Serve in cups or glasses garnished with a dusting of ground cinnamon or nutmeg.

TROPICAL FRUIT SMOOTHIE

THE AVERAGE blender can usually hold enough to make two servings of a smoothie at once, so if you are planning to make more, dice as much fruit as you need, then purée the smoothies in several batches.

MAKES 2 SERVINGS

1 cup diced pineapple

¼ cup diced mango

¼ cup diced papaya

¼ cup peeled and diced kiwi

½ cup fresh orange juice, divided use

¼ cup coconut milk

¼ cup plain nonfat yogurt, optional

⅓ cup ice

1 tbsp sugar, or as needed

¼ tsp vanilla extract

2 pineapple slices for garnish

Toasted shredded unsweetened coconut for garnish, optional

1. In a blender, combine pineapple, mango, papaya, kiwi, and ¼ cup orange juice; puree until smooth. With the machine running, add the remaining orange juice, coconut milk, yogurt (if using), ice, sugar, and vanilla extract. Blend until smooth and thick.

2. Serve the smoothies at once in chilled tall glasses garnished with a pineapple slice and a sprinkle of toasted coconut.

CAPPUCCINO SMOOTHIE

IF YOU don't have an espresso maker, use triple the amount of coffee you normally use to brew coffee.

MAKES 2 SERVINGS

1 cup espresso, cold

½ cup coffee ice cream

¼ cup crushed or cracked ice

⅓ cup whole milk

¼ cup heavy cream, whipped

¼ tsp ground cinnamon, or as needed

Blend the espresso, ice cream, ice, and milk in a blender until smooth. Serve at once in chilled tall glasses garnished with a dollop of whipped cream and a sprinkle of cinnamon.

MANGO LASSI

THIS TRADITIONAL Indian drink was originally made from yogurt, water, toasted cumin, salt, and chiles. Sweet lassis, such as this one, have become very popular in recent years. To make a mango puree, cut a very ripe mango into pieces and push the flesh through a wire-mesh sieve or a food mill. If you have any leftover puree, you can store it in the refrigerator or freezer.

MAKES 8 SERVINGS

4 cups mango puree

4 cups whole-milk yogurt

½ cup whole milk

½ cup water

4 tsp lime juice, about 1 lime

4 tsp honey, plus more if needed

¾ tsp ground cardamom

1. In a large mixing bowl, whisk together the mango puree, yogurt, milk, water, lime juice, honey, and cardamom thoroughly. Taste the mixture and add more honey if necessary.

2. Serve the lassi at once in chilled glasses.

GARLIC AND PARSLEY BUTTER

THIS COMPOUND BUTTER is an ideal base for crostini and canapés. For more information on compound butters, see the notes on page 202.

MAKES 2 CUPS

1½ bunches flat-leaf parsley, stems removed

4 garlic cloves, roughly chopped

1 tsp salt, or to taste

1 lb butter, diced into small cubes, cold

1. Place the parsley, garlic, and salt in a food processor fitted with a metal chopping blade and pulse until evenly minced and well blended.

2. Add the cubed butter to the parsley-garlic mixture. Process, scraping down the sides as needed, until the butter is softened and the mixture is well blended. The butter should be light green in color.

3. The butter may be placed into a ramekin or shaped into a log and rolled in plastic wrap. Refrigerate until ready for use, or the butter be can be held for at least a week in the refrigerator

Making Crostini or Canapés

Crostini and canapés are bite-size, open-faced sandwiches. Simple and quick to make, they offer the busy cook a wide range of flavors, textures, and colors.

All canapés have a base of bread, a spread, a main item, and a garnish. Crostini, meaning "little toasts" in Italian, are not held to the same rigid guidelines as a canapé. Crostini refers both to a toasted piece of Italian or French bread, and the hors d'oeuvre that is created when a savory item is placed on top of the toast.

Crostini and canapés should be easy to pick up, and small enough to eat in one or two bites. For the most appealing crostini and canapés, choose your ingredients with attention to color, shape, and texture. In the following recipes, the terms crostini and canapé can be used interchangeably.

PREPARE THE CROSTINI OR CANAPÉ BASE

Select the bread for your crostini or canapé base and cut it into shapes, if necessary. Cocktail rye or pumpernickel bread is easy to use for canapés, but you can use other breads as well. Trim away the crust, and cut the cocktail bread in half on the diagonal to make triangles. For an elegant affair, use small, round cutters to create a more uniform and finished-looking base. When making crostini, you can choose to toast, grill, or broil the bread slices for more flavor and texture.

ADD A FLAVORFUL SPREAD TO THE BASE

A spread acts as a moisture barrier between the main item and the bread, as well as to hold the topping in place. It also adds mouthfeel and flavor. Spread a thin layer of softened butter, cream cheese, mustard, a bean spread, or mayonnaise from edge to edge. Add flavoring ingredients to the spread if you like: minced garlic, shallots, or scallions; purees of roasted peppers or chiles, Parmesan cheese, or olives can be blended into the spread.

GARNISH THE CROSTINI OR CANAPÉ WITH THE TOPPING

Sliced toppings should be very thin and cut or trimmed so they won't hang over the edge of the base. Another option is to dice or mince the main item and fold it into the spread to make a flavorful salad topping for the base. When you plan to make larger numbers of crostini or canapés for a party or reception, you can add the spread and topping to an entire slice of bread, then use cutters to trim or cut them into shape. Garnishes like a bit of fresh fruit, vegetables, or herbs can add additional color, texture, and flavor.

BLACK BEAN AND AVOCADO CROSTINI

Crostini is a general term that refers to "little toasts" which are usually topped with one or more garnish items. This Southwestern version combines the creaminess of black beans with the heat from the guacamole for a terrific hors d'oeuvre or snack.

MAKES 8 SERVINGS

24 baguette slices, ¼-inch thick

¼ cup Garlic and Parsley Butter (page 13)

½ cup small-dice Vidalia onion

2 plum tomatoes, small dice

¾ cup cooked or canned black beans, drained and rinsed

4½ tsp chopped cilantro

1 tsp white wine vinegar

1 tsp salt, or to taste

½ tsp freshly ground black pepper, or to taste

2 avocados

2 tbsp lime juice

1 garlic clove, minced

¼ tsp chili powder

⅛ tsp ground cumin

24 cilantro or parsley leaves, washed, for garnish

1. Preheat the oven to 400°F.

2. Toast the baguette slices in the oven for 5 to 7 minutes, or until the outside edges of the slices are golden brown.

3. Spread each baguette slice with approximately ½ teaspoon of the garlic and parsley butter. Reserve the toasts until needed.

4. Combine the onion, tomato, black beans, cilantro, and vinegar. Season with salt and pepper.

5. Peel and core one of the avocados and dice into ¼-inch pieces. Combine the avocado with 1 tablespoon of the lime juice, garlic, chili powder, and cumin. Season with salt and pepper.

6. Peel and core the remaining avocado. Slice each half across the meridian into 8 slices. Sprinkle the avocado with the rest of the lime juice to prevent oxidation.

7. Spread 1 heaping teaspoon of the avocado mixture on each crostini. Top with 1 tablespoon of the black bean mixture.

8. Garnish with an avocado slice and a cilantro or parsley leaf.

PROSCIUTTO AND MELON CANAPÉ

The best time to serve this delicate, sweet and savory hors d'oeuvre is when melon varieties are in peak season, allowing you to enjoy the fullest contrast between juicy cantaloupe and lightly salty, paper-thin slices of prosciutto.

MAKES 8 SERVINGS

8 slices white bread

Olive oil, as needed

MASCARPONE CHEESE SPREAD

5 oz mascarpone cheese

¼ tsp Tabasco sauce

¼ tsp Dijon mustard

Dash salt, or to taste

Dash freshly ground black pepper, or to taste

1 cantaloupe, scooped into 24 small balls

8 thin slices prosciutto (about ¼ lb)

1 bunch mint leaves, chiffonade

1. Preheat the broiler.

2. Brush the bread slices lightly with olive oil and broil for 30 seconds per side until crisp.

3. Combine the mascarpone cheese, Tabasco, Dijon mustard, salt, and pepper. Mix well.

4. Using the small side of a melon baller, scoop approximately 24 balls out of the cantaloupe.

5. Spread the mascarpone mixture on the toasted bread slices. Lay a slice of prosciutto on each slice of bread, then cut canapés out of the bread using a round cutter.

6. Top each canapé with a cantaloupe melon ball. Garnish with mint chiffonade.

CROSTINI VARIATION: Spread the mascarpone cheese mixture onto toasted ¼-inch-thick baguette slices. Cut each prosciutto slice into thirds; top each of the crostini with a folded piece of prosciutto and a cantaloupe melon ball. Garnish with mint chiffonade.

LOBSTER AND PROSCIUTTO CROSTINI

T HIS VERY elegant hors d'oeuvre is so simple that even on a tight schedule you can achieve impressive results. Frozen lobster meat is generally of excellent quality, and since it is already cooked, it only requires thawing time. It you wish to substitute fresh lobster in this recipe, allow an additional 40 to 45 minutes cooking time for the lobster.

24 baguette slices, ¼-inch thick

¼ cup Garlic and Parsley Butter (page 13)

6 tbsp olive oil, for frying

24 large fresh sage leaves

½ cup goat cheese, soft

8 thin slices prosciutto (about ¼ lb)

1 cup cooked lobster meat (thawed if frozen)

1. Preheat the oven to 400°F.

2. Toast the baguette slices in the oven for 5 to 7 minutes, or until the outside edges are golden brown. Spread each baguette slice with approximately ½ teaspoon of the garlic butter. Reserve the toasts until needed.

3. Heat the olive oil in a small sauté pan over medium-high heat. Gently place the sage leaves in the oil and lightly fry for 2 to 3 minutes. Remove and drain on absorbent paper. Hold at room temperature until needed.

4. Spread each of the toasted baguette slices with 1 teaspoon of the goat cheese. Cut each prosciutto slice into thirds; top each crostini with a folded piece of prosciutto.

5. Place 2 teaspoons of the lobster meat on top of the prosciutto. Garnish each crostini with a fried sage leaf.

GUACAMOLE

Guacamole is a Mexican condiment made from mashed avocados, lemon or lime juice, and chile peppers. Variations can include tomatoes, cilantro, garlic, and scallion. It is important to remember that avocado begins to oxidize as soon as its flesh is exposed to air; cover your guacamole with a layer of plastic wrap pressed directly onto the surface of the mixture.

MAKES 8 SERVINGS

4 avocados, halved, pitted, and peeled

3 tbsp lime juice

2 plum tomatoes, diced, optional

1 jalapeño, seeded and minced, optional

½ cup sliced scallions

½ cup chopped cilantro

1 tsp Tabasco sauce, or to taste

Salt and pepper as needed

1. Mash the avocados with a fork. Add the remaining ingredients and adjust the seasoning with lime juice, salt, and spices.

2. The guacamole is ready to serve now or it can be held in a covered container for up to 8 hours.

Working with Avocados

The delicate flesh of an avocado will discolor rapidly if it is cut very far in advance or exposed to the air. Avoid cutting the avocado more than 1 hour before you will need it. Once you cut it, sprinkle the diced flesh with a little lemon or lime juice and toss gently to coat all the pieces. Cover the avocado and keep refrigerated until needed.

Crudités

Crudités is nothing more elaborate than fresh, raw vegetables served with a cold sauce for dipping. The name itself means "raw" in French. Nearly every cuisine has some corollary to the French crudités. Sometimes it's as simple as the "relish" platters popular in the 1950s that featured stalks of celery and radishes with the simplest of all sauces: salt. Sometimes it's an extensive selection of fresh and pickled vegetables, such as you might enjoy from an antipasto selection, or some tapas.

Crudités platters can be strictly vegetables or you might want to include pickles, olives, cured or smoked meats, and cheeses to turn your crudités into a more substantial appetizer, or even, if paired with good breads and some flavorful oils, to make into a simple supper.

SELECTING VEGETABLES FOR CRUDITÉS

The main criteria for selecting vegetables for a crudités platter are flavor and freshness. The best way to be sure your vegetables are the most flavorful is to choose them based on the season. Sniff or, if possible, taste vegetables.

The way vegetables look is important for a successful crudités platter. Look for vivid colors, good textures, and unblemished specimens. It's a good idea to be generous so you can create a bountiful array. Consider not only the flavor of the vegetables, but also the color.

PREPARING VEGETABLES FOR A CRUDITÉS PLATTER

Some vegetables are perfect to eat raw: cucumbers, tomatoes, peppers, zucchini, carrots, celery, and fennel are some exam-

CANNELLINI BEAN PUREE

Cannellini are flavorful, kidney-shaped beans which are found dried or canned. This puree would be an excellent spread for the base of a vegetarian canapé, or could be used as a vegetable dip.

MAKES 2 CUPS

⅔ cup chopped onion

¼ cup chopped carrot

½ cup chopped celery

1 tsp black peppercorns

6 garlic cloves, crushed

2 rosemary sprigs

2 thyme sprigs

2 bay leaves

1 lb canned cannellini beans

2 garlic cloves, roughly chopped

2 tbsp lemon juice

1 tsp salt, or to taste

½ tsp hot pepper sauce

½ tsp ground white pepper

¼ cup extra-virgin olive oil

1 tbsp chopped parsley

1. Tie the onion, carrot, celery, whole peppercorns, garlic cloves, rosemary, thyme, and bay leaf in a cheesecloth pouch, and combine with the canned beans in their liquid in a medium saucepan. Simmer for 15 minutes. Discard the cheesecloth bag and drain the beans, reserving the cooking liquid. Cool the mixture to room temperature.

2. Puree the beans in a food processor, using the reserved cooking liquid to adjust the texture to a spreadable consistency. Season with chopped garlic, lemon juice, salt, hot sauce, and pepper.

3. Garnish with olive oil and parsley.

ples. Rinse, peel, and cut or slice them so they are easy to pick up and eat.

Other vegetables, including green beans, sugar snap or snow peas, broccoli, cauliflower, and some baby vegetables, including zucchini, pattypan, or yellow squash, also are delicious raw, but you may prefer to quickly blanch them, and possibly even marinate them, before adding them to your platter. Blanching makes some vegetables brighter and more vivid. It also helps remove any bitterness from vegetables like cauliflower and broccoli. Blanched vegetables should be thoroughly drained and chilled so they are crisp, not waterlogged. If you are planning to pickle or marinate the vegetables, remember that the flavor is absorbed better when the vegetables are still warm. However, acids can change the colors in green vegetables, so it's best to chill them before you add any dressings or marinades.

ARRANGING VEGETABLES ON A CRUDITÉS PLATTER.

It really doesn't matter how you arrange the vegetables themselves. You can arrange them neatly for a sophisticate look or simply toss them together for a rustic presentation. There are a few guidelines to follow, however:

- *Dry the vegetables well so that the dips can cling.*

- *Chill the vegetables and the platter, as well as the bowls you plan to use for dips.*

- *Use strong or contrasting colors for a dramatic look.*

LIMA BEAN SPREAD

WHEN YOU make this delicious spread, double the recipe. Use the leftover spread to make a pasta sauce by adding enough of the reserved liquid (or broth or water) to the spread and simmering until you get a light, pourable consistency. Serve over hot tricolored pasta.

MAKES 2 CUPS

2 tbsp extra-virgin olive oil, divided use

½ cup minced onion

1 garlic clove, chopped

2 cups frozen lima beans, thawed

½ cup frozen peas, thawed

½ cup Vegetable Broth (page 65)

½ tsp salt

2 tsp coarsely chopped flat-leaf parsley

2 tsp lemon juice

1 tsp chopped rosemary

½ tsp freshly ground black pepper

1 tbsp grated Parmesan cheese

Coarse sea salt for garnish

1. Heat 1 tablespoon of the olive oil in a large sauté pan over medium heat. Add the onion and garlic and sauté until translucent, 3 to 5 minutes. Add the beans, peas, broth, and salt. Reduce the heat to low and simmer until heated through, about 5 minutes. Drain, reserving the remaining liquid.

2. While the mixture is still warm, puree in a food processor. Slowly drizzle in remaining olive oil while pureeing. Add the parsley, lemon juice, rosemary, and black pepper and continue to puree. Adjust the consistency with the reserved liquid, if needed; the spread should be thick but spreadable. Transfer to a bowl, add the cheese, and mix thoroughly.

3. Refrigerate at least 30 minutes before serving. Garnish with sea salt, if desired.

ONION DIP

IF YOU'VE never had a made-from-fresh onion dip, this recipe will convince you that it's well worth the few minutes of preparation time!

MAKES ABOUT 3 CUPS

2 tbsp olive oil

1½ cups diced onions

Salt and pepper as needed

1½ cups sour cream

¾ cup mayonnaise

¼ tsp garlic powder

1. Heat a sauté pan over medium heat. Add the oil and heat until it shimmers. Add the onions and season with a pinch of salt. Sauté, stirring frequently, until the onions are a deep, rich brown, about 20 minutes. Remove from heat and set aside to cool.

2. Mix the remaining ingredients in a bowl, and then add the cooled onions. Refrigerate for an hour. Stir and season with additional salt and pepper, if needed, before serving.

SPINACH DIP

YOU CAN bake this dip in small ramekins if you prefer, but we like it baked in a small, round pumpernickel, rye, or sourdough loaf.

MAKES ABOUT 3 CUPS

2 cups chopped spinach, cooked or thawed if frozen and squeezed dry and drained

1 cup finely chopped artichoke hearts or bottoms

1 cup sour cream

½ cup minced green chiles

⅓ cup grated Parmesan cheese

2 tsp minced garlic

1 cup coarsely grated Monterey Jack cheese

Salt and pepper as needed

1 small round bread loaf (rye, pumpernickel, or sourdough)

1. Preheat oven to 350°F.

2. Stir the spinach, artichoke, sour cream, chiles, Parmesan, and garlic together in an oven-proof bowl. Fold in the Monterey Jack cheese. Season to taste with salt and pepper. Bake until the mixture is very hot and bubbly, about 10 to 15 minutes.

3. To prepare the bread, cut a circle from the top of the loaf, keeping it intact to use as a lid. Pull out the bread from the center of the loaf to make room for the dip. Pour the dip into the bread bowl, re-place the "lid" and serve.

ARTICHOKE DIP

THIS DIP can be served hot or at room temperature. Just be careful not to leave it at room temperature for more than an hour or so because it does contain mayonnaise.

MAKES ABOUT 3 CUPS

1½ cups cooked artichoke hearts, drained and chopped

1 cup mayonnaise

1 cup grated Parmesan cheese

½ cup diced green chiles

3 tbsp sliced scallions, cut thin on the diagonal, optional

2 tbsp small-dice tomatoes, peeled and seeded, optional

1. Preheat oven to 350°F.

2. Combine the artichoke hearts, mayonnaise, cheese, and green chiles. Mix well and pour into a 2-quart casserole dish. Bake for 20 to 25 minutes or until lightly browned.

3. Garnish with chopped green onions and chopped tomato, if desired.

Peeling and Seeding Tomatoes

Bring a pot of water to a rolling boil. Fill a bowl with ice water and have it near the stove. Core the tomatoes and score an X through the skin at the bottom of each. Submerge a few tomatoes at a time in the boiling water for 15 to 30 seconds. Using a slotted spoon, transfer the tomatoes to the ice water. Drain the tomatoes and pull the skin away. Slice the tomatoes in half crosswise. Plum tomatoes should be halved from top to bottom. Squeeze or scrape out the seeds and chop the flesh.

SALSA FRESCA

UNLIKE JARRED, store-bought salsas, this salsa is at its best for only a brief period. Keep it chilled and use it within a day. You can use as much or as little of the jalapeño as you like. Try other chiles as well, including the smoky-hot canned chipotles with a little of their sauce (known as *adobo*) either instead of or in addition to the jalapeño. Other additions you might try include black beans, red peppers, or cucumbers.

MAKES 2 CUPS

1 cup seeded and diced tomatoes

¼ cup minced onion

2 tbsp small-dice green bell pepper

1 tbsp minced jalapeño

1 tbsp extra-virgin olive oil

1 garlic clove, minced

2 tsp chopped cilantro

½ tsp chopped oregano

1 tbsp fresh lime juice

½ tsp salt

⅛ tsp freshly ground black pepper

1. Combine the tomatoes, onion, green pepper, jalapeño, olive oil, garlic, cilantro, and oregano. Add lime juice, salt, and pepper to taste.

2. Let the salsa rest in a covered container in the refrigerator at least 30 minutes before serving.

BLACKENED TOMATO SALSA

BLACKENING THE tomatoes gives them a smoky taste, as well as making them easy to peel.

MAKES ABOUT 3 CUPS

5 plum tomatoes

1 tbsp olive oil

1 Spanish onion, sliced ¼ inch thick

½ dried chipotle chile

Salt to taste

1. Place the tomatoes on a wire rack directly over a gas burner or on a medium-high grill. Turn them frequently until they are blackened over their entire surface. Set aside.

2. Heat the oil in a large sauté pan over medium heat. Add the onion slices and cook on both sides until they are a very deep brown, about 15 to 20 minutes total cooking time.

3. Coarsely chop the tomatoes and onions. Combine the tomatoes, onions, chili, and salt in a blender or food processor. Puree the mixture in short pulses to make a chunky salsa. Serve the salsa warm or at room temperature.

CHIPOTLE PICO DE GALLO

MAKES 1 CUP

1 cup medium-dice tomatoes (seeded before dicing)

4 tsp minced red onion

½ tsp red wine vinegar

½ canned chipotle pepper, minced

Salt, to taste

1 tbsp cilantro chiffonade

Combine all the ingredients and mix well. The pico de gallo is ready to use now or it can be stored in a covered container in the refrigerator up to 2 days.

TOMATILLO SALSA

A TOMATILLO IS a fruit that resembles a small, unripe tomato with a papery husk. Tomatillos have a tart and lemony flavor and are commonly used in Southwestern and Mexican cuisines. This easy-to-make salsa is an excellent complement to grilled meats.

MAKES 2 CUPS

10 tomatillos

1 jalapeño

2 garlic cloves

1 teaspoon salt, or to taste

1 bunch cilantro

1. Remove the husks from the tomatillos.

2. Place the tomatillos and the jalapeño in a pot and cover them with water. Boil until the tomatillos are fully cooked and have become a dull olive green color, about 10 minutes.

3. Remove the stem, seeds, and veins from the jalapeño.

4. Strain the tomatillos from the water and place them directly into a food processor fitted with a metal chopping blade. Add the flesh from the jalapeño, the garlic cloves and the salt. Process the mixture until completely smooth.

5. Add the cilantro to the food processor and pulse to chop and incorporate.

6. Serve the salsa warm or chilled.

NOTE: To make a hotter salsa, do not remove the seeds and veins from the jalapeño.

SPICED MIXED NUTS

GOOD FOR cool autumn afternoons, or just about any time, this delicious nut mixture is great to have on hand for unexpected guests.

MAKES 1 POUND

½ tsp celery seed

½ tsp garlic powder

½ tsp chili powder

¼ tsp ground cumin

⅛ tsp cayenne pepper

1 tsp salt, or to taste

3 tbsp butter

1 tbsp Worcestershire sauce

1 lb unsalted raw whole mixed nuts

1. Preheat the oven to 375°F.

2. Combine the celery seed, garlic powder, chili powder, cumin, cayenne, and salt.

3. Melt the butter in a saucepan over medium heat. Add the Worcestershire sauce and bring to a simmer. Add the nuts and mix until evenly coated.

4. Sprinkle the combined spices over the nuts and stir. Place the nuts on a nonstick or well-greased baking sheet and bake, stirring occasionally, for 15 to 17 minutes, or until evenly browned.

5. Cool completely before serving. Store in an airtight container for up to 2 weeks.

NOTE: If saltier nuts are desired, sprinkle with kosher salt while still warm.

SPICY ROASTED CASHEWS

SPECIAL ENOUGH for the holiday season, these cashews, whether served as a snack or given as a small gift, can be made just as spicy as you like.

MAKES 1 POUND

1 lb whole raw cashews

2 tbsp butter, melted

1 tsp salt, or to taste

¼ tsp garlic powder

¼ tsp onion powder

⅛ tsp cayenne pepper

1. Preheat the oven to 375°F.

2. Toss the cashews and melted butter together until evenly coated. Place on a baking sheet and bake until golden brown, about 15 to 17 minutes.

3. While the cashews are in the oven, combine the salt and spices; reserve.

4. Remove the cashews from the oven and toss with the combined spices while still warm. Allow to cool before serving.

5. The cashews may be stored in an airtight container for up to 2 weeks.

VARIATION: For Spicy Curried Cashews, follow the same procedure, but simply add 1 tablespoon of curry powder to the spice mixture.

CHILI-ROASTED PEANUTS
with Dried Cherries

THE ADDITION of sweet and tart dried cherries gives a delicious twist to these lightly spiced, oven-roasted peanuts.

MAKES 1 POUND

2 tbsp butter

1 lb peanuts, raw

1 tbsp chili powder

2 tsp ground cumin

2 tsp ground white pepper

1 tbsp salt, or to taste

½ tsp dried oregano

½ tsp cayenne pepper

½ lb dried cherries (or raisins)

1. Preheat the oven to 325°F.

2. Melt the butter in a small sauce pan. Coat the raw peanuts with the melted butter.

3. Spread the peanuts on a large baking sheet and lightly toast for about 10 minutes, shaking the pan occasionally.

4. Mix together the remaining ingredients, except the cherries, in a large bowl. Transfer the toasted peanuts to the bowl and coat with the dry ingredients. Mix in the cherries.

5. Cool completely before serving. Store in an airtight container for up to 2 weeks.

CHAPTER
2

Appetizers
and Salads

Appetizers

Every culture and cuisine has its own tradition of "little foods," enjoyed before a meal or even on their own. Popular throughout the Mediterranean are *mezes* such as stuffed grape leaves, olives, and luscious garlicky bean or vegetable spreads. In Spain, the tradition of *tapas* runs a gamut from seafood to eggs to savory pastries. Throughout Mexico and South America, *antojitos* (or "little whims") are enjoyed in a wide range of forms, from tostadas to tacos. *Dim sum*, Cantonese for "heart's delight," includes steamed dumplings and pot stickers. The Russians enjoy a *zakuski* table, laden with preserved and pickled foods; while in Scandinavia, it is the *smörgåsbord*, with fabulous open-faced sandwiches and gravlax, that fills this culinary slot. Classic French *hors d'oeuvre* encompass a vast array of dishes, featuring a range of specialties from foie gras and oysters to marinated salads of lentils and celeriac. While these examples of "little foods" may seem daunting, the recipes included in this chapter are quick and easy to prepare.

A meal that includes an appetizer course is perceived as extraordinary; however, you need not reserve appetizers for special occasions or holidays. There are quite a number of simple foods that are quick to prepare and don't demand a lot of effort in the kitchen. With the addition of an appetizer, you can enhance ordinary meals, even on a workday evening.

ARTICHOKE CEVICHE
in Belgian Endive

A CEVICHE IS a marinated dish that you may be more familiar with when made with fish or seafood. In this all-vegetable dish, the lime juice is important both for its flavor and for its ability to keep the artichokes from turning brown when they are exposed to the air.

MAKES 4 SERVINGS

4 artichokes

1 lemon, sliced

Salt and pepper as needed

1 cup diced plum tomato

½ cup red onion julienne

1 scallion, split and sliced thinly on the diagonal

2 tbsp chopped cilantro, or as needed

2 tsp minced garlic

½ tsp minced jalapeño, or to taste

2 tbsp extra-virgin olive oil

1 tbsp lime juice, or as needed

12 Belgian endive spears

1. Trim the stems, leaves, and choke from the artichokes. Place the hearts in a small pot with enough water to generously cover. Add the lemon slices and salt to taste. Bring the water to a simmer over high heat. Reduce the heat to medium and simmer until the artichoke hearts are very tender, about 12 to 15 minutes. Cool the hearts and slice thinly or quarter.

2. Toss together the artichokes, tomato, red onion, scallion, cilantro, garlic, and jalapeño. Drizzle the olive oil and lime juice over the ceviche and season generously with salt and pepper. Toss until the ingredients are evenly coated. Cover the bowl and marinate the ceviche in the refrigerator for at least 2, and up to 12, hours.

3. Taste the ceviche just before serving and season with additional cilantro, lime juice, coarsely ground black pepper, and salt to taste. Spoon the ceviche into the endive spears and serve on a chilled platter or plates.

SMOKED TROUT

with Apple-Horseradish Cream

W HEN YOU apply the salt mixture, make it slightly heavier over the thickest portion of the fish and thinner where the fish begins to taper at the tail. The drying stage, where the fish is left uncovered in the refrigerator, develops a skin that picks up a lot of the smoky flavor. Garde-manger chefs refer to this stage as "forming a pellicle."

MAKES 6 SERVINGS

6 pan-dressed trout, 10 oz each

1 cup kosher salt

½ cup granulated sugar

1 tbsp garlic powder

1 tsp onion powder

1 tsp ground black pepper

Zest of 2 lemons

2 cups mixed baby greens

⅔ cup Lemon Vinaigrette (page 56)

2 Granny Smith apples, thinly sliced

1 cup Apple-Horseradish Cream (recipe follows)

1. Lay the trout on a baking sheet skin-side up. Scrape the skin lightly with the back side of a knife to remove the scales.

2. Combine the salt, sugar, garlic and onion powders, pepper, and lemon zest.

3. Cover the belly and tail sections of the trout with a ¹⁄₁₆-inch layer of the salt mixture and cover the thicker sections with a ¼-inch layer. Let the trout sit for 30 minutes in the refrigerator.

4. Rinse the trout in cold water and place on a wire rack. Let dry, uncovered, in the refrigerator for at least 6 and up to 12 hours.

5. Prepare a smoker according to the manufacturer's instructions or set up a disposable smoker as described below. Place the trout skin-side down in the smoker and let it smoke for 10 to 15 minutes at between 225° and 250°F. If you are using a disposable smoker, the cooking time is about 5 minutes. Remove from the heat and let cool.

LEFT TO RIGHT When placing the fish on the rack to form a pellicle, be sure not to crowd them; they need plenty of air to circulate around them so that they dry evenly. Place the trout skin-side down on the rack that is set over the smoking wood chips; it is important that the wood chips start smoking before adding the trout so that they will get the proper amount of flavor during the time they are in the smoker. Carefully pull the pin bones out with a pair of tweezers; this may take you a couple of tries, but your guests will appreciate it.

6. Toss the greens with the Lemon Vinaigrette. Serve the trout with the dressed greens, sliced apples, and the Apple-Horseradish Cream.

Making a Disposable Smoker

Grill smokers are used for adding intense smoky flavor to trout and other ingredients. If you don't have a traditional smoker available to you, you can easily set up a disposable smoker. You'll need two aluminum roasting pans, a rack, and hardwood chips.

Dampen the chips or chunks and then make an even layer of them in one of the pans. Set your rack over the chips, and top with the second pan, inverting it to make a domed lid.

Put this assembly over direct heat on the grill until you can smell the smoke. Lift off the lid, place the food you want to smoke on the rack, replace the lid, and continue to smoke for the length of time suggested in your recipe.

Apple-Horseradish Cream

MAKES 1 CUP

¼ cup heavy cream

¼ cup sour cream

¼ cup grated Granny Smith apple (peeled before grating)

2 tbsp prepared horseradish

¼ tsp salt

Whisk the heavy cream until medium-stiff peaks form. Fold in the sour cream, apple, horseradish, and salt. The sauce is ready to serve now or store in a covered container in the refrigerator for up to 2 days.

Smoked Fish Platter with Accompaniments

Smoked fish—salmon, trout, sturgeon, or whitefish—is easy on the cook. Buy the fish from a reputable source and keep it well-wrapped until you are ready to put your platter together.

SERVE ONE KIND OF FISH OR A VARIETY

Trout can be purchased whole. Cut the trout into pieces or present it as a whole "side." Smoked trout breaks easily into large flakes that you can mound or present in a bowl.

Smoked salmon is cured and then smoked; lox is a cured salmon that is not smoked. Both are usually cut into paper-thin slices. You can find packaged sliced smoked or cured salmon, but you may have a market or deli in your area that hand carves salmon. Good smoked salmon is smooth, silky, and supple. Shingle the slices or roll them into loose rosettes.

Experiment with other smoked fish, like sturgeon or white fish. Some fish varieties tend toward flakiness; others are firmer and easier to slice.

Although you should hold smoked fish in the refrigerator, it is a good idea to give it some time to come to room temperature to bring out the best flavor and texture.

ARRANGE THE FISH AND ACCOMPANIMENTS

Some traditional accompaniments to smoked fish include pumpernickel or rye bread. Whole-grain breads and crackers are also good choices. Bagels, of course, are the classic choice to serve with lox. Add chopped red onions, hard boiled eggs, a dish of capers, and lemon wedges so that everyone can season and garnish to suit themselves. Cream cheese, plain or seasoned with dill or chives, makes a great spread and also helps hold the fish on your bagel, bread, or cracker.

GREEN BEANS
with Frizzled Prosciutto and Gruyère

IF YOU can find slender little haricots verts, use them in this salad. Large green beans can be left whole or sliced on the diagonal if you wish. Cut the Gruyère into sticks that are about the same size and length as your green beans.

MAKES 8 SERVINGS

3 tbsp lemon juice, or to taste

1 tbsp white wine vinegar

2 tbsp minced shallots

Salt and pepper as needed

7 tbsp extra-virgin olive oil

1 lb green beans, ends trimmed

¼ lb prosciutto, thinly sliced

¼ lb Gruyère cheese cut into sticks

1. Combine the lemon juice, vinegar, shallots, ½ teaspoon salt, and ¼ teaspoon pepper. Gradually whisk in 6 tablespoons olive oil. Season with additional salt and pepper, if needed. Set aside.

2. Bring a large pot of salted water to a boil. Add the green beans and cook until bright green and just barely tender to the bite, about 3 minutes. Drain the green beans and rinse with cold water until they feel cool. Drain well.

3. Toss the greens beans and the dressing together and let them marinate at room temperature for 10 minutes.

4. Heat the remaining olive oil in a sauté pan over medium-high heat until it shimmers. Add the prosciutto to the hot oil and cook until it "frizzles," about 2 minutes. Add the prosciutto and the Gruyère to the beans. Season with additional salt and pepper if necessary. Serve at room temperature.

STUFFED CHERRY TOMATOES
with Minted Barley Cucumber Salad

THE BARLEY salad can be prepared up to 2 days in advance. You may want to double the ingredients for the filling to have on hand as an accompaniment to grilled or broiled salmon. The tomatoes can be stuffed up to 6 hours before they are served.

MAKES 8 SERVINGS

½ cup pearl barley

¼ cup diced tomato

¼ cup diced cucumber

⅓ cup chopped flat-leaf parsley

2 tbsp chopped mint

1 tbsp finely sliced scallions, white portion only

2 tsp extra-virgin olive oil

1 tsp lemon juice

Salt and pepper as needed

16 cherry tomatoes

1. Soak the barley in enough cold water to cover for 30 minutes and drain well.

2. Bring the barley and enough water to cover to a boil. Reduce the heat and simmer until tender, about 40 minutes. Strain through a sieve, transfer to a bowl of ice water, and let cool for 1 minute. Set the sieve over a bowl and let the barley drain.

3. Combine the barley, tomato, cucumber, parsley, mint, and scallions in a large mixing bowl. Stir in the olive oil, lemon juice, salt, and pepper.

4. Cut the core from the cherry tomatoes and make two cuts into the tomato to open it out like a flower. Stuff each cherry tomato with some of the salad, and serve on a chilled platter or individual chilled salad plates.

SATAY OF BEEF
with Peanut Sauce

WHILE THE beef is a classic to pair with the peanut sauce, lamb or chicken would be excellent substitutions.

MAKES 4 SERVINGS

Bamboo skewers, 8-inch, as needed

1½ lb top round of beef or beef flank steak, cut 1 x 5 inches and thinly sliced

MARINADE

4 tsp ginger, finely chopped

8 garlic cloves, minced

1 tsp crushed red pepper flakes

2½ tbsp curry powder

2 tbsp honey

½ cup fish sauce

½ cup soy sauce

PEANUT SAUCE

1½ tsp peanut oil

1½ tsp garlic, minced

¼ tsp crushed red pepper flakes

¼ cup coconut milk

2 tbsp lemon juice

½ cup smooth peanut butter

1 tbsp soy sauce

¼ cup water

1. Soak the skewers in water while you prepare the marinade. Combine the beef with the marinade ingredients in a zipper-lock bag and seal. Gently toss the beef with the marinade in the bag until coated evenly. Allow the meat to marinate at least 30 minutes and up to 12 hours.

2. While the beef is marinating, combine the ingredients for the Peanut Sauce in a small saucepan and bring to a slow boil. Simmer 4 to 5 minutes, adjusting consistency with more water or peanut butter as needed, and adjusting seasoning as needed.

3. Thread a piece of the marinated beef on each skewer. Grill or broil the skewered meat, cooking about 3 to 4 minutes per side. Serve with the warm Peanut Sauce.

DRIED SALT COD, MEXICAN-STYLE
Bacalao a la Mexicana

BASED UPON salt cod, or *bacalao*, and traditionally served at Mexican Christmas celebrations, this stew is made with a rich *mole* and finished with almonds. The usual accompaniment is toasted tortillas. To learn more about buying and preparing salt cod, see the note following this recipe.

MAKE 8 SERVINGS

2 lb dried salt cod

2 ancho chiles, toasted

4 cups diced plum tomatoes

½ cup olive oil

2 cups diced yellow onion

2 tbsp minced garlic

1 bay leaf

1 tsp ground cinnamon

1 tsp freshly ground black pepper

3 red bell peppers, roasted, peeled and diced

½ cup sliced almonds

¼ cup raisins

½ cup stuffed green olives

2 tbsp capers

2 tbsp chopped parsley

2½ cups diced cooked potatoes

1. Soak the cod in cold water for 12 hours, changing the water every 3 or 4 hours. Drain. Place the cod in a saucepan, add enough cold water to cover, and bring to a boil. Drain the cod, letting it cool until it is easy to handle, and then pull the cod apart into shreds; set aside.

2. Remove the stems and seeds from the ancho chiles and soak them in hot water for 10 minutes. Drain the chiles and purée with the tomatoes in a blender until smooth. Strain the mixture and set aside.

3. Heat the oil in a large skillet over medium heat until it shimmers. Add the onion and garlic and sauté until transparent, 6 to 8 minutes. Add the chile/tomato purée and cook over low heat, stirring occasionally, until the mixture thickens, 5 to 6 minutes. Add the cod, bay leaf, cinnamon, black pepper, bell peppers, almonds, raisins, olives, capers, and parsley. Cook over medium heat for 10 minutes, stirring occasionally. Add the potatoes, cover, and cook until heated through, about 12 minutes. Serve at once.

Salt Cod

Known as *baccala* in Italian, *bacalao* in Spanish, *bacalhau* in Portuguese, *morue* in French, and salt cod in English, this heavily salted fish is typically sold in Italian, Greek or Portuguese markets and at some larger grocery chains. When buying salt cod, look for uniform texture and color; avoid pieces with a yellowish tint. The flesh should be pliable and compact, not woody. Look for pieces that have a uniform thickness; they will soak evenly. Skinless and boneless salt cod is easier to handle.

Cooks disagree on the appropriate length of time to soak salt cod. Some suggest 8 hours while others soak the fish for up to 3 days. We feel that 12 hours is just enough time to remove the overpowering saltiness. Cut the cod fillets into chunks and put them into a large bowl. Add enough cold water to completely cover the fish and put the bowl in the refrigerator. Replace the water every 3 or 4 hours. After the fillets have been soaked and drained, the fish should feel soft and pliable, with only a hint of brininess. If your salt cod still has the skin and bones, pull off the skin, pick out the bones, and break the fish into flakes.

SPICY LAMB KEBABS
with Pickled Grapes

THE FLAVORS in this recipe are largely inspired by Greek cooking, but with the distinct influence of Asian cuisine as well, blending the refreshing bite of fresh herbs with the pungency of cinnamon and ginger, and the brilliant colors of saffron and turmeric.

MAKES 4 SERVINGS

1½ lb boneless leg of lamb

2 tbsp minced garlic

¼ cup olive oil

¼ cup lemon juice

4 tsp minced flat-leaf parsley

2 tbsp minced oregano leaves

1 tbsp ground coriander

2 tsp minced ginger

2 tsp Spanish-style paprika

2 tsp salt

1 tsp ground black pepper

½ tsp ground turmeric

½ tsp ground cayenne pepper

¼ tsp crushed saffron threads

16 bamboo skewers

32 Pickled Grapes, recipe follows

1. Trim the lamb and cut it into 1-inch cubes; you should have about 24 pieces.

2. Thoroughly combine all the remaining ingredients except the grapes. Coat the meat evenly with the mixture. Cover and marinate in the refrigerator for at least 2 and up to 12 hours.

3. Remove the lamb from the refrigerator 30 minutes before grilling. Soak the bamboo skewers in cool water for 30 minutes. Drain just before using.

4. Preheat a gas grill to medium-high. If you are using a charcoal grill, build a fire and let it burn down until the coals are glowing red with a moderate coating of white ash. Spread the coals in an even bed. Clean the cooking grate.

5. While the grill is heating, thread 3 pieces of meat and 2 grapes onto each skewer. Grill until the lamb is medium-rare, 2 to 3 minutes on each side. Serve at once.

Pickled Grapes

MAKES 2½ CUPS

1½ cups granulated sugar

¾ cup white wine vinegar

1 cinnamon stick

¼ tsp salt

1¼ cups seedless green grapes (about 32 grapes)

1¼ cups seedless black grapes (about 32 grapes)

1. Combine the sugar, vinegar, cinnamon stick, and salt in a saucepan. Simmer over medium heat until the sugar has completely dissolved, about 5 minutes.

2. Pour the mixture over the grapes, and allow the grapes to cool to room temperature. Refrigerate overnight, covered. The grapes are ready to use now or they can be stored in the refrigerator for up to 2 weeks.

MUSSELS WITH OLIVES
Mejillones al Estilo de Laredo

IN THIS Spanish-inspired recipe for mussels, a sauce enriched with olives and wine is a perfect counterpoint to the sweet and briny mussels. Serve this dish with lots of crusty bread for soaking up the sauce.

MAKES 4 SERVINGS

6 dozen mussels

2 tbsp olive oil

1 small yellow onion, sliced thin

2 anchovy fillets, chopped

⅛ tsp red pepper flakes

1 tbsp minced shallot

1 tsp minced garlic

1½ cups diced plum tomatoes

¼ cup dry white wine

1 bay leaf

Salt as needed

Freshly ground black pepper as needed

¼ cup chopped or sliced black olives, pitted and chopped

2 tbsp chopped flat-leaf parsley for garnish

1. Scrub the mussels under running cold water with a stiff-bristled brush and remove their beards (see note following this recipe). Set aside.

2. Heat the oil in a casserole or Dutch oven over high heat until it shimmers. Add the onion and sauté, stirring occasionally, until translucent, about 6 minutes. Add the anchovy fillets and red pepper flakes and stir until the anchovies break apart and "dissolve." Add the shallot and garlic and sauté, stirring constantly, until aromatic, about 30 seconds. Add the tomatoes, wine, bay leaf, and a pinch of salt and pepper. Bring to a boil over medium-high heat.

3. Add the mussels to the casserole, cover tightly, and steam until the mussels open, about 12 minutes. Discard any mussels that do not open. Scoop the mussels into a large heated bowl or individual bowls. Stir the olives into the sauce remaining in the casserole and season to taste with salt and pepper. Spoon the sauce over the mussels, garnish with parsley, and serve at once.

Cooking Mussels and Clams

Mussels and clams are both delicious and attractive. They are best when you give them appropriate care. Remember that they should be alive when you buy them and when they go into the pot. The first, and most important, step is buying them from a reliable source. The fish market, stall, or counter you visit should smell pleasantly of the sea and be very busy. Strong or unpleasant odors may be a sign that the fish is not fresh. The faster the fish is sold, the fresher it is likely to be.

Keep clams and mussels in paper bags or wrapping in the refrigerator until you are ready to cook them. Try to buy seafood the day you want to cook it, but if you need to hold it for a day or two, it will be fine.

When you are ready to cook mussels and clams, the first step is to clean them well. Put them in a colander, set them in the sink, and turn on the cold water tap. One by one, take the shellfish in one hand and a scrub brush in the other. Clean the shells thoroughly under running cold water. You may see that some of the shellfish has opened up. As long as the shell snaps shut again when you tap it, the mussel or clam is fine. If it stays open, throw it out.

Mussels require an extra step to clean them. Trap the hairy "beard" between the flat side of a paring knife blade and the pad of your thumb, then tug and pull the beard away.

Once the clams and mussels are cooked, the shells will open up and the edges of the meat inside should be curled. If any of them do not open, that is a sign that they were not alive. Don't serve unopened cooked shellfish; throw it out.

BLACK BEAN EMPANADAS

THESE EMPANADAS make great hors d'oeuvres. Serve with sour cream, Salsa Fresca (page 19), or guacamole. Assembled empanadas may be held refrigerated for up to 24 hours or frozen for up to 3 weeks.

MAKES 8 SERVINGS

EMPANADA FILLING

1 tbsp olive oil

¼ cup minced onion

¾ tsp minced garlic clove

¼ tsp ground cumin

¼ tsp dried Mexican oregano

1½ cups cooked or canned black beans, drained and rinsed

1 tsp salt

¼ tsp freshly ground black pepper

3 tbsp water, or as needed

¼ cup crumbled queso blanco or grated cheddar cheese

EMPANADA DOUGH

¾ cup all-purpose flour

½ cup masa harina

1½ tsp baking powder

¾ tsp salt

1 tbsp canola oil or lard, melted and cooled

2 large eggs

2 tbsp water

Egg wash of 1 large egg whisked with 1 tbsp water

3 cups canola oil or as needed for frying

Kosher salt for garnish

1. To make the filling, heat the olive oil in a medium sauté pan over medium-high heat. Add the onion and garlic and sauté, stirring frequently, until tender, 3 to 4 minutes. Stir in the cumin and oregano and cook for 30 seconds more. Add the beans to the onion mixture and season with the salt and pepper. Puree the bean mixture with 3 tablespoons water. If the beans are too stiff to puree easily, add additional water to thin them. Transfer the beans to a bowl and stir in the cheese. The filling is ready to use now, or it can be stored in a covered container in the refrigerator for up to 2 days.

2. To prepare the dough, combine the flour, masa harina, baking powder, and salt in a mixing bowl. Add the oil or lard and mix by hand with a wooden spoon until evenly distributed. In a small bowl, stir together the eggs and water. Add the egg mixture gradually to the flour mixture, stirring as you add. Knead the dough until it is pliable, about 3 minutes. Adjust the consistency of the dough with more flour or water if needed.

3. To assemble the empanadas, roll out the dough ¹⁄₁₆ inch thick. Using a 3-inch round cutter, cut the dough into circles, making 24 circles. Place 2½ teaspoons of the filling on each circle. Brush the edges of the dough with the egg wash, fold in half, and seal the edges by crimping with the tines of a fork.

4. Place the empanadas on parchment-lined baking sheets, cover, and refrigerate until ready to use. They may be held for up to 24 hours or frozen for up to 3 weeks.

5. Heat the oil in a deep fryer or deep skillet to 350°F. Add the empanadas to the hot oil and fry until golden brown and crisp, turning if necessary to brown both sides evenly, 3 to 4 minutes. Drain briefly on paper toweling. Sprinkle with a little kosher salt and serve very hot.

Principles for Presenting Appetizers

Use the following basic principles to help you select, prepare, and plate appetizers like the pros:

- *Serve appetizers at the proper temperature.* This allows the full flavor of each ingredient to be enjoyed fully.

- *Season all appetizer items with care.* Appetizers are meant to stimulate your taste buds, so proper seasoning is of the utmost importance.

- *Slice, shape, and portion appetizers carefully.* There should be just enough of every element to make the appetizer interesting and appealing from the first bite to the last.

- *Presentation counts.* Take the time to choose attractive plates, platters, serving utensils, and cups for dipping sauces. A beautifully presented item can excite the palate before the first bite.

MUSHROOM, LEEK, AND BRIE TURNOVERS

THIS SAVORY turnover recipe features the delicious flavors of sautéed mushrooms and creamy Brie cheese. As the mushrooms and leeks cook they will caramelize, developing a rich, smoky taste.

MAKES 12 TURNOVERS

1 tbsp extra-virgin olive oil

¾ cup coarsely chopped mushrooms

1 cup sliced leeks

1 tsp minced garlic

2 tbsp Madeira

½ tsp salt

¼ tsp freshly ground black pepper

1½ lb Blitz Puff Pastry (page 256)

Egg wash of 1 egg whisked with 2 tbsp cream or milk

3 oz ripe Brie cheese (rind removed)

1. Preheat the oven to 425°F. Line a baking sheet with parchment paper.

2. Heat the olive oil in a sauté pan over medium-high heat until it shimmers. Add the mushrooms to the pan and sauté until lightly caramelized, about 2 to 3 minutes. Add the leeks to the pan and reduce the heat to medium. Sauté the leeks until they are light golden brown, about 3 to 4 minutes. Add the garlic and cook for 1 minute.

3. Deglaze the pan with the Madeira and reduce until nearly dry, about 1 minute. Season the mixture with salt and pepper. Cool the mixture to room temperature.

4. Roll the dough into a rectangle (12 × 16 inches). Cut the dough into twelve 4-inch squares. Place the squares on the prepared baking sheet and let them chill in the refrigerator until firm, about 10 minutes.

5. Brush each square lightly with egg wash. Place 1 tablespoon of the mushroom filling in the center of each square. Top the filling with 1½ teaspoons Brie. Fold one corner of the dough over the filling and line it up with the opposite corner of the dough. Press the edges firmly together to seal the filling inside the puff pastry dough. Chill the turnovers for about 10 minutes before baking. Brush the turnovers lightly with egg wash. Cut a small opening in the center of each turnover to allow steam to vent.

6. Bake the turnovers until golden brown, about 20 to 25 minutes. Serve immediately.

Working with Prepared Phyllo Dough

Phyllo dough is nothing more than a simple flour-and-water dough stretched into thin sheets. Working with prepared phyllo is much easier than stretching it yourself. It is available in the freezer section of well-stocked supermarkets and from Greek and Middle Eastern groceries.

GETTING READY TO WORK

Thaw frozen phyllo dough either in the refrigerator overnight or at room temperature for 2 hours. Once thawed, the individual sheets should pull apart easily and be very flexible. However, contact with the air soon dries out phyllo unless it is covered. Set your work area up so that your phyllo stays moist and flexible as you work with it. Place a large baking sheet or a piece of plastic wrap down, remove the phyllo from the box, and unroll the number of sheets needed. Set the sheets flat on the baking sheet or plastic wrap. Cover the sheets completely with a large piece of plastic wrap, and then lay a piece of lightly dampened paper towel or a barely moistened kitchen towel over the plastic to keep the air around the phyllo moist.

LAYERING PHYLLO

Transfer one sheet of the phyllo at a time to your flat work area and immediately re-cover the remaining sheets. Brush or spray the entire sheet with butter or oil. For a very flaky texture and extra flavor in the finished dish, you can scatter bread crumbs over the sheet. Keep working this way, one sheet at a time, until you have the correct number of layers for your recipe. If necessary, cut the phyllo stack into strips to fold into triangles for appetizer-size portions.

SCORING PHYLLO

Large items that you will need to cut into portions should be scored before they go into the oven. Otherwise, the fragile, crisp pastry would shatter as you try to slice it. It is easiest to cut the dough when it is firm, so we suggest that you chill it first. The butter will firm up in about 20 minutes. Then use the tip of your sharpest paring knife to cut almost through the layers. It is best to leave a layer or two uncut so that the filling doesn't ooze out as the pie bakes, but if it should, the pie will still taste great.

FENNEL AND CHORIZO STRUDELS

THESE STRUDELS are very hearty and rustic, full of delicious and robust flavors. Be careful not to allow the phyllo sheets to dry out as you work.

MAKES 8 SERVINGS

¾ cup butter, melted

2 shallots, minced

4 oz chorizo, sliced thin, skin on

1⅔ cups fennel bulb, diced

1½ tbsp tarragon leaves, minced

½ tbsp chives, minced

1 egg

1 cup breadcrumbs

1 tsp salt, or to taste

¼ tsp freshly ground black pepper, or to taste

8 sheets phyllo dough, thawed

1. Preheat the oven to 400°F

2. Heat about 2 tablespoons of the butter in a sauté pan over medium heat. Add the shallots and sauté them until they are translucent.

3. Add the chorizo, lower the heat, and allow some of the fat to render. Add the fennel and gently cook until tender. It may be necessary to reduce the heat slightly so that the mixture does not burn.

4. Allow the mixture to cool to room temperature. Add the tarragon leaves, chives, egg, and enough breadcrumbs (about ½ cup) to lightly bind the mixture. Adjust the seasoning with salt and pepper.

5. To assemble each strudel, lay a sheet of phyllo dough on your work surface with the longer edge of the dough parallel to the edge of the work surface. As you work, keep the unused sheets of phyllo covered with plastic wrap to keep them from drying out.

6. Brush the dough with melted butter and sprinkle with about 1 to 1½ teaspoons of breadcrumbs. Top with another sheet of phyllo dough and repeat this process until a stack of 4 buttered phyllo sheets is formed.

7. Mound half of the chorizo-fennel mixture along the bottom of the phyllo, leaving a 2-inch border at the edges. Beginning with the bottom edge, carefully roll up the dough and filling, and seal. Repeat with the remaining dough and filling to make a second strudel. Transfer the strudels seam-side down to a parchment paper-lined baking sheet. Brush with the remaining melted butter, and score the dough on a diagonal to indicate 4 portions.

8. Bake in a 400°F oven until golden brown, about 10 to 15 minutes. Slice and serve immediately.

SPANAKOPITA

YOU CAN substitute two 10-ounce boxes of frozen spinach for the fresh. Place the frozen spinach in a colander; let it thaw completely and squeeze out the moisture before using.

MAKES 40 PIECES

2 lb fresh spinach

¼ cup olive oil

1 cup minced onions

2 tbsp minced garlic

Salt and pepper as needed

3 large eggs, beaten

Two 3-oz packages cream cheese, room temperature

1¼ cups crumbled feta cheese

¼ cup chopped dill

¼ cup chopped parsley

½ tsp ground coriander

¼ tsp grated nutmeg

One 1-lb box phyllo sheets, thawed

1½ cups melted butter

1. Rinse and drain the spinach until all traces of sand and dirt are gone. Bring a large pot of salted water to a rolling boil. Add the spinach (this can be done in two or more batches, if necessary). Stir the spinach until all of the leaves are submerged and wilted. Simmer, uncovered, until the spinach is just tender, about 3 minutes. Drain the spinach, rinse well with cold water to stop the cooking, and press or squeeze out as much additional moisture as possible. Chop the spinach and set aside.

2. To make the spinach filling: Heat the oil in a sauté pan over medium-high heat until it shimmers. Add the onions and garlic and sauté, stirring frequently, until the onions are tender and translucent, 4 to 5 minutes. Add the spinach and sauté until very hot, another 3 minutes. Season well with salt and pepper. Transfer to a bowl or plate and cool completely. Blend the eggs into the cream cheese until smooth, and then stir into the spinach mixture. Fold in the feta, dill, parsley, coriander, and nutmeg. The filling is ready to use now, or it may be stored in a covered container in the refrigerator for up to 24 hours.

3. To assemble the spanakopita: Set up the phyllo as described on page 33. Make a stack of three phyllo sheets, brushing each layer with melted butter. Cut the sheets into five strips with a sharp knife or pastry cutter. Mound about 1 tablespoon of the filling mixture at the base of each strip. Fold the dough up into triangles. Brush the top of each triangle with a little additional butter and transfer to a baking sheet. They can be placed fairly close together, but they should not be touching. The spana-

kopita is ready to bake now or they can be packed into a container and frozen for up to 1 month.

4. Preheat the oven to 375°F. Bake the spanakopita until the phyllo is crisp and golden brown and the filling is completely cooked and very hot, 16 to 18 minutes. Serve hot or at room temperature.

SEARED SCALLOPS
with Fiery Fruit Salsa

WHEN BUYING scallops, ask to smell them; scallops should have a pleasant briny scent of the ocean. Keep them refrigerated until cooking time.

MAKES 6 SERVINGS

SALSA

⅔ cup mango, peeled and diced

½ cup papaya, peeled and diced

¼ cup pineapple, canned or fresh, cored, peeled, and diced

¼ cup diced red bell pepper

⅓ cup diced red onion

1 tbsp chopped cilantro

½ tbsp lime juice

½ tbsp white wine vinegar

1 tsp jalapeño, seeded and minced

½ tsp extra-virgin olive oil

⅛ tsp salt, or to taste

Freshly ground black pepper, to taste

2 lb sea scallops

2 tbsp vegetable oil

1. Combine all the ingredients for the salsa in a medium bowl. Allow the salsa to sit for 15 minutes before serving.

2. Remove the muscle tabs from the scallops; blot the scallops dry. Heat a sauté pan on medium-high

heat. Add the oil to coat bottom of pan. Place the scallops in the pan and sauté on the first side for about 2 to 3 minutes, or until golden brown. Turn the scallops once and sauté on the second side. Do not overcrowd the scallops in the pan. If necessary, cook the scallops in batches, holding those that are cooked in a warm oven.

3. Serve the scallops with the tropical fruit salsa.

NOTE: The scallops will release from the pan when properly browned. Do not try to pry the scallops from the pan as they will tear. The pan should not be too hot because the scallops will get scorched before they're cooked.

VARIATION: To make a sweet salsa for desserts or as a filling for crêpes, substitute mint for the cilantro, strawberries for the red pepper, honey for the olive oil, and leave out the vinegar, salt, and pepper.

SPICY ASIAN GRILLED SHRIMP
and Marinated Vegetable Salad

THIS DISH adheres to the Asian principle of balancing all of the basic tastes. It is highly perfumed, almost heady, with only a suggestion of heat from the ginger and chili sauce.

MAKES 6 SERVINGS

12 bamboo skewers

2 tbsp rice wine vinegar

2 tbsp minced garlic

1 tbsp minced ginger

1 tbsp chili sauce

1 tbsp Thai fish sauce

2 tsp five-spice powder

2 tsp dark sesame oil

2½ lb shrimp (16/20 count), peeled and deveined

Marinated Vegetable Salad, recipe follows

1. Soak the bamboo skewers in cool water for about 30 minutes.

2. Combine the vinegar, garlic, ginger, chili sauce, fish sauce, five-spice powder, and sesame oil in a bowl. Add the shrimp and toss to coat all the shrimp evenly. Cover, and marinate in the refrigerator for at least 1 and up to 3 hours.

3. Preheat a gas grill to high. If you are using a charcoal grill, build a fire and let it burn down until the coals are glowing red with a light coating of white ash. Spread the coals in an even bed. Clean the cooking grate.

4. Remove the shrimp from the marinade and let any excess drain off. Thread the shrimp onto the skewers.

5. Place the skewers on the grill and cook on both sides until cooked through, about 3 to 4 minutes per side. Serve the skewers immediately on a bed of the Marinated Vegetable Salad.

Peeling and Deveining Shrimp

Most recipes using shrimp call for the raw shrimp to be peeled and deveined prior to cooking. Other recipes may call for the shrimp to be only deveined before cooking, cutting through the shells but leaving them intact for their flavor.

To peel shrimp, start from the belly side and peel away the legs along with the shell. Pull off the tail if desired, or leave it intact to serve as a handle for shrimp that is to be eaten with the fingers.

To devein shrimp, lay the peeled shrimp on a work surface. With the curved outer edge of the shrimp facing your cutting hand, use a paring knife to make a shallow cut along the shrimp's back. Use the tip of the knife to scrape out the gray or black vein, which is actually the shrimp's intestinal tract.

Marinated Vegetable Salad

LOOK FOR unsalted raw nuts at natural food stores. Remember to store any nuts you don't use for this recipe in the freezer, where they'll keep for up to 3 months; raw nuts which are stored at room temperature can quickly become rancid.

MAKES 6 SERVINGS

1½ cups grated carrot

1½ cups grated daikon radish

2 tbsp minced pickled ginger

¼ cup vegetable oil

1 tbsp olive oil

1 tbsp peanut oil

1½ tsp sesame oil

2 tbsp rice wine vinegar

1 tsp soy sauce

1 tsp Thai fish sauce

Pinch ground white pepper

Pinch cayenne pepper

1 tbsp chopped unsalted roasted peanuts

1½ tsp toasted sesame seeds

Toss together the carrot, daikon radish, and ginger in a bowl. Combine the remaining ingredients in a separate bowl and mix well. Pour over the carrot mixture, and toss to mix. Cover and refrigerate until ready to serve.

Trimming and Peeling Asparagus

To trim asparagus, hold a spear with both hands and bend the spear until it snaps. Discard the stem end. If your asparagus is too thick to bend easily, you can simply trim away the woody portion of the stem with a pairing knife.

Peel asparagus carefully. If you use too much pressure, you could remove too much of the flesh of the asparagus and the spear could snap again. Instead, lay the asparagus flat on your cutting board and then peel, rolling the asparagus to get to all sides. Peel the lower half of each spear. It's easiest if the surface you work on is about 3 inches higher than your worktable or counter. That way, you won't bang your knuckles.

CHILLED ASPARAGUS
with Mustard Herb Vinaigrette

IF YOU have a choice at the market, opt for larger asparagus. It has a richer, more satisfying flavor than very slender asparagus.

MAKES 8 SERVINGS

2 lb asparagus

MUSTARD HERB VINAIGRETTE

2 tbsp white wine or cider vinegar

2 tsp Dijon mustard

1 tsp chopped flat leaf parsley

½ tsp chopped tarragon leaves

Salt and pepper as needed

Dash of onion powder

Dash of garlic powder

¼ cup extra-virgin olive oil

1. Bring a large pot of salted water to a full rolling boil.

2. Trim the asparagus to remove the white, fibrous ends. Cut the asparagus into 2-inch pieces on the diagonal.

3. Add the asparagus to the boiling water and cook until the spears are bright green and just tender, 4 to 5 minutes. (If necessary, cook the asparagus in batches.) Drain the asparagus in a colander and rinse with cold water until the asparagus is chilled. The asparagus is ready to dress and serve now, or it can be

held in a covered container in the refrigerator for up to 6 hours.

4. To make the vinaigrette, whisk together the vinegar, mustard, parsley, tarragon, salt, pepper, onion powder, and garlic powder until blended. Add the oil to the vinegar mixture in a thin stream, whisking constantly. Season with additional salt and pepper, if needed.

5. Toss the chilled asparagus with the vinaigrette or pass it separately on the side. Serve immediately on a chilled platter or plates.

TOMATO SAMPLER
with Pan-fried Calamari

Some farm stands offer baskets of an assortment of tomato varieties with colors that range from a brilliant yellow to a deep, dusky maroon that is almost black. We especially enjoy the contrast of hot, crunchy, pan-fried calamari against the cool, juicy tomatoes.

MAKES 4 SERVINGS

¾ lb fresh calamari, cleaned and rinsed

½ cup all-purpose flour, or as needed for dredging

2 tsp Old Bay seasoning mix

Salt and pepper as needed

½ cup milk

1 cup olive or canola oil, or as needed for pan frying

¾ cup arugula leaves

3 cups torn frisée

1 cup Balsamic Vinaigrette (page 58)

1 yellow beefsteak tomato, sliced thick

1 red beefsteak tomato, sliced thick

½ cup red cherry tomatoes, halved

½ cup yellow cherry tomatoes, halved

1. Cut the squid's body into thin rings approximately ⅛ inch thick. Rinse the rings and tentacles thoroughly in cold water, then blot dry on absorbent toweling.

2. Combine the flour, Old Bay seasoning, salt, and pepper in a large plate or pan. Pour milk into a shallow bowl.

3. Add the oil to a skillet (there should be about ¼ inch covering the bottom) and preheat the oil over medium-high heat.

4. Dip the squid rings and tentacles into the milk first and then in the seasoned flour, turning to coat evenly. Immediately lower the coated calamari into the hot oil. Cook, turning occasionally, until the squid is golden brown on all sides, about 6 to 8 minutes. Remove the calamari from the oil and drain briefly on absorbent toweling.

5. Toss together the arugula and frisée with the vinaigrette and mound the dressed greens on a serving platter or individual plates. Add the tomatoes to the vinaigrette remaining in the bowl and very gently toss to coat. Top the greens with the tomatoes and calamari. Serve at once.

GRILLED SHRIMP PASTE ON SUGARCANE
with Hoisin Peanut Sauce

Don't let the long list of ingredients in this recipe put you off. The table salad called for in this recipe is a traditional Vietnamese accompaniment, and includes plenty of fresh herbs so your guests can flavor their food themselves at the table.

2 oz pork fatback

1 tbsp roasted peanut oil

¼ cup minced shallots

12 oz shrimp (31/35 count), peeled, deveined,
    and chopped

2 tbsp fish sauce

1 tbsp granulated sugar

1 tsp minced garlic

1 large egg

¼ tsp ground white pepper

2 tbsp cornstarch

½ tsp baking powder

¼ cup thinly sliced scallions

16 pieces canned sugarcane (see note)

8 leaves red-leaf lettuce

1 cup bean sprouts

1 cup European cucumber julienne, skin on

1 tbsp chopped mint

1 tbsp chopped cilantro

1 tbsp chopped Thai basil

3 tbsp Scallion Oil (recipe follows)

1¼ cups Hoisin Peanut Sauce (recipe follows)

NOTE: This recipe calls for canned sugarcane to be cut into pieces that you will mold the shrimp paste around. Since the stalks have different sizes, cut each piece as needed in order to make "skewers" that are about ¼ inch thick.

1. Bring a small pot of water to a boil. Boil the fatback until white and firm, about 10 minutes. Drain and cool the fatback, then mince.

2. Heat the peanut oil in a small pan over medium-high heat. Sweat the shallots in the oil until translucent, about 2 minutes. Transfer the fatback and shallots to a mixing bowl and allow them to cool to room temperature.

3. Add the shrimp, fish sauce, sugar, garlic, egg, pepper, cornstarch, and baking powder to the fatback mixture. Mix well to coat the shrimp evenly with all of the ingredients.

4. Transfer the mixture to the bowl of a food processor. Pulse into a smooth paste, about 30 seconds. (Do not overmix or the paste will toughen.) Transfer the mixture to a bowl and stir in the scallions.

LEFT TO RIGHT Mold the shrimp paste around the sugarcane using a little bit of pressure so that it adheres to the cane pieces. The shrimp paste should be opaque when it is properly steamed. Grilling the shrimp adds a great deal of flavor; it is important not to grill the shrimp too long or it will become tough and dry.

5. Wet your hands, and form about 2 tablespoons of the shrimp paste into a ball. Flatten the paste until it is about ½ inch thick, and place a piece of sugarcane in the center. Wrap the paste around the cane, making the paste about 1 inch thick and leaving about ½ inch of exposed cane on both ends to use for handles. Press the paste onto the cane so it sticks. Lightly oil your hands and smooth the surface. Set aside on an oiled plate. Finish molding all the paste onto the sugarcane pieces.

6. Preheat a gas grill to medium. If you are using a charcoal grill, build a fire and let it burn down until the coals are glowing red with a moderate coating of white ash. Spread the coals in an even bed. Clean the cooking grate.

7. Set the skewered shrimp paste in a steamer basket lined with lettuce leaves. Set over a pot of simmering water, cover, and steam the shrimp paste on the sugarcane until just cooked through and firm, 3 to 5 minutes. If unsure, break one open and check the middle for doneness and color.

8. Place the steamed shrimp pieces on the grill over direct heat. Grill for 1 minute, then give each piece a quarter turn. Grill for another minute. Flip each piece over and grill for another 3 minutes, or until the shrimp is heated through and there are ample grill marks.

9. To make the table salad: Arrange a lettuce leaf, a small pile of bean sprouts, and a small pile of cucumber on each plate. Combine the herbs and sprinkle on top of the bean sprouts and the cucumber. Drizzle the salads with the Scallion Oil. Place 2 pieces of the grilled shrimp on top of each salad. Spoon the Hoisin Peanut Sauce over the shrimp pieces. Serve immediately.

NOTE: These shrimp paste skewers could also be seared using a nonstick stovetop grill pan over medium-high heat.

Scallion Oil

MAKES 1 CUP

½ cup vegetable oil

½ cup thinly sliced scallions

1. Combine the oil and scallions in a small sauté pan and heat over medium flame until the oil begins to sizzle, about 1 minute.

2. Remove from heat and let cool to room temperature. The oil is ready to use now or it may be stored in the refrigerator for up to 3 days.

Hoisin Peanut Sauce

MAKES 1¼ CUPS

½ cup hoisin sauce

¼ cup water

¼ cup rice vinegar

¼ cup minced shallots

1 tbsp Vietnamese chili-garlic paste

1 tbsp chopped roasted unsalted peanuts

1. Combine the hoisin, water, rice vinegar, and shallots in a small sauté pan and bring to a boil over high heat. Reduce heat to medium and simmer for 5 minutes, until the sauce darkens slightly and lightly coats the back of a spoon.

2. Remove from heat and let cool to room temperature. Stir in the chili-garlic paste and peanuts. The sauce is ready to use now or it may be stored in a container in the refrigerator for up to 1 week.

Working with Artichokes

Before you serve whole artichokes or just their hearts, trim away the thorns and scoop out the choke.

TRIMMING WHOLE ARTICHOKES

Once artichokes are cut and exposed to air they start to turn brown. An acid such as lemon juice slows this discoloration. Whenever you are cutting artichokes, cut a lemon in half to rub on cut surfaces or fill a bowl with water and add a squeeze of lemon juice and salt to hold the artichokes after trimming.

Cut the stem flush with the base of the artichoke or leave it intact, but peel the stem and trim off the rough bottom. For artichokes served whole, use a chef's knife to cut off the top inch of the artichoke, and then use kitchen scissors to remove any remaining barbed leaf tips and create a neat appearance. For artichoke hearts, pull away the outer leaves, leaving only the tender inner leaves at the center. To remove the choke before cooking, spread open the leaves of the artichoke. Use a grapefruit spoon, tablespoon, or melon baller to scoop out and discard the pale, purple-tinged leaves.

TRIMMING ARTICHOKE BOTTOMS

To prepare artichoke bottoms, cut away the outer leaves with a paring knife at a point that stops just outside of the yellow center (below left). Trim and peel the stem (below center) or cut it flush with the artichoke base. Make a cut crosswise through the artichoke at its widest point. Scoop out the choke at the center with a grapefruit spoon or teaspoon (below right). The bottom should look like a bowl. Hold the trimmed artichoke bottoms in lemon water to prevent browning.

COOKING ARTICHOKES

Artichokes are typically cooked by boiling them. Fill a pot with enough water to completely submerge the artichokes and add salt and lemon juice to season the water. The taste of salt and lemon juice should be noticeable. (You can substitute other citrus fruits such as limes or grapefruits, or replace the lemon juice with a white vinegar.) When the water is simmering, add the artichokes and cover them with a clean plate small enough to fit down into the pot, so that it can keep the artichokes under the surface as they cook.

An alternative is to use thawed frozen artichokes, if you can find them in your market. Canned artichokes (both hearts and bottoms) are widely available as both brine-packed or marinated. Brine-packed versions can be used in most recipes with good results, as long as you carefully rinse the artichokes to remove the brine. Reserve marinated artichokes to feature in salads or antipasto platters, rather than use them in cooked dishes.

GRILLED ARTICHOKES
with *Hazelnut Romesco Sauce*

SELECT THE smallest artichokes you can find for this dish. Whatever the size of your artichoke, the leaves should be firmly attached.

MAKES 8 SERVINGS

2 bay leaves

1 lemon, halved

8 artichokes

½ tsp salt

½ tsp pepper

¾ cup olive oil

3 garlic cloves, sliced

2 cups Hazelnut Romesco Sauce (recipe follows)

1. Add the bay leaves and 1 lemon half to 2 quarts of water in a large stockpot. Season with the salt and pepper, and bring to a simmer.

2. Trim the stems of each artichoke and peel them to expose the tender flesh. Remove the outer petals to expose the soft, light green petals toward the center. Slice off the top 1 inch of each artichoke.

3. Add the artichokes to the simmering water. Cover the pan and simmer over medium-low heat until tender, about 20 minutes. Remove the artichokes from the water and allow to cool.

4. Quarter each artichoke and remove the hairy choke from the center of each. Place the artichoke quarters in a zip-close bag. Add the olive oil, garlic, and the juice of the remaining lemon half. Let marinate in the refrigerator for at least 30 minutes and up to 4 hours.

5. Preheat a gas grill to medium heat. If you are using a charcoal grill, build a fire and let it burn down until the coals are glowing red with a moder-

ate coating of white ash. Spread the coals in an even bed. Clean the cooking grate.

6. Remove the artichokes from the marinade and grill uncovered over direct heat, turning often, until golden, about 10 minutes.

7. Serve the artichoke quarters on serving plates with hazelnut romesco sauce drizzled over the top.

Hazelnut Romesco Sauce

THIS RICH sauce is an ideal accompaniment to grilled and broiled vegetables or savory vegetable entrees.

MAKES 2 CUPS

2 dried ancho chiles

Cold water as needed

2 cups chopped roasted red bell pepper

2 cups chopped hazelnuts, skinned

⅔ cup olive oil

2 tbsp tomato paste

2 tbsp red wine vinegar

1 tbsp minced garlic

1½ tsp Spanish paprika

¼ tsp cayenne pepper

Salt as needed

1. Put the ancho chiles in a small saucepan and cover with cold water. Bring to a boil over high heat, then immediately remove the pan from the heat. Let the chiles steep for 20 minutes. Strain the chiles from the water. Reserve some of the soaking liquid to adjust the consistency of the sauce.

2. Put the roasted red pepper, hazelnuts, olive oil, tomato paste, vinegar, garlic, paprika, and cayenne in a blender. Puree to a smooth consistency, adding a bit of the chile soaking liquid, if necessary, to puree the sauce and reach a soft, sauce-like consistency (about the same consistency as mayonnaise).

Place in a covered container, refrigerate, and allow to rest overnight to develop the best flavor. Adjust the seasoning with salt before serving.

PARMESAN-ROASTED WHITE ASPARAGUS
with White Truffle Oil

ROASTING ASPARAGUS is an unexpected and surprisingly delicious alternative to steaming. We've suggested white asparagus in this recipe, but green asparagus would be equally delicious.

MAKES 4 SERVINGS

2 bunches white asparagus, trimmed

2 tbsp walnut or extra-virgin olive oil

1 tbsp grated Parmesan cheese

½ tsp chopped thyme

Salt and pepper as needed

White truffle oil, optional

1. Preheat the oven to 425°F.
2. Place the asparagus on a baking sheet and drizzle with the oil, Parmesan, thyme, salt, and pepper. Roast, turning the asparagus once or twice as it roasts, until the asparagus is tender with a crisp coating of Parmesan, 12 to 15 minutes. Serve warm or at room temperature. Drizzle with a little truffle oil just before serving if desired.

SPINACH AND SAUSAGE STUFFED MUSHROOMS

TRY OTHER varieties of mushrooms in this dish, if you wish. You can stuff the mushrooms up to 2 days before baking them.

MAKES 6 SERVINGS

12 large white mushrooms

½ lb Italian sausage, sweet or hot

1 cup chopped chopped fresh spinach leaves

½ cup minced flat-leaf parsley

½ cup grated Parmesan cheese

½ cup minced scallions

1 large egg, lightly beaten

Salt and pepper as needed

¼ cup butter

¼ cup plain breadcrumbs

1. Preheat the oven to 400°F.
2. Cut the stems away from the mushroom caps and trim to remove any dirt or bruised portions. Chop the stems and reserve. Scrape the gills from the mushroom caps and reserve separately.
3. Remove the sausage from its casing and crumble. Heat a large skillet over medium-high heat. Add the sausage and cook, stirring with a wooden spoon to break up any large clumps, until the sausage is no longer pink, about 5 minutes. Use a slotted spoon to lift the sausage from the skillet. Drain the sausage in a sieve to allow any grease to drain away. Transfer to a mixing bowl when cool.
4. Return the skillet to medium-high heat. Add the chopped mushroom stems and sauté until they are tender and any moisture they release has cooked away, 2 to 3 minutes. Add the spinach and sauté until the spinach is tender, about 4 minutes. Add the spinach mixture to the sausage and stir to combine. When the mixture has cooled to room temperature, stir in the parsley, ¼ cup of Parmesan, the scallions, and egg. Stir until blended. Season to taste with salt and pepper.
5. Return the skillet to medium heat. Add the butter and heat until the butter is melted but not foaming.

Add the mushroom caps to the butter and roll or toss the caps in the butter until they are evenly coated. Continue to cook, partially covered, until the caps are heated through, 2 to 3 minutes. Remove them from the pan using a slotted spoon and transfer to a baking dish. Fill the mushroom caps with the sausage stuffing mixture. Combine the remaining ¼ cup Parmesan with the breadcrumbs and sprinkle evenly over the tops of the mushrooms. Bake until the tops of the mushrooms are golden and crisp, 10 to 12 minutes. Serve at once.

VEGETABLE TEMPURA

THE POPULARITY of these crisp, batter-dipped vegetables as an appetizer has spread beyond Japanese restaurants.

MAKES 4 TO 6 SERVINGS AS AN APPETIZER

DIPPING SAUCE

2 scallions, minced

¼ cup soy sauce, plus as needed

¼ cup water

2 tbsp rice vinegar

2 tbsp honey

1 tbsp minced fresh ginger

2 garlic cloves, minced

1 tsp dry mustard

1 tsp hot chili sauce, plus as needed

BATTER

2 cups all-purpose flour

4 tsp baking powder

2 cups cold water

¼ cup dark sesame oil

1 cup red pepper strips

1 cup yellow pepper strips

1 cup broccoli florets

1 cup quartered mushrooms

1 small zucchini, cut on the diagonal, ⅛ inch thick

1 small yellow squash, cut on the diagonal, ⅛ inch thick

Salt and pepper as needed

Vegetable oil for deep frying

1. For the dipping sauce: Combine the scallions, soy sauce, water, vinegar, honey, ginger, garlic, mustard, and hot sauce in a bowl. Cover and refrigerate to let the flavors blend for at least 1 hour or up to 12 hours. Taste and adjust the seasoning with soy sauce and hot sauce before serving.

2. For the batter: Whisk together the flour and baking powder. Add the cold water and sesame oil all at once and whisk until about the thickness of pancake batter and very smooth. Refrigerate until ready to prepare the tempura.

3. Pour the oil into a tall pot to a depth of 3 inches. Heat over medium heat until the oil registers 350°F on a deep-frying thermometer.

4. While the oil heats, blot the vegetables dry and season with salt and pepper. Dip the vegetables in the batter to coat evenly. Working in batches to avoid crowding. slip the batter-coated vegetables into the hot oil. Deep fry until the batter is golden brown and puffy, 3 to 4 minutes. Turn the vegetables, if necessary, to brown and cook evenly. Remove from the pot with tongs and drain briefly on absorbent towels. Serve at once with the dipping sauce.

How to Cut Vegetables for Tempura

You can take some liberties in how you prepare the vegetables for tempura, but be sure that they're cut so that they will be tender inside just when the batter is crisp and golden. Here are some suggested cutting techniques. Remember to dry all ingredients thoroughly before dunking them in the tempura batter.

ZUCCHINI AND YELLOW SQUASH: Cut on a sharp diagonal to make elongated ovals, ½ inch thick, or cut in lengthwise wedges, 3 to 4 inches long.

BELL PEPPERS: Core and seed, remove the ribs, and cut lengthwise into strips ½ inch wide.

SHIITAKE MUSHROOMS: Remove stems and fry the caps whole or cut out a decorative star on top.

GREEN BEANS: Trim ends and fry whole.

SWEET ONIONS: Before peeling, cut into rings 1 inch thick; then pull off outer layer of skin.

EGGPLANT: Cut in half lengthwise, cut half moons ¼ inch thick; sprinkle lightly with salt and let sit for 20 minutes to purge excess bitter juices; rinse and pat dry.

ASPARAGUS: Trim off the woody base with a diagonal cut.

SWEET POTATOES AND MOST ROOT VEGETABLES: Cut into slices, ¼ inch thick.

CARROTS AND PARSNIPS: Cut on a sharp angle to make elongated ovals, ¼ inch thick.

LOTUS ROOT: Cut in cross-sections to reveal the beautiful seed pod pattern, ¼ inch thick.

WARM BLACK-EYED PEA SALAD
with Lemon-Basil Vinaigrette

SUBSTITUTE OTHER herbs for the basil in the vinaigrette, if you wish, like thyme, oregano, or chives. Add a sprinkling of lemon zest to give additional color and appeal to the salad.

MAKES 8 SERVINGS

1 tbsp olive oil
1 cup minced onion
2 garlic cloves, minced
1 tbsp lemon zest

6 cups chicken broth, plus as needed
2 cups dried black-eyed peas, sorted and rinsed
2 sprigs thyme
2 sprigs rosemary
2 bay leaves

LEMON-BASIL VINAIGRETTE

½ cup extra virgin olive oil
¼ cup fresh lemon juice
½ cup basil, chiffonade
½ tsp salt
¼ tsp freshly ground black pepper

1. Heat the oil in a sauce pan over medium heat. Add the onions and sauté until translucent, about 5 minutes. Add the garlic and lemon zest and continue to sauté until aromatic, 2 minutes more.

2. Add the broth, black-eyed peas, thyme, rosemary, and bay leaves and bring to a boil. Reduce the heat and simmer until the peas are tender, about 1 hour. Add additional broth if necessary to keep the peas covered thoughout the cooking time.

3. While the peas cook, whisk together the olive oil, lemon juice, basil, salt, and pepper to combine.

4. Drain the black-eyed peas in a colander. Remove and discard the rosemary, thyme, and bay leaves. Add the hot peas to the lemon basil vinaigrette and toss gently until evenly coated. Serve warm or at room temperature.

PANZANELLA
Bread Salad with Fresh Tomatoes

PANZANELLA IS an Italian bread-and-tomato salad made with garlic, basil, parsley, olive oil, and vinegar. While this recipe calls for toasting the bread, other variations may call for soaking the bread in water before tossing it with the remaining ingredients.

MAKES 8 SERVINGS

1 baguette, 24-inch, preferably 2 days old

1 tbsp butter

½ cup plus 3 tbsp extra-virgin olive oil

¼ cup garlic, chopped

2 lb tomatoes

½ cup balsamic vinegar

2 tsp salt, or to taste

1 tsp freshly ground black pepper, or to taste

1 bunch basil

½ cup roughly chopped parsley

1. Cut the baguette into cubes 1-inch square. Toast in a 350°F oven for 1 to 2 minutes or until crisp and dry, stirring occasionally if necessary.

2. Place the butter and 2 tablespoons of the olive oil into a 10-inch sauté pan over medium low heat. Allow the butter to melt, then add the garlic. Sauté 2 to 3 minutes until translucent but not brown. Toss the garlic, butter, and oil with the diced bread.

3. Slice the tomatoes and place in a large bowl. Add the vinegar, remaining olive oil, salt, and pepper.

4. Layer one-quarter of the basil leaves on top of each other and roll into a tight bunch. Thinly slice the bunch of leaves crosswise to create long strips of basil approximately ⅛-inch thick.

5. Just before serving, toss the bread, basil, and parsley with the tomatoes. Adjust the seasoning with additional salt and pepper if necessary.

SOUTHWESTERN SLAW

THIS PIQUANT slaw is the perfect accompaniment to grilled meats or poultry.

MAKES 8 SERVINGS

2 cups fine-shredded green cabbage

2 tsp lime juice

2 tsp honey

2 tbsp minced red onion

2 tsp minced jalapeños

2 tsp chopped cilantro

Salt, to taste

Combine all the ingredients. Allow the mixture to marinate for at least 30 minutes and up to 8 hours before serving.

MOROCCAN CARROT SALAD

THIS UNUSUAL carrot salad gets its mysteriously rich taste in part from the dates, which infuse the onions with their sweetness as they cook.

MAKES 8 SERVINGS

2 lb carrots, peeled and thinly sliced

2 garlic cloves

4 tbsp olive oil

Juice of 1 lemon

1 tbsp ground cumin

Small pinch of cayenne pepper

1 tsp minced cilantro

1 tsp minced parsley

2 onions, finely chopped

1 cup chopped dates

1. In a medium saucepan, combine the carrots and garlic. Add water to cover by 1 or 2 inches. Bring to a simmer and cook until tender, about 5 minutes. Using a slotted spoon, transfer the carrots to a bowl.

2. Cook the cooking liquid over medium heat to reduce to ½ cup. Whisk in 2 tablespoons of the

olive oil and the lemon juice to the reduced cooking liquid. Pour the mixture over the carrots. Add the cumin, cayenne, cilantro, and parsley. Set aside.

3. Heat the remaining olive oil in a medium saucepan over medium heat. Add the onions and sauté until translucent, about 5 minutes. Add the dates and cook until the dates are softened. Toss the onion and date mixture with the carrots. Let cool. Cover the salad and refrigerate for 1 to 2 hours before serving.

CUCUMBER, TOMATO, AND FETA SALAD

THIS SALAD is simple to prepare and perfect for a summer lunch, when tomatoes and cucumbers are just waiting to be enjoyed.

MAKES 6 SERVINGS

3½ cups cucumbers, sliced and quartered

1½ cups tomatoes, diced

1/4 lb feta cheese

1 cup red onion, thinly sliced

¼ cup red wine vinegar

1 tbsp oregano, coarsely chopped

1 tsp salt, or to taste

1 tsp freshly ground black
    pepper, or to taste

½ cup extra-virgin olive oil

1. Combine the cucumbers, tomatoes, cheese, and onion in a salad bowl.

2. In a separate bowl, combine the vinegar, oregano, salt, and pepper. Stream in all of the olive oil while whisking constantly.

3. Toss the the salad ingredients with the dressing and serve.

FARRO SALAD
Insalata di Farro

FARRO IS an ancestor to the wheat grown today. It was the primary ingredient in *puls*, the polenta eaten for centuries by the Roman poor before corn was introduced from the New World. Farro has a pleasant, chewy texture and it absorbs other flavors beautifully. The salad also is delicious made with barley instead of farro.

MAKES 4 SERVINGS

3 cups water

Salt as needed

1 cup farro, soaked in cold water for 1 hour

¼ cup lemon juice

6 or 7 mint sprigs

¼ cup red wine vinegar

¼ cup chopped fresh mint

Pinch of sugar, or as needed

1¼ cups extra-virgin olive oil

Freshly ground black pepper as needed

2 beefsteak tomatoes, seeded and chopped

½ cup diced seeded cucumber

½ cup diced celery or fennel

½ cup diced red or yellow bell pepper

⅓ cup diced red onion

¼ cup chopped fresh basil or mint

¼ cup chopped flat leaf parsley

1. Bring 3 cups of lightly salted water to a boil over high heat in a saucepan. Add the farro and stir once or twice to separate the grains. Reduce the heat to medium and simmer, covered, until the farro doubles in volume and is tender to the bite, 25 to 30 minutes. Drain the farro, if necessary, transfer it to a salad bowl, and cool to room temperature. Set aside.

2. To make the dressing: Combine the lemon juice and mint sprigs in a small pan and bring to a boil over high heat. Immediately remove the pan from the heat, cover, and let the mint infuse the lemon juice until flavorful, about 10 minutes. Remove and discard the mint sprigs. Whisk in the vinegar, mint, and a pinch of sugar. Add the oil while whisking until the dressing is blended and lightly thickened. Season to taste with salt and pepper.

3. Add the tomatoes, cucumber, celery or fennel, bell pepper, red onion, basil or mint, and parsley to the farro. Pour the dressing over the salad ingredients and fold the salad together until it is evenly dressed. Serve on chilled plates.

FRENCH LENTIL SALAD

Lentils, available in many varieties, are quick-cooking legumes. Substitute red or yellow lentils for the brown French lentils to create a more vibrantly colored salad.

MAKES 8 SERVINGS

2 cups French lentils

4 cups water

¾ cup carrots, small dice

½ cup celery, small dice

1 cup red onion, small dice

¼ lb white mushrooms, thinly sliced

2 tsp mustard

2 tsp salt, or to taste

¼ cup cider vinegar

½ cup olive oil

1. Simmer the lentils in the water until they are tender, about 25 minutes. Rinse the lentils in cold water until they are slightly chilled and drain well.

2. Combine the lentils, carrots, celery, onion, and mushrooms.

3. Combine the mustard, salt, and vinegar. Stream in the olive oil while whisking to fully combine.

4. Toss the dressing with the lentil mixture.

MARINATED PEPPER SALAD
with Pine Nuts and Raisins

Feel free to add other ingredients to this dish, including thin slices of celery, fresh basil or cilantro, or red onions. It makes a great accompaniment to grilled, roasted, or baked meats, fish, or poultry.

MAKES 8 SERVINGS

4 red peppers, cored and quartered

4 yellow peppers, cored and quartered

¼ cup olive oil

2 tsp salt, or to taste

1 tsp ground black pepper, or to taste

½ cup extra-virgin olive oil

1 cup golden raisins

1 cup toasted pine nuts

⅓ cup chopped parsley

1 tbsp minced garlic

1. Preheat a gas grill to medium. If you are using a charcoal grill, build a fire and let it burn down until the coals are glowing red with a moderate coating of white ash. Spread the coals in an even bed. Clean the cooking grate.

2. Brush the peppers with the olive oil and season with the salt and pepper.

3. Grill the peppers until marked on each side and tender throughout but not mushy, about 5 minutes per side.

KIR ROYALE
(PAGE 2)

RASPBERRY
LEMONADE
(PAGE 4)

LEMONADE (PAGE 2)

GINGER LEMONADE
(PAGE 4)

SANGRIA (PAGE 5)

BUBBLE TEA (PAGE 8)

MANGO LASSI (PAGE 12)

BLACK BEAN AND AVOCADO
CROSTINI (PAGE 14)

PROSCIUTTO AND MELON
CANAPÉ (PAGE 14)

LIMA BEAN SPREAD (PAGE 18)

SALSA FRESCA (PAGE 19)

ARTICHOKE CEVICHE IN BELGIAN ENDIVE
(PAGE 24)

GREEN BEANS WITH
FRIZZLED PROSCIUTTO AND
GRUYÈRE (PAGE 27)

SMOKED TROUT WITH
APPLE-HORSERADISH CREAM
(PAGE 25)

STUFFED CHERRY TOMATOES WITH
MINTED BARLEY CUCUMBER SALAD
(PAGE 27)

SATAY OF BEEF WITH PEANUT SAUCE
(PAGE 28)

SPICY LAMB KEBABS WITH
PICKLED GRAPES (PAGE 29)

MUSSELS WITH OLIVES
(PAGE 30)

SEARED SCALLOPS WITH FIERY FRUIT SALSA
(PAGE 35)

TOMATO SAMPLER WITH
PAN-FRIED CALAMARI
(PAGE 38)

GRILLED SHRIMP PASTE ON SUGARCANE
WITH HOISIN PEANUT SAUCE (PAGE 38)

VEGETABLE TEMPURA
(PAGE 44)

PANZANELLA
(PAGE 45)

MARINATED PEPPER SALAD WITH
PINE NUTS AND RAISINS (PAGE 48)

TOMATO, AVOCADO, AND ROASTED CORN SALAD (PAGE 51)

ROASTED EGGPLANT SALAD (PAGE 53)

4. Cut the grilled peppers into ¼-inch-thick slices and drain in a sieve or colander for 2 hours.

5. Combine the peppers with the extra-virgin olive oil, raisins, pine nuts, parsley, and garlic. Adjust seasoning to taste with salt and pepper, if desired.

Roasting Peppers on the Stovetop

• Use tongs or a fork to hold a whole pepper in the flame of a gas burner, turning the pepper until all of its sides are blackened, or

• Cut the peppers in half, pull away the seeds, and rub the outsides lightly with oil. Place them, cut side down, on a baking sheet and broil until blackened.

Once the peppers are blackened (by either method), place them in a plastic bag and let them rest until they are cool enough to handle. Then pull away the charred skin, using a paring knife or your fingers to loosen the skin. Discard the seeds, ribs, and stems.

RADISH SALAD WITH PEARS

S ERVE THIS refreshing salad with slightly spicy foods. It's a great foil for bold flavors and brings a touch of sweetness to the plate.

MAKES 6 SERVINGS

36 small radishes, sliced thin

2 pears, peeled, quartered, and sliced thin

¼ cup distilled white vinegar

2 tbsp olive oil

1 tsp sugar, or to taste

Salt and freshly ground pepper, to taste

3 tbsp plain yogurt

Combine the sliced radishes and pears in a large bowl. Add the vinegar, oil, sugar, salt, and pepper.

Stir gently until well combined. Cover and marinate at room temperature for 15 minutes. Blend in the yogurt. Taste and adjust the seasoning, if necessary. Cover and refrigerate for at least 1 to 2 hours before serving.

SCALLION SALAD

MAKES 8 SERVINGS

½ tsp granulated sugar

¼ tsp sesame oil

1 tsp mirin (sweet rice wine)

½ tsp toasted sesame seeds, smashed

½ tsp Korean red pepper powder

1 tsp salt

2 cups scallion julienne

1. Combine the sugar, sesame oil, mirin, sesame seeds, red pepper powder, and salt.

2. Toss together the dressing with the scallions just before serving.

FRUIT SALAD
with Orange-Blossom Syrup

O RANGE-BLOSSOM WATER, generally available from health food stores and wholesalers, adds a fragrant touch to the delicious syrup. It is distilled from bitter orange flowers and is commonly used in beverages, confections, and baked goods.

MAKES 8 SERVINGS

¾ cup orange-blossom water

2 tbsp sugar

1 orange

1¼ cup diced cantaloupe

2 cups diced pineapple

1¼ cups red grapes

1½ cups quartered strawberries

1 cup blueberries

⅔ cup diced kiwi

¼ cup thi n sliced mint

1. To make the syrup, combine the orange-blossom water and the sugar in a small saucepan. Heat, stirring occasionally, until the sugar completely dissolves. Set aside until needed.

2. Zest the orange using the smallest holes on a grater. Reserve the orange for another use.

3. Combine all of the fruits except the kiwi in a large bowl.

4. Serve immediately or refrigerate until needed. For individual servings, place 1 cup of the fruit salad in a glass or serving dish. Top with 1 tablespoon of the syrup. Spoon 1 tablespoon of the diced kiwi on top of the fruit. Garnish the fruit with the orange zest and mint chiffonade. Alternately, the fruit salad can be garnished and served in a large bowl.

Composed Salads

Carefully arranging items on a plate, rather than tossing them together, forms a composed salad. A "main item," such as grilled chicken or shrimp, a portion of cheese or grilled vegetables, and so forth, is often set on a bed of greens.

The formulation of a composed salad is rather loose, but the following guidelines should be kept in mind when deciding upon the ingredients:

- *CONSIDER THE ELEMENTS: Contrasting flavors are intriguing, conflicting are not.*

- *REPETITION OF COLOR OR FLAVOR can contribute to the dish; too much of a good thing is just too much.*

- *ALL OF THE COMPONENTS should be capable of standing alone; however, the composition should be that each part is enhanced in combination with the others.*

- *THE SALAD SHOULD BE ARRANGED in a way that the textures and colors of the food are most attractive to the eye.*

BAKED GOAT CHEESE
with Mesclun, Pears, and Toasted Almonds

THE RICH and creamy texture of the cheese contrasts nicely with its crispy, baked crust. The almonds add a deep, rich flavor to the dish. The backdrop of the mesclun pulls all the elements together.

MAKES 8 SERVINGS

1¼ lb goat cheese, well chilled

1 cup dry breadcrumbs

1½ lb mesclun lettuce mix, or a mixture of mesclun and frisée

¾ cup extra-virgin olive oil

¼ cup lemon juice

Salt, to taste

Freshly ground black pepper, to taste

2 pears, cored, sliced into thin wedges

1 cup slivered almonds

1. Preheat the oven to 400°F. Slice the goat cheese into ½-inch thick discs. Gently coat the goat cheese with the breadcrumbs and place on a baking sheet. Bake the goat cheese in a 400°F oven until lightly browned, about 10 minutes. Allow the cheese to cool slightly while assembling the salads.

2. Toss the mesclun mix with the olive oil, lemon juice, salt, and pepper. Divide the lettuce into 8 portions and mound each portion on a plate. Top each portion with 3 or 4 pear slices, about 2 tablespoons of almonds, and 2 goat cheese rounds.

SALAD OF CRAB AND AVOCADO

THIS SALAD is substantial enough to serve as a summertime entrée when accompanied by Cornbread (page 244) to accent the salad's Southwestern flavor profile.

MAKES 8 SERVINGS

½ cup small diced red pepper

2 plum tomatoes, cored and chopped

2 scallions, sliced thinly on the diagonal

1 clove garlic, minced

2 tbsp chopped cilantro

2 tsp minced jalapeño, seeds and veins removed

1 tsp salt, or to taste

¼ tsp freshly ground black pepper, or to taste

2½ cups lump crabmeat, pasteurized, picked over to remove cartilage and shell

2 avocados, peeled and cut into small dice

3 tbsp lime juice

¼ cup sour cream

1. Toss together the red pepper, tomato, scallions, garlic, cilantro, and jalapeño to form a salsa. Season with ¼ teaspoon salt and a pinch of black pepper and let the mixture sit at room temperature while working on the rest of the appetizer (about 20 minutes). Combine the avocado, lime juice, ½ teaspoon salt, and a pinch of black pepper.

2. In a 6-fluid-ounce glass, layer ¼ cup of the tomato salsa, about 5 tablespoons of crab, and 2 tablespoons of the avocado mixture. Spoon approximately 1 teaspoon of sour cream on top of the avocado layer. Garnish with a little bit of the salsa.

NOTE: Be sure to wear gloves while mincing the jalapeño to prevent irritation of your skin.

TOMATO, AVOCADO, AND ROASTED CORN SALAD

IF YOU have the grill going, you can cook the corn on the grill instead of in the oven.

MAKES 8 SERVINGS

4 ears corn on the cob with husks still attached

Salt, as needed

6 cups mesclun lettuce mix, rinsed and dried

1 cup Chipotle-Sherry Vinaigrette (page 56)

3 red beefsteak tomatoes, sliced ¼ inch thick

2 avocados, cut into slices

1 medium red onion, sliced thin

1 cup small-diced aged Cheddar cheese

2 tsp freshly ground black pepper

1. Preheat oven to 400°F. Roast the unhusked ears of corn until tender, about 45 minutes. Check their doneness after about 45 minutes; pull the husk partially away from the biggest ear. If you can pierce a kernel easily with a fork, it is done. Remove from the oven and cool completely.

2. Shuck the corn and cut the kernels from the cobs. Place the corn kernels in a mixing bowl and toss with 1 teaspoon of the salt. Keep the corn at room temperature if you are making the salad right away, or cover and refrigerate for up to 12 hours.

3. Toss the mesclun mix with ½ cup vinaigrette. Mound the dressed mesclun on a chilled platter or individual plates. Arrange the tomatoes, avocados, and red onion over the mesclun. Sprinkle with the cheese and reserved corn. Drizzle with the remaining ½ cup dressing. Season to taste with salt and pepper. Serve immediately.

Selecting and Preparing Salad Greens

Salad greens include lettuce of all types, as well as other leafy vegetables, such as Belgian endive and watercress. The selection of greens and their complementary dressings lend themselves to many forms and appearances. In its most basic form, a green salad is one or two lettuces tossed with a dressing and garnished with vegetables, croutons, or cheeses. More complex or composed salads usually are served as main-course meals or appetizers rather than an accompaniment.

Today, you can feature a wider variety and better quality of greens than ever before in your salad bowl. Salad greens can be grouped according to their flavors and/or textures:

MILD GREENS: Bibb, Boston, green or red leaf, iceberg, mâche, oak, romaine, various baby varieties of cooking greens

SPICY GREENS: Amaranth, arugula, mizuna, tat-soi, watercress

BITTER GREENS AND CHICORIES: Belgian endive (or witloof), curly endive (known as chicory or frisée), radicchio

HERBS AND FLOWERS: Basil, chives, chervil, mint, parsley, chrysanthemums, nasturtiums, pansies

Lettuce blends are readily available in virtually every market. You can select from precut lettuces such as romaine, iceberg, or baby spinach; or try more exotic blends, sometimes referred to by their French name, *mesclun*. These precut and cleaned greens can be purchased in your local market. A great boon to the time-challenged cook, precut and packaged salad greens still need a thorough rinse and a few turns in your salad spinner. If you have a bit more time, you can prepare your own blend from individual greens, using the preceding list as a flavor guide and your own sense of color to guide you. Using more than one color, flavor, or texture is a great way to make your own custom blend.

CLEAN THE GREENS

Nothing is worse than a gritty salad or one that forces your friends and family to use a knife to cut the lettuce. All greens, including prepackaged salad mixes and "triple-washed" bagged spinach, must be washed and dried prior to serving and should be kept properly chilled until ready to eat.

Salad greens are highly perishable and require proper handling. More tender greens, such as Boston lettuce or mâche, last only a day or two; romaine and iceberg are heartier and last much longer. If you purchase your fresh produce at a weekly farmer's market, be sure to enjoy tender greens right away and save the longer-lasting ones for later in the week.

The salad spinner is a relatively inexpensive piece of time-saving equipment for salad washing. Through centrifugal force, the salad spinner cleans the greens while spinning away water. This ensures the greens will have better flavor and the dressing will cling to them more evenly. Wash the greens thoroughly in plenty of cool water to remove all traces of dirt and sand:

1. Separate the greens into leaves, and trim coarse rims or stem ends or ribs.

2. Fill a large bowl or a clean sink with cold water, then add the lettuce. Swish it gently through the water and lift it away. Check the bottom of the bowl or sink; if you feel any grit or sand, drain the water and repeat until all traces of grit are gone.

3. Dry the greens completely. Greens that are properly dried have more flavor and, when stored, last longer. Fill the basket of a salad spinner and spin until the leaves are dry.

4. Store cleaned and dried greens in the refrigerator until ready to dress and serve. Keep them in plastic containers or zipper-lock bags with a piece of paper towel to absorb any excess moisture, or in your salad spinner. Use the greens within a day or two.

CUT OR TEAR THE GREENS INTO BITE-SIZE PIECES

Use clean fingers to tear lettuce into pieces or use a knife to cut greens into pieces or to shred them. If you are using a knife, make it a habit to sharpen the blade before you begin. A sharp edge will cut cleanly through the leafy greens and you won't bruise or crush the lettuce. Use a high-carbon, stainless steel blade so you don't discolor the leaves.

TOMATO SALAD
with Warm Ricotta Cheese

TRY THIS unique and interesting way of serving ricotta cheese for a twist on a favorite summer treat. You can use all extra-virgin olive oil as we do here, or use a blend of olive oils to achieve a lighter flavor if you prefer.

MAKES 6 SERVINGS

2 lb ricotta cheese

1 tsp salt, plus additional to taste

1¼ cups extra-virgin olive oil

1 tsp coarse-grind black pepper, plus additional to taste

3 tbsp fine-dice shallots

3 tbsp red wine vinegar

2 tbsp sherry vinegar

1 basil sprig

2 lb red, yellow, and orange cherry and pear tomatoes

3 tsp minced basil

1. To make the ricotta cheese, preheat the oven to 350°F. Mix the ricotta and ½ teaspoon of the salt together well. Put the mixture in a small baking dish or casserole. Drizzle with ¼ cup of the olive oil and sprinkle with ½ teaspoon of the pepper. Bake until browned on top and bubbling around the edges, about 20 minutes. Let sit for about 10 minutes before serving.

2. Meanwhile, combine the shallots, vinegars, ½ teaspoon salt, ½ teaspoon pepper, and the basil sprig in a bowl; let sit for 20 minutes.

3. Remove and discard the basil sprig. Whisk in the remaining oil. Adjust the flavor as necessary with additional vinegar, salt, and pepper.

4. Cut any large tomatoes into halves or quarters; leave small ones whole. Add the tomatoes to the vinaigrette and toss to coat them evenly. Divide the tomatoes among six salad plates. Add a spoonful of the warm ricotta to each. Scatter the minced basil over the top of the salads.

ROASTED EGGPLANT SALAD

THIS EGGPLANT salad makes a great dip or even a filling for a sandwich, but to make it the center of a meal, serve it with plenty of pita bread, olives, feta cheese, and nuts.

MAKES 4 SERVINGS

3 lb eggplant (1 large or 2 medium)

2 to 3 lemons

¼ cup extra-virgin olive oil, plus as needed

4 tbsp finely chopped flat-leaf parsley

4 garlic cloves, minced

2 tsp ground cumin

Salt as needed

Freshly ground black pepper as needed

½ cup crumbled feta cheese

1 cup thinly sliced cucumber

4 plum tomatoes, sliced thin

¼ cup cured olives

1 green pepper, roasted, seeded, and cut into strips

½ cup coarsely chopped toasted walnuts

4 pita breads, warmed

1. For a smoky taste, grill eggplants under the broiler, turning often, or cook them slowly on a stovetop cast iron griddle. You also can bake them at 400°F until the eggplants are soft throughout. Drain in a colander.

2. Halve the lemons and squeeze the juice. Set the juice aside and put the peels into a small bowl of

cold water. When the eggplants are cool enough to handle, strip away the skin and scoop out and discard any large seed pockets. Place remaining eggplant pulp in the lemon water. After a few minutes, drain the eggplant pulp and squeeze dry.

3. Mash the eggplant in bowl and blend in the olive oil, lemon juice, chopped parsley, garlic, and cumin. Season to taste with additional olive oil, lemon juice, salt, and pepper.

4. Chill well before serving on chilled plates garnished with feta cheese, slices of cucumber, tomato, olives, green pepper, and walnuts. Accompany the salad with warm pita bread.

CUCUMBER RAITA

RAITA IS an East Indian yogurt-based salad that most commonly features cucumber, eggplant, potatoes, or spinach. These salads are typically flavored with cumin or *garam masala*, an Indian spice mixture that includes fenugreek, ginger and garlic, among other spices.

MAKES 8 SERVINGS

2 cups plain yogurt

½ cup peeled and diced seedless cucumber

2 minced garlic cloves

1 tbsp chopped mint

½ tsp ground cumin

¼ tsp salt, or to taste

¼ tsp freshly ground black pepper,
     or to taste

Dash cayenne pepper

1. Drain the yogurt through a cheesecloth-lined colander for 30 minutes. Transfer to a bowl.

2. Mix in the ingredients and serve.

NOTES: For a thicker, creamier result, drain the yogurt through a cheesecloth-lined colander in the refrigerator overnight before preparing the raita.

A quick and easy way to prepare the cucumbers is to peel them and chop them in the food processor. Excess water may be drained before the cucumbers are added to the yogurt.

To remove the sharp garlic "bite" and impart a more subtle garlic flavor, toss the garlic cloves in a small pot of boiling water for a minute, drain them and repeat the process. The garlic may then be chopped in the food processor with the cucumber, or minced separately.

TRADITIONAL COBB SALAD

COBB SALAD was created at the Brown Derby Restaurant in Hollywood, California. Various interpretations may call for either chicken or turkey. The garnish suggestions here are typical, but some versions have included watercress, celery, Cheddar cheese, hard-boiled eggs, black olives, or alfalfa sprouts.

MAKES 8 SERVINGS

2 lb chicken breasts, boneless and skinless

2 tsp salt, or to taste

1 tsp freshly ground black pepper, or to taste

1 tbsp vegetable oil

16 bacon slices

1 lb romaine lettuce, washed, dried, and torn
     into pieces

½ cup Cobb Salad Vinaigrette (page 56)

1½ cups diced tomatoes

2 cups crumbled blue cheese

2 halved avocados, cut into ¼-inch-thick slices

½ cup scallions, sliced on diagonal

8 eggs, hard-boiled, quartered

1. Preheat the oven to 400°F.

2. Season the chicken breasts with salt and pepper. Heat the vegetable oil in a large sauté pan over medium-high heat and sauté the chicken breasts until golden brown, about 2 to 3 minutes on each side. Place the pan in a 400°F oven and finish cooking the chicken to an internal temperature of 165°F. Cool and cut into ¼-inch-thick slices on the bias.

3. Sauté the bacon until crisp. Drain on absorbent paper and crumble into small pieces.

4. Toss the romaine with the vinaigrette and divide between 8 chilled plates. Top each individual salad with 5 or 6 chicken slices, 3 tablespoons diced tomato, ¼ cup blue cheese, ¼ avocado, 1 tablespoon scallions, 4 hard-boiled egg quarters, and 2 tablespoons crumbled bacon. Serve at once.

Step-by-Step Vinaigrettes

Many of our salads feature freshly made, flavorful vinaigrettes. Most vinaigrette recipes can be doubled, tripled, or even quadrupled without any problem. Making a large batch of vinaigrette gives you a head start on a variety of dishes—vinaigrettes are used as a marinade or a dip, as well as to dress salads.

DETERMINE THE BALANCE OF ACID AND OIL

A good vinaigrette balances the sharpness of the vinegar or juice by combining it with oil. One of the simplest of all recipes, a basic vinaigrette is a combination that you can express as a ratio: three parts oil to one part acid.

This works well as a starting point, but you may find with experience that you prefer a combination that changes the ratio slightly. If your oil is so strongly flavored that it could overpower the vinegar, you may wish to replace some of the intensely flavored oil with a more subtly flavored one. Very sharp or strong vinegars can be adjusted by either adding a bit of water to dilute them or sugar to soften their acidity.

ADD ANY ADDITIONAL INGREDIENTS

When preparing a vinaigrette, add the salt, pepper, herbs, mustard, or other ingredients to the vinegar before adding the oil so they will be blended evenly throughout the sauce. Herbs give vinaigrettes a wonderful flavor and color. However, if they are added too far in advance, the vinegar can start to discolor them and flatten their lively flavors. When preparing a large batch of vinaigrette that you want to last through several meals, you might prefer to add the herbs to the dressing just before you serve it.

GRADUALLY ADD THE OIL

Slowly pour or ladle a few droplets of oil at a time into the bowl, whisking constantly. Once the vinaigrette starts to thicken, you can add the oil more quickly. If the vinaigrette sits for a short time, it will start to separate. Whisk it vigorously before using.

Use a handheld or countertop blender to make a vinaigrette quickly. Vinaigrettes made with a blender will be thicker, and can hold their emulsion longer than those that are simply whipped together.

CHECK THE SEASONING

To be certain your dressing is balanced, put a few leaves of lettuce in a small bowl and add a teaspoon of the vinaigrette. Toss the greens until they are lightly coated and then taste them. If you taste a vinaigrette full strength, it may seem too strong or biting; once on your greens, however, the flavor may be perfect. Adjust the seasoning or the ratio of oil to vinegar, if necessary, whisk well, and serve.

COBB SALAD VINAIGRETTE

THIS VINAIGRETTE is also versatile enough to be used on most green salads.

MAKES 2 CUPS

¼ cup water

6 tbsp red wine vinegar

½ tsp sugar

2½ tsp lemon juice

1¼ tsp salt, or to taste

½ tsp freshly ground black pepper, or to taste

½ tsp coarse grain mustard

2 minced garlic cloves

1¼ cups extra-virgin olive oil

Whisk together all the ingredients except the olive oil. Allow the flavors to marry for 5 minutes. Gradually whisk in the oils until all of the oil has been added and the vinaigrette is smooth and has thickened. Taste and adjust the seasoning. The vinaigrette is ready to use now or it may be stored in a covered container in the refrigerator for up to 3 days. Blend the dressing together again before serving.

CHIPOTLE-SHERRY VINAIGRETTE

MAKES 1 CUP

3 tbsp sherry vinegar

1 tbsp fresh lime juice

1 tbsp minced shallots

1 tbsp chopped cilantro

2 canned chipotles, drained and minced

1 garlic clove, minced

1 tsp real maple syrup

¾ cup olive oil

Salt and pepper as needed

1 tsp chopped thyme

1 tbsp chopped parsley

1. Whisk together all the ingredients except the olive oil. Gradually whisk in the olive oil until all of the oil has been added and the vinaigrette is smooth and has thickened.

2. Just before serving, whisk the vinaigrette to recombine the oils and vinegar. Taste and adjust the seasoning and add the herbs. The vinaigrette is ready to use now or it may be stored in a covered container in the refrigerator for up to 3 days.

GARNISH AND DRESS YOUR SALADS just before serving. Add just enough dressing for the greens. Plan on about 2 to 3 tablespoons for each serving. Use less if the dressing is thin, like a vinaigrette, or a bit more if the dressing is heavier. Use clean hands, tongs, or a salad spoon and fork and a lifting and tossing motion until each piece of lettuce is coated completely.

LEMON VINAIGRETTE

MAKES 2 CUPS

⅓ cup lemon juice

3 tbsp white wine vinegar

1 tsp honey

1½ tsp salt

½ tsp ground black pepper

1½ cups extra-virgin olive oil

3 tbsp minced parsley or chives, optional

1. Whisk together all the ingredients except the olive oil. Gradually whisk in the olive oil until all of the oil has been added and the vinaigrette is smooth and has thickened.

2. Just before serving, whisk the vinaigrette to re-combine the oils and vinegar. Taste and adjust the seasoning and add the herbs, if using. The vinaigrette is ready to use now or it may be stored in a covered container in the refrigerator for up to 3 days.

LEMON-PARSLEY VINAIGRETTE

SIMILAR TO many store-bought varieties, this homemade version is quick and easy to make and well worth the extra effort.

MAKES 2 CUPS

¾ cup lemon juice

2 tbsp balsamic vinegar

1½ tbsp parsley, chopped

1 tsp salt, or to taste

½ tsp freshly ground black pepper, or to taste

¾ cup canola oil

5½ tbsp olive oil

Whisk together all the ingredients except the oils. Gradually whisk in the olive oil until all of the oil has been added and the vinaigrette is smooth and has thickened. Taste and adjust the seasoning. The vinaigrette is ready to use now or it may be stored in a covered container in the refrigerator for up to 3 days. It may be necessary to blend the dressing together again before serving.

TANGERINE-PINEAPPLE VINAIGRETTE

IN THIS vinaigrette, the sweetness of the tangerine and pineapple juice is is kept from becoming overwhelming with the addition of Dijon mustard.

MAKES 2 CUPS

½ cup plus 2 tbsp tangerine juice

5 tbsp pineapple juice

1 tbsp lemon juice

1 tsp balsamic vinegar

1 tsp Dijon mustard

½ tsp garlic, minced

1 tsp salt, or to taste

½ tsp freshly ground black pepper, or to taste

½ cup plus 2 tablespoons vegetable oil

5 tbsp olive oil

Whisk together all the ingredients except the olive oil. Gradually whisk in the olive oil until all of the oil has been added and the vinaigrette is smooth and has thickened. Taste and adjust the seasoning. The vinaigrette is ready to use now or it may be stored in a covered container in the refrigerator for up to 3 days. It may be necessary to blend the dressing together again before serving.

LIME-CILANTRO VINAIGRETTE

MAKES 2 CUPS

½ cup lime juice

½ tsp honey

¼ cup cilantro, chopped

1 tsp salt, or to taste

½ tsp freshly ground black pepper, or to taste

¾ cup peanut oil

¾ cup vegetable oil

Whisk together all the ingredients except the oils. Allow the flavors to marry for 5 minutes. Gradually whisk in the oils until all of the oil has been added and the vinaigrette is smooth and has thickened.

Taste and adjust the seasoning. The vinaigrette is ready to use now or it may be stored in a covered container in the refrigerator for up to 3 days. It may be necessary to blend the dressing together again before serving.

PORT WINE VINAIGRETTE

Port, a sweet fortified wine from Portugal, adds a luscious sweetness to this vinaigrette.

MAKES 2 CUPS

½ cup tawny port

½ cup red wine vinegar

¼ tsp salt, or to taste

Freshly ground black pepper, or to taste

1 cup vegetable oil

Whisk together all the ingredients except the olive oil. Gradually whisk in the olive oil until all of the oil has been added and the vinaigrette is smooth and has thickened. Taste and adjust the seasoning. The vinaigrette is ready to use now or it may be stored in a covered container in the refrigerator for up to 3 days. It may be necessary to blend the dressing together again before serving.

RED WINE VINAIGRETTE

Try substituting other oils, like walnut or peanut, for the ones called for here.

MAKES 2 CUPS

½ cup red wine vinegar

1 tsp Dijon-style mustard

Salt and pepper as needed

¾ cup extra-virgin olive oil

¾ cup corn or safflower oil

2 to 3 tbsp minced herbs, optional

Whisk together all the ingredients except the olive oil. Gradually whisk in the olive oil until all of the oil has been added and the vinaigrette is smooth and has thickened. Taste and adjust the seasoning. The vinaigrette is ready to use now or it may be stored in a covered container in the refrigerator for up to 3 days. It may be necessary to blend the dressing together again before serving.

BALSAMIC VINAIGRETTE

Balsamic vinegar is a speciality of the town of Modena in Italy, where it is aged in wooden barrels for several years, resulting in its characteristic dark caramel color and rich flavor.

MAKES 2 CUPS

¼ cup red wine vinegar

¼ cup balsamic vinegar

1 tsp salt

¼ tsp freshly ground black pepper

1½ cups extra-virgin olive oil

Whisk together all the ingredients except the olive oil. Gradually whisk in the olive oil until all of the oil has been added and the vinaigrette is smooth and has thickened. Taste and adjust the seasoning. The vinaigrette is ready to use now or it may be stored in a covered container in the refrigerator for up to 3 days. It may be necessary to blend the dressing together again before serving.

Broths and Soups

Soup Basics

Though the methods used for making different soups vary, there are some general guidelines that apply to all soups. From ingredient and equipment selection through cooking, storing, and serving, this chapter will explore some of the basic principles of making soup.

INGREDIENTS

The long history of soup-making should reassure any cook that lack of the right ingredients is no deterrent to putting a pot on the stove. Indeed, soups are good storage vehicles for abundant harvests; freeze a bumper crop of tomatoes or cucumbers, for example, in soup form and you can be assured that nothing will go to waste.

The best soups are made from the best available ingredients. Since soups are mostly liquid, it stands to reason that the flavor of the liquid used to make the soup will strongly influence its overall flavor. If you start with a wonderful homemade broth, your soup will be distinguished by its fragrance. A very small number of soups call for so few ingredients other than broth that an insipid liquid will be quite noticeable. This is not to say, though, that commercially prepared broths and soup bases are never appropriate. These products are convenient and can be very necessary time savers under the right circumstances. Depending on the soup, they might be used as is, or you might choose to fortify and enhance their flavor first by simmering them with a few fresh aromatic ingredients (herbs, vegetables, etc.). Many soups are based on milk or the juices or cooking liquids of fresh fruits or vegetables. Still others are made with plain water to allow the flavor of the main ingredients to shine through.

The meats you choose for soup-making should be flavorful and mature. Generally, these cuts are the least expensive. Meats with a great deal of flavor, such as the neck, short ribs, hocks, or shank, are preferred for beef soups. Stewing hens are best for chicken-based soups. Fish or shellfish should be perfectly fresh.

Another important component is vegetables. The most frequently used vegetables are onions, leeks, carrots, and celery, but there are virtually no vegetables that cannot be included in a soup. Vegetable soups are an excellent way to use up wholesome odds and ends in your refrigerator, cooked or raw. Remember, though, that no soup can resurrect an over-the-hill ingredient. When you cut vegetables for soups, try to be as uniform as possible in the size of the pieces. The size affects the rate at which the vegetable will cook— evenly sized pieces will cook at the same speed.

Herbs, spices, and other aromatic ingredients (lemon grass or chiles, for example) are added to soups to increase flavor and, many times, to reduce or eliminate the need for salt. They are frequently tied in a small piece of cheesecloth, which is then known as a sachet d'épices (bag of spices), hereafter referred to as a sachet. By leaving a long tail of string on the sachet, you can tie one end to the handle of your soup pot. This makes it easier to find and remove the sachet when the spices have contributed the desired flavor to the soup. A large teaball can be used in place of cheese cloth and string to make a sachet.

EQUIPMENT

Soup-making equipment is simple. Most of the soups in this book require just a single vessel for cooking the soup, though some do require the use of a second, usually smaller, vessel. You can make soup in just about any container large enough to accommodate the ingredients, so the recipes in this book simply call for a soup pot. Your soup pot should have a heavy bottom (to protect against scorching) and a capacity of about one gallon or more (most of the recipes yield two to three quarts). If, as in the French onion soup or shrimp bisque, the recipe calls for caramelizing or searing an ingredient before liquid is added, you should choose a pot with a wide bottom to expose more of that ingredient to direct heat than a narrow pot would. Otherwise, your soup pot should be taller than it is wide. This configuration results in less surface area, which means that less liquid will evaporate during cooking. It is best to avoid aluminum pots, particularly for cream soup, because the action of spoons and whisks against the pot can cause the soup to take on a grayish cast. Pots made of (or at least lined with) a nonreactive material, such as stainless steel, anodized aluminum, or enameled cast iron, are better choices.

For pureed and cream soups, you will need a strainer and equipment to do the pureeing. This can be a blender, hand-held blender, food processor, or food mill. A blender will give you the finest puree, followed by the food mill, food processor, and, finally, the hand-held blender. If you use a blender or food processor, be sure the lid is securely closed before turning it on. An explosion of hot soup may cause severe burns, will definitely make you unhappy as you clean up your wasted soup. To be on the safe side, let the soup cool a bit before pureeing it.

Finally, you will also need a variety of small equipment: spoons and other stirring implements, tongs, a whisk, a ladle, measuring cups (for both liquid and dry ingredients), and measuring spoons. You might also need storage containers or bags for storing extra soup. And, of course, you will need something in which to serve the soup: a tureen and/or cups, bowls, soup plates, mugs, or crocks, depending on the soup.

COOKING

Most soups are cooked at a gentle simmer, just long enough to develop good flavor and body. Unless specifically instructed to do so, don't boil soups. An even simmer prevents scorching vegetables and thick soups at the bottom of the pot, and minimizes the rate of liquid evaporation. If a soup is accidentally allowed to boil and the liquid level drops dramatically, replace the amount lost with broth or water.

To preserve fresh flavors, cook ingredients only until tender. Add vegetables according to their cooking times. Add herbs and spices when the recipe instructs, unless you want to change the flavor of the soup. There is a direct relationship between the length of time the seasonings simmer and the

quality and intensity of flavor they add. Fresh herbs lose flavor with long cooking times while spices become more intense. Wrapping herbs and spices in cheese cloth or a teaball to make a sachet allows you to remove them without straining the soup.

Stir soups from time to time to prevent starchy ingredients from sticking to the bottom of the pot. Throughout the cooking process, a shallow kitchen spoon or similar skimming utensil should be used to remove any scum or foam which forms on the surface so that the best flavor, texture, and appearance is obtained.

Taste a soup frequently and, when the flavor is fully developed and all of the ingredients are tender, serve it right away or cool and store it as described below. Although some soups may develop a more rounded, mellow flavor if served the day after they are prepared, no soup benefits from hours on the stove. Not only will the flavor become dull and flat, but the nutritive value will also be greatly decreased.

ADJUSTING CONSISTENCY

Thick soups, especially those made with starchy vegetables or dried beans, may continue to thicken during cooking and storage. As a general rule, creams and bisques should be about as thick as cold heavy cream and liquid enough to pour from a ladle into a bowl. Purees should be somewhat thicker.

For a soup that has become too thick, add an appropriately flavored broth in small amounts until the proper consistency is reached. Check the seasoning before serving.

For a soup that is too thin, dissolve a small amount of cornstarch or arrowroot in a little broth or water to make a starch slurry. Add the slurry a little at a time to the simmering soup, stirring constantly. After each addition, let the soup simmer for a minute or two, so that you can assess the thickness. Keep adding the slurry gradually until the soup has reached its desired thickness.

Soups should be seasoned throughout the cooking process. There are dozens of ways to adjust the flavor of a soup. Powdered or cubed meat or poultry base may be added to bolster a weak broth; however, this will affect the clarity. Chopped fresh herbs, a few drops of lemon or lime juice, Tabasco sauce, Worcestershire sauce, or grated citrus zest may be added to brighten a soup's flavor. These items should be added a little at a time, and the seasoning carefully checked after each addition. Salt and pepper to taste should be added just prior to serving, when the soup is at the correct temperature.

COOLING AND STORING

Most soup recipes can be doubled or tripled to make extra quantities to refrigerate or freeze until needed. If you are planning to store a soup, prepare it just up to the point at which final adjustments are made—seasoning, finishing with cream, or adding garnishes. Make the final adjustments after you have reheated the soup, just before serving.

One of the leading causes of foodborne illness is the failure to properly cool foods. There is a specific temperature range, from 41 to 140°F, often referred to as the danger zone, which is particularly hospitable to a variety of illness-causing bacteria and viruses. In order to be certain that your soups remain wholesome and flavorful in the refrigerator over the course of several days, it is critical that you understand how to handle hot liquids in a way that will avoid the proliferation of harmful microbes.

In order to rapidly cool soups (or any other liquid) and speed their progression through the danger zone, the following procedures should be followed. First, transfer the hot soup to a clean container. The container selected should be metal, because it is a good heat conductor. Plastic is fine for storage, but is a poor choice for actually cooling the soup. Next, place the entire container in a cold-water bath, with enough water to come up to the level of the hot soup in the container. Adding ice to the water will also help to reduce the length of time it takes to cool the liquid. If you cool the soup in a sink, you can use bricks or a rack to elevate the container so that cold water is able to circulate beneath it. Stirring the soup as it cools helps to speed the process, as well as to prevent anaerobic bacteria (which thrive in the absence of oxygen) from growing in the center of the container. The larger the batch, the longer the soup will take to cool, and the more important it is to take every possible step to accelerate the cooling.

Once the liquid has cooled to about 45°F, it is ready to be refrigerated or frozen. Depending on the ingredients, refrigerated soups will remain wholesome for three to five days. Frozen soups can be stored for four to five months. Label the storage container with the name of the contents and the date of preparation, so you can keep track of what you have and how long it's been there.

CHICKEN BROTH

CHICKEN BROTH is a crucial ingredient in soup making, and the flavor of homemade is hard to beat. You can double, or even quadruple, this recipe and freeze the extra so that you always have some on hand. If you freeze the broth in ice-cube trays, then transfer the cubes to freezer bags, it's easy to thaw exactly the amount you need. If you're short on time and must use canned broth, choose the all-natural or fat-free, reduced-sodium varieties.

MAKES ABOUT 2 QUARTS

4 lb stewing hen or chicken parts or meaty bones, such as backs and necks

3 quarts cold water

1 large onion, diced (about 1¼ cups)

1 carrot, diced (about ⅓ cup)

1 celery stalk, diced (about ½ cup)

5–6 whole black peppercorns

3–4 parsley stems

1 bay leaf

1 sprig fresh thyme

1½ tsp salt, or to taste

1. Place the chicken and water in a large pot (the water should cover the chicken by at least 2 inches; add more if necessary). Bring the water slowly to a boil over medium heat.

2. As the water comes to a boil, skim any foam that rises to the surface. Adjust the heat once a boil is reached, so that a slow, lazy simmer is established. Cover partially, and simmer 2 hours, skimming as often as necessary.

3. Add the remaining ingredients. Continue to simmer, skimming the surface as necessary, until the broth is fully flavored, about 1 hour.

4. If using hen or chicken parts, remove them and cool slightly. Dice or shred the meat, and reserve to garnish the broth or save for another use. Discard the skin and bones.

5. Strain the broth through a fine sieve or cheese-cloth-lined colander into a large metal container. Discard the solids.

6. If you are using the broth right away, skim off any fat on the surface. If you are not using the broth right away, cool it quickly by transferring it to a metal container (if it's not in one already) and placing the container in a sink filled with ice-cold water. Stir the broth as it cools, and then transfer it to storage containers. Store in the refrigerator, up to 5 days, or in the freezer, up to 3 months. Label and date the containers clearly before putting them into the freezer.

NOTES: To make a double chicken broth, use cold chicken broth instead of water.

Some stores sell packages of necks and backs that can be used to prepare broth. This broth can also be made with the carcasses of roasted birds. Save the bones after all of the meat has been pulled or carved away (freeze them if you will not be making the broth within a day or two). You will need the carcasses of about 3 birds.

If the broth is allowed to chill in the refrigerator overnight, the fat will rise to the surface and harden. It is then easy to lift away. The broth will then be completely fat free, and will only have the salt that you have chosen to add.

If, after straining the broth, you find the flavor to be weaker than you would like, simply put the broth back on the stove and boil it down until the flavor has concentrated.

BEEF BROTH

FOR THE clearest broth, be sure to skim frequently as it comes to a simmer, and as often as necessary thereafter. Never let it reach a boil; this will make the broth cloudy. In describing the proper state of a broth as it simmers, the French use the verb *fremir*—to tremble. This means that there should be movement on the surface, but only a few lazy bubbles should actually be seen breaking the surface.

MAKES ABOUT 2 QUARTS

4 lb beef (chuck, ribs, shank, or neck)

3 quarts water

1½ medium onions, coarsely chopped (about 2 cups)

1 leek, white and light green part, coarsely chopped (about 1¼ cups)

1 carrot, coarsely chopped (about ⅓ cup)

1 celery stalk, coarsely chopped (about ½ cup)

¼ cup celery leaves

3–4 parsley stems

3–4 black peppercorns

1 bay leaf

2 tsp salt, or to taste

½ tsp dried or 1 sprig fresh thyme

1. Preheat the oven to 400°F.

2. Put the beef in a roasting pan and place in the oven. Roast until deep brown, 45 minutes to 1 hour.

3. Transfer the beef to a soup pot. Pour 1 cup water into the hot roasting pan and scrape the bottom to loosen any drippings; pour over the beef. Add the remaining water (there should be enough to cover the beef by 2 inches; add more water if necessary) and bring to a simmer. Cover partially and simmer gently, 2 hours. Skim frequently any scum that rises to the surface.

4. Add the remaining ingredients. Continue to simmer gently until the broth has developed a full, rich flavor, about 2 hours. Remove the meat and reserve to garnish the broth or save for another use.

5. Strain the broth through a fine sieve or cheese-cloth-lined colander into a large metal container. Discard the solids.

6. If you are using the broth right away, skim off any fat on the surface. If you are not using the broth immediately, cool it quickly by placing the container in a sink filled with ice-cold water. Stir the broth as it cools, and then transfer it to storage containers. Store in the refrigerator, up to 5 days, or in the freezer, up to 3 months. Label and date the containers clearly before putting them into the freezer. Remove any fat that has hardened on the surface before reheating.

FISH BROTH

Use only the bones from mild, lean white fish, such as halibut or sole, to make this broth. Bones from oily fish, like salmon, will make a broth that is overpowering. The bones must be perfectly fresh. If you won't be able to prepare it right away, store the bones in the freezer. Shells from shrimp, crab, and lobsters can be substituted for the bones to prepare a crustacean broth. They can be stored in the freezer, too, until you have enough ingredients and time to make a batch. This recipe, as well as those for other broths, can easily be multiplied if you have a good quantity of ingredients on hand. It takes no longer to simmer a gallon of broth than it does two quarts. Freeze any that you don't plan to use right away—frozen homemade broth is a great convenience food to have on hand for meal preparation on busy nights.

MAKES ABOUT 2 QUARTS

2 tbsp vegetable oil

5 lb fish bones from lean, white fish

2 onions, thinly sliced (about 2½ cups)

2 leeks, white and light green parts, thinly sliced (about 2½ cups)

2 celery stalks, thinly sliced (about 1 cup)

1 cup white mushrooms or mushroom stems, thinly sliced, optional

1 cup dry white wine, optional

2½ quarts cold water

10 black peppercorns

6 parsley stems

2 sprigs fresh thyme, tarragon, or dill

2 bay leaves

1. Heat the oil in a soup pot over low heat. Add the fish bones, onions, leeks, celery, and mushrooms, if using. Stir until all the ingredients are evenly coated with oil. Cover the pot and cook, without stirring, about 5 minutes.

2. Add the wine, if using, and simmer until the wine is reduced by half. Add the water, peppercorns, parsley stems, fresh herbs, and bay leaves. Bring the broth just up to a simmer. Continue to simmer gently, 35 to 45 minutes.

3. Strain the broth through a fine sieve or cheesecloth-lined colander. Discard the solids. If the broth is not to be used right away, cool it thoroughly before storing it in the refrigerator, up to 3 days, or in the freezer, up to 6 weeks. Label and date the containers clearly before putting them into the freezer.

VEGETABLE BROTH

THE LIGHT flavor of this vegetable broth is far superior to that of commercially prepared vegetable broths, which always seem to taste like the can they came in. In addition to its role in making soup, vegetable broth can be used to prepare grain or bean dishes, instead of water or chicken broth. It is also good as the cooking liquid for pan-steamed vegetables. The vegetables listed here should be thought of as suggestions. Feel free to use other vegetables, as long as they will not give the finished broth a strong odor or color (for instance, beets and beet greens might not be appropriate). Starchy vegetables may make the broth foam over as it simmers. Beyond that, let your own taste be your guide.

MAKES ABOUT 2 QUARTS

2 tsp olive or corn oil

1–2 garlic cloves, finely minced

2 tsp minced shallots

3 quarts water

1 large onion, thinly sliced (about 1¼ cups)

1 leek, white, light green, and dark green parts, trimmed and sliced (about 3 cups)

1 celery stalk, thinly sliced (about ½ cup)

1 carrot, thinly sliced (about ⅓ cup)

1 parsnip, thinly sliced (about ⅓ cup)

1 cup thinly sliced broccoli stems

1 cup thinly sliced fennel, with some tops

½ cup dry white wine or vermouth, optional

1 tbsp salt or to taste

4–5 whole black peppercorns

½ tsp juniper berries

1 bay leaf

1 sprig fresh or ¼ tsp dried thyme

1. Heat the oil in a soup pot over medium heat. Add the garlic and shallots and cook, stirring frequently, until they are translucent, 3 to 4 minutes.

2. Add the remaining ingredients and bring slowly to a simmer. Cook until the broth has a good flavor, about 1 hour.

3. Strain the broth through a sieve. Allow it to cool completely before storing in the refrigerator.

NOTES: This broth can be prepared in large batches, then frozen for later use. Be sure to label and date the containers so that you use the oldest broth first. Freeze the broth in ice cube trays, then store the frozen cubes in large freezer bags so you can thaw exactly the amount needed at any given time.

When preparing vegetables for other dishes, save any wholesome trim or peels that you want to put into the broth. Then every few days, put on a pot of broth. You will get a nutrient boost, as well as avoiding the use of canned broths that might be higher in sodium that you'd like.

CHILLED CUCUMBER SOUP
with Shrimp and Dill

USING THE same broth to cook the shrimp and make the soup infuses this elegant soup with a bold shrimp flavor.

MAKES 8 SERVINGS

4 cups fish, chicken, or vegetable broth

¾ lb medium shrimp, peeled and deveined

2 tbsp butter

1 cup chopped yellow onions

¾ cup diced celery

6 medium cucumbers, peeled, seeded, and chopped

2 tsp salt, divided use

½ tsp freshly ground white pepper, divided use

1½ tsp cornstarch dissolved in 2 tsp water

1½ cups sour cream

½ cup heavy cream

½ cup chopped dill

2 tbsp lemon juice, or as needed

1/2 tsp Tabasco sauce, or as needed

½ cup small-diced cucumber for garnish

Dill sprigs for garnish

1. Heat the broth in a large stockpot until simmering. Add the shrimp and cook for 2 to 3 minutes, or just until they turn opaque. Remove the shrimp from the broth, cut in half lengthwise, refrigerate, and reserve for garnish. Reserve the broth.

2. Heat the butter in a soup pot over medium heat. Add the onions and celery and sauté, stirring frequently, until the onions are translucent, 5 to 7 minutes. Add the reserved broth and the cucumbers. Add 1 teaspoon of salt and ¼ teaspoon pepper. Bring to a boil, then reduce the heat so that the soup simmers gently. Simmer until the cucumbers are tender, about 10 minutes.

3. Remove the soup pot from the heat and let it cool slightly. Puree the soup until smooth. Return the soup to medium heat and bring to a simmer. Stir in the dissolved cornstarch and simmer, stirring constantly, until thickened, about 2 minutes. Chill the soup at least 4 and up to 24 hours.

4. Combine the sour cream, heavy cream, dill, lemon juice, and Tabasco in a small bowl and stir until evenly blended. Whisk the sour cream mixture into the chilled soup. Taste and adjust the seasoning with the remaining salt and pepper. Add additional lemon juice or Tabasco if needed.

5. Serve the soup in chilled cups garnished with the reserved shrimp and diced cucumbers. Top with a dill sprig.

WHITE GRAPE GAZPACHO
with Toasted Almonds and Dill

WHITE GRAPES are a surprising ingredient in this refreshing soup. Cream cheese, an unusual soup ingredient, gives the soup body. English cucumbers, otherwise known as hothouse or seedless cucumbers, are less bitter than regular cucum-

About Cold Soups

Just as a steaming hot bowl of soup can warm you to the core on a freezing winter's day, so a cold soup holds the power to cool you on a blazing hot summer's day. Cold soups are usually served as appetizers or desserts, though they are refreshing whenever they are served.

Many of the soups in this chapter will take very well to being served cold. Cold soups can be rich, as in the case of cream soups, or bold and robust, as in the case of pureed soups. Whenever you intend to serve any food chilled, be sure to taste it carefully at the correct serving temperature. Cold foods often require stronger seasoning than hot foods. Remember to allow soups sufficient time to develop their flavor. Some soups are at their best and ready to serve as soon as they are prepared. Other soups develop a more complex and satisfying flavor if they are allowed to mellow in the refrigerator for several hours or overnight.

COLD VEGETABLE AND FRUIT SOUPS

Cold vegetable and fruit soups are often popular hot-weather offerings around the world. Many cuisines have special cold soups featuring a seasonal vegetable or fruit.

Vegetable or fruit soups are usually made by pureeing or chopping vegetables and/or fruits fine enough to reach a soup-like consistency. These soups range in texture from the appealing coarseness of a gazpacho to the velvety smoothness of a chilled melon soup. Broth or juice is often added to the vegetables or fruits to loosen the puree enough to create a good consistency. Other ingredients, such as cream, milk, buttermilk, garnishes, or granités can be added to the soup for extra flavor, color, or texture.

COLD CREAMED SOUPS

Vichyssoise (page 69) is a classic example of a cold creamed soup. It is made by preparing a chilled purée of potato and leek that is enriched with half-and-half. Other cold creamed soups are made by preparing a cream or velouté soup, as illustrated in chapter 3. After chilling, they are typically finished by adding chilled cream, yogurt, or creme fraîche.

When you taste and evaluate your cold cream soup, pay attention to the texture and consistency. Cold cream soups should have the same velvety, smooth texture as hot cream soups. Cold soups may thicken as they cool, so be certain that you have adjusted the consistency to make a soup that is creamy but not stiff. Good cold creamed soups should not leave your mouth feeling coated with fat, so keep the amount of cream in proportion to the other ingredients.

COLD CLEAR SOUPS

Cold clear soups require a rich, full-bodied, clarified broth or juice. Infusions, essences, or well-strained purees are often used to the create the special character of these soups. Some clear soups are thickened with a little gelatin. Jellied clear soups should barely hold their shape, and should melt in the mouth instantly.

bers and have very few seeds. Because they are not coated with food-grade wax like most regular cucumbers found in supermarkets, they can be used peel and all.

MAKES 10 TO 12 SERVINGS

2 lb white seedless grapes, rinsed well (about 6½ cups)

1 English cucumber, diced (do not peel, about 3 cups)

4 scallions, green parts only, sliced (about ⅓ cup)

2½ cups half-and-half

1¼ cups plain yogurt

¼ cup cream cheese (about 2 oz)

2 tbsp white-wine vinegar

2 tbsp extra-virgin olive oil

½ cup plus 2 tbsp chopped fresh dill

Salt, to taste

Freshly ground white pepper, to taste

¼ cup sliced almonds, toasted

1. Peel and halve 18 grapes. Reserve for garnish.

2. Puree the remaining grapes with the cucumber, scallions, half-and-half, yogurt, cream cheese, vinegar, olive oil, and ½ cup of the dill.

3. Season the soup with salt and white pepper. Chill thoroughly.

4. Serve in chilled bowls, garnished with the remaining chopped dill, grape halves, and almonds.

GAZPACHO

THIS TANGY marriage of fresh tomato, cucumber, pepper, and onion is a summer favorite. Gazpacho's flavor improves if allowed to chill overnight, but thereafter this soup has a short shelf life because the tomatoes sour very quickly. It is best prepared no more than a day or two before it will be eaten.

MAKES 8 SERVINGS

3 cups finely diced plum tomatoes, juices reserved

2 cups finely diced cucumbers, peeled and seeded

1¼ cups finely diced onion

1 cup finely diced red bell pepper

1 tsp minced garlic

2 tbsp tomato paste

2 tbsp extra-virgin olive oil

2 tbsp minced fresh herbs (tarragon, thyme, or parsley)

3 cups canned tomato juice

¼ cup red wine vinegar, or as needed

Juice of ½ lemon, or as needed

¼ tsp salt, or as needed

¼ tsp cayenne pepper, or as needed

1 cup tiny croutons

½ cup thinly sliced chives or scallion greens

1. Reserve 2 tablespoons each of the tomatoes, cucumbers, onion, and pepper for the garnish.

2. Puree the remaining tomato, cucumber, onion, and pepper in a food processor or blender along with the garlic, tomato paste, olive oil, and herbs until fairly smooth but with some texture remaining.

3. Transfer the puree to a mixing bowl. Stir in the tomato juice, the red wine vinegar, and lemon juice. Season with salt and cayenne to taste. Cover and chill thoroughly, at least 3 hours but preferably overnight.

4. After chilling, check the seasoning and adjust as needed. Serve in chilled bowls, garnished with the reserved vegetables, croutons, and chives.

NOTE: If the soup is too thin for your taste, add about 1 cup of freshly made white bread crumbs before chilling. If it's too thick, the consistency can be thinned by adding more tomato juice or water. Part of the tomato juice can be replaced with fish broth or clam juice, if desired.

COLD ROASTED TOMATO AND BASIL SOUP

ROASTING THE tomatoes (see page 81) before you make the soup intensifies their flavor and adds an additional level of complexity to this soup.

MAKES 8 SERVINGS

12 plum tomatoes

4 tbsp extra virgin olive oil, divided use

2 tsp salt, divided use

½ tsp freshly ground black pepper, divided use

1 cup small-diced onion

1 cup chopped celery

½ cup chopped leeks, white part only

4 garlic cloves, minced

4 cups vegetable broth

1 bay leaf

¼ cup chopped basil

Halved yellow pear tomatoes for garnish

Shredded basil leaves for garnish

1. Preheat the oven to 375°F.

2. Core the tomatoes and cut them in half lengthwise. Place the tomato halves on a baking sheet or in a baking dish large enough to accomodate them. Brush them with 3 tablespoons of the olive oil and season with ½ teaspoon of the salt and a pinch of the ground pepper. Roast the tomatoes until they are browned and have a rich, roasted aroma, approximately 1 hour. Set aside.

3. Heat the remaining olive oil in a soup pot over medium heat. Add the onion, celery, and leeks and sauté, stirring frequently, until the onion is translucent, 5 to 7 minutes. Add the garlic and sauté until aromatic, 2 minutes. Add the reserved tomatoes, broth, and bay leaf. Season with 1 teaspoon salt and

¼ teaspoon pepper. Bring to a boil, then reduce the heat so that the soup simmers gently; simmer until the vegetables are tender, about 30 minutes.

4. Remove the soup pot from the heat. Remove and discard the bay leaf. Add the chopped basil and puree the soup until smooth. Chill the soup at least 4 and up to 24 hours. Season with the remaining salt and pepper, if needed, just before serving.

5. Serve the soup in chilled cups garnished with yellow pear tomatoes and shredded basil.

VICHYSSOISE

THIS IS the Culinary Institute of America's rendition of the traditional classic, first prepared by French chef Louis Diat at New York City's Ritz Carlton Hotel in 1917. Diat's chilled potato-and-leek soup sprinkled with chives was inspired by a favorite hot soup made by his mother in France.

MAKES 8 SERVINGS

1½ tbsp vegetable oil

3 leeks, white parts only, finely chopped (about 3 cups)

½ onion, minced (about ¾ cup)

5 cups Chicken or Vegetable Broth (pages 63, 65)

3 russet potatoes, peeled and diced (about 3 cups)

Sachet: 2 whole cloves, 2 parsley stems, 2 black peppercorns, and ½ bay leaf enclosed in a large teaball or tied in a cheesecloth pouch

1½ cups half-and-half, chilled

1 tsp salt, or to taste

Freshly ground white pepper, to taste

¼ cup thinly sliced chives

1. Heat the oil in a soup pot over medium heat. Add the leeks and onion and cook until tender and translucent, 4 to 5 minutes.

2. Add the broth, potatoes, and sachet. Bring to a simmer and cook until the potatoes are starting to fall apart, about 25 minutes. Remove the sachet from the pot and discard.

3. Puree the soup. Cool the soup properly (see page 62), then chill thoroughly.

4. Just before serving, add the cold half-and-half to the soup and season with salt and white pepper. Serve in chilled bowls, garnished with chives.

FRESH CORN CHOWDER
with Green Chiles and Monterey Jack

THIS CHOWDER is best made with fresh corn on the cob, since you can only get corn milk from the whole ear. After you cut the kernels away, hold the cob over a bowl and use the spine of your knife to scrape out the flavorful juices. Add this corn milk along with the cream when you puree the kernels.

MAKES 8 SERVINGS

6 ears of corn, shucked, or 4 cups frozen kernels

1 cup heavy cream

2 slices bacon, minced

1¼ cups minced onion

1 cup minced red bell pepper

½ cup minced celery

½ tsp minced garlic clove

6 cups chicken broth

3 cups diced yellow or white potatoes

3 cups chopped tomatoes, peeled and seeded

One 4-oz can green chiles, drained and chopped

1 cup grated Monterey Jack cheese

Salt and freshly ground black pepper, to taste

Tabasco sauce, to taste

1 cup corn tortilla strips, toasted, optional

2 tbsp chopped cilantro

1. Cut the corn kernels from the cobs with a sharp knife, capturing as much of the juice as possible. Reserve ¾ cup of the corn kernels for later use. Puree the remaining corn kernels with the heavy cream in a food processor or blender; set aside.

2. Cook the bacon in a soup pot over medium heat until crisp, about 8 minutes. Add the onion, pepper, celery, and garlic. Reduce the heat to low and cover.

3. Cook, stirring occasionally, until the vegetables are tender, 10 to 12 minutes. Add the broth, potatoes, and tomatoes. Bring to a simmer and cook, covered, until the potatoes are tender, about 20 minutes. Skim any fat from the surface and discard.

4. Add the pureed corn and cream, the reserved corn kernels, chiles, and cheese. Cook on low heat just until the corn is warmed, about 5 minutes. Season to taste with salt, pepper, and Tabasco. Serve garnished with tortilla strips and cilantro.

FRENCH ONION SOUP

THE SECRET to making a fine French onion soup is to give it lots of time to develop flavor. The onions should be cooked slowly, until they become deeply caramelized, then simmered in broth to allow their flavors to permeate the broth. If you have the time, make the soup the day before you serve it to allow the flavor to mature and mellow.

MAKES 8 SERVINGS

¼ cup olive or vegetable oil

4 medium onions, thinly sliced (about 5 cups)

2 garlic cloves, minced (about 1 tsp)

½ cup brandy

1½ quarts Chicken or Beef Broth, heated
    (page 63)

Sachet: 3 to 4 parsley stems, ½ tsp each dried thyme and tar-
    ragon, and 1 bay leaf enclosed in a large teaball or tied in a
    cheesecloth pouch

Salt, to taste

Freshly ground black pepper, to taste

8 slices French bread

1 cup grated Gruyère cheese, or as needed

1. Heat the oil in a soup pot over medium-low heat. Add the onions and cook without stirring until the onions begin to brown on the bottom. Raise the heat to medium, stir, and continue to cook, stirring occasionally, until the onions are deeply caramelized (dark golden brown). The total cooking time will be 30 to 45 minutes. If the onions begin to scorch, add a few tablespoons of water and continue cooking.

2. Add the garlic and continue to cook an additional minute. Add the brandy and simmer until the liquid has nearly evaporated, 2 to 3 minutes.

3. Add the broth and sachet. Bring to a simmer and cook, partially covered, for 45 minutes to 1 hour, skimming the surface as necessary and discarding any fat. Remove the sachet and discard. Season with salt and pepper.

4. When ready to serve, preheat the oven to 350°F and bring 2 quarts water to a boil. Ladle the soup into individual ovenproof soup crocks. Top each crock with a slice of bread and sprinkle with grated cheese, covering the bread completely, and allowing the cheese to touch the edge of the crock.

5. Set the soup crocks in a baking dish and add enough boiling water to reach ⅔ up the sides of the crocks. Bake until the soup is thoroughly heated

and the cheese is lightly browned, 10 to 15 minutes. Serve immediately.

STRACCIATELLA

THE NAME of this simple soup literally means "rags." By whipping the soup as you add beaten eggs and Parmesan cheese, the eggs cook into threads, hence the name. For the best flavor, start with a homemade chicken or beef broth.

MAKES 6 TO 8 SERVINGS

6 cups Chicken or Beef Broth (page 63)

2 whole eggs

¼ cup freshly grated Parmesan cheese

Salt, to taste

Freshly ground white pepper, to taste

6–8 slices Italian bread

Extra-virgin olive oil, as needed

1 garlic clove, halved

1 tbsp chopped parsley, optional

1. Preheat the oven to 375°F. Bring the broth to a simmer in a soup pot.

2. Whisk the eggs and cheese together in a small bowl. Whisk the broth constantly as you add the egg mixture to broth in a thin stream. Season soup with salt and pepper. Keep warm.

3. Brush each slice of bread with olive oil and rub with the cut side of the garlic clove. Place on a baking sheet, and toast in the oven until lightly browned and crisp, 4 to 5 minutes.

4. Place a piece of toasted bread in the bottom of each heated soup bowl and ladle the soup over the bread. Sprinkle the stracciatella with parsley, if using, and serve immediately.

CREAM OF BROCCOLI SOUP

This velvety soup is the essence of broccoli. It's relatively simple to make, yet tastes very elegant and refined. Try serving this soup as a first course for company.

MAKES 8 SERVINGS

2 lb broccoli

¼ cup vegetable or olive oil

1¼ cups chopped onions

½ cup chopped celery

1¼ cups chopped leeks, white and light green parts only

¼ cup all-purpose flour

6 cups Chicken Broth (page 63)

½ cup heavy cream, heated

Fresh lemon juice, to taste

Salt and pepper as needed

1. Separate the broccoli into stems and florets. Trim away the tough outer parts of the stems. Set aside 1 cup of the nicest-looking small florets for garnish. Coarsely chop the remaining broccoli florets and the stems.

2. Heat the oil in a soup pot over medium heat. Add the onions, celery, leeks, and chopped broccoli. Sauté, stirring frequently, until the onions are softened and translucent, about 5 minutes. Add the flour and stir well to combine. Cook, stirring frequently, for 4 minutes. Gradually add the broth to the pot, whisking to work out any lumps of flour. Bring the soup to a simmer and cook for 45 minutes. Stir frequently and skim as needed.

3. Remove the pot from the heat and let the soup cool for at least 10 minutes before pureeing with a handheld blender. Strain the soup through a sieve and reserve the liquid if you are using a countertop blender or food processor. Add the solids to the blender jar or food processor bowl; do not overfill. Add a little of the liquid, replace the cover (without the vent from the lid or feed tube) and puree until smooth. Add more liquid if necessary to help puree the solids. Transfer the pureed soup to a clean pot. Continue to puree until all of the solids are pureed. Blend the soup and adjust the consistency by adding some of the remaining reserved liquid. (The soup is ready to finish now or it can be cooled and stored up to 2 days in the refrigerator or up to 1 month in the freezer.)

4. Meanwhile, steam or boil the reserved broccoli florets until just tender.

5. Return the soup to a simmer over low heat and add the heated cream. Season to taste with the lemon juice, salt, and pepper. Serve in heated bowls, garnished with the florets.

CREAM OF MUSHROOM SOUP

So-called exotic varieties of mushrooms, such as cremini and oyster, work well in this soup, as do regular white mushrooms. Use a combination or a single variety, depending on your taste and what's available at the market.

MAKES 2 QUARTS

2 tbsp butter

2 garlic cloves, chopped

1 cup onions, chopped

½ cup celeriac, chopped

2 quarts mushrooms, sliced

¼ cup all-purpose flour

¼ cup sherry wine

The Basic Steps for a Cream Soup

1. Select and prepare the vegetables for cooking (see *Main Ingredient Options*).

2. Sweat the aromatic ingredients, including onions, shallots, celery, or leeks, along with the main ingredient.

3. Add flour to make a roux. (See *Thickening Options*)

4. Add the liquid to the pot and bring the soup to a very gentle simmer.

5. Skim and stir the soup frequently and season throughout cooking time.

6. Puree until smooth, finish, and serve at the best temperature. (See *Finishing and Service Options*, page 74.)

MAIN INGREDIENT OPTIONS

You can use almost any fresh vegetable to make a cream soup using the method outlined above. The amount to choose depends upon the density of the vegetable. Vegetables that are similar in texture to broccoli (asparagus, cauliflower, artichokes, or peas, for example) can be interchanged easily. Replace the broccoli with an equal weight of any of those vegetables.

High moisture vegetables, like tomatoes or mushrooms, call for slightly more in order to get a rich flavor and a creamy consistency. Use 1½ times the weight of the broccoli.

THICKENING OPTIONS

The recipe for Cream of Broccoli Soup (opposite) is thickened with a classic roux using a technique known to chefs trained in classic European technique as singer. Flour is the thickener, but there are other options. One option is to use more of the basic ingredient and let the texture of the vegetable thicken the soup.

Another option calls for replacing the flour with a potato. Use a medium-size starchy potato, like an Idaho or russet, to thicken 2 quarts of soup (the amount made in this recipe). Peel the potato and cut it into thin slices or small dice. Add it along with the broccoli. It will fall apart as it cooks, thickening the soup.

Still another option is to add a little cornstarch or arrowroot to the soup after you have pureed it. Make a slurry by combining about ¼ cup of cornstarch or 2 tablespoons of arrowroot with enough cold water or broth to make it pourable. Add the slurry to the simmering soup a little at a time as you stir it. It only takes a minute or two to thicken the soup,

LEFT TO RIGHT Aromatics are cooked to the desired stage before the liquid is added; cream is added to the soup before adjusting the final consistency; the final consistency of the cream soup. The soup is garnished before being brought to the table.

so keep adding small amounts until the soup is the thickness you like.

Cream soups can be served hot or cold. To make a cold version of your favorite cream vegetable soup, chill the soup just after you have pureed it. Once the soup is well-chilled, stir in the cold cream and then taste the soup to be sure it is properly seasoned. Cold foods often need heavier seasoning, since cold temperatures dampen flavors slightly.

Finish a cream soup by stirring in heavy cream that has been blended with an egg yolk (see *Finishing Soups with a Liaison*), but be sure you don't boil the soup once the liaison goes in. Instead of adding heavy cream, try substituting a dollop of lightly whipped unsweetened cream to finish the soup. Add a slice or rosette of plain or flavored butter to the soup just before you serve it and allow it to melt over the surface for extra richness.

Substitute crème fraîche, sour cream, or even plain yogurt for the heavy cream for a different flavor, or omit the cream altogether, for a soup that is "creamy" in texture, but not loaded with cream.

FINISHING SOUPS WITH A LIAISON

A mixture of egg yolk and cream called a liaison may be used at the end of cooking to add body and sheen to a dish. Mixing cream with egg yolks makes the yolks less likely to curdle when hot liquid is added. Adding the hot liquid carefully, as described below, "tempers" the liaison by heating it up gradually for a second line of defense against curdling.

In a large bowl, whisk the cream and egg yolk together until evenly blended. To temper the liaison, gradually add some of the hot soup you want to finish, a ladleful at a time, to the egg mixture while whisking constantly to temper the eggs and prevent curdling.

Slowly pour the tempered mixture into the pot of hot liquid while stirring constantly. Gently warm the mixture, stirring frequently, until it thickens slightly. Do not allow it to go above 185°F, or the egg yolks can still curdle. Serve as soon as possible to ensure the safety and quality of the finished dish.

6 cups Vegetable Broth (page 65)

¾ cup heavy cream

Chives, sliced, as needed

⅛ tsp nutmeg, optional

1. In a large soup pot, melt the butter and sweat the garlic, onions and celeriac until translucent, about 5 to 7 minutes.

2. Add the mushrooms and cook until tender, about 5 minutes.

3. Sprinkle the mixture with flour and mix well.

4. Add the sherry wine and vegetable broth and simmer everything until the mushrooms are completely tender, approximately 25 minutes. Allow the soup to cool slightly before pureeing.

5. Puree the soup with a handheld blender, or in batches in a food processor or countertop blender. Strain the pureed soup through a colander or sieve, then return it to a simmer.

6. Gently simmer the heavy cream before adding it to the soup. Adjust the consistency of the soup with a little more broth, if needed. Season to taste with salt and pepper.

7. Pour into warmed soup cups or bowls and garnish with sliced chives and the nutmeg, if using.

CHEDDAR CHEESE SOUP

THIS SOUP does not have any cream in it, but the cheese makes it plenty rich. If you make this soup in advance, reheat it in a double boiler over simmering water, or in a microwave at medium power, so that the cheese doesn't separate from the soup, giving it a curdled appearance. Try other cheeses, such as Brie, Camembert, or even a mild goat cheese.

MAKES 6 SERVINGS

½ cup butter (1 stick)

2 leeks, white and light green parts, finely diced (about 2½ cups)

1 onion, finely diced (about 1¼ cups)

1 celery stalk, finely diced (about ½ cup)

¼ cup flour

2 tsp dry mustard

1 cup ale or white wine

6 cups Chicken or Vegetable Broth (pages 63, 65)

3 cups grated cheddar or Monterey jack cheese (about 1 lb)

Tabasco sauce, to taste

Salt, to taste

Freshly ground white pepper, to taste

¼ cup finely diced canned green chiles

2 tbsp minced cilantro or parsley

2 tbsp finely diced pickled jalapeños, optional

1. Melt the butter in a soup pot over medium heat. Add the leeks, onion, and celery. Stir to coat. Cover the pot and cook until the vegetables are tender, 4 to 5 minutes.

2. Add the flour and stir well with a wooden spoon. Cook, 4 to 5 minutes, stirring almost constantly. Add the dry mustard and ale, stirring to make a thick paste. Add the broth in batches, using a whisk to work out any lumps between each addition.

3. Bring the soup to a simmer and continue to simmer gently, 1 hour. Stir the soup occasionally, and skim as necessary.

4. Strain the soup through a sieve, reserving the liquid. Puree the solids and return to the soup pot. Add enough of the reserved liquid to achieve a soup consistency and strain once more.

5. Return the soup to a simmer. Whisk in the cheese and simmer until the cheese melts, about 1 minute. Season with the Tabasco sauce, salt, and

white pepper. Serve in heated bowls, garnished with chiles, cilantro, and jalapeños, if using.

NEW ENGLAND CLAM CHOWDER

THIS IS the Culinary Institute of America's rich, creamy version of the American classic. Paired with a salad and bread, it becomes a hearty meal.

MAKES 2 QUARTS

1¼ lb canned clams, minced, juices reserved

2–3 cups bottled clam juice

2 bacon slices, minced

1 onion, diced

2 tbsp all-purpose flour

1 bay leaf

½ tsp thyme leaves, chopped

1 lb potatoes, peeled, diced

3 cups heavy cream or half and half

6 tbsp dry sherry, or to taste

Salt, to taste

Freshly ground black pepper, to taste

Tabasco sauce, to taste

Worcestershire sauce, to taste

Oyster or saltine crackers, as needed

1. Drain the clam juice from the minced clams and combine with enough bottled juice to equal 3 cups of liquid.

2. Cook the bacon slowly in a soup pot over medium heat until lightly crisp, about 8 minutes.

3. Add the onion and cook, stirring occasionally, until the onion is translucent, about 5 to 7 minutes. Add the flour and cook over low heat, stirring with a wooden spoon, for 2 to 3 minutes.

4. Whisk in the clam juice, bring to a simmer, and cook for 5 minutes, stirring occasionally. The liquid should be the consistency of heavy cream. If it is too thick, add more clam juice to adjust the consistency. Add the bay leaf and fresh thyme.

5. Add the potatoes and simmer until tender, about 15 minutes.

6. Meanwhile, place the clams and cream in a saucepan and simmer together until the clams are cooked, about 5 to 8 minutes.

7. When the potatoes are tender, add the clams and cream to the soup. Simmer for 1 to 2 minutes.

8. Stir in the sherry. Season to taste with salt, pepper, Tabasco, and Worcestershire sauce. Serve in bowls with the crackers on the side.

MANHATTAN CLAM CHOWDER

THIS IS the classic mid-Atlantic clam chowder, not to be confused with New England's version. So controversial was the inclusion of tomatoes to New Englanders that a piece of legislation attempting to ban tomatoes from any true chowder was once introduced in Maine. Fresh clams taste great in the chowder, and leaving them in the shell provides a dramatic presentation. In the interest of time, you can substitute 1 cup canned clam meat and an additional 1 cup bottled clam juice for the fresh clams and juice.

MAKES 2 QUARTS

1 tbsp canola oil

2 leeks, white and green parts, diced

1 onion, diced

1 carrot, diced

1 celery stalk, diced

1 red bell pepper, seeds and ribs removed, diced

2 garlic cloves, minced

2 plum tomatoes, canned, coarsely chopped

2 white or yellow potatoes, peeled and diced

3 cups clam juice

1 cup tomato juice

1 bay leaf

Pinch dried thyme leaves

3 dozen chowder clams, shucked, chopped, juices reserved

Salt, to taste

Freshly ground black pepper, to taste

Tabasco, to taste

1. Heat the oil in a large soup pot over medium-high heat. Add the leek, onion, carrot, celery, pepper, and garlic. Cover the pot and cook over medium-low heat, stirring occasionally, until the vegetables are soft and translucent, about 8 to 10 minutes.

2. Add the tomatoes, potatoes, clam juice, tomato juice, bay leaf, and thyme. Bring to a simmer and cook until the potatoes are tender, about 15 minutes.

3. Add the clams with their juices and simmer until the clams are cooked, another 1 to 2 minutes more. Using a shallow, flat spoon, remove any surface fat and discard. Remove the bay leaf and season to taste with salt, pepper, and Tabasco.

VARIATION: Replace the clams with one pound of lean boneless fish such as fresh cod, Pollock or haddock, cut into a 1-inch dice. Use fish broth instead of the clam juice.

THAI HOT AND SOUR SOUP

THAI HOT and Sour Soup creates a complex interplay of spicy hot chile and sour citrus flavors on the palate. All of the ingredients are crucial to the overall flavor, so try not to leave anything out. You can find the ingredients at Asian groceries and some specialty markets.

MAKES 2 QUARTS

2 oz thin rice noodles (vermicelli)

2 quarts Chicken Broth (page 63)

1 stalk lemon grass, cut into 2-inch pieces and smashed

2 tbsp Thai fish sauce (nam pla)

1 tbsp chili oil

2 tsp lime zest

2 tbsp canned jalapeños, minced

3 tbsp lemon juice

1½ tbsp lime juice

½ lb shrimp (30–35 count), peeled and butterflied

8 oz straw mushrooms, canned, drained

¼ cup cilantro, chopped

1. Bring a medium-sized pot of water to a boil. Add the rice noodles and boil until tender, about 3 to 4 minutes. Drain, rinse under cold water, and drain again. Set aside.

2. Combine the chicken broth with the lemon grass, fish sauce, chili oil, lime zest, jalapeños, lemon juice, and lime juice in a wok or soup pot. Bring to a simmer and cook for 7 minutes. Strain or use a slotted spoon to remove the lemon grass.

3. Add the shrimp and cook 3 minutes.

4. Distribute the rice noodles, shrimp, mushrooms, and cilantro evenly between 8 heated soup bowls. Pour the broth into the bowls and serve.

THAI FRESH PEA SOUP

THIS SOUP adds a subtle twist to the delicate taste of peas. It is a great recipe if you have a bumper crop of fresh peas (although frozen peas work equally well), or if you are looking for an easy starter course for an evening of Thai cuisine.

SERVES 6 TO 8

6 cups Vegetable Broth (page 65), plus as needed

1 cup chopped onions

4 garlic cloves, finely minced

2 tsp green curry paste

8 cups shelled peas (thawed if frozen)

Salt and pepper as needed

1 tsp lightly toasted mustard seeds

¼ cup chopped mint

1. Add about ½ cup of the broth to a soup pot and bring to a simmer over medium heat. Add the onions, garlic, and curry paste. Sauté, stirring frequently, until the onions are softened and translucent, about 5 minutes. Add the remaining broth to the pot and bring to a boil. Add the peas, cover the soup, and simmer over low heat for 10 minutes.

2. Remove the pot from the heat and let the soup cool for at least 10 minutes before pureeing with a handheld blender. Strain the soup through a sieve and reserve the liquid if you are using a countertop blender or food processor. Add the solids to the blender jar or food processor bowl; do not overfill. Add a little of the liquid, replace the cover (without the vent from the lid or feed tube), and puree until smooth. Add more liquid if necessary to help puree the solids. Transfer the pureed soup to a clean pot. Continue to puree until all of the solids are pureed. Blend the soup and adjust the consistency by adding some of the remaining reserved liquid. (The soup is ready to finish now or it can be cooled and stored up to 2 days in the refrigerator or up to 1 month in the freezer.)

3. Return the soup to a simmer over low heat. Season to taste with salt and pepper and reheat the soup, if necessary. Serve the soup in heated bowls, garnished with the toasted mustard seeds and chopped mint.

CREAM OF TOMATO SOUP
with Rice and Basil

THIS DELICIOUS version of an old favorite is full of tomato flavor and is sure to bring back memories of home. If you have really flavorful, ripe tomatoes, use them in place of canned tomatoes. Otherwise, canned tomatoes offer the best flavor and consistency.

MAKES 2 QUARTS

2 tbsp olive oil

1½ cups onions, chopped

1 tbsp garlic, chopped

1 quart Vegetable Broth (page 65)

¼ cup basil, chopped

28 oz canned plum tomatoes

1 cup heavy cream

2 cups rice, cooked

1 tbsp basil, chiffonade

1. Sweat the onions and garlic in a little olive oil until translucent, about 5 to 7 minutes. Add the broth, fresh basil, and tomatoes, reserving some of the juice from the tomatoes. Simmer until everything is tender, about 20 minutes.

2. Puree the soup with a handheld blender, or in batches in a food processor or countertop blender.

3. Return the pureed soup to a low simmer. In a small pan, gently simmer the heavy cream before adding it to the soup, then use the reserved tomato juice to adjust the final consistency. Add the rice just before serving.

4. Serve the soup in preheated soup cups or bowls and garnish with the chiffonade of basil.

INDONESIAN CHICKEN, NOODLE, AND POTATO SOUP
Soto Ayam

D on't let the long list of ingredients and steps deter you from making this soup. It's truly delicious and not all that much trouble to make, despite appearances. Any of the ingredients you can't find at your supermarket are available at Asian groceries. To crush the aromatic ingredients, cover them with a piece of plastic wrap and smash with the bottom of a heavy pot or skillet.

MAKES 8 SERVINGS

One 3-lb chicken

2 tsp salt

1 tbsp vegetable oil

4 shallots, chopped

2 stalks fresh lemongrass, bottom 4 or 5 inches only, crushed

1 garlic clove, crushed

One 1-inch slice fresh ginger, crushed

½ tsp crushed black peppercorns

¼ tsp turmeric

6 cups chicken broth

1¼ cups diced yellow or white potatoes

1 oz dried mung bean threads (cellophane noodles)

2 tbsp soy sauce

1 tbsp red chili or hot bean paste

½ tsp sugar

4 scallions, thinly sliced

2 hard-boiled eggs, chopped

½ cup diced celery

1 tsp lemon juice or as needed

Fried Shallots for garnish (page 96)

1 lemon, cut into wedges for garnish

1. Remove the giblets from the chicken; discard or save the liver for another use. Wash the chicken and rub it with ½ teaspoon of the salt. Set aside.

2. Heat the oil in a skillet over high heat. Add the chopped shallots, lemongrass, garlic, ginger, black peppercorns, and turmeric. Cook, stirring constantly, until the aroma is apparent, about 30 seconds. Remove the skillet from the heat.

3. Combine the broth and remaining 1½ teaspoons salt with the chicken, giblets, and shallot mixture in a soup pot. Bring to a simmer and cook, skimming often to remove any foam that rises to the surface, until the chicken is cooked through and tender, about 45 minutes.

4. Remove the chicken from the broth and set aside. When cool enough to handle, remove the bones from the chicken. Return the bones to the broth and continue to simmer, skimming as needed, about 1 hour. Meanwhile, dice the chicken meat and set aside.

5. Place the potatoes in a saucepan, cover with cold water, and bring to a simmer. Cook until tender, about 20 minutes. Drain and spread the potatoes in a single layer to cool.

6. Soak the bean threads in hot water to cover until tender, about 5 minutes. Rinse and separate the strands under cool running water. Chop them into 2-inch pieces and set aside.

7. When the broth has simmered for an hour, strain it through a fine sieve, and return it to the pot. Mix the soy sauce, chili paste, and sugar together; stir into the strained broth. Add the diced chicken meat, cooked potatoes, soaked bean threads, scallions, chopped eggs, and celery to the broth.

Bring the soup to a simmer and add a squeeze of lemon to taste.

8. Serve in heated bowls, garnished with the fried shallots. Pass the lemon wedges on the side.

HAM BONE AND COLLARD GREENS SOUP

THIS HEARTY Southern-style soup is packed with vitamin- and mineral-rich collard greens. Ham bone soup was originally a means of getting the most meal mileage from a ham, but we have developed this recipe using a smoked ham hock (which should be available from your supermarket), so you don't have to purchase and eat a whole ham to make the soup. If you do happen to have a meaty ham bone, though, by all means use it instead of the ham hock. Ham hocks can be quite salty, so use salt-free homemade broth or a reduced-sodium canned variety to make this soup.

MAKES 8 SERVINGS

1 smoked ham hock

12 cups Chicken Broth (page 63)

1¼ lb collard greens

1 tbsp vegetable oil

¼ cup minced salt pork

1¼ cups minced onion

½ cup minced celery

½ cup all-purpose flour

Sachet: 5 to 6 black peppercorns, 4 parsley stems, 1 fresh thyme sprig or ½ tsp dried enclosed in a large tea ball or tied in a cheesecloth pouch

½ cup heavy cream

4 tsp malt vinegar, or as needed

Tabasco sauce as needed

1. Place the ham hock and broth in a pot large enough to accommodate both. Bring to a simmer and cook, partially covered, for 1½ hours. Remove the ham hock from the broth and allow both to cool slightly.

2. Bring a large pot of salted water to a boil. Cut the tough ribs and stems away from the collard greens and discard. Plunge the greens into the boiling water and cook for 10 minutes. Drain and cool slightly. Chop the greens coarsely and set aside.

3. Heat the oil in a soup pot over medium heat. Add the salt pork and cook until crisp, 3 to 5 minutes. Add the onion and celery and cook, stirring occasionally, until tender, about 5 minutes.

4. Add the flour and cook, stirring frequently, for 5 minutes. Gradually add the broth, whisking constantly to work out any lumps of flour, and bring to a simmer. Add the collard greens, ham hock, and sachet; simmer for 1 hour.

5. Remove and discard the sachet. Remove the ham hock and cool slightly. Trim away the skin and fat and discard. Dice the lean meat, and return it to the soup.

6. Add the cream and season to taste with the vinegar and Tabasco. Serve in heated bowls.

TOMATO AND ESCAROLE SOUP

TO GIVE this soup extra richness, we used canned "fire-roasted tomatoes." If you can find them in your market, give them a try. Or, try roasting your own fresh tomatoes to deepen their flavor.

MAKES 4 TO 6 SERVINGS

3 tbsp extra-virgin olive oil

1¼ cups large-dice onions

1 tbsp minced shallots

1 tsp minced garlic

6 cups coarsely chopped escarole, stemmed and washed

2 cups Chicken Broth (page 63)

1½ cups chopped tomatoes (peeled and seeded)

½ cup tomato sauce

Salt and pepper as needed

1. Heat the oil in a soup pot over medium-high heat. Add the onions, shallots, and garlic and stir to coat with the oil. Sauté, stirring frequently, until the onions are softened and translucent, about 5 minutes.

2. Add the escarole and cook, stirring frequently, until it wilts, about 5 minutes.

3. Add the broth, chopped tomatoes, and tomato sauce. Bring the soup to a boil, skimming the surface to remove any foam, and then reduce the heat to low and simmer until the escarole is very tender and all of the ingredients are very hot, about 10 minutes.

4. Season to taste with salt and pepper. Serve in heated bowls or cups.

Oven-Roasting Tomatoes

Choose ripe, flavorful tomatoes for oven roasting. Plum tomatoes are a great choice since they have more flesh and less "water" than other varieties, but you will get excellent results from virtually any variety, including cherry or grape tomatoes.

First, wash the tomatoes well. Cut the core out of larger tomatoes before slicing them or cutting them into wedges. Smaller varieties, like cherry tomatoes, need only to be cut in half.

Arrange the tomatoes on an oiled baking sheet. Turn the tomatoes so they are lightly coated with the oil, then put them into a 350°F oven until they darken in color and have a sweet, rich aroma. Larger tomato slices or wedges may take up to 30 minutes, thin slices or small tomatoes will take 15 to 20 minutes.

If you want to add even more flavor, season the tomatoes before you put them into the oven with salt, pepper, minced garlic, or chopped herbs.

TORTILLA SOUP

THIS SOUP, fragrant with the aromas of cilantro, chili powder, and cumin, is both flavored and thickened with corn tortillas. Toasting the tortillas before grinding them helps develop the fullest flavor. Garnished with avocado, cheese, chicken, and toasted tortilla strips, this soup is a delicious light meal.

MAKES 6 SERVINGS

4 corn tortillas

2 tsp vegetable oil

¾ cup finely grated or pureed onion

½ tsp minced garlic

¾ cup tomato puree

1 tbsp chopped cilantro leaves

1½ tsp mild chili powder

1 tsp ground cumin

6 cups Chicken Broth (page 63)

1 bay leaf

1 cup shredded cooked chicken breast

2 tbsp grated Cheddar cheese

½ cup diced avocado

1. Preheat the oven to 300°F. Cut the tortillas into matchsticks. Place them in an even layer on a baking sheet and toast them in the oven for about 15 minutes. Or, toast the strips by sautéing them in a dry skillet over medium heat, tossing frequently. Reserve about ½ cup of the strips for a garnish. Crush the remainder in a food processor or blender.

2. Heat the oil in a soup pot over medium heat. Add the onion and garlic and cook, stirring frequently, until they release a sweet aroma, 5 to 6 minutes. Add the tomato puree and continue to cook for another 3 minutes. Add the cilantro, chili powder, and cumin and cook for another 2 minutes.

3. Add the broth, crushed tortillas, and bay leaf and bring the soup to a simmer, stirring well. Continue to simmer for 25 to 30 minutes. Strain the soup through a sieve, and serve immediately in heated bowls, garnished with the shredded chicken, cheese, reserved tortilla strips, and diced avocado.

POTAGE AU PISTOU
Vegetable Soup with Garlic and Basil

PISTOU IS both the name of this soup and the garlic-and-basil condiment used to season it. Pistou, the condiment, is the French version of Italy's pesto. Pistou, the soup, is the French version of Italy's minestrone. You can substitute 1½ cups canned navy beans, drained and rinsed, for dried. Simply add them to the soup, along with the vermicelli. This soup is best in late summer, when many of the ingredients can be purchased from your local farmstand or picked from your garden. Served with a loaf of crusty bread (with olive oil for dipping) and a bottle of chilled dry white wine, it makes a fine meal.

MAKES 8 TO 10 SERVINGS

¾ cup dried navy beans, soaked overnight in 3 cups of water

2 tbsp olive oil

3 carrots, diced (about 1 cup)

2 leeks, white and light green parts, diced (about 2½ cups)

1 onion, diced (about 1¼ cups)

2½ quarts Chicken Broth (page 63), heated

Pinch saffron threads, optional

6 oz green beans, cut into 1-inch lengths (about 1 cup)

1 yellow or white potato, peeled and diced (about 1 cup)

1 medium zucchini, diced (about 1 cup)

2 oz vermicelli or angel-hair pasta, broken into 2-inch lengths (about ¾ cup)

2 ripe tomatoes, peeled, seeded, and diced (about 2 cups)

Salt, to taste

Freshly ground black pepper, to taste

1 recipe Pistou (recipe follows), or to taste

1. Drain the beans and place in a large saucepan. Add 1 quart water, and bring to a simmer. Cook until tender, about 1 hour, adding more water, if necessary, to keep the beans covered.

2. Heat the oil in a soup pot over medium heat. Add the carrots, leeks, and onion. Cook until the onion is translucent, about 10 minutes. Add the broth and the saffron, if using, to the vegetables, bring to a simmer, and cook, 10 minutes.

3. Add the green beans, potato, and zucchini. Continue to simmer, 10 minutes.

4. Add the vermicelli and simmer until tender, about 8 minutes.

5. Drain the beans of their cooking liquid and add them to the soup along with the tomatoes. Season to taste with salt and pepper and continue to simmer, 1 minute.

6. Add the pistou, to taste, just before serving. Serve in heated bowls.

Pistou

MAKES ABOUT 3/4 CUP

½ cup fresh basil leaves, chopped

½ cup grated Parmesan cheese

2 tablespoons pinenuts, toasted

2 garlic cloves, chopped

⅓ cup olive oil

1. To toast the pinenuts, spread them in a single layer in a pie plate and roast in a 350°F oven until they are golden, 7 to 10 minutes; stir the nuts frequently and watch carefully, as they can burn quickly. You can also toast the nuts in a heavy, dry skillet over medium-low heat. Toss them often. Remove them from the skillet as soon as they are golden or they will continue to brown. Allow the nuts to cool.

2. Puree the basil, Parmesan, toasted pinenuts, and garlic to a fine paste in a food processor or blender.

3. With the machine running, add the olive oil in a thin stream. Scrape the sides of the bowl or blender jar as necessary. Puree until the oil is completely incorporated.

MUSHROOM BARLEY SOUP

Fresh white mushrooms are used in this version of a traditional winter soup, but feel free to bolster the flavor by incorporating your favorite fresh or dried wild mushrooms. A splash of sherry added at the last moment brings this humble dish up to a whole new level. This soup will mellow and deepen in flavor if it is prepared a day ahead. It will also thicken slightly; to adjust the consistency, add a little water or broth and reheat.

MAKES 8 SERVINGS

1 tbsp vegetable oil

1 onion, finely diced (about 1¼ cups)

1 carrot, finely diced (about ⅓ cup)

1 celery stalk, finely diced (about ½ cup)

1 parsnip, finely diced (about ⅓ cup), optional

3 cups sliced white mushrooms (about 10 ounces)

2 quarts Chicken Broth (page 63)

¾ cup pearl barley

½ tsp salt, or to taste

½ tsp freshly ground black pepper, or to taste

1 tbsp chopped parsley

2 tbsp dry sherry or sherry wine vinegar, optional

1. Heat the oil in a soup pot over medium heat. Add the onion and cook, stirring frequently, until golden brown, about 10 minutes.

2. Add the carrot, celery, parsnip, if using, and mushrooms. Stir well to combine with the onion. Cover and cook over low heat, for 3 to 4 minutes.

3. Remove the cover and add the broth and barley. Bring to a simmer and cook until the barley is tender, about 30 minutes.

4. Season with salt and pepper. Stir in the parsley. Stir in the sherry or vinegar, if using, just before serving. Serve in heated bowls.

HLELEM
Tunisian Vegetable and Bean Soup

Harissa is a Tunisian hot sauce or paste usually made with hot chiles, garlic, cumin, coriander, caraway and olive oil. It's available in cans, jars, or tubes from Middle Eastern markets and specialty stores.

MAKES 2 QUARTS

2 tbsp olive oil

4 tsp garlic, minced

¼ cup celery stalk, large outer veins trimmed, diced

¼ cup onion, minced

1 quart Chicken Broth (page 63)

6 tbsp tomato paste

⅔ cup canned lima beans, drained, juices reserved

⅔ cup canned chickpeas, drained, juices reserved

7 cups Swiss chard leaves, stems removed and cut into
    1-inch pieces, leaves shredded, lightly packed

½ cup angel hair pasta, dry, broken into
    bite-sized pieces

½ tbsp red curry paste or harissa

Salt, to taste

Freshly ground black pepper, to taste

¼ cup parsley, chopped

1. Heat the olive oil in a soup pot over medium heat. Add the garlic, celery, and onion. Cook, stirring occasionally, until the onion is translucent, about 5 to 7 minutes.

2. Combine ½ cup of the reserved chickpea liquid with ½ cup of the reserved lima bean liquid. Add the broth, reserved bean liquid, and the tomato paste. Mix together until well blended and bring to a simmer for 10 minutes.

3. Approximately 10 minutes before serving, add the cooked beans and chickpeas, the Swiss chard, and the pasta. Simmer until the pasta and chard stems are tender, about 10 minutes.

4. Add the red curry paste and stir until blended. Season to taste with the salt and pepper. Garnish with the chopped parsley.

MINESTRONE

Minestrone, literally "big soup," is an Italian classic packed with vegetables, pasta, and beans. There is no one right way to make minestrone. Recipes vary from cook to cook according to individual preferences, so feel free to improvise with other vegetables, beans, or pasta shapes to suit your taste. Pancetta is a type of Italian bacon. It can usually be found in delis and butcher shops, but if it is unavailable in your area, you can omit it or substitute regular bacon.

MAKES 8 SERVINGS

2 tbsp olive oil

1 slice pancetta (or 2 strips bacon), chopped

1½ cups chopped green cabbage

1 cup chopped onion

1 cup sliced carrot

¼ cup chopped celery

2 garlic cloves, minced

8 cups Chicken Broth (page 63)

½ cup peeled, diced potato

One 3-inch piece Parmesan cheese rind

¾ cup vermicelli or angel hair pasta, broken into
    2-inch pieces

½ cup chopped plum tomatoes

¼ cup drained canned chickpeas

⅓ cup drained canned kidney beans

⅓ cup Pesto (recipe follows)

Salt as needed

Freshly ground black pepper as needed

Freshly grated Parmesan cheese as needed

1. Heat the oil in a soup pot over medium heat. Add the pancetta and cook until the fat melts, 3 to 5 minutes. Do not allow the pancetta to brown. Add the cabbage, onion, carrot, celery, and garlic and cook until the onion is translucent, about 6 to 8 minutes.

2. Add the broth, potato, and Parmesan cheese rind. Bring to a simmer and cook until the vegetables are tender, about 30 minutes. Do not overcook.

3. Meanwhile, cook the vermicelli according to package directions until tender; drain and reserve.

4. When the vegetables in the soup are tender, add the cooked vermicelli, tomatoes, chickpeas, and kidney beans. Cook just until heated through. Remove and discard the Parmesan rind.

5. Season the soup to taste with the pesto, salt, and pepper. Serve in heated bowls, sprinkled with Parmesan cheese.

Pesto

MAKES 1 CUP

2 cups packed basil leaves

3 garlic cloves, peeled

Zest and juice of 1 lemon

5 tbsp toasted pine nuts

⅔ cup grated Parmesan cheese

¼ tsp salt

¼ tsp freshly ground black pepper

¼ to ⅓ cup extra-virgin olive oil

Combine the basil, garlic, lemon juice and zest, pine nuts, Parmesan, salt, and pepper in a food processor, pulse until finely chopped. Add ¼ cup of the olive oil in a thin stream until fully incorporated and a thick paste forms; add more olive oil if necessary.

Using Bacon as a Flavoring in Soups

A bit of bacon, salt pork, or the end of a piece of cured ham such as Prosciutto or Smithfield adds depth and flavor to soups. Bacon is especially good at flavoring soups since you can gently cook out some of the fat, a procedure know as rendering, and use that fat to cook the aromatic base of your soup.

The kind of bacon you choose depends upon the flavor profile of your soup. Smoked bacons have a distinctive taste. Cured but unsmoked bacon, like pancetta, has a more subdued flavor. Pancetta is a type of Italian bacon that usually can be found in delis and butcher shops. If it is unavailable in your area, you can omit it or substitute regular bacon.

If you are choosing a bacon to render and use both as a cooking fat and for flavor, choose fatty slices, if you have an option. Put the bacon into a soup pot with a tablespoon or two of water, and then put the pot over low heat. Starting in a cold pot gives the bacon fat time to melt before the bacon gets too crisp. Stir the bacon as it cooks. The liquid will turn a cloudy color at first. Once the bacon seems to have given up most of its fat, turn the heat up a bit and keep cooking long enough for the bits to turn brown and crisp. The fat will turn clear as any moisture in the pan cooks away.

MUSSEL SOUP

THE HAIRY, inedible filaments that protrude from a mussel are known as a "beard." To debeard a mussel, pinch the filaments between thumb and forefinger and pull firmly. Debearding a mussel kills it, so wait until just before cooking to perform this step. You can substitute a variety of seafood for the mussels if you like. Any white fish, such as flounder, halibut, or monkfish, works well, as does shelled and deveined shrimp.

MAKES 2 QUARTS

½ cup white wine

1 medium onion, minced

1 bay leaf

2 fresh thyme sprigs, optional

1–2 cups water, as needed

3 lb mussels, debearded and scrubbed well under
  cold running water

2 tbsp olive oil

1 leek, white and light green parts, finely diced

1 celery stalk, finely diced

2 garlic cloves, minced

2 cups plum tomatoes, drained, seeded, and chopped, juices reserved

1 tsp dried basil

Salt, to taste

Freshly ground black pepper, to taste

½ tsp lemon zest, grated

¼ cup basil or parsley, chopped

1. In a pot large enough to accommodate the mussels, combine the wine, ¼ cup of the onion, bay leaf, thyme sprig (if using), and enough of the water to raise the liquid level to about 1 inch. Bring to a boil. Add the mussels, cover, and steam until the mussels open, about 5 minutes. Use a slotted spoon to transfer the mussels to a bowl and allow them to cool slightly. Remove the mussels from their shells and set aside. Discard the shells. Strain the cooking liquid, including the liquid released by shucked mussels, through a coffee filter and set aside.

2. Heat the olive oil in a soup pot over medium heat. Add the remaining onion, leek, celery, and garlic. Cover the pot, reduce the heat to medium-low, and cook until the vegetables are translucent, about 5 to 7 minutes.

3. Combine the mussel cooking liquid with the reserved tomato juice. Add enough water to bring the amount of liquid to 4 cups. Add this mixture along with the tomatoes and the dried basil to the soup pot. Bring to a simmer and cook, partially covered, for 10 to 12 minutes.

4. Add the mussels to the soup pot and cover the pot. Simmer until the mussels are heated through, about 2 minutes.

5. Season to taste with the salt, pepper, and lemon zest. Garnish with the basil or parsley.

VARIATIONS: Substitute ¼ cup Pernod and ¼ cup dry vermouth for the white wine.

Add ½ teaspoon of saffron along with the tomatoes.

Add a sachet containing ½ teaspoon each of anise seeds and fennel seeds and 1 clove of peeled garlic, at the same time that the tomatoes are added.

POTAGE SOLFERINO
Puree of Vegetable and Potato

A SMALL DICE of parboiled vegetables brings fresh color and texture to this humble puree. For a garnish, you might use a slotted spoon to remove the crisp bacon bits in step 1, drain on paper towels, and sprinkle over the soup just before serving.

MAKES 4 TO 6 SERVINGS

2 tbsp unsalted butter

4 slices bacon, diced

1 carrot, sliced (about ⅓ cup), plus ¼ cup finely diced

1 stalk celery, diced (about ½ cup)

1 leek, white and green parts, sliced (about 1¼ cups)

1 medium onion, diced (about 1¼ cups)

1 small yellow turnip, peeled and diced (about 1½ cups)

¼ head cabbage, shredded (about 2 cups)

1 quart Chicken or Vegetable Broth (pages 63, 65)

2 yellow or white potatoes, peeled and diced (about 2 cups)

Sachet: 1 bay leaf, 1 tsp chopped fresh or ½ tsp dried oregano, 4–5 black peppercorns, 1 garlic clove, and 1 tsp chopped fresh marjoram or ½ tsp dried leaves enclosed in a large teaball or tied in a cheesecloth pouch

¼ cup sliced green beans

1 small tomato, peeled, seeded, and chopped

1 tbsp chopped parsley

Salt and freshly ground black pepper, to taste

1. Melt the butter in soup pot over medium heat. Add the bacon and cook until the bacon is crisp and brown, 6 to 7 minutes.

2. Add the carrot, celery, leek, onion, turnip, and cabbage; stir to coat evenly. Cover and cook until the onion is tender and translucent, 4 to 5 minutes.

3. Add the broth, potatoes, and sachet. Bring to a simmer and cook until the vegetables are tender, 25 to 30 minutes.

4. Meanwhile, boil or steam separately the diced carrots and sliced green beans until just tender. Set aside to cool.

5. Remove the sachet and discard. Strain soup through a sieve, reserving liquid. Puree solids and return to the pot. Add enough of the reserved liquid to achieve a thick soup consistency.

6. Add the diced carrot, green beans, tomato, and parsley. Season with salt and pepper. Simmer the soup until heated through, about 5 minutes. Serve in heated bowls.

Pureeing Soups

You can puree soups by a variety of means: using a handheld blender directly in the soup pot, in a countertop blender, with a sieve or a food mill, or in a food processor. Follow these guidelines to avoid scalds and burns.

For all soups, the first step in pureeing a soup, regardless of what piece of equipment you intend to use, is to pull the soup pot off the heat and allow the soup to cool for at least 10 minutes. Besides possible scalds or burns from the hot soup, boiling hot liquids can splash up unexpectedly when agitated by a food processor or blender.

USING A HANDHELD BLENDER

Be sure that the soup pot is not too full. You should have at least 4 inches of space between the top of the soup and the top of the pot. If the soup fills the pot more than that, transfer some of the soup to a bowl or a pot. Put the head of the blender under the surface of the soup before you turn it on. Continue to run the blender until the soup is smooth. You can strain the soup through a fine sieve after pureeing it this way, if necessary, to remove any fibers from the vegetables.

USING A COUNTERTOP BLENDER OR A FOOD PROCESSOR

Strain the soup through a sieve to separate the solids and liquids; reserve the liquid separately. Add enough of the solids to the blender jar or bowl of the food processor to fill it by about half. Remove the "funnel" from the lid of the blender or feed tube of a food processor, to allow steam from the hot soup to escape; otherwise, pressure will build up and the soup might burst up when you remove the lid. It also permits you to add some of the reserved liquid so the soup purees more easily.

Turn the motor on at a low setting. Gradually ladle some of the liquid into the soup so the blades can turn more easily. You can increase the blender speed once the soup has become a coarse puree. After the soup is smooth, transfer it to a clean pot.

Continue to puree the soup, working in batches. After all of the soup is pureed and combined in the clean pot, stir it well and, if necessary, add more of the reserved liquid or additional broth to thin the soup.

BLACK BEAN SOUP

THIS VEGETARIAN version of a traditional Mexican favorite removes the time-consuming steps required in preparing dried black beans, and develops excellent flavor using garlic, dried herbs, peppers and sun-dried tomatoes.

MAKES 2 QUARTS

¼ lb onion, diced

2 tbsp garlic, minced

2 tbsp olive oil

½ tsp cumin, ground

1 lemon, thickly sliced

1 oz sun-dried tomatoes, chopped

1 tsp jalapeños, minced

1 tsp dried oregano

½ tsp salt, or to taste

3 lb canned black beans, drained and rinsed

2 quarts Vegetable Broth (page 65)

1½ tbsp sherry vinegar

1. In a 3 quart pot, sauté the onions and garlic in the oil until translucent. Add the ground cumin and continue to sauté until fragrant, about 1 minute.

2. Add the lemon slices, tomatoes, jalapeños, oregano, salt, beans, and vegetable broth. Simmer for 15 minutes.

3. Remove and discard the lemon slices. Use a handheld blender, or a food processor or countertop blender, to partially puree 3 cups of the soup (it should be thick and chunky), and add it back to the pot. Cook for an additional 10 minutes.

4. Finish the soup by adding the vinegar.

PUREE OF SPLIT PEA SOUP

THE BACON and ham hock add a traditional smoky flavor to this thick and heart-warming puree of vegetable and split peas. However, if you prefer a meatless version, omit the bacon and ham hock, substitute vegetable broth for the chicken broth, and replace the bacon fat with vegetable oil.

MAKES 8 SERVINGS

4 strips bacon, minced

1 medium onion, diced (about 1¼ cups)

1 carrot, diced (about ⅓ cup)

1 celery stalk, diced (about ½ cup)

1 leek, white and light green part, diced (about 1¼ cups)

6 cups Chicken Broth (page 63)

2 yellow or white potatoes, peeled and diced (about 2 cups)

½ lb split green or yellow peas, or lentils

1 smoked ham hock

Sachet: 1 bay leaf, 1 whole clove, 1 garlic clove, and 4–5 peppercorns enclosed in a large teaball or tied in a cheesecloth pouch

Salt, to taste

Freshly ground black pepper, to taste

1 cup Croutons (page 96)

1. Cook the bacon in a soup pot over medium-high heat until crisp and brown. Remove the bacon with a slotted spoon; drain on paper towels and set aside. Pour off all but 3 tablespoons of the bacon fat. Add the onion, carrot, celery, and leek; stir to evenly coat with fat. Cover the pot and cook the vegetables over medium-low heat, stirring occasionally, until the onion is tender and translucent, 6 to 8 minutes.

2. Add the broth, potatoes, peas, and ham hock. Bring to a simmer and cook over medium heat, 20 minutes, stirring occasionally. Add the sachet and

simmer until the split peas are soft, about 30 minutes. Skim away any scum during simmering.

3. Remove the sachet from the pot and discard. Remove the ham hock and set aside to cool. When cool enough to handle, cut the ham off the bone, dice, and set aside.

4. Strain the soup through a sieve, reserving the liquid. Puree the solids and return them to the pot. Add enough of the reserved liquid to achieve a thick consistency. Blend well. Stir in the ham and bacon. Season with salt and pepper. Serve in heated bowls, garnished with croutons.

Evaluating the Quality of Puree and Cream Soups

Cream soups and purees are best when they are intensely flavored and lightly thickened with a good color and an appealing aroma. Soups should be made with quality ingredients, from the aromatics through to the main ingredient, and on to the finishing ingredients. Be sure that the vegetables, meats, and cream are fresh and flavorful. Trimming and cutting them properly before you add them to the soup pot allows them to release their flavors quickly, without overcooking or turning a muddy or grayish color.

TOO THICK: These soups should pour easily from the ladle or spoon; a soup thick enough to hold the spoon upright is too thick. And because they contain starchy ingredients, these soups may keep getting thicker as they simmer, or during storage. If your soup is too thick, use additional broth or water to thin it and adjust the seasoning again once the texture is right.

BURNT OR SCORCHED FLAVOR OR AROMA: Stir soups as they simmer so that they don't scorch. As you stir, check the way the spoon feels against the bottom of the pot. If the soup has started to thicken and stick, transfer it to a clean pot to prevent it from burning.

HARSH FLAVOR: If the flavor is too harsh, the ratio of ingredients used was incorrect. The vegetables may not have been properly sweated or the soup might not have been cooked long enough. Taste the soup as it simmers to determine when the flavor is best.

RED LENTIL SOUP

O F ALL VEGETABLES, lentils, at approximately twenty-five percent, are second only to soybeans in protein content. They have been cultivated by humans for millennia, as evidenced by their presence at ancient Egyptian and prehistoric European sites. Today, lentils are available in several varieties, such as the yellow lentil and the green (French) lentil. The red (Egyptian) lentil is the quickest cooking of all lentils, and lends itself well to soup making because, as it cooks, it tends to fall apart and practically purees itself.

MAKES 8 SERVINGS

3 tbsp unsalted butter

½ large onion, minced (about 1 cup)

2 garlic cloves, minced (about 1 tsp)

½ celery stalk, diced (about ¼ cup)

1 lb red lentils

1 tsp ground cumin

2 tbsp long-grain white rice

2½ quarts Chicken Broth (page 63), or as needed

Juice of ½ lemon

Salt, to taste

Freshly ground white pepper, to taste

1. Melt the butter in a soup pot over medium heat and add the onion, garlic, and celery. Cook until the onion is translucent, 4 to 6 minutes. Reduce heat to low, add the lentils and cumin, and stir to coat evenly with butter. Cook, 4 to 5 minutes.

2. Add the rice and 5 cups of the chicken broth. Bring to a simmer and cook, stirring often to avoid scorching, until the lentils dissolve and begin to look like a pureed soup, 30 to 45 minutes. Add the remaining broth as needed to adjust the consistency. Heat through.

3. Season with the lemon juice, salt, and pepper. Serve in heated bowls.

UDON NOODLE POT

UDON NOODLES are sold as both a fresh and dry pasta. We used fresh noodles in this recipe, but you can substitute dried udon noodles. To learn about preparing them, see the note below.

MAKES 6 SERVINGS

24 oz fresh udon noodles

1 tbsp peanut or canola oil

6 cups dashi (recipe follows)

2 dozen littleneck clams

12 oz boneless skinless chicken thighs, cut into bite-size pieces

12 oz small shrimp (31/36 count), peeled and deveined

1½ cups sliced shiitake mushroom caps

1½ cups finely shredded Napa cabbage

1½ cups finely shredded spinach

1 cup thinly sliced carrots

1 cup snow peas, trimmed

⅓ cup soy sauce

1 tbsp mirin

2 scallions, thinly sliced on the diagonal

1. Bring a large pot of salted water to a boil. Cook the noodles until just tender, about 2 to 3 minutes. Drain the noodles and rinse under cold water. Drain the noodles again, toss with the oil, and reserve.

2. Bring the dashi to a simmer in the pot. Add the clams, chicken, shrimp, and mushrooms to the pot and ladle the simmering dashi over the top. Cover and cook until the clams are open and the chicken is cooked through, 10 to 12 minutes. Discard any clams that do not open. Transfer the clams, chicken, shrimp, and mushrooms to a bowl and keep warm.

3. Add the cabbage, spinach, carrots, and snow peas to the pot and simmer until all of the vegetables are cooked through and very hot, about 10 minutes. Return the noodles to the pot and simmer until they are very hot, 3 to 4 minutes. Add the soy sauce and mirin and continue to simmer until the soup is very flavorful, 2 to 3 minutes.

4. Serve the clams, chicken, shrimp, and mushrooms over the noodles and vegetables and ladle the broth over the top. Garnish with the scallions.

Dashi

MAKES 6 CUPS

6½ cups cold water

One 3-inch piece dried kombu seaweed

2 oz bonito flakes

Combine the water, kombu, and bonito flakes in a large saucepan. Bring the water to a simmer over medium-high heat. Continue to simmer until the broth is very flavorful, 20 to 25 minutes. Strain the dashi and use as directed, or store in a clean, covered container in the refrigerator for up to 1 week.

Preparing Udon Noodles

To prepare fresh udon noodles: bring a large pot of salted water to a rolling boil over high heat. Add the noodles, stir to separate the strands, and cook until they are tender to the bite, but not mushy, 2 to 4 minutes.

To prepare dried udon noodles, begin as you do for fresh noodles by bringing water to a rolling boil and adding the noodles. Then, once the water returns to a boil, add 1 cup of cold water. Repeat the process of bringing the water back to a boil and adding a cup of cold water two or three more times or until the noodles are tender.

ROAST TURKEY BROTH
with Caramelized Butternut Squash and Sage Dumplings

THIS DOUBLE broth is perfect for a cold winter's day. If you happen to have the carcass of a roast turkey on hand, chop it into large pieces and roast it instead of using fresh bones. You can also add leftover roast turkey meat to the soup. If you are not serving all the soup at once, refrigerate the broth, squash, and dumplings separately, and reheat only as much as you need.

MAKES 8 SERVINGS

4 lb turkey legs or meaty turkey bones (wings, backs, and necks) and giblets (excluding the liver)

3 quarts Chicken Broth (page 63), or as needed

1 large onion, thinly sliced (about 1¼ cups)

1 carrot, thinly sliced (about ⅓ cup)

1 celery stalk, thinly sliced (about ½ cup)

5–6 whole black peppercorns

3–4 parsley stems

1 bay leaf

1 sprig fresh thyme

Salt, to taste

2 tbsp unsalted butter

2 cups diced butternut squash (about 1 lb)

Freshly ground white pepper, to taste

1 recipe Sage Dumplings (page 92)

1. Preheat the oven to 400°F. Spread the turkey legs or bones in a single layer in a roasting pan. Roast until deep golden brown, about 1 hour.

2. Transfer the turkey legs or bones to a large soup pot. Add 2 cups of the broth to the hot roasting pan and scrape the bottom of the pan with a wooden spoon to loosen any drippings. Pour over the turkey legs or bones.

3. Add enough broth to cover by at least 2 inches. Bring slowly to a boil over medium heat. As the liquid comes to a boil, skim any foam that rises to the surface. Adjust the heat once a boil is reached, so that a slow, lazy simmer is established. Simmer 1 hour, skimming as necessary.

4. Add the onion, carrot, celery, peppercorns, parsley stems, bay leaf, thyme, and salt. Continue to simmer, skimming the surface as necessary, until broth is fully flavored, about 1 hour.

5. While the broth is simmering, heat the butter in a large ovenproof skillet over medium heat. Add the squash and cook, stirring occasionally, until brown on all sides, 15 to 20 minutes. Season the squash with salt and pepper and place the skillet in the preheated oven. Roast the squash until tender, about 10 minutes. Remove the squash from the oven, drain off any excess fat, and set aside.

6. When the broth is fully flavored, strain it through a fine sieve or cheesecloth-lined colander into a clean soup pot. If you used turkey legs, remove the skin, pull the meat from the bones, dice, and return it to the broth, or save for another purpose. Discard the remaining solids.

7. Add the squash and the dumplings to the broth. Return to a simmer briefly to heat through. Season with salt and pepper. Serve in heated bowls.

Sage Dumplings

THESE DUMPLINGS are an herbed version of Italian gnocchi (potato dumplings). You can substitute any other fresh herb for the sage, if you like. There are two keys to making the dumplings light and fluffy. First, mix the dough until the ingredients just come together. Overmixing will develop the gluten in the flour and make the dumplings tough. Second, don't let the water simmer too quickly while you cook the dumplings. Vigorous simmering will rough up the dumplings and misshape them. If you plan on storing the cooked dumplings rather than adding them directly to soup, rinse them under cold water, drain, and lightly toss them in olive oil to keep them from sticking together.

MAKES ABOUT 60 PIECES

1¼ lb yellow potatoes (about 4)

¾ cup all-purpose flour (4 oz)

1 egg

1 tbsp extra-virgin olive oil, plus more as needed

1 tbsp salt

½ cup grated dry jack or Parmesan cheese

2 tbsp chopped fresh sage

1. Peel the potatoes and cut into sixths. Place in a pot of cold, salted water. Bring to a simmer over medium heat and cook gently until just tender, about 20 minutes. Drain and return the potatoes to the pot. Place over medium heat again for a few minutes to drive off any excess moisture. Shake the pot frequently until steam no longer rises from the potatoes.

2. Pass the potatoes through a medium-holed food mill or potato ricer. Spread the potatoes in a thin layer on a baking sheet and refrigerate or set aside until cool.

3. Place the cooled potatoes in a large bowl. Add the flour. Chop the flour into the potatoes with a rubber spatula until a grainy texture has formed.

4. Mix the egg, oil, and salt together. Add to the potato mixture along with the cheese and sage. Mix gently by hand until just incorporated.

5. Place the dumpling dough in a pastry bag without a tip and pipe the dough into 6-inch logs onto a floured cutting board. Gently roll the dough by hand into smooth logs approximately the diameter of a dime.

6. Cut the logs into ½-inch lengths and roll onto a fork to imprint with ridges. Store the dumplings in a single layer on a floured jellyroll pan until ready to cook.

7. Cook the dumplings in heavily salted, gently simmering water until just firm, about 90 seconds. Lift the dumplings out of the water with a slotted spoon and add directly to soup.

POSOLE-POBLANO SOUP
with Smoked Pork and Jalapeño Jack Cheese

TRADITIONALLY SERVED at Christmas, this thick Mexican soup is full of deep, complex flavors. Some of the ingredients may be unfamiliar to you, but they should not be difficult to find either at a supermarket or Latin-American grocery. Poblanos are dark-green fresh chiles that range from mild to quite spicy. Anchos are dried, ripe poblanos. Roasting (the poblanos) and toasting (the anchos) intensifies their flavors. Hominy (corn from which the hull and germ have been removed) is available canned in either gold or yellow varieties. If you have a good butcher or smokehouse nearby, you might be able to get some smoked pork shoulder. Otherwise, most supermarkets sell smoked pork chops. Masa harina (dough flour) is made from the dried dough used to make corn tortillas. It provides flavor and a slight thickening effect, but you can omit it and still have a delicious soup. Quaker makes masa harina, but purchase a Mexican brand, such as Manteca, if you can.

MAKES 6 SERVINGS

2 poblano chiles

4 tsp corn oil

1 ancho chile

10 oz smoked pork, diced (about 2½ cups)

Salt, to taste

Freshly ground black pepper, to taste

1 onion, diced (about 1¼ cups)

2 garlic cloves, minced

1 jalapeño pepper, seeded and minced

3 tbs masa harina, optional

2 tbs tomato paste

1½ quarts Chicken Broth (page 63)

1 tsp dried oregano

1 tsp dried thyme

¾ cup canned hominy, rinsed and drained

Juice of 1 lime, or to taste

½ cup grated jalapeño jack cheese

2 tbsp chopped fresh cilantro

½ cup diced jicama, optional

1 tomatillo, papery hull removed, washed, and diced, optional

2–3 radishes, diced or cut into matchsticks, optional

1. Preheat the broiler. Brush the poblanos with 1 teaspoon of the oil. Place the poblanos under the broiler and turn them as they roast so that they blacken evenly on all sides. Put the poblanos in a bowl and cover, letting them steam for 10 minutes, then remove them from the bowl and pull off the skins. Use the back of a knife to scrape away any bits that don't come away easily. Remove the seeds, ribs, and stem from poblanos. Chop flesh coarsely. Set aside.

2. Heat a cast-iron or other very heavy skillet over high heat. Remove the stem and seeds from the ancho and straighten it into a single layer. Toast the ancho by placing it in the hot skillet and pressing down hard with a metal spatula, until it crackles and a wisp of smoke rises, 3 to 5 seconds. Flip over and repeat on the other side. Chop the ancho coarsely and set aside.

3. Heat the remaining oil in a soup pot over medium heat. Season the pork cubes with salt and pepper and add to the pot. Cook until the pork is well browned, about 5 minutes. Add the onion and continue to cook, 5 minutes. Add the garlic and jalapeño pepper and cook, 1 minute more. Add the masa harina, if using, and cook for 1 minute. Add the tomato paste and cook for 1 minute.

4. Add 4½ cups of the broth along with the oregano and thyme. Bring to a simmer and cook, at least 20 minutes.

5. Meanwhile, place the remaining broth and the ancho chile in a saucepan. Bring to a simmer and cook until the chile is quite tender, about 15 minutes. Puree the ancho and broth in a blender.

6. When the soup has simmered for at least 20 minutes, add the ancho puree. Continue to simmer, 15 minutes.

7. Add the poblanos and hominy, and simmer an additional 10 minutes.

8. Just before serving, season with lime juice, salt, and pepper. Serve in heated bowls, garnished with cheese and cilantro, as well as the jicama, tomatillo, and radish, if using. Or, put the garnishes in small bowls and pass them on the side.

SALMON MISO SOUP

Miso, which is fermented soybean paste, is a principle ingredient in Japanese cooking. It comes in a variety of flavors and colors. Most miso is quite salty, though low-salt varieties are available. Containing large amounts of protein and B vitamins, it's also highly nutritious. The variety called for in this soup, yellow (shinshu) miso, is very mellow as misos go. Daikon is a large, white Asian radish with a sweet flavor and crisp texture. Look for daikon and miso, as well as many of the other ingredients called for here, in Asian groceries and health-food stores.

MAKES 8 SERVINGS

3 tsp vegetable oil

1 egg, lightly beaten

3 tbsp thinly sliced scallion greens

½ tsp minced fresh ginger

¼ cup diced carrot

¼ cup diced daikon

1½ quarts Chicken Broth (page 63)

5 tbsp yellow miso (shinsu)

2¼ tsp instant dashi

¼ cup dried wakame seaweed, broken into 1-inch pieces, optional

1 cup diced soft tofu

½ cup finely diced, fresh, boneless, skinless salmon fillet (about 3 oz)

2¼ tsp dark Asian sesame oil

¼ tsp freshly ground black pepper

1. Heat 1 teaspoon of the oil in a nonstick omelet pan or small skillet over medium-low heat. Add the egg and cook until set on the bottom, about 1 minute. Flip the omelet and cook until completely set, 1 to 2 minutes. Transfer the omelet to a cutting board, dice, and set aside.

2. Heat the remaining 2 teaspoons oil in a large wok or soup pot. Add 1½ tablespoons of the scallion, and the ginger. Stir-fry briefly, about 30 seconds. Add the carrots and daikon. Stir-fry until tender, about 3 minutes.

3. Add the broth, miso, and dashi. Stir to combine and dissolve. Add the seaweed, if using.

4. Bring the soup to a simmer. Add the tofu, salmon, sesame oil, and black pepper. Simmer until the salmon is just cooked, about 1 minute.

5. Serve in heated bowls, garnished with the remaining scallions and the diced omelet.

FISHERMAN'S SOUP WITH SHRIMP AND FRESH HERBS
Canh Chua Tom

It is worth the effort to find a fresh pineapple for this delicious Vietnamese sweet-and-sour soup. You may be able to find peeled and cored fresh pineapple in the produce section of your grocery store.

MAKES 6 SERVINGS

2 tbsp peanut oil

2 tbsp Vietnamese chili paste

2 tsp minced garlic

10 cups Chicken Broth (page 63)

2 cups quartered cherry tomatoes

1 cup diced pineapple

¼ cup tamarind pulp

2 tbsp Vietnamese fish sauce, plus additional as needed

1 tbsp sugar

1 lb shrimp (31/35 count), peeled, deveined, halved lengthwise

½ cup diced taro root

2 tbsp lime juice, or as needed

Salt as needed

Freshly ground black pepper as needed

¾ cup bean sprouts, trimmed

¼ cup cilantro leaves

6 Thai basil leaves, cut in halves

Fried Shallots (see page 96)

1. Heat the oil in a soup pot over medium heat. Add the chili paste and garlic, and sauté until fragrant, stirring constantly, about 20 seconds. Add the chicken broth, tomatoes, pineapple, tamarind, 2 tablespoons of the fish sauce, and the sugar. Bring the broth to a boil, stirring to dissolve the tamarind paste into the broth.

2. As soon as the soup comes to a boil, reduce the heat and simmer until flavorful, about 5 minutes. Add the shrimp and taro root, and simmer just until the shrimp is barely cooked through, 5 minutes.

3. Season the soup to taste with the lime juice, additional fish sauce, salt, and pepper. Divide the shrimp, bean sprouts, cilantro, and basil equally among 6 warmed soup bowls. Ladle the warm broth over the shrimp and garnishes, top with the fried shallots, and serve at once.

CIOPPINO

A SAVORY TOMATO broth full of seafood and vegetables, cioppino is an American original created in San Francisco by Italian immigrants. Although not traditional, you can substitute 1 cup of lump crab meat for the crabs. If you purchase fennel with the tops still attached, save some of the nicest looking sprigs for a garnish. Serve the cioppino with large garlic toasts or crusty sourdough bread.

MAKES 8 TO 10 SERVINGS

2 tbsp olive oil

1½ cups sliced scallions

2 cups diced green pepper

1¼ cups diced onion

1¼ cups diced fennel bulb

2 tsp minced garlic

1 cup dry white wine

4 cups Fish Broth (page 64)

8 cups chopped plum tomatoes, fresh or canned

½ cup tomato puree

2 bay leaves

Salt as needed

Freshly ground black pepper as needed

20 littleneck clams, scrubbed well

3 steamed hard-shell crabs, cooked

20 medium shrimp, peeled and deveined

1¼ lb swordfish or halibut steaks, diced

3 tbsp minced basil

1. Heat the oil in a soup pot over medium heat. Add the scallions, pepper, onion, and fennel. Cook, stirring occasionally, until the onion is translucent, 6 to 8 minutes. Add the garlic and cook another minute. Add the white wine, bring to a boil, and cook until the volume of wine is reduced by about half, 4 to 6 minutes.

2. Add the fish broth, tomatoes, tomato puree, and bay leaves. Cover and slowly simmer the mixture for about 45 minutes. Add a small amount of water, if necessary. Cioppino should be more a broth than a stew.

3. Season to taste with the salt and pepper. Remove and discard the bay leaves. Add the clams and simmer for about 10 minutes. Discard any clams that do not open.

4. Separate the claws from the crabs and cut the bodies in half. Add the crab pieces, shrimp, and swordfish to the soup. Simmer until the fish is just cooked through, about 5 minutes.

5. Add the basil and adjust the seasoning to taste, if necessary. Serve in heated bowls or soup plates.

CROUTONS

CROUTONS KEEP well for several days in an airtight container, so the recipe can easily be multiplied. Cut the croutons into any size you like, from tiny cubes for garnishing soups in cups to large cubes for bowls of soup or for salads—just don't make them any bigger than a soup spoon, and adjust the baking time appropriately.

MAKES ABOUT 2 CUPS ½-INCH CROUTONS

3 slices white bread

1½ tbsp melted unsalted butter or olive oil

¼ tsp salt, or to taste

1. Remove the crust from the bread, if desired. Cut the bread into cubes. (If the bread is very fresh, dry the cubes in a 200°F oven, 5 minutes.)

2. Preheat the oven to 350°F. Toss the bread, butter or oil, and salt in a bowl.

3. Spread the bread cubes in a single layer on a baking sheet. Bake until golden, 8 to 10 minutes. Stir the croutons once or twice during baking so that they brown evenly.

Garlic Croutons

Mince 1 clove garlic. Sprinkle with ¼ teaspoon kosher salt and mash to a paste with the side of a large knife. Add the garlic paste to the butter or oil before tossing with bread cubes. Bake as directed.

Cheese Croutons

After the bread cubes have been tossed with butter, toss them with ½ cup very finely grated Parmesan, Romano, or other hard grating cheese (a rotary cheese grater or a microplane grater will give you the finest texture and help the cheese adhere to the bread). Bake as directed.

Herb Croutons

Add 3 tablespoons chopped fresh or dried herbs (such as oregano or rosemary) to the butter or oil. Toss with the bread cubes. Bake as directed.

FRIED SHALLOTS

THIS CRISPY garnish makes a delicious finishing touch for various soups. If you don't have a thermometer, test the temperature of the oil by adding one shallot ring. If the oil is hot enough, it will immediately bubble around the shallot.

MAKES 8 GARNISH SERVINGS

2 shallots

½ cup all-purpose flour

Salt, to taste

Cayenne pepper, to taste, optional

½ cup milk

2 cups vegetable oil, or as needed, for frying

1. Peel and slice the shallots into ⅛-inch-thick rings. Separate the rings.

2. Season the flour with salt and cayenne, if using.

3. Dip the shallot rings in the milk, then strain or use a slotted spoon to remove them, and dredge them in the flour.

4. Fry the shallots in 325°F oil until golden, about 5 minutes. Drain on paper towels. Season with salt.

Pastas, Casseroles, and Light Fare

VEGETARIAN MOUSSAKA

S EITAN IS a protein-rich food made from wheat, with a dense, meaty texture that makes it an ideal vegetarian substitute in traditionally meat-based dishes. You can find it in the produce section of many larger supermarkets, or in natural or health food stores.

MAKES 8 SERVINGS

3 lb eggplant (2 large or 3 medium)

2 tsp kosher salt, to taste

3 tbsp butter

¼ cup flour

3 cups milk

½ tsp ground black pepper, to taste

1½ lb potatoes

3 tbsp olive oil, or as needed

1 cup minced onion

1½ tsp minced garlic

2 cups chopped plum tomatoes

1 cup dry white wine

6 cups Vegetable Broth (page 65)

2 cups crumbled seitan

⅓ cup dark raisins

¼ cup toasted pine nuts

2 tbsp chopped flat-leaf parsley

2 tsp chopped thyme

2 tsp chopped oregano

1 tsp ground cinnamon

2 egg yolks, beaten

1. Peel and slice the eggplant about ¼ inch thick. Place in a colander, sprinkle liberally with kosher salt, and let rest until the salt begins to draw out some of the liquid, about 20 minutes. Rinse the eggplant thoroughly, let drain, and blot dry. (See note "Preparing Eggplant for Cooking," opposite.)

2. While the eggplant is draining, prepare a white sauce: Melt the butter in a saucepan over medium

LEFT TO RIGHT Keeping the eggplant slices in a single layer in the pan, sauté until golden brown. When assembling the moussaka, make sure that the eggplant and potato slices are evenly spaced and layered. Add the white sauce to the dish one ladle at a time, allowing it a chance to infuse through the layered vegetables and reach the bottom; if desired, you could also gently tap the bottom of the dish against a hard surface to force any trapped air out of the casserole. The finished moussaka should have a slightly bubbly sauce and rich golden brown color.

heat. Add the flour and stir well to make a smooth paste. Continue to cook, stirring frequently, until the mixture has a light blond color, 5 to 6 minutes. Add the milk gradually, whisking as you add it, until it is all incorporated and the sauce is smooth. Simmer over medium-low to low heat until the sauce is thick and smooth. Taste and adjust the seasoning with salt and pepper. Remove from the heat and reserve.

3. Put the potatoes in a pot and add enough water to cover them; bring to a simmer over medium-high heat. Simmer until a skewer or paring knife can be easily inserted about halfway into the potato, about 20 minutes. Drain the potatoes and set aside until they are cool enough to handle. Remove the skin and slice the potatoes into ¼-inch-thick rounds; set aside.

4. Heat 2 tablespoons oil in a skillet over medium high heat. Add the eggplant slices in batches (do not allow the slices to touch or pile up on top of each other). Fry on the first side until a light golden brown, about 2 minutes. Turn and fry on the second side until golden brown, another 2 minutes. As the slices are cooked, remove them to a paper lined pan to absorb any excess oil. Add more oil to the pan as necessary as you fry the eggplant. Continue to fry until all of the slices are done. Set aside.

5. In the same pan, heat enough of the oil to generously coat the pan until the oil shimmers. Add the onion and sauté, stirring frequently, until golden brown, about 10 to 12 minutes. Add the garlic and continue to sauté, stirring frequently, until there is a good aroma from the garlic, another 1 or 2 minutes. Add the tomatoes and cook over medium heat, stirring from time to time, until the tomatoes have a rich aroma and turn a deep rust color, 5 to 6 minutes. Add the wine and broth and simmer until

the liquid reduces by about half. Add the crumbled seitan and continue to cook just until evenly moistened and heated through, about 2 minutes. Stir in the raisins, pine nuts, parsley, thyme, oregano, and cinnamon. Taste the mixture and adjust as necessary with salt and pepper.

6. Preheat the oven to 350°F.

7. To assemble the moussaka, brush a casserole or baking dish with oil. Add a thin layer of the seitan mixture, followed by a layer of potatoes, then another thin layer of the seitan mixture, followed by a layer of eggplant. Continue to layer in this sequence until you have used all of the ingredients, ending with a layer of the seitan.

8. Blend the egg yolks into the white sauce and pour in an even layer over the top of the moussaka. Bake until the potatoes are very tender and easy to pierce with the tip of a paring knife, 1 to 1¼ hours. (Cover the moussaka loosely with foil if the top layer is browning too quickly.)

9. Remove the moussaka from the oven and let it rest for 15 minutes before slicing and serving.

Preparing Eggplant for Cooking

Many recipes instruct you to salt eggplant before you cook it. Some say this step is necessary because it draws out any bitterness in the eggplant. We think it's a good idea, even if the eggplant isn't large or bitter. Drawing out some of the moisture in eggplant collapses the vegetable a little, so it doesn't act as much like a sponge for oil when you fry it.

Peel the eggplant if you wish and slice the eggplant to the required thickness. Place the slices in a colander and put the colander in a large bowl. Sprinkle the slices liberally with kosher salt and let them rest until the salt begins to draw moisture to the surface, about 20 minutes. Rinse the eggplant thoroughly, let drain, and blot dry.

LAMB AND EGGPLANT MOUSSAKA

Making moussaka is something of an undertaking—a rich meat sauce (made here with lamb, but you can substitute other ground meats such as turkey, veal, or even pork, if you prefer), layered with tender eggplant (see note, page 99) and a cheese sauce. You can make the moussaka in two smaller casserole dishes to serve one now and freeze one to bake later.

MAKES 12 TO 14 SERVINGS

3 lb eggplant (2 large or 3 medium)

Salt as needed

⅓ cup olive oil, or as needed

2 cups diced onion

1¼ lb ground lamb (or substitute beef, turkey, pork, or combination)

2 cups chopped plum tomatoes

2 tsp minced garlic

2 cloves

Small piece cinnamon stick (or ¼ tsp ground cinnamon)

1 bay leaf

Pinch ground allspice

Freshly ground black pepper, as needed

½ cup water

2 tbsp tomato paste

¼ cup dry red wine

¼ cup plain bread crumbs

2 cups Cheese Sauce (recipe follows)

1. Peel, salt, and rinse the eggplant if desired (see note "Preparing Eggplant for Cooking").

2. Heat about 1 tablespoon of olive oil in a skillet over medium-high heat until it shimmers. Add the eggplant to the hot oil a few slices at a time and sauté the eggplant slices, turning as necessary, until tender and lightly colored, 2 to 3 minutes on each side. Transfer to a rack to drain while you sauté the remaining eggplant, adding more oil to the skillet as necessary.

3. To prepare a meat sauce: Heat 1 tablespoon of olive oil in a skillet. Add the onion and cook over medium high heat, stirring frequently, until tender, 10 to 12 minutes. Add the ground meat and cook over medium heat, stirring frequently, until the meat loses its raw appearance, about 5 minutes. Add the tomatoes, garlic, cloves, cinnamon, bay leaf, allspice, salt, pepper, and about ½ cup water. Simmer until thick and flavorful, about 30 minutes. Add the tomato paste and red wine and continue simmering until the wine has developed a sweet aroma, about 10 minutes.

4. Preheat the oven to 350°F.

5. To assemble the moussaka: Scatter the bread crumbs in a deep, rectangular baking dish. Place a layer of half of the eggplant slices over the bread crumbs. Add the meat sauce and spread it into an even layer. Add the remaining eggplant in an even layer over the meat sauce. Pour the cheese sauce over the eggplant. Bake, uncovered, until the cheese sauce is thick and golden brown and the eggplant is very tender, about 45 minutes. Let the moussaka rest for about 20 minutes before cutting and serving.

Cheese Sauce

MAKES 2 CUPS

5 tbsp butter

5 tbsp all-purpose flour

2½ cups milk

Few grains of nutmeg

Salt as needed

Freshly ground black pepper as needed

2 egg yolks

½ cup grated kefalotyri or Parmesan cheese

1. Heat the butter in a saucepan over medium heat. Add the flour and stir well. Cook for about 5 minutes, stirring constantly. Gradually whisk in the milk, working out any lumps that form. Bring to a full boil, then reduce the heat to low and gently simmer, stirring frequently, until thickened, about 30 minutes.

2. Remove the sauce from the heat and add nutmeg, salt, and pepper to taste. Whisk the egg yolks in a small boil and add a bit of the hot sauce to the yolks. Blend well, and return the yolk mixture to the rest of the béchamel. Stir in the cheese and blend well. Keep warm while preparing the moussaka.

SPRING GREENS AND CANNELLINI GRATIN

Y OU CAN used canned beans in this gratin as we do here, but if you have the time, cooking up a pot of beans means that you'll have some of the savory broth from the beans to replace the vegetable broth for a more intensely "beany" taste. Feel free to experiment with other cooking greens, such as escarole, tat soi (flat black cabbage), turnip, dandelion, or beet greens, but note that your cooking times may vary from those we give here.

MAKES 4 TO 6 SERVINGS

4 cups cooked cannellini, white kidney, or Great Northern beans, rinsed and drained

1 cup Vegetable Broth (page 65)

1 cup tomatoes, peeled, chopped, and seeded (see note on page 19)

Salt and pepper as needed

2 lb chard or collard greens, rinsed and drained

2 tbsp olive oil

1 tsp red pepper flakes, or to taste

1 tbsp minced garlic

2 cups lightly toasted bread crumbs

1. Combine the beans, broth, tomatoes, and a generous pinch of salt and pepper in a saucepan and cook over medium heat, stirring occasionally, until the beans are completely tender and very flavorful, about 20 minutes. Season with additional salt and pepper and reserve.

2. Preheat the oven to 350°F.

3. Trim the stems of the chard or collard greens. Cut the stems away from the leaves and keep the stems and leaves separate. Chop the stems and greens into ½-inch pieces, and reserve.

4. Heat the olive oil in a large sauté pan over medium heat. Add the red pepper flakes and garlic and sauté until the aroma of the garlic is released, about 1 minute. Add the chard or collard green stems to the pan first and cook until they are wilted, about 4 minutes. Add the leaves to the sauté pan and season with salt and pepper. Continue to sauté, tossing occasionally, until the greens are tender, 10 to 12 minutes. Combine the greens with the beans and tomatoes and mix thoroughly. Season with additional salt and pepper if needed.

5. Put the greens and beans in a 9 × 13-inch baking dish or a 1½-quart ceramic casserole. Make an even layer over the top of the casserole with the bread crumbs. Bake until the crumbs are golden brown and the entire dish is very hot, about 45 minutes. If the crumbs begin to brown before the cooking time is complete, cover the pan loosely with aluminum foil. Serve hot directly from the baking dish or casserole on heated plates.

ROASTED EGGPLANT STUFFED WITH CURRIED LENTILS

S MALL GLOBE eggplants are the perfect size for this dish and sometimes can be found in the supermarket produce section or at farm stands. If you cannot find them, however, use a larger eggplant, leaving the same size wall but cooking for up to 10 minutes longer; cut it into serving portions after baking.

MAKES 4 SERVINGS

½ cup brown lentils

2 cups Vegetable Broth (page 65) or water

2 small globe eggplants

1 tbsp olive oil, plus more for greasing pan

¼ cup minced yellow onion

2 tsp minced garlic

½ tsp grated gingerroot

½ cup minced white mushrooms

½ tsp lemon zest

½ tsp curry powder

¼ tsp ground cinnamon

Selecting and Preparing Legumes

As with grains, choose dried legumes from a store with high turnover. Beans, lentils, and dried peas can be stored in plastic bags or other airtight storage containers for a few months and don't require refrigeration.

Although it is fine to substitute one bean for another in many recipes, there is a noticeable difference in taste between favas and limas, black beans and kidney beans, and navy beans and black-eyed peas. If time is short, use canned beans instead of cooking dried beans from scratch.

SORTING AND RINSING

Pour the legumes onto a baking sheet and, working methodically from one end to the other, carefully sort through them, removing discolored or misshapen pieces. Submerge the sorted legumes in cold water, then remove and discard any that float to the surface. Drain and rinse well with cold running water.

SOAKING

Some chefs believe that soaking dried beans and other legumes before cooking gives a better texture. Place the sorted and rinsed legumes in a container and add enough cool water to cover them by a few inches, about four times the volume of water to beans. Let the legumes soak in the refrigerator for at least 4 hours or overnight.

For a quicker soak, place the sorted legumes in a pot and add enough water to cover by a few inches. Bring the water to a simmer. Remove the pot from the heat, cover, and let steep for 1 hour.

COOKING

Drain the soaked legumes, put in a large pot, and add enough water to cover the beans by about 2 inches. Bring the liquid to a full boil and then reduce the heat to maintain a simmer. Stir the legumes occasionally as they cook and add more liquid if the level starts to drop.

Most recipes tell you when to add various seasonings and flavorings, but the general rule is to add salt and any other acidic flavoring ingredients, such as tomatoes, vinegar, or citrus juices, only after the beans are nearly tender to preserve their smooth, creamy consistency

¼ tsp ground turmeric

Salt and pepper as needed

1. Bring the lentils and broth or water to a boil in a small pot. Cover and reduce the heat to low. Simmer until the lentils are tender to the bite, 25 to 30 minutes. Remove from the heat and set the lentils aside, still in their cooking liquid.

2. Preheat the oven to 350°F. Grease an 8 × 11-inch baking pan. Halve the eggplants lengthwise and scoop out some of the flesh, leaving a ½- to ¾-inch wall. Mince the scooped flesh and set aside. Transfer the eggplant halves to the prepared baking pan, skin side down.

3. Heat a large skillet over medium heat. Add the oil and heat until it shimmers. Add the onion, garlic, and ginger. Sauté, stirring occasionally, until the onion is golden brown, 6 to 8 minutes. Add the minced eggplant, mushrooms, lemon zest, curry, cinnamon, turmeric, and salt and pepper to taste. Sauté over medium heat, stirring occasionally, until the mushrooms begin to release some moisture, about 5 minutes.

4. Drain the lentils, reserving the cooking liquid, and add the lentils to the eggplant and mushroom mixture. Add enough of the cooking liquid (about ¼ cup) to moisten the vegetables well, and then simmer until the liquid is reduced, 6 to 8 minutes.

5. Fill the hollowed eggplant halves with the lentil mixture. Cover with aluminum foil and bake until the eggplants are tender and cooked through, 35 to 40 minutes. Serve immediately.

EGGPLANT PARMESAN

THIS EGGPLANT recipe includes a creamy ricotta layer for a moist dish with a lighter texture than a typical eggplant Parmesan. Assemble individual servings in ovenproof gratin dishes, if you wish.

MAKES 8 SERVINGS

1¼ lb sliced eggplant (about 1 large or 2 medium)

1½ cups ricotta cheese

1 cup grated Parmesan

½ cup minced flat-leaf parsley

Freshly grated nutmeg as needed, optional

Salt as needed

Freshly ground black pepper as needed

4 large eggs

⅔ cup milk

2 cups flour

2 cups dry bread crumbs, or as needed

4 cups canola oil, use as needed

3 cups Tomato Sauce (page 144), heated

2 cups grated mozzarella cheese

1. Peel, salt, and rinse the eggplant if desired (see "Preparing Eggplant for Cooking" on page 99).

2. Blend the ricotta, ½ cup Parmesan, the parsley, nutmeg, if using, ½ teaspoon salt, ¼ teaspoon pepper, and 1 egg until smooth. Keep refrigerated until needed.

3. Blend the remaining 3 eggs with the milk in a shallow bowl to make an egg wash. Put the flour in a second shallow bowl and season with a pinch of salt and pepper. Put the bread crumbs in a third shallow bowl.

4. Dip the eggplant slices one at a time into the flour, then the egg wash, and last, the bread crumbs, patting the crumbs evenly over all sides of the eggplant. Transfer the eggplant slices to a plate or baking sheet.

5. Pour about ½ inch of oil into a deep skillet and heat over medium high heat until the oil shimmers.

Add the breaded eggplant slices to the hot oil, a few pieces at a time, and fry on the first side until golden brown, about 2 minutes. Turn the eggplant and continue to fry until golden and crisp on the second side, 2 minutes. Transfer to a plate lined with paper towels; continue until all of the eggplant is fried.

6. Preheat the oven to 350°F.

7. Spread some of the tomato sauce in a lasagna pan, rectangular baking dish, or individual casseroles. Assemble the dish in layers: a layer of fried eggplant, a layer of the ricotta mixture, another layer of eggplant, topped with more tomato sauce. Sprinkle the assembled dish evenly with the mozzarella and the remaining Parmesan.

8. Cover the eggplant and bake until the ricotta mixture is very hot and the mozzarella cheese has melted, 20 to 25 minutes. Remove the cover and continue to bake until the cheese is golden brown, another 10 minutes. Let the dish rest for 10 minutes before cutting and serving.

BROCCOLI RAAB AND CANNELLINI BEANS

with Pancetta

MAKES 8 SERVINGS

2 tbsp olive oil

¼ cup diced pancetta or bacon

½ cup minced yellow onion

2 tsp minced garlic

2 bunches broccoli raab, trimmed

2 cups cooked or canned cannellini beans, drained and rinsed

½ cup chicken or vegetable broth

1 tsp salt

½ tsp ground black pepper

1. Heat the olive oil in a large sauté pan over me-

dium heat. Add the pancetta or bacon and sauté until the fat renders and the pancetta is translucent, about 1 minute.

2. Add the onion and sauté, stirring frequently, until golden brown, about 5 to 6 minutes. Add the garlic and continue to sauté until the garlic is aromatic, about 1 minute more.

3. Add the broccoli raab by handfuls, stirring and sautéing until the leaves just wilt before adding more. Add the cannellini beans and the broth.

4. Bring to a simmer and cook until the broccoli raab is bright green and tender, about 3 to 4 minutes. Season the mixture with salt and pepper. Keep warm until ready to serve.

VEGETARIAN STIR-FRIED TOFU AND RICE NOODLES

Pad Thai

SMOKED TOFU has a rich flavor that adds to this dish. It also has a firmer texture than regular tofu. If you can't locate smoked tofu, you can use firm tofu that you've pressed.

MAKES 4 SERVINGS

2 tbsp roasted chili paste (nahm prik pow)

4 tbsp light soy sauce

¼ cup rice wine vinegar

¼ cup palm sugar

2 tsp salt

1½ lb rice noodles, ¼-inch wide

¼ cup vegetable oil

1 lb smoked tofu, cut into sticks

1 leek, white and light-green portions, julienne

2 tbsp chopped garlic

3 large eggs, lightly beaten

2 scallions, sliced into thin 1-inch-long strips

2 cups vegetable or mushroom broth

½ lb bean sprouts

¼ cup roughly chopped cilantro

½ cup coarsely chopped pan-roasted peanuts (see page 132)

8 lime wedges

1. Whisk together the chili paste, soy sauce, rice wine vinegar, palm sugar, and salt to make a seasoning mixture. Set aside. Put the rice noodles in a bowl and add enough warm water to cover them. Let the noodles soften for 30 minutes, drain, and set aside.

2. Heat a wok over high heat, add 3 tablespoons of oil, and heat until nearly smoking. Add the tofu, leek, and garlic. Stir-fry until the leek brightens in color and softens slightly and the garlic is light gold, about 3 minutes.

3. Add the noodles and stir-fry until hot and coated with the oil. Push the noodles to the upper edge of one side of the wok. Add the remaining 1 tablespoon oil to the wok. Add the beaten eggs to the empty space in the wok. Fold the noodles over the eggs and let the mixture cook, undisturbed, for 20 seconds. Then, begin to stir-fry the noodle-egg mixture again.

4. Add the seasoning mixture and the scallions. Stir-fry until the noodles are soft, adding broth as necessary to moisten the noodles.

5. Fold in the sprouts and cilantro. Garnish with peanuts and lime wedges and serve at once on heated plates.

Working with Tofu

Tofu is sold in blocks that usually weigh about 12 ounces. It is packed in liquid to keep it fresh and to prevent it from drying out. Tofu is a perishable food that will be best if you pre- pare it within 2 days of purchase. Tofu is available in a variety of firmnesses: silk, which is very soft and slippery almost like a custard; medium, and firm. For tofu that you plan to sauté or stir-fry, buy firm tofu. You also can press the tofu to firm it up even more as follows:

Put 3 or 4 layers of paper towels in a plate or baking pan. Remove the tofu from the package and put it on the plate. Add 3 or 4 more layers of paper towels to cover the tofu. Next, put something flat, like a baking pan, on top of the stack. Set a few cans in the pan for weight. Put the whole assembly into the refrigerator and let the tofu drain for about 1 hour.

Many recipes call for the tofu to be cut into triangles. First, cut the block in half width-wise. Now cut the two large rect- angles in half, cutting from one corner to its opposite on the diagonal.

GREEN ENCHILADAS
Enchiladas Verdes

A GREEN ENCHILADA, stuffed with chicken and farmer's cheese, is a meal that's quick to as- semble and bake. The fresh cilantro and mint give the sauce exceptional brightness, a perfect counter- point to the rich and creamy filling.

MAKES 6 SERVINGS

2 tsp corn or olive oil

1 onion, medium dice

1 garlic clove, finely minced

1 cup farmer's or pot cheese

⅓ cup heavy cream

2 cups shredded or diced cooked chicken meat

3 tbsp sliced almonds, toasted

2 cups quartered tomatillos

1 cup sliced scallions

⅔ cup chopped fresh cilantro

2 whole roasted jalapeños, seeded, diced

2 tbsp chopped fresh mint

½ tsp ground cumin seed

½ tsp ground coriander seed

12 corn tortillas

6 oz Monterey Jack cheese, coarsely shredded

1. Preheat the oven to 350°F.

2. Heat the oil in a small skillet over medium heat until it shimmers. Add the onion and garlic, and sauté until the onion is a light golden brown, about 6 to 8 minutes. Remove the onion from the heat, spread it in a thin layer on a plate, and allow to cool completely.

3. Puree the farmer's cheese in a food processor until smooth. With the machine running, add the heavy cream in a stream. Remove the cheese mixture from the processor to a bowl. Fold in the chicken, almonds, and sautéed onion. Keep the filling in the refrigerator until ready to fill the enchiladas.

4. Place the tomatillos, scallions, cilantro, jalapeños, mint, cumin, and coriander in the food processor or blender and puree to form a sauce. Place the sauce in a shallow bowl.

5. Heat a cast iron skillet or other heavy-bottomed skillet over medium heat until quite hot. Soften the tortillas one at a time by toasting in the skillet for about 15 seconds on each side. Immediately dip the tortilla into the sauce to coat it very lightly and then set it on a work surface. Place a spoonful of the filling slightly to one side of the center of the tortilla and roll up into a cylinder. Place the filled and rolled enchilada in a buttered or oiled baking dish. Repeat with the remaining tortillas until all have been filled and rolled. Spoon the remaining sauce over the enchiladas.

6. Sprinkle the cheese over the enchiladas, cover the pan, and bake until the filling is hot, about 15

minutes. Remove the cover and bake long enough for the cheese topping to melt. Let the enchiladas rest for 5 minutes before serving on heated plates.

MACARONI AND CHEESE
Pasta Quattro Formaggi

FOUR CHEESES combine in this dish for a complex flavor. We've chosen fusilli pasta instead of ordinary elbows, but any short pierced pasta shape will be good.

MAKES 6 SERVINGS

2¾ cups heavy cream

1 cup Emmenthaler cheese

1 cup Gruyère cheese

1 cup Danish blue (Danablu) cheese

¾ cup grated Parmesan

1¼ lb fusilli (corkscrew pasta)

2 tsp freshly ground black pepper, or to taste

1. Preheat the oven to 350° F. Bring a large pot of well salted water to a boil for the pasta.

2. Pour the cream into a large saucepan and place it over medium heat, watching carefully to avoid scorching. Bring the cream to a simmer and reduce it by ¼, about 5 minutes. Reduce the heat to low and add the cheeses, stirring occasionally while the cheese melts, about 10 minutes.

3. While the cheese is melting, cook the pasta until it is tender to the bite, about 8 to 10 minutes. Drain well.

4. Add the cooked pasta to the cream sauce mixture, toss to coat, and season with pepper. (Salt should not be needed due to the saltiness of the water used for cooking the pasta and the saltiness of the cheese.)

5. Transfer to a greased casserole dish or baking pan. Bake until the macaroni and cheese is hot and creamy and a golden crust has formed on the top, about 20 minutes.

SHRIMP WITH TOMATOES, OREGANO, AND FETA CHEESE

To make this dish even more interesting, you may want to quickly broil it once you've added the cheese. Feta cheese doesn't melt the way cheddar or mozzarella does. It simply softens and begins to brown around the edges.

MAKES 4 SERVINGS

1½ lb large shrimp (16/20 count), shelled and deveined

Salt as needed

Freshly ground black pepper as needed

2 tbsp olive oil

1 cup chopped yellow onion

2 tsp minced garlic

¼ tsp ground cayenne

2 tbsp chopped oregano

1 cup Tomato Sauce (page 144)

1 tsp sugar

1 cup crumbled feta cheese

¼ cup chopped flat-leaf parsley

4 slices crusty bread

1. Season the shrimp with salt and pepper. Heat the oil in a large sauté pan over high heat until it shimmers. Add the shrimp and sauté, turning as necessary, until the shrimp are a bright pink, 2 to 3 minutes. Transfer the shrimp to a plate and keep warm.

2. Add the onion, garlic, cayenne, and oregano to the pan and sauté, stirring constantly, until ar-omatic, about 1 minute. Add the tomato sauce, reduce the heat to low, and bring to a simmer. Season the sauce to taste with sugar, salt, and pepper. Return the shrimp to the sauce and simmer very slowly until the shrimp is completely cooked, about 5 minutes.

3. Transfer the shrimp to a serving dish (or individual gratin dishes). Top the shrimp with the sauce and sprinkle the cheese evenly over the top. Serve very hot, topped with the chopped parsley. Serve with crusty bread.

PAELLA CON VERDURAS

There are several versions of paella enjoyed throughout Spain. This one takes advantage of a variety of fresh vegetables. Feel free to add whatever vegetables inspire you: green beans, chunks of zucchini or yellow squash, or cubes of pumpkin or Hubbard squash.

MAKES 6 SERVINGS

3 tbsp extra-virgin olive oil

2 cups small-dice onions

2 cups thinly sliced leeks, white part only

2 cups chopped plum tomatoes, peeled and seeded

2 tbsp minced garlic

1½ cups medium-grain rice

2 cups cauliflower florets

1 cup sliced or quartered cooked artichoke hearts

1 cup fresh or frozen green peas

4 cups Vegetable Broth (page 65)

Salt and pepper as needed

1 cup roasted red peppers strips

¼ cup chopped parsley

1. Heat the oil in a paella pan or a wide skillet. Add the onions, leeks, tomatoes, and garlic. Cook, stirring frequently, until the juices from the tomatoes have cooked away and the onions are tender, about 5 minutes.

2. Add the rice and stir to coat well. Continue to sauté until lightly toasted, 2 to 3 minutes.

3. Add the cauliflower, artichoke hearts, peas, and enough broth to cover the rice and vegetables. Season with salt and pepper and bring to a boil. Reduce the heat to low, cover the paella pan or skillet, and cook until the rice has absorbed most of the broth, about 20 minutes.

4. Add the remaining broth, cover the pan, and continue to cook until the rice is very tender. Season to taste with additional salt and pepper.

5. Serve the paella directly from the pan garnished with the roasted pepper strips and chopped parsley.

EGGPLANT ROLLATINI

INSTEAD OF eggplant, you can make this dish with large zucchini or yellow squash. If you wish, add chopped vegetables to the filling mixture for a heartier entrée.

MAKES 6 SERVINGS

18 eggplant slices, cut lengthwise

1½ cups ricotta cheese

2 cups grated mozzarella cheese

½ cup grated Romano

½ cup minced flat-leaf parsley

Salt and pepper as needed

4 large eggs

⅔ cup milk

2 cups flour

2 cups dry bread crumbs, or as needed

4 cups canola oil, use as needed

3 cups Tomato Sauce (page 144), heated

1. Peel, salt, and rinse the eggplant if desired (see the note on preparing eggplant on page 99.)

2. Blend the ricotta, 1 cup mozzarella cheese, the Romano, parsley, ½ teaspoon salt, ¼ teaspoon pepper, and 1 egg until smooth. Keep refrigerated until needed.

3. Blend the remaining 3 eggs with the milk in a shallow bowl to make an egg wash. Put the flour in a second shallow bowl and season with a pinch of salt and pepper. Put the bread crumbs in a third shallow bowl. Dip the eggplant slices one at a time into the flour, then the egg wash, and last, the bread crumbs, patting the crumbs evenly over all sides of the eggplant. Transfer the eggplant slices to a plate or baking sheet.

4. Pour about ½ inch of oil into a deep skillet and heat over medium-high heat until the oil shimmers. Add the breaded eggplant slices to the hot oil, a few pieces at a time, and fry on the first side until golden brown, about 2 minutes. Turn the eggplant and continue to fry until golden and crisp on the second side, 2 minutes. Transfer to a plate lined with paper towels; continue until all of the eggplant is fried.

5. Preheat the oven to 350°F.

6. Spread some of tomato sauce in a rectangular baking dish or individual casseroles. Spread 2 or 3 tablespoons of the filling mixture over a slice of fried eggplant and roll the slice up lengthwise. Place the roll into the baking dish seam side down. Continue until all of the eggplant slices are filled and rolled. Spoon the remaining tomato sauce over the rolls, top with the remaining mozzarella. Cover the baking dish loosely with foil and bake

until the ricotta mixture is very hot and the mozzarella cheese has melted, about 20 minutes. Remove the cover and continue to bake until the cheese is golden brown, another 10 minutes. Serve directly from the baking dish or casserole on heated plates.

STIR-FRIED GLASS NOODLES
Jap Chae

IF YOU can locate Korean glass noodles, also known as dang myun, use them in this dish. They are similar to cellophane or glass noodles made from mung beans, but they are slightly thicker and chewier.

MAKES 4 SERVINGS

10 dried oak mushrooms

1 oz dried wood ear mushrooms

One 18-oz package glass noodles or Asian vermicelli

3 scallions, sliced thin

½ cup light soy sauce

1 tbsp dark sesame oil

2 tbsp sugar

½ cup vegetable oil

1 cup thinly sliced onion

1 tbsp minced garlic

1 cup red bell pepper julienne

2 cups shredded green cabbage

1 cup carrot julienne

Salt as needed

Freshly ground black pepper as needed

5 large eggs, lightly beaten

1. Rehydrate the oak mushrooms and wood ears separately in cool water (see page 130). Drain and reserve the soaking liquid to moisten the noodles if necessary. Cut off the stems and any hard portions of the mushrooms and discard them. Cut the caps into ⅛-inch wide strips. Set aside.

2. Pour enough boiling water over the noodles to cover them by at least 2 inches. Soak until rehydrated and elastic, about 15 minutes. Drain, rinse with cool water, and reserve.

3. Stir together the scallions, soy sauce, sesame oil, and sugar in a small bowl. Set aside.

4. Heat the oil in a wok or skillet over high heat until it shimmers. Add the onion and garlic and stir-fry until tender, about 2 minutes.

5. Add the red bell pepper, cabbage, carrot, and mushrooms. Stir-fry until the vegetables are very hot, about 5 minutes. Add the scallion-soy sauce mixture and stir-fry until all of the ingredients are evenly coated. Add the noodles and stir-fry until very hot, 4 to 5 minutes. Season with to taste with salt and pepper.

6. Pour the eggs over the noodles and vegetables and stir-fry until the eggs are thickened and set, another 3 minutes. Serve immediately.

FARFALLE
with Asparagus, Shiitakes, and Spring Peas

THE APPEARANCE of peas at the farmer's market signifies the arrival of spring, and this dish takes advantage of three different varieties. Green peas quickly lose their freshness after being picked, so frozen green peas actually offer the best quality unless you are able to obtain them extremely fresh. Asparagus is best in the late spring, when the most flavorful and tender sprouts are readily available.

MAKES 8 SERVINGS

3 lb asparagus, peeled, trimmed

3 tbsp olive oil

2 tsp salt, or to taste

1 cup snow peas

1 cup sugar snap peas

2 cups green peas, frozen

1 lb farfalle (bowtie pasta), dried

1 tbsp butter

3 cups shiitakes, sliced

3 tbsp shallots, minced

3 tbsp marjoram, chopped

¼ tsp freshly ground black pepper, or to taste

2 bunches scallions, split lengthwise, thinly sliced

Parmesan cheese, shaved, to taste

1. Bring a medium saucepan of salted water to a boil to blanch the peas and a large pot of salted water to boil to cook the pasta. Preheat the broiler.

2. Toss the asparagus with the oil and 1 teaspoon of the salt. Place in a baking pan under the broiler for 8 minutes, until tender. Slice the asparagus into 1-inch pieces.

3. Cook each type of pea separately in the boiling water until almost tender, about 2 minutes each. Remove them from the water using a slotted spoon or small strainer. Reserve.

4. Cook the pasta in boiling water until tender to the bite, about 10 to 12 minutes. Drain.

5. Heat the butter in a sauté pan until it begins to turn brown. Add the shiitakes and shallots. Sauté until the shallots and mushrooms are slighly brown.

6. Add the asparagus, green peas, snow peas, sugar snap peas, marjoram, pepper, and 1 teaspoon of salt. Heat the vegetables thoroughly.

7. Toss the pasta with the cooked vegetables and scallions.

8. Just before serving, place a few shavings of Parmesan cheese on each portion.

TORTELLI
with Bitter Greens and Ricotta

THIS RECIPE uses just the leaves from a selection of cooking greens: beet greens, dandelion greens, and mustard greens are used here, but we like to change the combination, or feature just one, depending on what looks good at the market.

MAKES 8 SERVINGS

FRESH PASTA DOUGH

3 cups all-purpose flour

1 tsp salt

5 eggs

4 tbsp olive oil

1 cup dandelion greens, leaves only

1 cup beet greens, leaves only

1 cup mustard greens, leaves only

2 tbsp olive oil

½ cup minced onions

¼ cup minced garlic

1½ cups whole milk or part-skim ricotta

1 cup grated mozzarella

Salt and pepper as needed

¼ cup butter

Grated Parmesan to pass on the side

1. To make the pasta dough in a food processor, place the flour and salt in the bowl and turn the food processor on. Add the eggs and olive oil through the feed tube with the processor running and continue to mix just until the mixture is evenly blended. It will look like a damp, coarse meal. If the mixture forms a ball that rides on top of the blade, it is too wet. In that case, add a few teaspoons of flour and continue to process briefly. If the dough will not hold together when you press it in your hand, add more water a

teaspoon at a time. Remove the dough from the processor, knead it once or twice to make a smooth ball, and wrap in plastic wrap. Let the dough rest at room temperature for 1 hour before rolling it out.

2. Bring a large pot of salted water to a rolling boil over high heat. Add the dandelion, beet, and mustard greens, and cook until they are wilted and tender, about 3 minutes. Drain in a colander, rinse with cold water, and drain again. Gather the leaves into a ball, place them on a clean dish towel, and twist the towel to squeeze out the excess moisture. Chop the squeezed greens finely.

3. To make the filling, heat the olive oil in a sauté pan over medium-high heat. Add the onions and garlic and sauté, stirring frequently, until the onions are tender and translucent, 3 to 4 minutes. Transfer to a bowl and cool to room temperature. Stir in the chopped greens, ricotta, and mozzarella. Season generously with salt and pepper.

4. Divide the pasta dough in half. Working with one piece of dough at a time, roll out the dough using a pasta machine or a rolling pin. Cut each sheet of dough in half, so that you have two pieces of roughly the same dimensions. Drop generous tablespoons of the filling mixture onto one half of the dough sheet, spacing them about 3 inches apart. Gently lay the second half of the sheet over the filling, letting the dough drape over the filling. Use your fingers to gently press the dough around the filling and press out any air. Use a sharp knife or a rotary cutter (pizza wheel) to cut the tortelli apart. Use the tines of a fork to seal all around the edges. Transfer the filled tortelli to a sheet pan lined with parchment or waxed paper. Continue until you have filled all of the pasta.

5. Simmer the pasta in salted water until tender, 8 to 10 minutes. Drain and dress with butter and Parmesan cheese. Serve at once.

FETTUCCINE

with Corn, Squash, Chiles, Crème Fraîche, and Cilantro

CRÈME FRAÎCHE is a cultured cream very similar in flavor to sour cream. Its rich texture softens the spiciness of the chiles and provides a velvety sauce for this luscious dish.

MAKES 8 SERVINGS

1 lb fettuccine noodles

2 tbsp olive oil

2 onions, diced

2 zucchini, diced

4 cups corn kernels, frozen or fresh

2 jalapeños, diced

2 tsp garlic, minced

2 cups Vegetable Broth (page 65)

1 tbsp salt, or to taste

¼ tsp freshly ground black pepper

½ cup crème fraîche

¼ cup cilantro, chopped

1. Bring a large pot of salted water to a boil for pasta. Heat the olive oil in a large saucepan or Dutch oven. Sauté the onions and zucchini until the onions are translucent and the zucchini is tender, approximately 8 to 10 minutes. Add the corn, jalapeños, and garlic. Cook for another 5 minutes.

2. Add the vegetable broth and season with the remaining salt and pepper. Cook the pasta until tender to the bite, about 8 to 10 minutes. Drain the pasta, add it to the sauté pan, and mix with the sauce.

3. Portion into pasta bowls and add a dollop of crème fraîche to each serving. Garnish each portion with the cilantro.

SPICY BUCATINI WITH MUSSELS AND CLAMS

Bucatini Arrabiata con Cozze e Vongole

PIERCED SPAGHETTI, called *bucatini*, looks like fatter-than-usual spaghetti. Its hollow center lets sauce coat the pasta on the inside and outside for even more flavor.

MAKES 8 SERVINGS

3 tbsp extra-virgin olive oil

1 cup minced yellow onion

8 garlic cloves, sliced thin

1 tsp red pepper flakes

6 cups finely chopped plum tomatoes, peeled and seeded

½ cup basil chiffonade

¼ cup chopped flat-leaf parsley

Salt as needed

Freshly ground black pepper as needed

2 lb dry bucatini pasta

2 dozen mussels, rinsed, debearded (see page 31)

2 dozen littleneck clams, rinsed

1. Heat the oil in a skillet over large saucepot. Add the onion and cook until tender and limp, about 5 minutes. Add the garlic and continue to sauté, stirring frequently, until aromatic, another 2 minutes. Add the red pepper flakes and cook over low heat until very flavorful, about 5 minutes.

2. Add the tomatoes to the pan and bring to a slow simmer. Cook over low heat, stirring from time to time, until the sauce has a good consistency and flavor, about 20 minutes. Add the basil, parsley, salt, and pepper to taste.

3. Bring a large pot of water to a rolling boil while the sauce simmers. Salt generously (the water should taste noticeably salty). Add the pasta and cook until it is tender to the bite, about 8 minutes. Drain well and keep hot.

4. Add the mussels and clams to the sauce. Cover the pot and simmer until the mussels and clams open, about 10 minutes. Discard any that remain closed.

5. Return the cooked pasta to the pot and gently stir and toss to coat the pasta. Serve the pasta at once in heated bowls topped with clams, mussels, and additional sauce.

ORECCHIETTE

with Peas, Mushrooms, Tomatoes, Ham, and Pecorino

ORECCHIETTE ARE little ear-shaped pastas, whose broad surfaces are perfect to pair with a chunky "sauce" of vegetables, ham, and cheese.

MAKES 6 SERVINGS

4 cups dry orecchiette pasta

2 tbsp butter

1 tbsp minced shallots

3 cups quartered or sliced white mushrooms

Salt as needed

Freshly ground black pepper as needed

6 oz Smithfield ham, cut into julienne

3 fresh or canned plum tomatoes, peeled, seeded, and chopped

1½ cups green peas (thawed if frozen)

2 cups heavy cream

3 tbsp chopped sage

½ cup pecorino Romano cheese

3 tbsp chopped flat-leaf parsley

1. Bring a large pot of water to a rolling boil. Salt generously (the water should taste noticeably salty).

Add the orecchiette, stir once or twice, and cook until tender to the bite, about 8 minutes. Drain well and keep hot.

2. Heat the butter in the pasta pot over medium heat until it stops foaming. Add the shallots and cook, stirring frequently, until tender and limp, about 2 minutes. Add the mushrooms and continue to sauté, stirring frequently, until the mushrooms are tender and cooked through, about 5 minutes. Season the mushrooms with salt and pepper to taste.

3. Add the ham, tomatoes, peas, and cream to the pan and bring to a simmer. Cook over low heat, stirring from time to time, until the sauce has a good consistency and flavor, about 3 minutes. Add the sage and half of the Romano cheese. Stir well and adjust the seasoning to taste with salt and pepper if necessary.

4. Return the cooked orecchiette to pot and gently stir and toss to coat the pasta. Serve the pasta at once in heated bowls topped with the remaining Romano cheese and the parsley.

PENNE PUTTANESCA
with Sautéed Shrimp

PUTTANESCA IS an Italian sauce that sometimes includes tomatoes, onions, capers, olives and anchovies and is generally served with pasta. This version adds delicious sautéed shrimp for a quick and easy, yet hearty, pasta dish.

MAKES 8 SERVINGS

2 tbsp olive oil

4 garlic cloves, minced

28 oz diced tomatoes, canned

3 tbsp Niçoise olives, pitted, chopped

3 tbsp capers, drained

½ cup parsley, chopped

2 tsp red pepper flakes

Salt, to taste

1 lb penne pasta

1 lb shrimp, peeled, deveined (31/40 count)

Parmesan cheese, grated, to taste, optional

1. Bring a large pot of salted water to a boil for the pasta. Heat 1 tablespoon of the oil in a large sauté pan over low heat; add 2 teaspoons of garlic and cook, stirring, for 1 minute. Add the tomatoes, olives, capers, ¼ cup of parsley, and the red pepper flakes. Increase the heat to medium and bring the mixture to a simmer. Cook, uncovered, stirring occasionally until thickened, about 10 minutes. Set the sauce aside.

1. Meanwhile, cook the pasta in the boiling water until tender to the bite, approximately 10 to 12 minutes. Drain well. .

2. Heat the remaining oil in a large sauté pan over medium heat. Add the reserved garlic and cook for 1 minute. Add the shrimp and the remaining parsley, sauté for 1 to 2 minutes and add the tomato sauce. Cook the shrimp for an additional 3 to 5 minutes, or until opaque in the center.

3. Add the sauce and shrimp mixture to the drained pasta and top with grated cheese, if desired.

SEMOLINA PIZZA DOUGH

ADDING A bit of semolina to the pizza dough makes a great crust with a crisp texture and a wonderful flavor. The dough can also be rounded into individual balls and frozen in zip-close bags to be used at another time.

3½ cups bread flour, plus as needed

½ cup semolina or durum flour

1½ tsp active dry yeast

1½ cups room-temperature water (68–76°F)

3 tbsp olive oil, plus as needed

2 tsp salt

Cornmeal for dusting

1. To prepare the dough, combine the flours and yeast in the bowl of a stand mixer fitted with the dough hook. Add the water, olive oil, and salt and mix on low speed for 2 minutes.

2. Increase the speed to medium and knead until the dough is quite elastic but still a little sticky, 4 minutes.

3. Transfer the dough to a lightly oiled bowl, turn the dough to coat it with the oil, cover with plastic wrap or a damp towel, and allow to rise in a warm place until nearly doubled in size, about 30 minutes.

4. Fold the dough gently, cover, and let rest until relaxed, 15 to 20 minutes. If making two crusts, cut the dough into 2 equal pieces. Round each piece of dough into a smooth ball.

5. Cover the dough and let rest another 15 to 20 minutes before shaping into a pizza crust.

Shaping a Pizza Crust

To shape a pizza crust, press the dough into a disk, stretching and turning the dough as you work. You may finish stretching the dough by flipping it: With the dough resting on the backs of your hands, simultaneously spin the dough and toss it into the air. As it falls back down, catch it on the backs of your hands once more. Continue until the crust is evenly thick, about ⅛ to ¼ inch. If you prefer, you can pull and stretch the dough directly on a lightly floured work surface until it is an even thickness.

Transfer the pizza to a prepared baking sheet. Top the dough as directed, leaving the outer rim of the crust ungarnished.

ROASTED VEGETABLE PIZZA

ROASTING THE vegetables removes some of their moisture, for a pizza topping full of flavor that won't weigh down the crust. Cooking the vegetables on a grill will give them a bit of extra texture and a wonderful smoky taste.

MAKES 4 SERVINGS

2 small yellow squash, sliced 1/4 inch thick on a diagonal

2 small zucchini, sliced ¼ inch thick on a diagonal

2 medium Vidalia onions, sliced ¼ inch thick

1 medium eggplant, sliced ¼ inch thick

Salt and pepper as needed

1 cup extra-virgin olive oil, or as needed

2 tbsp minced garlic

Cornmeal for dusting

Semolina Pizza Dough (page 113)

1 cup ricotta cheese

1½ cups shredded mozzarella

3 tbsp chopped parsley

1. Preheat the oven to 425°F or preheat a gas grill to medium-high.

2. Put the sliced vegetables in a large colander and sprinkle them generously with salt. Allow the vegetables to rest for 15 minutes to begin extracting water. Rinse the salt from the vegetables. Drain and blot the vegetables dry to remove excess water before roasting.

3. Arrange the vegetables on baking sheets in a single layer and drizzle with the olive oil and garlic, reserving about 2 tablespoons of the oil.

4. Roast the vegetables in the oven or grill them over direct heat until lightly charred and tender, about 15 to 20 minutes. When the vegetables are cool enough to handle, cut them into thin strips if desired. (This can be done in advance and the vegetables held in a covered container in the refrigerator for up to 2 days.)

5. When you are ready to assemble and bake the pizza, preheat the oven to 425°F. Scatter a thin coating of cornmeal on baking sheets (or preheat pizza stones in the oven if they are available). Stretch the pizza dough into either 1 large round or 4 individual rounds and place on the prepared baking sheet. Spread the ricotta on the pizza dough in a thin layer and top with the chopped or sliced roasted vegetables and the mozzarella. Drizzle with a little of the remaining olive oil and top with the parsley.

6. Bake the pizza until the crust is crisp and golden brown and the cheese has melted, about 15 minutes. Cut into wedges and serve immediately.

NEOPOLITAN-STYLE PIZZA
with Mozzarella, Prosciutto, and Roasted Red Pepper

FRESH MOZZARELLA, prosciutto, and a drizzle of fruity, extra-virgin olive oil give this pizza a special character.

MAKES 4 SERVINGS

2 red bell peppers

Semolina Pizza Dough (page 113)

½ cup Tomato Sauce (page 144)

¾ lb sliced fresh mozzarella

8 thin slices prosciutto

Extra-virgin olive oil as needed

Salt as needed

Freshly ground black pepper as needed

1. Preheat the oven to 450°F. Prepare baking sheets by scattering them with cornmeal.

2. Char the red peppers directly in a gas flame until they are charred and blistered on all sides. Immediately place in a bowl or plastic bag and cover the peppers. Once they are cool enough to handle, pull away the skin and cut out the stem, ribs, and seeds. Cut into strips. Set aside.

3. Shape the pizza dough into two 12-inch rounds. Transfer the dough rounds to the cornmeal-scattered baking sheets. Bake the crust until firmed and set, about 10 minutes.

4. Spread ¼ cup tomato sauce on each pizza. Layer the cheese, prosciutto, and peppers on the pizza crusts. Drizzle with a little olive oil and season with salt and pepper.

5. Bake the pizza until the crust is golden brown and crisp, 12 to 14 minutes. Let the pizza rest for 5 minutes before serving.

GRILLED PIZZA
with Basil and Onion

SAUTÉ OR grill the onions for the pizza before you begin. You can use uncooked onions, if you prefer. In that case, use a sweet onion like Walla Walla or Vidalia. The tomato sauce that you use for the pizza should not be too watery.

MAKES 8 SERVINGS

2½ tsp active dry yeast

2 cups warm water

3½ cups all-purpose flour

1 cup semolina flour, plus extra for dusting

1 tbsp salt

¼ cup olive oil

1½ cups tomato sauce

2 cups grated mozzarella

¼ cup sautéed diced onions

2 tbsp basil chiffonade

1. Combine the yeast and water in a bowl and stir to dissolve. Let the mixture sit until a thick foam forms.

2. Add the flours and the salt to the yeast and stir by hand, or mix on medium speed in an electric mixer using the dough hook attachment, until the dough is smooth and elastic, about 5 minutes.

3. Transfer the dough to a second bowl that has been lightly oiled. Cover the dough with a clean kitchen towel and let rest at room temperature until nearly doubled in size, about 1½ hours.

4. Gently fold the dough over and allow it to rise for another 45 minutes.

5. Preheat a gas grill to high. If you are using a charcoal grill, build a fire and let it burn down until the coals are glowing red with a moderate coating of white ash. Spread the coals in an even bed. Clean the cooking grate.

6. Roll or stretch the dough into a 12-inch round. Lightly dust a 12-inch pizza pan with semolina flour and lay the dough round on top. Brush some of the olive oil over the entire dough round.

7. Lift the dough from the pan and place the pizza dough directly on the grill with the oiled side face-down. Brush the dough with the remaining olive oil. Grill the pizza until the dough is marked and it puffs up slightly, 3 to 4 minutes. Flip the pizza over and spread the sauce evenly over the round, leaving a ½-inch border around the outside edges. Evenly sprinkle the cheese over the sauce and top with the on-ions. Close the lid on the grill. Cook the pizza until the crust is golden brown and the cheese is slightly brown and bubbly, about 2 to 3 minutes more.

8. Remove the pizza from the grill and sprinkle the basil chiffonade on top. Cut the pizza into 8 slices and serve immediately.

BIBIMBAP

Contrasting temperatures and textures make this dish an adventure. Freshly fried eggs and marinated strips of steak are served on a bed of cool, crisp vegetables, atop a mound of hot steamed rice.

MAKES 4 SERVINGS

BEEF MARINADE

¼ cup Korean soy sauce

2 tsp sugar

¼ cup minced scallions

1 tbsp minced garlic

2 tsp minced ginger root

2 tsp ground toasted sesame seeds

Few drops dark sesame oil, as needed

Freshly ground black pepper, as needed

1 lb beef skirt steak, cut into strips

¼ cup peanut or canola oil, as needed

2 cups steamed medium-grained rice

2 cups iceberg lettuce chiffonade

1 cup julienned or grated red radish

1 cup julienned or grated daikon

1 cup julienned or grated carrot

1 cup julienned or grated seedless cucumber

4 shiso leaves, cut into fine shreds

4 large eggs

2 tbsp Korean red pepper paste (gochujang), or as needed

1. Combine the soy sauce and sugar in a bowl. Add the scallions, garlic, ginger, and sesame seeds. Add the sesame oil and pepper to taste. Add the skirt steak and toss until evenly coated. Cover, refrigerate, and let the steak marinate for at least 1 and up to 8 hours.

2. Heat 2 tablespoons oil in a wok over high heat until it is nearly smoking. Add the beef strips to the hot oil and stir-fry until the beef is cooked, about 4 minutes. Transfer to a bowl and keep warm.

3. Divide the rice evenly among 4 bowls. Top the rice with the lettuce. Toss together the red radish, daikon, carrot, cucumber, and shiso leaves. Divide the vegetables evenly among the bowls. Top the vegetables with the skirt steak and season each serving with a few drops of dark sesame oil.

4. Wipe out the wok and return it to the burner. Add 1 table-spoon oil to the wok and heat over medium heat until the oil ripples. Add the eggs to the hot oil one at a time and fry, basting the top with a little oil, until the whites are set and the yolk is hot, 2 to 3 minutes. Top each serving with a fried egg and serve at once, accompanied by the Korean red pepper paste.

Shiso Leaves

Shiso leaves, sometimes known as perillo, come from an herb related to both basil and mint. In fact, it is similar in flavor to those herbs, although most would agree that shiso leaves have a more complex flavor than either herb.

Green shiso leaves are typically used in salads, stir-fries, or in tempura. Red shiso leaves are used to flavor and color Japan's famous pickled plums, umeboshi. If you can't find shiso leaves, you can use either basil or mint, or both.

HUE CHICKEN SALAD
Ga Bop

YOU CAN use either poached or roasted chicken to make this salad. If you can't find *rau ram* (see page 118), substitute an equal quantity of basil and mint. Vietnamese *sambal* is a fiery hot chile paste. You can substitute a good hot sauce if it cannot be found.

MAKES 4 SERVINGS

½ medium onion, sliced thin

1½ lb shredded cooked chicken meat

¼ cup rau ram leaves, torn

¼ cup mint leaves, torn

¼ cup minced cilantro leaves and stems

2 Thai bird chiles, thinly sliced

2 tbsp lime juice

1 tbsp peanut oil

1 tbsp fish sauce

1 tbsp Vietnamese sambal

2 tsp sugar or as needed

Salt as needed

Freshly ground black pepper as needed

4 banana leaves, cut into large triangles

4 Boston lettuce leaves

2 cups steamed jasmine rice

½ cup Fried Shallots (page 96)

1 red Fresno chile, sliced paper thin

1. Combine the onion slices with enough cold water to cover and refrigerate for at least 30 minutes and up to 2 hours.

2. Combine the chicken, rau ram, mint, cilantro, and Thai bird chiles in a large bowl. Drain the onion slices and add them to the chicken. Add the lime juice, peanut oil, fish sauce, and sambal to the

salad and toss gently until combined. Season to taste with sugar, salt, and pepper.

3. Arrange the banana leaves and Boston lettuce on chilled plates. Top with the salad and serve with steamed rice, fried shallots, and the Fresno chile.

MINTY THAI-STYLE CHICKEN SALAD

THE QUANTITY of mint in this salad is significant. Throughout Southeast Asia herbs often are included as a major ingredient in dishes, rather than being relegated to a supporting role as a garnish or decoration.

MAKES 4 TO 6 SERVINGS

1 tbsp canola oil

1 tbsp dried red pepper flakes

½ tsp mild or hot paprika

⅔ lb minced chicken breast or thigh meat

3 tbsp fish sauce

2 tsp brown sugar

2 beefsteak tomatoes, seeded and chopped

¼ cup minced scallion

⅓ cup lime juice

½ cup mint leaves, torn

1 tbsp minced lemongrass

3 wild lime leaves, cut into fine slivers

4 to 6 red-leaf lettuce leaves

½ head Napa cabbage, cored and cut into 2-inch-wide wedges

12 cilantro sprigs

1. Heat the oil in a sauté pan over low heat. Add the red pepper flakes and paprika and sauté, stirring constantly, until aromatic, about 10 seconds. Add the chicken, fish sauce, and brown sugar and increase the heat to medium. Sauté, stirring frequently, until chicken is no longer pink, 4 to 5 minutes.

3. Transfer the chicken to a bowl and add the tomatoes, scallion, lime juice, mint leaves, lemongrass, and lime leaves. Toss the salad until all ingredients are evenly coated.

4. Serve the salad on lettuce leaves accompanied with a wedge of cabbage. Drizzle some of the juices from the bottom of the salad bowl over each serving. Garnish with cilantro.

VIETNAMESE SALAD ROLLS

DESPITE ITS common name of Vietnamese mint (or hot mint), *rau ram* is not related to the mint family, but is actually a member of the buckwheat family. Rau ram has long, smooth green leaves on a purple tinged stem. Its aroma is described as a combination of lemon and coriander-cilantro aroma and it has a bitter, peppery flavor. If you cannot locate rau ram, you can substitute ordinary mint.

MAKES 8 SERVINGS

DIPPING SAUCE

¼ cup fish sauce

¼ cup sugar, plus 2 tbsp for rice wrappers

¼ cup water

3 tbsp rice vinegar

4 tsp chili sauce

2 tsp minced garlic

Juice of 1 lime

4 oz rice noodles

2 cups carrot julienne

Salt as needed

½ bunch green-leaf lettuce, cut into thin strips

¼ bunch rau ram (or mint leaves), torn in thin strips

4 cups warm water

8 rice paper rounds, 12-inch diameter

16 small cooked shrimp (30/35 count), peeled, deveined, and halved lengthwise

¼ bunch cilantro leaves

1. Combine the fish sauce, ¼ cup sugar, ¼ cup water, the vinegar, chili sauce, garlic, and lime juice to make the dipping sauce. Mix well and chill if made ahead of time. The sauce may be held for up to 24 hours.

2. Bring a large pot of salted water to a boil. Add the rice noodles, stir once or twice, and cook until tender, about 3 minutes. Drain the noodles and then rinse with cool water until they are chilled. Drain well and set aside.

3. Marinate the carrot with 2 teaspoons salt for 10 minutes. Rinse in cool water to remove the salt and squeeze out the juice from the carrots. Set aside.

4. Combine the rice noodles, marinated carrots, lettuce, and mint to make the noodle filling. Set the filling aside.

5. Combine 4 cups warm water with 2 tablespoons sugar in a bowl. Place the rice papers, one at a time, in the water until they soften, about 10 seconds. Remove the rice paper, blot on paper toweling, and transfer to a work surface. Spoon ½ cup of the filling in the center of each rice paper. Roll the rice paper around the filling halfway. Put two pieces shrimp and two or three cilantro leaves on the inside of the unrolled part of the wrapper and finish rolling.

6. Cut each roll in half and serve on chilled platters or plates with the dipping sauce.

LEFT TO RIGHT To prepare the vegetables for the Vietnamese Salad Rolls, julienne them into matchsticks about two inches long and ⅛-inch thick. Rice paper is made pliable and easy to work with when it is rehydrated in cold water just before use. When rolling the fillings up inside the rice paper, begin at the bottom of the rice paper and roll away from you. As you pass the middle, bring both sides of the paper in to the center, then keep them tucked in as you complete the roll.

NIÇOISE-STYLE GRILLED TUNA

ORIGINATING IN Nice, on the Mediterranean coast in the south of France, this ubiquitous salad gained its name and popularity from its specific combination of ingredients, as well as the inclusion of an olive known also as *niçoise*, a variety native to the region.

MAKES 8 SERVINGS

2 lb tuna fillet, trimmed of silverskin

16 baby red potatoes, halved

6 tbsp olive oil

2 tbsp salt, or to taste

1 tbsp freshly ground black pepper, or to taste

1 lb mixed salad greens

1 lb haricots verts, cooked

½ cup Port Wine Vinaigrette (page 58)

1 quart cherry tomatoes

32 Niçoise olives

4 hard-boiled eggs, cut into eighths

1 cup Tomatillo Salsa (page 20)

1. Preheat the oven to 350°F.

2. Cut the tuna into eight 4-ounce portions and refrigerate until needed.

3. Coat the potatoes in the olive oil and about half of the salt and pepper. Roast the potatoes in a 350°F oven for 30 to 35 minutes, or until tender.

4. When the potatoes are about halfway cooked, toss 2 cups of the greens and ½ cup haricots verts with 3 tablespoons of the vinaigrette. Assemble the salads while the potatoes cook: Mound the greens and beans on each plate; arrange ½ cup cherry tomatoes, 4 olives and 4 pieces of egg on the greens.

5. Season the tuna with the remaining salt and pepper. When the potatoes are finished cooking, grill the tuna to the desired doneness, about 2 to 3 minutes on each side for medium rare. Slice the tuna into ¼-inch thick slices and fan the tuna on top of the greens. Spoon 2 tablespoons of the to-matillo salsa across the tuna. Place 4 of the potato halves around the tuna on each plate.

POTATO SALAD WITH TUNA, OLIVES, AND RED PEPPERS
Rin Ran

THIS SALAD is best if the potatoes are warm when you dress and toss the salad. We recommend that you search out good quality oil-packed tuna for this recipe. Specialty shops and delicatessens are a good source. Water-packed tuna, especially albacore, is fine, but the salad won't be quite as luscious.

MAKES 4 SERVINGS

1 lb new potatoes

Salt as needed

2 large red bell peppers, seeded and diced

1 cup pitted green olives

One 8-oz can oil-packed tuna, drained

6 tbsp extra-virgin olive oil

2 tbsp red wine vinegar

1 tsp ground cumin

1 tsp mild paprika

Freshly ground black pepper as needed

¼ cup coarsely chopped flat leaf parsley

1. Cook the potatoes in lightly salted water until they are just done, tender but firm enough to slice, 20 to 25 minutes. Let cool slightly, then peel and dice.

2. Combine the warm potatoes, peppers, and olives in a salad bowl. Break the tuna up with your fingertips as you add it to the salad. Set aside.

CHILLED CUCUMBER SOUP WITH
SHRIMP AND DILL (PAGE 66)

THAI FRESH PEA SOUP (PAGE 77)

INDONESIAN CHICKEN, NOODLE,
AND POTATO SOUP (PAGE 79)

CREAM OF BROCCOLI SOUP
(PAGE 72)

UDON NOODLE POT
(PAGE 90)

POTAGE AU PISTOU (PAGE 82)

MINESTRONE
(PAGE 84)

CREAM OF TOMATO SOUP WITH
RICE AND BASIL (PAGE 78)

FRESH CORN CHOWDER WITH
GREEN CHILES AND MONTEREY JACK (PAGE 70)

MANHATTAN CLAM CHOWDER
(PAGE 76)

FISHERMAN'S SOUP WITH SHRIMP
AND FRESH HERBS (PAGE 94)

VEGETARIAN MOUSAKKA
(PAGE 98)

ROASTED EGGPLANT STUFFED
WITH CURRIED LENTILS (PAGE 102)

STIR-FRIED GLASS NOODLES
(PAGE 109)

MACARONI AND CHEESE
(PAGE 106)

GREEN ENCHILADAS (PAGE 105)

ROASTED VEGETABLE PIZZA (PAGE 114)

FARFALLE WITH ASPARAGUS, SHIITAKES,
AND SPRING PEAS (PAGE 109)

LEMON-INFUSED GREEK SALAD WITH
STUFFED GRAPE LEAVES (PAGE 121)

BIBIMBAP (PAGE 116)

VIETNAMESE SALAD ROLLS (PAGE 118)

MADEIRA-GLAZED PORTOBELLO
SANDWICH (PAGE 125)

HUE CHICKEN SALAD
(PAGE 117)

BAJA-STYLE FISH TACOS WITH
SOUTHWESTERN SLAW (PAGE 127)

3. Combine the oil, vinegar, cumin, paprika, black pepper, and salt in a small bowl, whisking until the dressing is combined and thickened. Pour this over the salad ingredients and toss gently until all the ingredients are evenly dressed. Serve on a chilled platter or plates garnished with parsley.

LEMON-INFUSED GREEK SALAD
with Stuffed Grape Leaves

SIMPLE MEDITERRANEAN flavors come together in this easy-to-make salad. The recipe for the Stuffed Grape Leaves requires a little extra preparation time, but their flavor will be superior to store-bought stuffed grape leaves and worth the effort.

MAKES 8 SERVINGS

1½ lb romaine hearts

1 cup Greek olives, pitted and sliced in half lengthwise

½ cup Lemon-Parsley Vinaigrette (page 57)

4 pita bread, toasted, cut into 16 wedges

1 European cucumber, peeled, sliced ⅛-inch thick

1 lb cherry tomatoes, halved

1 yellow pepper, thinly sliced

1 red onion, peeled, sliced ⅛-inch thick

¾ lb feta cheese, crumbled

16 Stuffed Grape Leaves (recipe follows)

1. Remove about a third of the stem from the romaine lettuce. Wash and spin-dry. Slice the romaine or tear it into bite size pieces. Place the cleaned romaine into a large serving bowl.

2. Add the sliced olives, cucumbers, cherry tomatoes, peppers, and red onions; toss with the vinaigrette. Top with the feta cheese and garnish with pita wedges and the stuffed grape leaves.

STUFFED GRAPE LEAVES

PLAN TO make this recipe the day before you want to serve it so that the stuffed grape leaves can rest overnight; this allows them to firm up and their flavor to develop more fully. You can keep cooked stuffed grape leaves in the refrigerator to add to salads or enjoy on their own. Adding a layer of potatoes to the baking dish keeps the grape leaves from sticking as you cook them.

MAKES 8 SERVINGS

½ cup olive oil

1 cup minced onions

½ cup minced fennel

2 tbsp minced garlic

1 cup short-grain rice

1½ cups fine-dice tomatoes

Salt and pepper as needed

¼ cup minced scallions, white portion only

¼ cup minced parsley

¼ cup chopped dill

¼ cup chopped mint

18 to 20 brine-packed grape leaves, rinsed and drained

2 cups thinly sliced potatoes

4 cups Vegetable Broth (page 65) or water, as needed

¼ cup lemon juice

Lemon wedges for garnish

Plain yogurt for garnish

1. Heat 2 tablespoons of the oil in a sauté pan over medium-high heat. Add the onions, fennel, and garlic and sauté, stirring frequently, until they are fragrant and just starting to become translucent, about 4 minutes.

2. Add the rice and stir to coat completely with the oil. Continue to sauté, stirring constantly, until the rice develops a toasty flavor, about 2 minutes. Add the tomatoes and season with salt and pepper. Continue to cook until the tomatoes are very hot, another 3 minutes. Remove the pan from the heat and stir in the scallions, parsley, dill, and mint. Season with additional salt and pepper, if needed.

3. Cool the rice mixture to room temperature; it can be kept in the refrigerator in a covered container for up to 12 hours, if you want to prepare the rice ahead of time and assemble the grape leaves later.

4. Bring a pot of water to a boil. Add the grape leaves and cook until they are softened, about 5 minutes. Drain well.

5. Arrange the sliced potatoes in a rectangular baking dish and add enough of the broth to barely cover them (this will prevent the potatoes from discoloring as you fill and roll the grape leaves).

6. Spread each grape leaf flat on a work surface. The veins should be facing up and the smooth side of the leaf facing down. Place 1 tablespoon of the rice mixture in the center of the leaf. Fold in the sides and then roll up the leaf like a cigar so that the rice is completely encased in the leaf. Place the filled grape leaves in the baking dish, with the seam facing down so the grape leaves won't unroll. The grape leaves can be close to each other, but should not be touching.

7. Season the grape leaves with lemon juice and a little salt and pepper. Add the remaining olive oil, the lemon juice, and enough additional broth

Building a Fire in a Charcoal Grill

A good fire burns evenly and lasts long enough to cook everything completely. While gas grills may take as little as 15 minutes to heat up, a fire typically takes at least 35 to 45 minutes before it is ready for cooking.

Lighter fluid and treated charcoal briquettes may be simpler to use, but they can leave a distinct flavor on foods. We strongly recommend avoiding lighter fluid. Never use gasoline or kerosene to start a fire.

To start a fire, open the vents in the grill to let the air in. Crumple a few sheets of newspaper and place them on the fuel grate. Add hardwood chips, briquettes, or kindling to the paper to make a mound, and set the paper on fire. Let it burn, but keep an eye on it. Fires at this stage can go out easily if there is too much or too little air blowing on them. If you are using logs instead of briquettes or chunks, add them once the kindling has started to flame.

Let the fire burn without disturbing it. Add more wood or briquettes carefully when the flames start to die down until you have enough fuel to last for a cooking session.

testing the temperature of your grill

Some grills have built-in thermometers to make it easy to monitor how hot the grill is. If you don't have such a feature on your grill, you can use a time-honored test:

Hold your hand, palm facing down, over the heat source just above the grill rack. Count how many seconds it takes before you have to take your hand away from the grill.

- 2 seconds equals high heat
- 3 seconds equals medium-high heat
- 4 seconds equals medium heat
- 5 seconds equals medium-low heat
- 6 seconds equals low heat

or water to barely cover the grape leaves. Cover the grape leaves with a clean, heat-proof plate (this will keep them submerged as they cook). Place over medium heat and bring the broth or water to a simmer. Reduce the heat to low and cook until the rice filling is very tender, 30 to 45 minutes.

8. Remove the grape leaves from the pan, cool to room temperature, and then chill for at least 8 hours in a covered container in the refrigerator. You may wish to add some of the broth to the storage container to keep the grape leaves moistened. Serve the stuffed grape leaves chilled or at room temperature with lemon wedges and yogurt.

PAKISTANI-STYLE LAMB PATTIES

PINE NUTS, garlic, aromatic herbs and seasonings, and ground lamb combine in these savory patties for a delicious Middle Eastern-inspired taste.

MAKES 8 SERVINGS

6 tbsp fresh white breadcrumbs

¼ cup cold water

2 tbsp vegetable oil

3 tbsp minced yellow onion

1½ tsp minced garlic

2½ lb lean ground lamb

2 eggs, lightly beaten

3 tbsp toasted pine nuts

3 tbsp chopped parsley

2 tbsp tahini

2 tbsp grated ginger

2 tbsp ground cumin

¾ tsp ground coriander

¾ tsp ground fennel seeds

1½ tsp salt

¾ tsp ground black pepper

1. Soak the breadcrumbs in the water until well moistened, about 2 minutes. Squeeze out any excess moisture. Transfer to a bowl and reserve.

2. Heat the oil in a sauté pan over medium-high heat. Add the onion and sauté, stirring frequently, until translucent, about 4 to 5 minutes. Add the garlic and sauté until aromatic, about 1 minute. Remove from heat and transfer to a plate to cool.

3. Combine the onion-garlic mixture and the reserved breadcrumbs together with the lamb, eggs, pinenuts, parsley, tahini, ginger, cumin, coriander, fennel seeds, salt, and pepper. Mix gently until the ingredients are evenly blended.

4. Shape the lamb mixture into 8 patties about 4 inches in diameter and ¾ inch thick, and chill them in the refrigerator.

5. Preheat a gas grill to medium-high. If you are using a charcoal grill, build a fire and let it burn down until the coals are glowing red with a moderate coating of white ash. Spread the coals in an even bed. Clean the cooking grate.

6. Grill the patties over direct heat until medium, about 4 to 5 minutes on each side.

Herb Skewers

Rosemary sprigs can grow large enough to be used as flavorful herb skewers. Tarragon or oregano sprigs that are sturdy enough could also be used as skewers.

Strip all the leaves from an herb sprig, leaving just a few leaves on the top inch or so. The leaves you strip from the stem can be used for other dishes or you can add them to any marinade you might be using. Thread the food onto the skewer, filling the skewer from the bottom to the top.

ROSEMARY-SKEWERED CHICKEN AND MUSHROOMS
with Grill-Baked Naan

MAKING SKEWERS from the stems of herbs gives the dish an additional layer of flavor that isn't released until you bite into the food.

MAKES 6 SERVINGS

½ cup olive oil

3 tbsp lemon juice

1 tbsp chopped Mediterranean oregano

1 tsp minced garlic

1 tsp salt

½ tsp ground black pepper

12 boneless, skinless chicken thighs

1½ lb mushrooms

12 rosemary skewers (page 123)

12 Grill-Baked Naan (page 247)

1. Whisk together the olive oil, lemon juice, oregano, garlic, ½ tsp of the salt, and ¼ tsp of the pepper to make a marinade.

2. Trim any fat from the chicken meat. Cut the thighs in half and place in a zip-close bag. Pour ⅔ of the marinade over the chicken and toss to coat well. Seal the bag, pressing out the air. Let marinate in the refrigerator for at least 1 and up to 12 hours.

3. Place the mushrooms in another zip-close bag and add the remaining marinade. Toss to coat the mushrooms evenly. Seal the bag, pressing out the air. Let marinate in the refrigerator for 1 hour.

4. Preheat a gas grill to medium. If you are using a charcoal grill, build a fire and let it burn down until the coals are glowing red with a moderate coating of white ash. Spread the coals in an even bed. Clean the cooking grate.

5. Thread the chicken and mushrooms on the rosemary skewers, alternating them. Season the kebabs with the remaining salt and pepper.

6. Grill the kebabs over direct heat, covered, turning to cook evenly, until the chicken is browned and cooked through and the mushrooms are tender, about 15 to 20 minutes. Serve the kebabs (removed from the skewers, if desired) with warm naan.

TURKEY BURGER

A LEAN AND healthy base for a wide variety of toppings, this recipe is full of flavor.

MAKES 8 SERVINGS

2 lb ground turkey

1 garlic clove, minced

½ tsp salt, or to taste

¼ tsp freshly ground black pepper, or to taste

2 tbsp parsley, chives, or basil, chopped

2 tsp vegetable oil

8 provolone or Monterey Jack cheese, sliced

8 sandwich rolls, split and toasted

BURGER GARNISH ITEMS (OPTIONAL)

1 avocado, sliced just before serving

1 tomato, sliced

1 red onion, sliced

8 romaine lettuce leaves

1. Preheat the grill. Gently blend the ground turkey with the garlic, salt, pepper, and herbs. Shape into 8 patties and chill in the refrigerator until the grill is very hot.

2. Brush the grill rods with the oil. Grill the turkey burgers on the first side until browned, about 5

minutes. Carefully flip the burgers over, and grill on the second side until browned and cooked through, another 5 minutes. Top with the cheese during the final 2 to 3 minutes of grilling.

3. Serve the burgers on the toasted buns, topped with sliced avocado, tomato, onion, and lettuce.

GRILLED FOCACCIA SANDWICH
with Bacon and Avocado

I F YOU want to make your own focaccia for these sandwiches, use the recipe for Semolina Pizza Dough (page 113), but shape the dough to fit into an 8- or 9-inch round baking pan. Dimple the top of the dough after it has nearly doubled in size, drizzle generously with olive oil, and add any other toppings you wish, such as sautéed onions, roasted garlic, or minced herbs. Bake the focaccia at 375°F until the crust is golden brown, about 20 minutes.

MAKES 6 SERVINGS

¼ cup extra-virgin olive oil, or as needed

1 tbsp balsamic vinegar

3 beefsteak tomatoes, sliced thin

2 ripe Haas avocados, sliced

1 tsp lemon juice

1 tbsp minced garlic

1 tsp salt

¼ tsp ground black pepper

6 onion or plain focaccia squares or two 8-inch round focaccia

¼ to ½ cup mayonnaise

6 lettuce leaves, rinsed and dried

12 slices cooked bacon

1. Combine 2 tablespoons olive oil and the vinegar. Add the sliced tomatoes and toss gently to coat them. Set aside. Slice the avocados and sprinkle with the lemon juice to keep them from turning brown. Set aside.

2. Heat a griddle or cast iron skillet over medium heat or preheat the broiler to high. In a small bowl, combine the remaining olive oil with the garlic. Season with salt and pepper. Set aside.

3. Cut the focaccia in half horizontally and brush with the garlic oil mixture. Griddle or broil, oiled sided facing down, until toasted, about 4 minutes

4. Spread the mayonnaise on the focaccia and then layer the sandwich filling on top of the bread: lettuce leaves, sliced tomatoes, bacon, and sliced avocado. Close the sandwich and serve at once.

MADEIRA-GLAZED PORTOBELLO SANDWICHES

P ORTOBELLO MUSHROOMS are actually mature cremini mushrooms and have a dense, meaty texture when cooked. They can easily be prepared for this recipe a day ahead. Cool the broiled mushroom caps completely and refrigerate until needed. Slice the mushrooms and allow them to return to room temperature prior to assembling the sandwiches.

MAKES 8 SERVINGS

8 portobello mushrooms

¼ cup Madeira

3 tbsp olive oil

2 garlic cloves, bruised

½ tsp dried oregano

2 tsp salt, or to taste

1 tsp freshly ground black pepper, or to taste

3 cups sliced onion

8 hard rolls, split

8 thin slices Swiss cheese

4 cups mixed baby greens

1. Preheat the broiler and place the oven rack in the upper third of the oven.

2. Remove the stems from the mushrooms, use a sharp paring knife to cut away the gills, and discard. Combine the Madeira, 2 tablespoons of the olive oil, garlic cloves, oregano, 1 teaspoon of salt, and ½ teaspoon of the pepper in a large bowl. Add the mushrooms and toss to coat. Set aside for 10 minutes to marinate.

3. Heat the remaining tablespoon of olive oil in a sauté pan set over medium-high heat. Add the onion and sauté until soft and translucent, 5 to 6 minutes. Season with the remaining 1 teaspoon of salt and ½ teaspoon of pepper.

4. Place the mushrooms on a baking sheet, brush with the marinade, and broil until browned and tender, about 4 minutes on each side. When cool enough to handle, thinly slice each mushroom and place one entire sliced mushroom on the bottom half of each roll. Top with 1 slice of cheese.

5. Place the bottom half of each roll with the mushroom and cheese on a baking pan and broil until the cheese is melted, about 2 minutes.

6. Top each sandwich with ¼ cup of the onions, ½ cup of the greens, and the top half of the roll.

OYSTER PO' BOY
with Rémoulade

THERE ARE several explanations about its origin, but one popular theory reports that the po' boy sandwich—a true New Orleans specialty—was invented in 1920 by Benny and Clovis Martin at Martin Brother's Grocery where it was offered to street-car workers then on strike. In this version, oysters are rolled in fresh bread crumbs, sautéed, and served in French rolls with a classic rémoulade sauce.

MAKES 8 SERVINGS

REMOULADE

½ cup mayonnaise

2 scallions, minced

¼ cup minced celery

2 tbsp minced parsley

2 tbsp dill pickle relish

2 tbsp red wine vinegar

4 tsp Dijon mustard

4 tsp minced capers, drained

2 tsp Worcestershire sauce

4 dashes hot pepper sauce, optional

1½ cups bread crumbs

¾ cup all-purpose flour

1 tsp freshly ground black pepper, or to taste

½ tsp cayenne pepper

4 dozen oysters, shucked

4 large eggs, beaten

½ cup canola oil, or as needed

8 crusty French rolls, cut in half

2 beefsteak tomatoes, thinly sliced

1 cup shredded romaine lettuce

2 lemons, cut into wedges

1. To prepare the rémoulade: Combine the mayonnaise, scallions, celery, parsley, relish, vinegar, mustard, capers, Worcestershire sauce, and pepper sauce, if using, in a bowl. Set aside.

2. Combine the bread crumbs, flour, black pepper, and cayenne. Toss with your fingertips to combine. Drain the oysters of any liquid and dry thoroughly. Dip the oysters, one at a time, into the beaten egg

and roll in the bread crumb mixture. Heat ¼ cup of the oil in a large skillet until it shimmers. Add half of the oysters and fry, turning once, until the oysters are browned and cooked through, 4 to 5 minutes. Repeat with the remaining oil and oysters.

3. Toast the roll halves. Layer the oysters, tomato slices, and lettuce evenly on 8 halves and top with the remaining halves. Serve with the rémoulade and lemon wedges.

EGGPLANT AND PROSCIUTTO PANINI

Panini is the Italian word for rolls or sandwiches. Today "panini" usually refers to rustic sandwiches that are grilled.

MAKES 8 SANDWICHES

1 cup ricotta cheese

1 tsp freshly ground black pepper, or to taste

2 tbsp basil, chopped

22 oz jarred eggplant caponata

8 sandwich rolls (hoagie, ciabatta, sourdough), sliced in half lengthwise

¼ lb prosciutto, thinly sliced

1. In a bowl, combine the ricotta cheese, pepper, and basil. Mix together well and refrigerate until ready to use.

2. Preheat a grill or sandwich press to high.

3. Spread the eggplant caponata evenly on one half of each roll. Spread the ricotta mixture evenly on the other half. Top the ricotta side with the prosciutto slices, and invert the eggplant side on top.

4. Grill each sandwich for 3 to 4 minutes. Slice each sandwich into 4 pieces, and serve.

BAJA-STYLE FISH TACOS
with Southwestern Slaw

Put the ingredients for this classic fish taco out on the table and let your family and friends build their own. The combination of fish and coleslaw is heady and robust, a perfect match to the rich taste of the pico de gallo and the lime-scented Mexican crema. If you cannot find Mexican sour cream, substitute regular sour cream. Mexican sour cream has a milder acidic bite and a little more salt.

MAKES 8 SERVINGS

2 lb mahi-mahi

½ cup vegetable oil

3 tbsp lime juice

5 tsp chili powder

1½ tsp ground cumin

1½ tsp ground coriander

1½ tsp minced garlic

Salt, to taste

8 flour tortillas, 8 inches in diameter

Southwestern Slaw (page 46)

1 cup Chipotle Pico de Gallo (page 20)

½ cup Mexican Crema (recipe follows)

1. Preheat a gas grill to medium-high. If you are using a charcoal grill, build a fire and let it burn down until the coals are glowing red with a moderate coating of white ash. Spread the coals in an even bed. Clean the cooking grate.

2. Cut the mahi-mahi into 16 equal slices.

3. Combine the oil, lime juice, chili powder, cumin, coriander, garlic, and salt. Coat the mahi-mahi with the marinade.

4. Grill the fish on the first side over direct heat until the flesh is firm and well marked, about 2 min-

utes. Turn the fish and grill until cooked through, about 1½ to 2 minutes more.

5. Grill the tortillas until they have light grill marks and are heated through, about 15 seconds on the first side. Turn the tortillas and grill them until they just start to bubble, another 15 seconds.

6. Center 2 pieces of grilled fish on each tortilla, and top with the Southwestern Slaw and Chipotle Pico de Gallo. Add a dollop of Mexican Crema, fold in half, and serve immediately.

Mexican Crema

MAKES ½ CUP

½ cup Mexican sour cream

½ tsp finely grated lime zest

2 tsp lime juice

Combine all the ingredients and mix well. The cream is ready to use now or it can be stored in a covered container in the refrigerator for up to 2 days.

CHAPTER

5

Main Dishes

Rehydrating Dried Mushrooms

Place the mushrooms in a small bowl and add enough in warm water to cover them. Let them rest until they are softened, about 30 minutes. Lift the mushrooms from the water, letting it drain away. Save the liquid; you can strain it through a coffee filter and add it to any simmered dishes that could benefit from a touch of mushroom essence. You may need to cut away tough stems (especially with shiitake mushrooms). You can simply discard the stems, but if you make stocks and broths, you may want to save the stems to use in those recipes.

BRAISED BEEF SHORT RIBS
Kalbi Jim

KALBI JIM is a Korean dish made with short ribs that are cooked in a mirin-and-soy sauce until the sauce reduces to a mahogany glaze, and the meat is tender enough to fall from the bone.

MAKES 8 SERVINGS

8 beef short ribs, bone-in, cut into 3-inch lengths

Salt as needed

Freshly ground black pepper as needed

1½ cups mirin

¾ cup light soy sauce

2 cups large-dice yellow onion

2 slices ginger root (¼-inch-thick), peeled and lightly crushed

2 tsp minced garlic

½ cup jujube (Chinese red dates)

8 dried shiitake mushrooms, rehydrated and chopped, liquid reserved (see note)

2 cups sliced daikon

2 cups thinly sliced carrots, cut on diagonal

2 tsp sugar or as needed

¼ cup pine nuts, toasted

1 tbsp dark sesame oil

One 3-egg omelet, cut into diamonds or strips (see note)

1. Season the short ribs with salt and pepper and place in a casserole or Dutch oven. Add the mirin, soy sauce, onion, ginger, garlic, jujube, and reserved mushroom-infused water; there should be enough liquid to just cover ribs. Bring the liquid to a boil and then immediately lower the heat until the liquid is at a gentle simmer. Simmer, skimming as necessary and turning the ribs to keep them moist, until fork tender, about 2 hours.

2. When meat is fork tender add the mushrooms, daikon, and carrots and simmer until the vegetables are tender, about 10 minutes. Remove and discard the crushed ginger. Season to taste with additional soy sauce and sugar.

3. Stir in the pine nuts and sesame oil; simmer until heated through, about 5 minutes. Serve the ribs and vegetables on heated plates garnished with omelet diamonds or strips

An Omelet Garnish

Several Asian recipes call for eggs. They may be stirred into soups or stir fries, but another popular option is making an omelet that can be cut into shapes.

First, heat a sauté pan over medium-high heat. Add enough oil to lubricate the pan well so the omelet won't stick. For this recipe, beat three eggs until they are frothy; the Chinese use chopsticks to avoid working in too much air. Season the eggs with a pinch of salt and pepper and pour them into the pan. The eggs will begin to set almost immediately. Use a heatproof spatula to push the cooked eggs away from the bottom. The uncooked eggs will flow to the bottom of the pan and cook. When the eggs are fully cooked, turn the omelet out of the pan onto a plate. Roll or fold it into a neat shape and let it rest until it is cool. Then, cut it into ribbons, diamonds, or other shapes.

CARBONNADES OF BEEF FLAMANDE

THIS COMBINATION of beef and onions, cooked in dark, rich ale, is a classic example from the Belgians of how to make the most from the ingredients at hand. If you can find stout or porter, use it in this hearty braised dish. Broad noodles, steamed potatoes, or potato croquettes would make an excellent accompaniment to this dish.

MAKES 4 SERVINGS

4 beef chuck steaks (about 5 to 6 oz each)

Salt as needed

Freshly ground black pepper as needed

3 tbsp canola oil

4 medium-size yellow onions, sliced thick

2 tbsp tomato paste

¼ cup water

2 tbsp firmly packed dark brown sugar

12 oz dark beer

2 cups Beef Broth (page 63)

1 tbsp Dijon-style mustard

2 tsp balsamic vinegar

1. Preheat oven to 300°F.

2. Season the steaks generously with salt and pepper. Heat the oil in a cast-iron skillet over high heat until it shimmers. Add the steaks to the skillet and sear them on both sides, about 2 minutes per side. Remove the steaks from the skillet and hold them on a warmed plate.

3. Add the onions to the hot oil in the skillet and sauté them until they are a deep golden brown, 8 to 10 minutes. As they cook, stir them from time to time to prevent scorching.

4. Add the tomato paste to the onions and sauté for about 3 minutes over medium heat, stirring frequently. Add the water and brown sugar to the pan and stir well.

5. Add the beer and stir to blend. Allow the beer to reduce to half its original volume. Add the broth and bring the mixture to a simmer.

6. Return the steaks to the skillet along with any juices they have released. Cover the skillet and place in the oven. Braise the steaks, turning from time to time to keep them evenly moistened, until they are very tender, about 1½ hours.

7. Remove the steaks and keep them warm. Place the pan over medium heat and bring the sauce to a simmer. Remove any fat from the surface and add the mustard and balsamic vinegar. Allow the sauce to reduce slightly over high heat and adjust the seasoning with additional salt and pepper if necessary. Ladle the sauce over the steaks and serve on heated plates.

BEEF IN MUSSAMAN CURRY SAUCE
Kaeng Mussaman

MUSSAMAN CURRY is the mildest of the Thai curries. You can find prepared curry pastes in large grocery stores or shops that specialize in Asian products, or you can make your own—a recipe follows.

MAKES 4 SERVINGS

5 cups coconut milk

2 lb boneless beef chuck, cut in 2-inch chunks

⅓ cup Mussaman Curry Paste (recipe follows, or substitute prepared red curry paste)

4 cups large-dice potatoes

3 tbsp fish sauce plus as needed

3 tbsp tamarind pulp

2 tbsp palm sugar plus as needed

6 cinnamon sticks

1 tsp ground cardamom

¾ cup large-dice yellow onion

½ cup pan-roasted peanuts (see note below)

2 tsp lime juice or as needed

1. Heat the coconut milk in a large saucepot over medium heat until it comes to a gentle boil, about 10 minutes. Skim off any cream that rises to the surface and transfer it to a small, heavy bottomed saucepan or skillet.

2. Add the beef chunks to the coconut milk in the saucepot and continue to simmer until the beef is tender, about 1 hour.

3. Bring the coconut cream to a gentle boil over medium heat. Adjust the heat to maintain a gentle boil and cook, stirring occasionally, until the coconut cream becomes thick and fragrant and tiny pools of oil glisten on the surface, 6 to 8 minutes. Add the curry paste and stir to dissolve it in the coconut cream. Simmer the mixture until it has a rich aroma, 3 to 4 minutes.

4. Add the curry paste mixture to the beef and coconut milk; stir well. Add the potatoes, fish sauce, tamarind, palm sugar, cinnamon, and cardamom and simmer until the potatoes are par-cooked, about 10 minutes. Add the onion and peanuts and simmer until the potatoes are tender, about 5 minutes more. Season to taste with additional fish sauce, palm sugar, and lime juice. It should have a pleasing, sweet, sour, and salty balance.

Pan-Roasting Nuts

You can buy roasted peanuts and cashews to garnish some Southeast Asian stews like this curry. For the best flavor and texture, however, consider toasting your own. You use the same technique to pan-roast spices and seeds for a depth of flavor you simply can't find in store-bought spice blends.

Let a heavy-bottomed skillet or sauté pan get very hot over high heat. Add the nuts, spices, or seeds to the pan in an even layer. Swirl the pan gently to keep the ingredients in motion constantly. The aromas will open up and deepen dramatically.

Once the nuts, spices, or seeds begin to give off a noticeable aroma, keep a close eye on them. They can go from perfect to overdone in a few seconds. Pour them out of the pan into a bowl just before they are the shade of brown you want.

Mussaman Curry Paste

MUSSAMAN CURRY PASTE, or *phrik kang mussaman*, has a distinct aroma, due to the number of spices it contains. It is usually based on dried chiles and contains coriander and cumin. The measurements given here are just a starting point.

MAKES ½ CUP

1 tbsp coriander seeds

1 tsp cumin seeds

1 tsp fennel seeds

1 tsp cloves

2 dried red chiles

Two 1-inch pieces dried galangal

1 stalk lemongrass

1 bunch cilantro

6–7 cloves garlic, minced

¼ small onion, minced

1 tsp shrimp paste

½ tsp freshly ground black pepper

½ tsp freshly ground nutmeg

1. Toast the coriander seeds, cumin seeds, fennel seeds, and cloves in a dry skillet or wok over moderate heat until very fragrant, about 2 minutes. Immediately transfer the spices to a bowl and set aside.

2. Remove the stems and seeds from the chiles. Soak the chiles and the galangal in warm water for 20 minutes. Transfer the chiles and galangal to a mortar or a blender. Discard the soaking water.

3. Chop the tender inner portion of the stalk of lemongrass. Scrape the well-rinsed roots from the bunch of cilantro and add them to the chiles.

4. Add the garlic and onion to the chiles, along with the spice mixture, shrimp paste, black pepper, and nutmeg. Grind to a smooth paste. (If you are using a blender, you might have to add a few teaspoons of water.)

5. Use the curry paste immediately or store it in a closed container in the refrigerator for up to 2 weeks or in the freezer for up to 6 months.

Toasting Curry Paste

Toasting curry paste intensifies its flavor, whether you are using your handmade version or a good quality brand that you've purchased.

Let a saucepan get very hot over high heat. Add the paste to the pan and stir it constantly. The aromas will open up and deepen dramatically.

For the Mussaman Curry Sauce in the previous recipe, add the coconut cream to the toasted curry paste and stir well to blend the curry into the cream. It's now ready to add to your simmering curry.

BOLIVIAN BEEF STEW

THERE ARE many variations of this spicy, slow cooking, one-pot meal. Serve it with warm cornbread and salad greens dressed with lemon juice. Adjust the amount of jalapeño pepper to suit your family and friends.

MAKES 4 SERVINGS

1 lb boneless lean beef round, cut into 2-inch cubes

Salt to taste

Freshly ground black pepper to taste

1 tbsp canola oil

2 cups diced yellow onion

½ cup chopped red or green bell pepper

1 jalapeño pepper, seeded, deveined, and chopped

2 cups chopped plum tomatoes, fresh or canned

1 cup low-sodium beef broth

2 cups diced acorn or winter squash

2 red potatoes, diced

2 small ears of corn, sliced into 1-inch-thick rounds

2 tbsp minced cilantro

1. Season the cubes of beef generously with salt and pepper.

2. Heat the oil in a Dutch oven or casserole over medium high heat until it shimmers. Sauté the beef in the oil, stirring frequently, until the beef is browned on all sides, 8 to 10 minutes. Transfer the beef to a pan and keep warm.

3. Return the same pan to the heat. Add the onion, bell pepper, and jalapeño. Sauté, stirring frequently, until the onion is lightly browned, 8 to 10 minutes. Add the tomatoes and broth. Bring the liquid to a boil, and reduce the heat to low. Return the beef and any juices it may have released to the casserole. Simmer, covered, stirring occasionally, until the beef is tender, 1 to 1½ hours. Season to taste as the stew simmers with additional salt and pepper.

4. Add the squash, potatoes, and corn to the stew. Simmer, covered, until the vegetables are tender,

about 20 minutes. Season to taste with additional salt and pepper. Divide the stew evenly among 4 heated bowls, sprinkle each serving with some of the cilantro, and serve.

Pitting Olives for Cooking

You don't have to take the pits out of your olives, but when cooking with them, it does make them a little easier to eat. You can buy cherry and olive pitters at most stores that carry cookware appliances or gadgets. If you don't have a pitter, though, you can either cut the olive away from the pit using a sharp paring knife, or you can fish the pit out of the olive using a paper clip. Open the paper clip out so that you have two hooks. Insert the rounded end of one of the hooks into the olive; catch the pit in the bend of your hook, and pull it out of the olive.

CATALAN BEEF STEW
with Orange Peel and Black Olives

THE CUISINE of Spain is rapidly becoming more familiar to cooks and restaurant-goers. This typical dish marries a flavorful cut of beef from the shoulder with some typical Catalonian ingredients. Bitter oranges are traditional, but if you don't have access to a bitter orange, use a Valencia (juice) orange and a touch of lime juice for nearly the same flavor profile.

MAKES 4 SERVINGS

1 tbsp olive oil

5 slices bacon, thick-cut, diced

2 lb boneless beef chuck or bottom round, cut into
    2-inch pieces

Salt as needed

Freshly ground black pepper as needed

2 cups chopped yellow onion

2 cups red wine

2 tbsp orange peel julienne

2 bay leaves

2 tsp minced garlic

2 parsley sprigs, minced

1 cup Spanish black olives, pitted

1. Heat the oil in a casserole or Dutch oven over medium-high heat until it shimmers. Add the bacon, and sauté until the bacon is crisped and browned, 5 minutes. Transfer the bacon to a bowl with a slotted spoon, letting the oil drain back into the casserole.

2. Return the casserole to the heat and heat the oil until it shimmers. Season the beef generously with salt and pepper. Add the beef (working in batches to avoid crowding the pan) and sear on all sides until brown, about 8 minutes. Transfer the beef to the bowl with the bacon using a slotted spoon, letting the oil drain back into the casserole. Add the onion and sauté, stirring occasionally, until deeply caramelized, 25 to 30 minutes.

3. Return the beef and bacon to the casserole, add the red wine, orange peel, bay leaves, garlic, and parsley; bring the liquid to a boil. Immediately adjust the heat for a gentle simmer. Season the stew to taste with salt and pepper throughout cooking time. Simmer the stew, covered, until the beef is nearly tender, about 2 hours. Add the olives and continue to simmer until the beef is fork tender, 1 to 1½ hours. Serve in heated bowls.

NOTE: To be sure that this dish is as moist and succulent as possible, use this tip: Cut a piece of cooking parchment that will fit snugly inside your casserole or Dutch oven. Once the stew is simmering very slowly, carefully push the paper down onto the surface of the stew to keep the meat completely submerged. Professional chefs refer to this paper lid as a *cartouche*.

OXTAIL STEW IN RED WINE
Rabo de Toro

OXTAIL STEWS have incredible body and flavor. We recommend that you make this a day or two before you plan to eat it—the flavor deepens as it rests. Boiled, mashed, or pan-fried potatoes are good accompaniments to this dish, along with a glass of the wine you used to make the stew.

MAKES 6 SERVINGS

¼ cup olive oil

2¾ lb oxtail pieces

Salt as needed

Freshly ground black pepper as needed

2 cups chopped yellow onion

1½ cups chopped leek, white and light green portions

1 tsp minced garlic

½ cup diced plum tomato

1 tbsp sherry vinegar or as needed

1 tbsp honey

2 cups dry red wine, such as a good-quality Rioja

3 cups Beef Broth or as needed (page 63)

4 parsley sprigs

4 thyme sprigs

1 bay leaf

2 tbsp chopped parsley, for garnish

1. Heat the oil in a casserole or Dutch oven over high heat until it shimmers. Season the oxtail pieces generously with salt and pepper; add in a single layer to the hot oil. (Work in batches if necessary to avoid crowding the pieces.) Sauté the oxtail, turn-ing as necessary, until browned on all sides, about 10 minutes. Transfer to a plate, letting the oil drain back into the casserole. Cover the oxtail loosely and set aside.

2. Return the casserole to high heat until the oil shimmers. Add the onion, leek, and garlic and sauté, stirring occasionally, until golden brown, about 15 minutes. Add the diced tomato and cook until it deepens in color and smells sweet, about 2 minutes.

3. Add 1 tablespoon sherry vinegar and the honey and stir until the honey is dissolved. Return the ox-tail pieces and any juices they may have released to the casserole and fold the oxtail into the vegetables gently with a wooden spoon.

4. Add the red wine and enough of the broth to cover the oxtail. Bring to a simmer over low heat. Tie the parsley, thyme, and bay leaf together into a bouquet garni and add to the stew. Cover the casse-role and simmer very gently over low heat until the meat on the oxtail is nearly falling from the bone, 2 to 3 hours.

5. Transfer the oxtail pieces to a heated serving bowl and keep warm. Remove and discard the bou-quet garni. Return the casserole to the heat. Skim the fat and oil from the surface and bring to a sim-mer over medium-high heat. Simmer rapidly until the sauce thickens slightly, about 5 minutes. Sea-son to taste with additional sherry vinegar, salt, and pepper. Pour the sauce over the oxtail pieces, gar-nish with parsley, and serve at once.

SAIGON BEEF STEW
with Lemongrass and Anise

SLICE THE onion and carrots paper-thin for this dish. Cutting the carrots on the diagonal gives them a pleasing shape. You can make plain round slices into flowers by cutting three or four evenly-spaced grooves into the carrot with a paring knife before you slice it.

MAKES 6 SERVINGS

3 tbsp annatto oil

2 tbsp chopped shallots

2 tsp minced garlic

1 tbsp curry powder

2 tsp minced Thai bird chiles or as needed

½ tsp ground anise

Salt as needed

Freshly ground black paper as needed

1½ lb beef chuck roast, cut into 1½-inch cubes

3 cups Beef or Chicken Broth (page 63)

3 lemongrass stalks, crushed and cut into 3-inch pieces

2 tbsp fish sauce or as needed

1 tbsp soy sauce or as needed

1 tbsp sugar

2 cups thinly sliced carrots, cut on the diagonal

1 cup thinly sliced yellow onion

½ cup loosely packed Thai basil leaves, torn into pieces

½ cup loosely packed cilantro leaves, torn into pieces

1. Heat the annatto oil in a casserole or Dutch oven over high heat until it shimmers. Add the shallots and garlic and stir until fragrant, about 30 seconds. Add the curry powder, chiles, anise, and a pinch of salt and pepper. Sauté, stirring frequently, until aromatic, about 1 minute. Spoon half of this shallot-spice mixture into a bowl and set aside.

2. Add the beef to the casserole and stir until evenly blended with the remaining shallot-spice mixture. Sauté until the beef has lost its raw look, about 5 minutes. Add the broth, lemongrass, fish sauce, soy sauce, and sugar and bring to a boil over high heat. Immediately reduce the heat until the stew is simmering gently. Continue to simmer, skimming occasionally, until the beef is nearly tender, about 15 minutes. Add the carrots and onion and simmer until the beef and carrots are tender, about 15 minutes.

3. Stir in the reserved shallot-spice mixture. Season to taste with salt, pepper, and additional fish sauce or soy sauce. Serve in heated soup plates garnished with basil and cilantro leaves.

Annatto Oil

Brightly colored, aromatic annatto oil makes this dish unusual. If you can't find annatto oil, make your own: Heat 1 cup canola oil in a small saucepan. When it is shimmering, add 5 tablespoons annatto seeds. The seeds will foam up and sputter. Immediately pull the pan off the heat, let the seeds steep for 10 minutes, and then strain out and discard the seeds.

STIR-FRY CITRUS BEEF

STIR-FRYING IS a quick cooking method that produces delicious results and eye-appealing presentations. If you're not in the mood for beef, substitute 2 pounds of boneless, skinless chicken breasts, cut into ¼-inch-thick slices.

MAKES 8 SERVINGS

2 lb oranges

6 tbsp dry sherry

6 tbsp soy sauce

1 tbsp vegetable oil

2 lb sirloin, trimmed of fat and cut across the grain into ¼-inch-thick slices

¼ cup ginger, minced

½ tsp red pepper flakes

3 cups bean sprouts

3 cups snow peas, ends and strings removed

8 cups steamed rice

2 tsp sesame oil, optional

4–6 tbsp cilantro leaves

1. Zest half of the oranges and juice them all. Measure the juice and add enough water to equal 2 cups. In a small bowl, stir together zest, juice, sherry and soy sauce. Reserve.

2. Heat a wok or nonstick pan over high heat. When pan is hot, add the oil, then add the beef, ginger, and pepper flakes. Cook, stirring occasionally until beef is browned, about 3 to 4 minutes. With a slotted spoon, transfer beef to a bowl. Pour off any excess oil

3. Pour orange juice mixture into wok and bring to a simmer. Add bean sprouts and pea pods; cook, stirring, until pea pods turn a brighter green (about 1 minute).

4. Return the beef and any juices to the pan and cook long enough to reheat the beef. Serve over steamed rice. If desired, finish with sesame oil. Garnish with cilantro.

Clay Pots

Clay is an ancient cooking medium. You may have even seen some contemporary recipes that call for foods to be wrapped in wet clay and then roasted or baked. Clay pots give foods a distinctive flavor, but they require careful handling.

Be sure to buy your clay pot from a reputable source. Some unglazed clay cooking equipment may contain harmful or toxic substances. Before you use a clay pot for the first time, let it soak in cold water overnight. The next day, let it air dry. After that, you will only need to soak the pot for 15 minutes before starting to prepare a dish.

Once you've added all of your ingredients to the pot, place the covered clay pot into the center of a cold oven. As the oven heats up, it will gradually bring the pot up to the desired temperature. If you put a cold clay pot into a hot oven, you risk cracking the pot. Most clay pot recipes call for a temperature of at least 400°F.

Never place a hot clay pot on a cold or wet surface. It will surely crack. Use a hot pad or wooden cutting board. Some clay cookers are flameproof for use on a stovetop or even a grill, but be sure that your clay pot can handle direct heat.

CHICKEN CLAY POT

Cooking in clay pots is an important technique in some Chinese cuisines. The unglazed cooker can go from the oven to the table, and it retains heat to keep foods hot at the table.

MAKES 4 SERVINGS

1¼ lb boneless skinless chicken breast

Salt as needed

Freshly ground black pepper as needed

⅔ cup water

½ cup fish sauce

⅓ cup tightly packed brown sugar

1 tbsp canola oil

6 sprigs fresh cilantro, chopped (including roots and stems)

2 Thai bird chiles, chopped

1 tsp garlic, minced

1 tsp minced ginger root

1 tsp lime juice

1 tsp red wine vinegar

2 tbsp chopped cilantro leaves

1. Cut the chicken into ½-inch cubes. Season well with salt and pepper.

2. Stir together the water, fish sauce, brown sugar, oil, cilantro, Thai bird chiles, garlic, ginger, lime juice, and vinegar in a small bowl until the sugar is completely dissolved.

3. Put the chicken in a soaked clay pot (see note for pot preparation) or an ovenproof casserole with a lid. Pour the fish sauce mixture over the chicken pieces.

4. Put the clay pot into a cold oven and set the temperature for 400°F. (If you are using an ovenproof casserole, put it into a preheated oven.) Cook in the oven until the chicken is cooked through and the liquid has thickened and coats the chicken, 12 to 15 minutes. Garnish with cilantro and serve immediately directly from the clay pot or casserole.

MOROCCAN LEMON CHICKEN
with Spicy Mango Chutney

FRESH LEMON, chickpeas, and a dash of spice create the Moroccan flavors in this one-skillet meal. The flavor of this dish improves with time, so feel free to prepare it a day in advance of serving.

MAKES 8 SERVINGS

1 lemon

8 chicken breast halves, boneless

1 tbsp salt, or to taste

Freshly ground black pepper, to taste

2 tsp curry powder

2 tbsp olive oil

2 cups onion, thinly sliced

1¼ cups Chicken Broth (page 63) or water

2 bunches asparagus, white and green

1½ cups chickpeas, drained and rinsed

Spicy Mango Chutney (recipe follows)

¼ cup parsley, chopped

1. Bring a large pot of salted water to a boil. Cut the lemon in half. Juice one half and thinly slice the remaining half in rounds. Reserve.

2. Season the chicken with salt, pepper, and a little curry powder. Heat the oil in a large nonstick skillet over medium-high heat. Add the chicken and cook until golden, about 2 minutes per side. Transfer the chicken to a platter.

3. Pour off excess fat from the pan and return to the heat. Add the onion, the remaining curry powder, and ½ cup of broth or water to the skillet. Bring to a boil, scraping up browned bits from the bottom. Cover and cook over medium heat, stirring occasionally, until onions are almost tender, about 5 minutes.

4. Return the chicken to the pan, along with I cup broth or water, the reserved lemon slices, and ½ teaspoon salt. Bring to a boil. Reduce the heat, cover, and simmer 15 to 20 minutes, turning the chicken and stirring occasionally during cooking.

5. Meanwhile, trim 1 to 2 inches off the asparagus, and cook in boiling salted water until just tender. Drain the asparagus and reserve.

6. Stir the chickpeas and ⅓ cup of the mango chutney in with the chicken. Simmer for 5 minutes or until the chickpeas are heated through. Stir in the reserved lemon juice to taste.

7. Serve the chicken with the chickpeas, garnished with chopped parsley and the asparagus, with additional mango chutney on the side.

Spicy Mango Chutney

MAKES 1¾ CUPS

2 cups mango, chopped (about 2 medium)

⅔ cup dark brown sugar

2 tbsp cider vinegar

½ cup raisins

1 tbsp jalapeño, minced

1 tbsp garlic, minced

1 tbsp ginger, minced

¼ tsp salt, or to taste

⅛ tsp freshly ground black pepper, or to taste

1. Combine the mangos and brown sugar in a 2½ quart saucepan. Add the vinegar, raisins, jalapeño, garlic, ginger, salt, and pepper, bring to a boil and simmer 15 minutes.

2. Transfer to clean storage container. Cover and refrigerate for up to 2 weeks.

Smen

Smen is a traditional butter-based cooking oil featured in Moroccan dishes. It is made in the same basic manner as ghee (page 152), but instead of using butter made from cow milk, smen is made from sheep or goat milk. While you may think of butter as something perishable, this preserved butter is prepared in such a way that it can last for several months. The deep, pungent aroma is used to enhance many savory dishes, especially couscous.

CHICKEN WITH ALMONDS AND CHICKPEAS
Djeg Kdra

A TRADITIONAL MOROCCAN dish, *kdra* is a slowly braised dish made in a tagine. Tagines have cone-shaped lids that capture the steam released by the dish as it cooks. The steam falls back onto the food, basting and flavoring it throughout the cooking time.

MAKES 4 SERVINGS

1 cup whole almonds, blanched

3 or 4 saffron threads

¼ tsp ground turmeric

2 tbsp clarified butter or smen (see note)

4 chicken legs (drumstick and thigh)

Salt as needed

Freshly ground black pepper as needed

½ tsp ground ginger

1 cinnamon stick

½ cup minced yellow onion

2 cups thinly sliced yellow onion

½ cup cooked chickpeas, drained and rinsed

4 cups Chicken Broth (page 63) or as needed

¼ cup chopped flat-leaf parsley

2 tsp lemon juice or as needed

1. Place the almonds in a small sauce pan and add enough cold water to cover them. Bring to a gentle simmer over low heat, cover, and immediately remove from the heat. Let the almonds soak in the hot water until softened, about 1 hour.

2. Crush the saffron threads together with the ground turmeric in a small dish and reserve.

3. Heat the butter or smen in a casserole or tagine over medium-high heat until hot but not smoking. Season the chicken with salt and pepper and sear in the hot butter, turning as necessary, until the chicken is lightly colored on all sides, 8 to 10 minutes. Transfer to a plate and keep warm.

4. Add half of the saffron-turmeric mixture, the ginger, and cinnamon stick to the butter in the casserole and sauté, stirring constantly, until aromatic, about 30 seconds. Add the minced onion and sauté, stirring frequently, until the onion is translucent, about 6 minutes.

5. Add the reserved chicken along with any juices it may have released, the sliced onion, and chick-

peas to the casserole or tagine. Add enough of the broth to barely cover the chicken. Cover the casserole and braise over very low heat until the chicken is very tender, 45 to 50 minutes.

6. Drain the almonds and add them to the sauce, along with the parsley and the remaining saffron-turmeric mixture. Simmer the sauce long enough to heat the almonds, 1 to 2 minutes. Season to taste with lemon juice and additional salt and pepper. Serve directly from the tagine or casserole on heated plates.

About Beer Can Chicken

"Beer Can" Chicken was a popular trend in outdoor cooking. The idea was that you could replicate a spit by making the chicken stand upright. A typical beer can was just the right size and height. Although it might seem primitive, you can still use a beer can if you don't have the roasting tool we show in our photos. If you like the flavor and the incredibly moist bird you get from "beer can" roasting, it's worth the money to get a vertical roaster, if for no other reason than that you can use all those fabulous juices to baste the bird as it cooks.

BEER CAN CHICKEN

Use a clean cotton mop to daub the chicken with the mopping sauce as it roasts on the grill.

MAKES 8 SERVINGS

2 fryer chickens, about 4 lb each

4 tsp salt

2 tsp ground black pepper

Two 12-oz cans lager- or pilsner-style beer

10 tbsp lemon juice

¼ cup Barbecue Sauce, plus additional (recipe follows)

1. Preheat a gas grill to medium-high; leave one burner off. If you are using a charcoal grill, build a fire and let it burn down until the coals are glowing red with a moderate coating of white ash. Spread the

LEFT TO RIGHT Position the back of the bird on the vertical roaster and gently roll the front of the chicken over the roaster; push the drumsticks forward until they are almost touching to properly balance the bird. Baste the chicken over medium-high heat until it turns golden brown. As the layers of the mopping sauce build up and caramelize, a rich, flavorful, mahogany crust will form on the chicken.

coals in an even bed on one side of the grill. Clean the cooking grate.

2. Blot the chickens dry and season with 2 teaspoons of the salt and 1 teaspoon of the pepper.

3. To make the mopping sauce: Pour half the beer from each can into a bowl. Add the lemon juice, barbecue sauce, the remaining 2 teaspoons salt, and the remaining 1 teaspoon pepper. Leave each beer can half full of beer and set aside.

4. If you are using vertical roasters, add the reserved beer to the reservoirs in the roasters, assemble the roasters, and set the chickens on the roasters. If cooking the chickens on the beer cans, set the cans on the grill over direct heat and carefully lower the chickens onto them. Position the legs so that they balance the chickens. Grill over direct heat, covered, until golden, mopping the chickens every 10 minutes with the mopping sauce, about 30 minutes.

5. Move the chickens to indirect heat, cover, and continue to cook until brown, mopping every 10 to 15 minutes, until they are a rich brown and cooked through (165°F), another 30 to 35 minutes.

6. Remove the chickens from the beer cans or roasters, transfer to a platter, and allow them to rest 15 minutes.

7. Cut each chicken into quarters with a kitchen fork and boning knife. Serve on a heated platter or plates, accompanied by additional barbecue sauce.

Barbecue Sauce

MAKES 3 CUPS

1⅔ cups ketchup

½ cup white vinegar

¼ cup water

¼ cup packed brown sugar

2 tbsp Worcestershire sauce

4½ tsp paprika

4½ tsp chili powder

4½ tsp dry mustard

1 tsp salt

¾ tsp ground cayenne pepper

Combine all the ingredients in a mixing bowl. Whisk until thoroughly mixed. Serve immediately or store in the refrigerator for up to 3 weeks.

GRILLED CHICKEN BULGOGI-STYLE

BULGOGI, ALSO spelled *bool kogi*, is a traditional Korean dish consisting of grilled meat served in a wrapper. Usually, bulgogi features beef, a popular meat in Korean cooking, but we've adapted it to chicken thighs. The word *bulgogi* translates as "fire meat," so you can expect some heat. The marinade contains sugar, which can burn quickly over the hot fire necessary to grill the bulgogi, so keep an eye on it as it cooks and move the chicken pieces to a cooler spot if the marinade starts to scorch.

MAKES 8 SERVINGS

1 cup minced scallions

3 tbsp minced ginger

1 tbsp minced garlic

⅓ cup light soy sauce

5 tbsp mirin (sweet rice wine)

1 tbsp vegetable oil

4 tsp toasted sesame seeds

2 tbsp granulated sugar

2 tsp Korean red pepper powder

8 boneless, skinless chicken thighs

½ cup Korean red pepper paste

16 leaves Napa cabbage or iceberg lettuce

Scallion Salad (recipe follows)

3 garlic cloves, thinly sliced and blanched (see note)

1. Whisk together the scallions, ginger, garlic, soy sauce, 3 tablespoons of the mirin, the oil, 3 teaspoons of the sesame seeds, 1 tablespoon of the sugar, and the red pepper powder to make a marinade.

2. Trim the chicken thighs to remove any pockets of fat and pound them until they are an even 1/2 inch thick. Cut each thigh in half. Add the pounded chicken thighs to the marinade and turn to coat the chicken evenly. Let marinate in the refrigerator for at least 1 and up to 12 hours.

3. Smash the remaining 1 teaspoon sesame seeds and whisk together with the red pepper paste, the remaining 2 tablespoons mirin, and the remaining 1 tablespoon sugar to make a sauce. Refrigerate the sauce in a covered container until ready to serve.

4. Preheat a gas grill to high. If you are using a charcoal grill, build a fire and let it burn down until the coals are glowing red with a moderate coating of white ash. Spread the coals in an even bed. Clean the cooking grate.

5. Remove the chicken from the marinade, letting any excess marinade drain off. Grill the chicken until browned and cooked through, about 4 to 5 minutes per side.

6. Arrange 2 cabbage or lettuce leaves on each plate. Place a chicken thigh on top, spoon some of the Scallion Salad over it, and garnish with slices of the garlic and the reserved sauce.

To blanch the garlic, bring a small pan of water to a boil. Add the sliced garlic and simmer for 30 seconds. Drain the garlic, rinse with cool water, and drain and rinse again. You can blanch the garlic ahead of time and keep it in the refrigerator until you are ready to use it.

Scallion Salad

MAKES 8 SERVINGS

½ tsp granulated sugar

¼ tsp sesame oil

1 tsp mirin (sweet rice wine)

½ tsp toasted sesame seeds, smashed

½ tsp Korean red pepper powder

1 tsp salt

2 cups scallion julienne

1. Combine the sugar, sesame oil, mirin, sesame seeds, red pepper powder, and salt.

2. Add the scallions and toss together just before serving.

LEMON-GINGER GRILLED CHICKEN

INSPIRED BY the Lemon Chicken which is a Chinese-restaurant favorite, this heavenly, slightly tart dish can be made on the grill or under the broiler, and is delicious served hot or cold.

MAKES 8 SERVINGS

4 tbsp lemon zest

⅔ cup lemon juice

4 tsp ginger, peeled and minced

4 tsp light brown sugar, firmly packed

1 tbsp peanut oil

1 tbsp salt, or to taste

4 Szechuan chili peppers, dried, seeds removed

3 lb chicken thighs, boneless, skinless

1. Combine the lemon zest, lemon juice, ginger, brown sugar, oil, salt, and chiles in a zip-close plastic bag. Add the chicken, squeeze out the air, and seal

the bag; turn to coat the chicken. Refrigerate, turning the bag occasionally, at least 15 minutes.

2. Spray the grill or broiler rack with nonstick spray. Preheat the grill or broiler on high. If broiling, position the rack about 5 inches from the heat source. Grill or broil the chicken until cooked through, about 6 minutes per side.

CHICKEN MOLE
Mole Poblano de Pollo

IN OAXACA, a state in southeastern Mexico, you can find dozens of different kinds of moles— some even claim that mole got its start in Oaxaca. This traditional mole is a rich harmony of spices, chiles, chocolate, nuts, and seeds.

MAKES 4 SERVINGS

3 tbsp olive oil

4 chicken legs (thigh and drumstick)

Salt as needed

Freshly ground pepper as needed

1 yellow onion, finely diced

1 green bell pepper, finely diced

1 jalapeño, finely chopped

¼ cup blanched almonds, chopped

3 garlic cloves, smashed

2 tbsp chili powder

1 tsp grated ginger root

½ tsp minced thyme

¼ tsp aniseed

¼ tsp ground cinnamon

3 plum tomatoes, peeled, seeded, and chopped

1 cup Chicken Broth (page 63), plus more as needed

3 tbsp almond butter

2 tablets Mexican chocolate, chopped (see note)

2 tbsp toasted sesame seeds

1. Preheat the oven to 350°F.

2. Heat the oil in a large Dutch oven over medium-high heat. Season the chicken with salt and pepper and then sear, turning as necessary, until browned on all sides, about 10 minutes. Remove and set aside.

3. Add the onion to the hot pan and sauté, stirring frequently, until golden brown, 10 to 12 minutes. Add the bell pepper, jalapeño, almonds, and garlic to the pan and sauté until aromatic, 3 to 4 minutes. Add the chili powder, ginger, thyme, aniseed, and cinnamon and sauté until aromatic, about 30 seconds, being careful not to burn the mixture. Add the tomatoes and stir to combine.

4. Pour in 1 cup of the broth and stir to dissolve any browned bits in the pan. Whisk in the almond butter, return the chicken to the pan along with any juices it may have released, and bring to a boil. Cover the pan and transfer to the oven. Braise the chicken, turning it occasionally, until tender, about 1 hour. Add a little more broth as needed throughout the cooking time to keep the chicken evenly moistened.

5. Remove the chicken from the pot and cover to keep warm. Add the chocolate to the sauce, stirring until melted. Season to taste with additional salt and pepper.

6. Return the chicken to the sauce and turn to coat evenly. Bring the mixture to a simmer over medium heat to heat the chicken through, and then serve at once. Garnish with the sesame seeds.

Mexican Chocolate

Look for flat cakes of Mexican chocolate, flavored with sugar, cinnamon, and finely ground almonds, in the ethnic foods section of large supermarkets or in Latin American markets.

SAUTÉED CHICKEN

with Moroccan Hot-and-Sweet Tomato Sauce

GINGER AND cinnamon give the tomato sauce its heat, while dark honey gives it a touch of sweetness. If you can't find the dark honey called for in the recipe, try using either Grade B maple syrup or molasses.

MAKES 4 SERVINGS

½ cup chopped onion

2 tsp minced garlic

4 boneless skinless chicken breast pieces (about 6 oz each)

Salt as needed

Freshly ground black pepper as needed

2 tbsp olive oil, plus as needed

2 tbsp butter

¾ tsp ground cinnamon

¼ tsp ground ginger

Pinch cayenne pepper or as needed

1 cup Tomato Sauce (recipe follows)

1 tbsp dark honey

1 tbsp sesame seeds, toasted

2 tbsp chopped cilantro leaves

1. Puree the onion and garlic in a food processor until a coarse paste forms. Set aside.

2. Blot the chicken dry and season with salt and pepper. Heat the olive oil in a casserole or Dutch oven over medium-high heat until it shimmers. Add the chicken pieces (do not overcrowd the pan; work in batches until all chicken is prepared and add more oil as needed) and sauté on the first side until about 2 to 3 minutes. Turn the chicken and sauté on the second side for another 3 minutes. Lower the heat if necessary to avoid scorching the chicken. Transfer to plate and keep warm.

3. Heat the butter in the pan over medium heat. Add the onion and garlic puree and cook, stirring frequently, until the onion is tender and has a sweet smell, about 10 minutes. Stir in the cinnamon, ginger, and cayenne and cook for another 2 to 3 minutes. Add the tomato sauce and honey to the pan and simmer for another 5 minutes. Season to taste with salt and pepper.

4. Return the chicken to the pan. Spoon the sauce over the chicken pieces, cover, and cook over low heat until the chicken is fully cooked, about 20 minutes. Sprinkle the sesame seeds and cilantro over the chicken before serving.

Tomato Sauce

MAKES 2 CUPS SAUCE

2 cups whole plum tomatoes, peeled and seeded

1 cup tomato puree

2 tbsp butter, sliced and chilled

Salt as needed

Freshly ground black pepper as needed

Puree the whole tomatoes in a food processor until a coarse paste forms. Transfer the tomatoes to a saucepan and bring to a simmer over low heat. Add the tomato puree and continue to simmer for another 10 minutes. Scatter the sliced butter over the sauce and swirl the pan until the butter is incorporated. Season to taste with salt and pepper.

PAN-SMOKED CHICKEN
with Apricot-Ancho Barbecue Glaze

P AN-SMOKING THE chicken leaves the flesh moist with a delicious smoky flavor. To learn more about pan-smoking and how to set up a portable smoker, see the sidebar *Making a Disposable Smoker* (page 26).

MAKES 8 SERVINGS

8 boneless chicken breasts

2 tsp salt

1 tsp ground black pepper

1¼ cups vegetable oil

½ cup cider vinegar

2 tbsp Worcestershire sauce

1 tbsp brown sugar

2 tsp dry mustard

1 tsp Tabasco sauce

1 tsp garlic powder

1 tsp onion powder

1 tbsp minced garlic

1 cup Apricot-Ancho Barbecue Glaze (recipe follows),
    or as needed

1. Season the chicken with the salt and pepper.

2. Combine the oil, vinegar, Worcestershire, sugar, mustard, Tabasco, garlic powder, onion powder, and minced garlic to make a marinade. Pour the marinade over the chicken, turning the chicken pieces to coat evenly. Cover and let marinate in the refrigerator for at least 3 hours or up to overnight.

3. Preheat the grill to medium. If you are using a charcoal grill, build a fire and let it burn down until the coals are glowing red with a light coating of white ash. Spread the coals in an even bed.

4. Place a rack over lightly dampened hardwood chips in an aluminum pan and place the smoker setup on the grill. Allow the chips to start smoking. Place the chicken on the rack and cover tightly. Smoke until the chicken is light golden brown, about 3 minutes.

5. Remove the chicken from the smoker and finishing grilling over direct heat until done (165°F), about 8 to 10 minutes more. Brush the chicken with barbecue glaze about halfway through the cooking time and again before removing it from the grill. Serve immediately, with additional barbecue sauce on the side if desired.

LEFT TO RIGHT Place the chicken on the smoker setup on the grill; leave enough space around the chicken to make sure that the smoke circulates properly. Do not smoke the chicken too long or the outside of the chicken will dry out.

Apricot-Ancho Barbecue Glaze

MAKES 4 CUPS

6 strips bacon, chopped

1½ cups small-dice yellow onion

1 tbsp minced garlic

¾ cup ketchup

¾ cup orange juice

¾ cup packed dark brown sugar

⅓ cup chopped dried apricots

¼ cup malt vinegar

2 ancho chiles, diced

1 tsp sweet or hot paprika

1 tsp dry mustard

1 tsp Tabasco sauce

1 tsp ground cayenne pepper

2 tsp salt

1 tsp ground black pepper

1. Sauté the bacon in a large sauté pan over medium heat until almost crisp, about 4 minutes. Add the onions and sauté until browned, about 5 minutes. Add the garlic and sauté until aromatic, about 1 minute.

2. Add all the remaining ingredients. Simmer until the apricots are very soft, about 10 minutes. Taste the sauce and season with additional salt and pepper, if needed.

3. Transfer to a blender and purée until relatively smooth. The glaze is ready to use now, or it can be cooled and stored in a covered container in the refrigerator for up to 1 week.

CHICKEN WITH OKRA

CHICKEN PIECES braise in an aromatic tomato sauce with okra in this intensely flavored dish.

Giving the okra a quick flash in the hot oil results in an interesting texture and flavor that you might not expect.

MAKES 4 SERVINGS

Salt as needed

¾ lb small okra pods, trimmed (see note opposite)

3 tbsp cider vinegar

¼ cup olive oil

4 whole chicken legs (drumsticks and thighs)

¾ cup minced onion

¼ cup minced green frying pepper

½ tsp dried oregano

⅛ tsp hot pepper flakes

1 pinch cinnamon

2 cups diced plum tomatoes

¾ tsp sugar, or as needed

2 tbsp lemon juice, or as needed

Freshly ground black pepper as needed

½ cup Chicken Broth (page 63) or water or as needed

3 tbsp chopped parsley

1. Fill a small dish with enough salt to make an even layer, about ¼ inch deep. Dip the trimmed ends of the okra into salt. Put the okra in a single layer on a baking sheet and sprinkle with the vinegar. Let the okra rest at room temperature for 1 hour. Rinse the okra and let it dry.

2. Preheat the oven to 375°F.

3. Heat half of the oil in a casserole or Dutch oven over medium-high heat until it shimmers. Sear the chicken in the oil, turning as necessary, until the chicken is lightly colored on all sides, 8 to 10 minutes. Transfer to a plate and keep warm.

4. Add as much of the remaining oil as needed to generously coat the casserole. Add the okra (working in batches to avoid crowding the pan) and sear on all sides until brown, about 4 minutes. Transfer to a plate and keep warm.

5. Add the onion and pepper to the casserole and sauté over medium heat, stirring frequently, until the onion is golden brown, about 10 minutes. Add the oregano, pepper flakes and cinnamon; sauté, stirring frequently, until aromatic, about 30 seconds. Add the tomatoes and cook until soft, thick, and lightly caramelized, about 10 minutes. Season to taste with the sugar, lemon juice, and additional salt and pepper.

6. Add the okra to the tomato sauce, pushing them under the surface, then arrange the chicken pieces on top of the okra. Add enough broth or water to bring the level of the liquid up to partially cover the chicken pieces. Bring the sauce up to a simmer. Immediately cover the casserole, transfer to the oven, and braise, basting the chicken legs occasionally, until the chicken is tender, about 45 minutes.

7. Transfer the chicken to a heated platter or plates. Return the casserole to high heat and simmer long enough to slightly reduce the sauce. Skim away any fat that rises to the surface and season to taste with additional lemon juice, salt, and pepper.

8. Ladle the sauce over the chicken pieces, sprinkle with parsley, and serve at once.

Okra

Choose small, young okra pods that are no more than 3 inches long. The pods should be clean and fresh; the pods will snap crisply when you bend them in half. Over-the-hill okra looks dull and dry.

Keep okra dry until just before you cook it; moisture will cause the pods to become slimy. You can store untrimmed, uncut okra in a paper or plastic bag in the refrigerator crisper drawer for up to three days, so plan on preparing okra very soon after you buy it.

GREEN CHILE AND PORK STEW WITH POTATOES

POBLANO CHILES and jalapeños give this dish its color and flavor. Whenever you work with hot chiles, wear gloves to protect your hands and be diligent about washing your hands, your tools, and the cutting board when you are done. Serve warm flour tortillas and a little grated Monterey Jack cheese to accompany this stew.

MAKES 6 SERVINGS

2 tbsp canola oil

2 lb boneless pork shoulder, cut into 1-inch cubes

Salt as needed

Freshly ground black pepper as needed

2 large yellow onions, cut into ¾-inch dice

1 tbsp minced garlic

6 cups Chicken Broth (page 63)

¼ cup tomato purée

3 to 4 fresh poblano chiles, roasted, seeded, peeled, and cut into ½-inch pieces (page 49)

2 tbsp mild red chili powder

1 tbsp ground cumin

2 tsp ground Mexican oregano

2 fresh jalapeño peppers, seeded, finely minced

2 tbsp green Tabasco sauce

1 tsp white vinegar

3 cups cubed russet potatoes, peeled

2 cups cooked cannelini beans, rinsed and drained

⅓ cup chopped cilantro

3 tbsp chopped flat-leaf parsley

1. Heat the oil in a casserole or Dutch oven over medium heat until it shimmers. Season the pork with salt and pepper and sauté until lightly colored on all sides. Transfer the pork to a plate or dish using

a slotted spoon, allowing most of the oil to drain back into the casserole. Return the casserole to the heat, add the onions and garlic and sauté, stirring frequently, until translucent, 6 to 8 minutes.

2. Return the pork and any juices it may have released to the casserole. Add the broth, tomato purée, poblanos, chili powder, cumin, and oregano; bring the liquid to a boil. Immediately adjust the heat for a gentle simmer. Simmer the stew, covered, for 1 hour, stirring occasionally.

3. Add the jalapeños, Tabasco, vinegar, potatoes, and beans. Continue to simmer, covered, until the potatoes and pork are very tender, about 20 minutes. Stir in the cilantro and parsley, and season to taste with additional salt and pepper.

4. Serve in heated bowls.

JERKED GAME HENS
with Rice and Beans and Grilled Pineapple–Jícama Salsa

Y OU CAN substitute chicken breast, pork chops, or rabbit for the game hens in this recipe; adjust the cooking times accordingly.

MAKES 6 SERVINGS

6 game hens

¾ cup Jerk Rub (recipe follows)

½ tsp salt

Rice and Beans (page 185)

2 cups Grilled Pineapple–Jícama Salsa (recipe follows)

1. Remove the backbone of each game hen by holding it upright, with the backbone facing you. Run a knife down either side to remove the bone, then lay it on its back and press on the breast to flatten the hen.

2. Rub the jerk rub on the game hens to coat evenly. (Wear gloves when working with the rub.) Transfer to a shallow pan, cover, and let marinate in the refrigerator for at least 8 and up to 12 hours.

3. Preheat a gas grill to medium. If you are using a charcoal grill, build a fire and let it burn down until the coals are glowing red with a moderate coating of white ash. Spread the coals in an even bed. Clean the cooking grate.

4. Brush off any excess rub from the game hens. Season the hens with the salt. Grill the game hens over direct heat until marked, about 4 minutes per side. Move the hens to indirect heat and continue to grill, covered and turning as needed, until cooked through (165°F), about 12 to 15 minutes more.

5. Serve the game hens on a heated platter or individual plates with the rice and beans on the side and the salsa spooned on top of the hens.

Grilled Pineapple–Jícama Salsa

WHILE YOU have the grill fired up, toss on a few items to have on hand for this quick and delicious salsa.

MAKES 4½ CUPS

3 tbsp lime juice

2 tbsp olive oil

2 tbsp chopped cilantro

½ tsp salt, or to taste

½ tsp black pepper, or to taste

2 cups diced grilled pineapple

1 cup jícama julienne

¾ cup small-dice red onion

¾ cup small-dice red pepper

2 tsp minced jalapeño, or to taste

Whisk together the lime juice, oil, cilantro, salt, and pepper in a salad bowl. Add the pineapple, jícama, onion, and peppers, and toss to combine well. Adjust seasoning to taste with salt and pepper. Refrigerate the salsa until ready to use. Store any unused salsa in a covered container in the refrigerator for up to 2 days.

Jerk Rub

MAKE SURE you wear gloves when working with the rub; if the oil from those Scotch bonnets comes anywhere near sensitive skin, it burns like fire.

MAKES ¾ CUP

½ medium yellow onion, chopped

3 scallions, chopped

1 Scotch bonnet, chopped

2 tbsp chopped thyme

2 tsp ground allspice

1½ tsp ground cinnamon

½ tsp ground cloves

½ tsp grated nutmeg

¼ cup dark rum

¼ cup soy sauce

¼ cup vegetable oil

Combine all the ingredients in a blender and purée to a smooth, thick paste. Refrigerate until ready to use. Store any unused rub in a covered container in the refrigerator for up to 3 days.

SEARED COD
in a Rich Broth with Fall Vegetables

ONE OF the more common varieties of fish, here cod is seared after being coated with a fine powder of ground, dried shiitake mushrooms. Autumn vegetables and pasta garnish this rich broth for an uncommon twist to a common fish.

MAKES 6 SERVINGS

1¼ lb fettuccine pasta

2¼ lb cod fillet

4 oz dried shiitake mushrooms

½ tsp salt, or to taste

½ tsp ground white pepper

2 tbsp olive oil

5 cups Vegetable Broth (page 65)

1 lb haricots verts, cut into 1-inch lengths, blanched

5 oz carrot, cut into thin strips, blanched

5 oz yellow turnip, cut into thin strips, blanched

5 oz white turnip, cut into thin strips, blanched

1 tbsp ginger, minced

3 oz enoki mushrooms, cut into 1½-inch lengths

3 tbsp chives, cut into ½-inch lengths

3 tbsp scallions, thinly sliced

1. Preheat the oven to 450°F.

2. Bring a large pot of salted water to a boil. Cook the pasta for 8 to 10 minutes, or until tender to the bite. Reserve.

3. Cut the cod into six portions. Refrigerate until needed.

4. Grind the dried shiitake mushrooms to a powder in a spice grinder. Blot the cod pieces with paper toweling to remove excess moisture, and season with a small amount of salt and pepper. Dredge each piece in the ground mushrooms. Add the oil to a preheated sauté pan over medium-high heat, and sauté the cod until browned, about 2 minutes per side.

5. Transfer the cod to a baking dish and bake in the 450°F oven until thoroughly cooked, about 6 to 7 minutes.

6. While the cod is baking, bring the broth to a simmer in a saucepan. Add the pasta, haricots verts, carrots, turnips, and ginger. Simmer until heated through, 3 to 4 minutes.

7. Transfer the broth, pasta, and vegetables to large soup plates. Arrange the pasta to make a bed for the cod in the center of the plate. Place the cod on the pasta and garnish with the enoki mushrooms and 1 teaspoon of both chives and scallions.

SAUTÉED DUCK BREAST
with Pinot Noir Sauce

Most recipes for duck involve a step designed to render away much of the fat during cooking, leaving the skin deliciously crisp.

MAKES 6 SERVINGS

1 bottle Pinot Noir wine (750 ml)

6 cups Chicken Broth (page 63)

2 tbsp vegetable oil

1 onion, diced

4 celery stalks, diced

2 carrots, diced

3 tbsp tomato paste

1 crushed garlic clove, 4 parsley stems, 6 black peppercorns, ¼ tsp dried thyme, 1 bay leaf, tied in a cheesecloth to make a pouch

½ tsp olive oil

2¾ tsp salt, or to taste

2 tsp freshly ground black pepper, or to taste

2¼ lb duck breast, boneless, skin on, trimmed of excess fat

3 tbsp butter

1. Preheat the oven to 400°F.

2. Bring the wine and the broth to a boil separately and reduce for 10 minutes.

3. While the liquids are reducing, heat the vegetable oil in a large sauté pan over medium-high heat. Add the onions and cook for 5 minutes, or until slightly translucent. Add the celery and the carrot and sauté until lightly caramelized, about 10 minutes.

4. Add the tomato paste to the caramelized vegetables and cook to a deep red-brown, stirring constantly, about 5 minutes.

5. Deglaze the pan with the reduced wine and simmer until reduced by half. Add the reduced broth and the cheesecloth pouch and simmer until the sauce lightly coats the back of a spoon, about 15 to 20 minutes.

6. While the sauce is simmering, heat the olive oil over medium heat in a large sauté pan. Season the duck with half of the salt and pepper. Sauté the duck breasts, skin side down, until the fat has rendered and the skin is dark golden brown, about 8 to 10 minutes. Turn the duck breasts skin side up and roast in the oven until cooked through, about 5 to 6 minutes. Hold the duck in a warm place if the sauce is not ready.

7. Season the sauce with the remaining salt and pepper, and swirl in the butter just before serving.

FLOUNDER SAUTÉ
à la Meunière

À la meunière—in the style of the miller's wife—means to dredge in flour, sauté in butter, and serve with brown butter sauce and parsley. Browning the butter gives it a rich, nutty flavor that pairs well with mild flounder. Serve with lightly garnished boiled potatoes and steamed vegetables.

MAKES 8 SERVINGS

3 lb flounder fillet

2 tbsp extra-virgin olive oil

7 tbsp butter

1 tsp salt, or to taste

½ tsp freshly ground black pepper, or to taste

½ cup all-purpose flour

Juice of 1 lemon

¼ cup parsley, chopped

1. Cut the flounder into eight 6-ounce portions.

2. Season the flour with salt and pepper.

3. Heat the oil and 3 tablespoons butter in a large sauté pan.

4. Season the fish with some of the salt and pepper, and dredge in the flour.

5. Sauté the fish for 1 to 2 minutes on each side, until lightly browned and crisp. Transfer the fish to a heated platter or plates and keep warm. Be very careful not to overcook fish.

6. Pour out any excess oil from pan, if necessary.

7. Add the remaining butter to the sauté pan and place over medium-high heat until the butter turns brown and has a nutty aroma, 2 minutes. Add the lemon juice and parsley and swirl the pan to blend the sauce. It should be almost foamy.

8. Spoon or pour the sauce over the flounder and serve at once

BAKED HAM
with Mustard Sauce

I F YOU think of baked ham only in terms of a shiny glazed roast with pineapple rings and maraschino cherries, this will be a revelation. The sauce has a delightful chunky texture. Its piquant flavors set off the smoky ham beautifully.

MAKES 8 SERVINGS

1 tbsp vegetable oil

1 cup minced onion

1 tbsp minced garlic

½ cup white wine vinegar

⅓ cup spicy brown mustard

2 tbsp sugar

½ tsp celery seed

½ tsp salt

¼ tsp ground black pepper

3 lb boneless ham roast

1. Preheat the oven to 350°F.

2. To make the mustard sauce, heat the oil in a medium sauté pan over medium heat. Add the onion and garlic and cook, stirring from time to time, until the onion becomes soft and translucent, about 5 minutes.

3. Add the white wine vinegar, mustard, sugar, and celery seed. Bring to a simmer over low heat, stirring to completely dissolve the sugar. Simmer until flavorful and very hot, about 3 minutes. Taste the sauce and season it with salt and pepper.

4. Score the ham with a wide crosshatch pattern, making incisions about ¼ inch deep. Set the ham on a rack in a roasting pan and spoon enough sauce over the ham to coat it evenly and lightly. Bake the ham, spooning a little additional sauce over the ham every 10 to 15 minutes, until it is heated through and the sauce forms a glaze, about 1 hour.

5. Allow the ham to rest for 5 to 10 minutes before slicing and serving. Return the remaining sauce to a simmer and serve it with the ham.

Ghee

Ghee, a type of cooking butter used in Indian cooking, can be purchased in jars at Asian or Indian markets, but it is easy to make yourself.

Cube 1 pound of cold unsalted butter, place in a saucepan, and set over low heat. Once the butter has melted, increase the heat slightly. The pure butterfat will become very clear. Some foam will rise to the top; skim it away.

Increase the heat slightly and continue to cook the butter until the milk solids that have fallen to the bottom of the pan turn a deep golden color.

Immediately remove the pan from the heat. Ladle the clear butterfat, or ghee, into a clean container; discard the liquid at the bottom of the pan. You can keep ghee in the refrigerator for up to 2 weeks.

LAMB KHORMA

LAMB KHORMA is a sensuous curry made by simmering lamb pieces with yogurt and cream, and thickening the sauce with a cashew paste. If you can find goat or sheep's milk yogurt, it will make a discernable difference in the taste.

MAKES 8 SERVINGS

2½ lb boneless lamb leg, cut into 1½-inch cubes

Salt as needed

Ground white pepper as needed

1½ cups plain yogurt

2 tbsp minced ginger root

1 tbsp minced garlic

2 tsp ground cardamom

12 oz cashew nuts

¼ cup ghee (see note) or canola oil

3 cups small-dice yellow onion

1 tsp ground cumin

1 tsp ground cardamom

1 tsp ground fennel

2 tbsp ground coriander

6 Thai bird chiles, chopped, or to taste

⅓ cup chopped cilantro stems

1 cup heavy cream

½ cup chopped cilantro leaves

1 cup pan-roasted cashews (see note, page 32)

4 cups steamed saffron rice (see note, opposite)

1. Trim the lamb and cut it into large pieces. Season with salt and pepper and put in a bowl. Add the yogurt, 1 tablespoon ginger, the garlic, and cardamom. Stir or toss until the ingredients are evenly distributed and the lamb is coated. Cover and refrigerate for at least 30 minutes and up to 3 hours.

2. Put the cashews in a small bowl and add enough hot water to cover them. Let the cashews soak for 30 minutes and then drain. Grind the drained cashews to a coarse paste in a food processor. Set aside.

3. Heat the ghee or oil in a casserole or Dutch oven over medium heat until it shimmers. Add the onion and sauté until transparent, 6 to 8 minutes. Add the cumin, cardamom, fennel, the remaining ginger, and the coriander. Cook, stirring often until aromatic, about 2 minutes. Add the chiles, cilantro stems, and cashew paste and stir well to be sure that nothing is sticking. Sauté, stirring frequently and adding water a tablespoon at a time if necessary, until the mixture is very aromatic, about 2 minutes.

4. Add the lamb and the yogurt marinade, increase the heat, and stir until the pieces are evenly coated. Once the meat's juices begin to flow, reduce heat to low, cover, and simmer very slowly, stirring occasionally, until the meat is nearly tender, about 1½ hours.

5. Add the cream and continue to simmer until the

curry is flavorful and thickened and the lamb is tender, 10 to 15 minutes. Season to taste with salt, pepper, and the Thai chiles. Garnish with cilantro leaves and cashews, and serve with saffron rice.

Steamed Saffron Rice

Steamed rice is a perfect backdrop to many of the dishes featured in this book. Perfectly steamed rice should be hot and fragrant. The type of rice you choose will have an effect on the cooked grain's texture. Jasmine or basmati rice has long kernels that are dry and have a tendency to separate. Sticky rice, as well as short- and medium-grain varieties, is moister with a greater tendency to hold together. Saffron rice has a rich golden hue.

Measure the rice, planning on about 1 cup dried rice for 6 people. Combine the rice and 2 cups cold water in a sauce pan. Add about 1 teaspoon salt (more or less to your taste) and bring the water to a boil over high heat. For saffron rice, add 4 or 5 crushed saffron threads. Immediately turn the heat to low, cover the pan tightly, and cook until the rice is tender. Check the rice from time to time as it steams; you may need to add a bit more water if the pot is dry but the rice is still crunchy. White rice usually take about 15 minutes. Brown rice can take anywhere from 35 to 45 minutes.

BROILED LAMB CHOPS
with White Bean and Rosemary Ragout

A SIMPLE RAGOUT of cannellini beans and fresh, pungent rosemary provides an ideal accompaniment to the full flavor of roasted lamb. This elegant, easy-to-prepare dish is great for entertaining.

MAKES 8 SERVINGS

6 tbsp reduced-sodium soy sauce

2 tbsp Dijon mustard

2 tbsp Worcestershire sauce

2 tbsp vegetable oil

1 tsp freshly ground black pepper, or to taste

2 tbsp chopped rosemary

4 tsp chopped thyme

4 tsp chopped sage

16 double lamb chops (rib or loin), frenched

1¾ cup cannellini beans, drained, juices reserved

1 tbsp demi-glace concentrate

1 tsp lemon zest

Salt, to taste

Freshly ground black pepper, to taste

1. Combine the soy sauce, mustard, Worcestershire sauce, vegetable oil, 1 teaspoon pepper, 1 tablespoon rosemary, and the thyme and sage in a zip-close bag; add the lamb. Squeeze out the air and seal the bag; turn to coat the lamb with the marinade ingredients. Refrigerate for 30 minutes.

2. While the lamb is marinating, prepare the white bean ragout. Combine the cannellini beans, ½ cup of their reserved juices, 1 tablespoon rosemary, the demi-glace concentrate, and the lemon zest in a saucepan.

3. Bring the mixture to a simmer, stirring constantly. Reduce the heat to medium low and continue to simmer the ragout for 10 minutes, stirring occasionally. If the ragout becomes too thick, add 2 to 3 tablespoons of the reserved juices from the beans to restore consistency. Keep warm.

4. Spray the broiler rack with nonstick cooking spray; preheat the broiler.

5. Remove the lamb chops from the marinade. Discard the marinade and brush off any excess herbs that may have stuck to the lamb. Be sure to wipe any excess marinade off the bones or else they will burn under the broiler. Season the chops with salt and pepper.

6. Broil the lamb chops 5 inches from the heat until done to taste, 2 to 3 minutes on each side for medium.

7. Spoon about ¼ cup of the white bean ragout onto a warm plate and nestle 2 of the lamb chops in the sauce.

BERBERE GRILLED LEG OF LAMB

THE COOKING time suggested here should produce a nice rare doneness, not bloody. However, it is hard to gauge how fast things will cook over indirect heat, so it is important to use an accurate meat thermometer.

MAKES 8 SERVINGS

1 leg of lamb, boneless roast, about 3 lb

1½ tsp salt

¾ tsp coarse-ground black pepper

¼ cup olive oil

¼ cup slivered garlic

½ cup Berbere Spice Paste (opposite)

Grilled Potato and Red Onion Fans (page 188)

Grilled Leeks (page 194)

1. Unroll the leg of lamb and make cuts as necessary to butterfly the leg (see note opposite). It should be an even thickness throughout, about 1½ to 1¾ inches. Blot dry with paper towels and season with salt and pepper. Brush the top with half of the olive oil, sprinkle with half of the garlic, and spread with half of the spice paste. Turn the lamb over and repeat with the remaining oil, garlic, and spice paste.

2. Marinate the lamb, covered, in the refrigerator for at least 6 and up to 12 hours.

3. Preheat a gas grill to medium-high. Leave one burner off. If using a charcoal grill, build a fire and let it burn down until the coals are glowing red with a moderate coating of white ash. Push the coals to one side of the grill. Clean the cooking grate.

4. Grill the lamb over direct heat until marked, about 3 minutes on each side. Move the lamb to the cool side of the grill. Continue to cook, turning every 15 minutes, until desired doneness is reached, about 1 hour and 10 minutes for medium-rare.

5. Remove the lamb from the grill and allow it to rest at least 10 minutes before slicing. Serve with the potatoes and leeks.

ABOVE Evenly spread the Berbere Spice Paste over the butterflied lamb to ensure that the flavor of the marinade is evenly distributed.

Berbere Spice Paste

MAKES 2⅔ CUPS

4 pequin chiles, seeds and stem removed

2 tsp cardamom seeds

1 tsp coriander seeds

1 tsp cumin seeds

1 tsp fenugreek seeds

1 tsp black peppercorns

¼ tsp allspice berries

¼ tsp whole cloves

1 cup coarsely chopped yellow onion

2 tbsp garlic cloves

2 tbsp Hungarian paprika

1 tbsp cayenne

½ tsp ground ginger

¼ tsp ground cinnamon

¼ tsp grated nutmeg

¼ cup red wine vinegar

¼ cup vegetable oil

1 cup water, as needed

1. Toast the pequin chiles, cardamom seeds, coriander seeds, cumin seeds, fenugreek seeds, black peppercorns (whole), allspice berries, and cloves in a dry skillet until aromatic, 4 minutes. Transfer to a bowl and let the spices cool to room temperature.

2. Grind the whole spices and chiles in a food processor until coarsely ground. Add the onion, garlic, paprika, cayenne, ginger, cinnamon, and nutmeg. Process to a coarse, heavy paste.

3. Add the vinegar and oil with the machine running. Add the water gradually, stopping when you have a loose paste.

4. The mixture is ready to use now or it can be transferred to a container and stored in the refrigerator for up to 3 weeks.

Butterflying Meats

The idea behind butterflying a cut of meat is to create an evenly thin cut with lots of surface area from a cut that is not naturally thin and flat in shape.

To butterfly a leg of lamb, unroll a boneless leg roast so that it lies flat, with the smooth side of the meat facing down. The rougher side, the side that was next to the bone, should be facing up. You'll see that some parts of the roast are thicker than others. Rest your hand over that part of the roast, keeping it parallel to the cutting surface. Holding a boning or filleting knife parallel to the work surface, make a horizontal slice into the meat. The cut should go from the interior toward the outside edge of the roast. Continue cutting just through the thicker portion. Stop cutting about ½ inch away from the edge of the meat to make a hinge.

Open out the meat flat, just the way you would open a book. Press the meat flat. Keep making cuts like this over the surface of the roast until you have a piece that has an even thickness. Pound the meat slightly to be sure that it cooks evenly on the grill.

LAMB MEATBALLS STEWED WITH HOT TOMATOES
Kefta

FRAGRANT AND flavorful meatballs like these are a staple in many Mediterranean cuisines. Be sure to keep the ingredients for the meatballs very cold until you are ready to mix them. It helps the meatballs hold together as they simmer.

MAKES 6 SERVINGS

MEATBALLS

1 lb ground lamb or beef

½ cup coarsely grated yellow onion

¼ cup dry bread crumbs

¼ cup chopped flat-leaf parsley

1 tsp minced garlic

¾ tsp ground cumin

¾ tsp paprika

½ tsp minced ginger root

¼ tsp ground cardamom

3 tbsp water

¼ chopped cilantro

1 tsp salt or as needed

¼ tsp ground black pepper or as needed

2 tbsp olive oil

½ cup chopped yellow onion

¼ tsp harissa

¼ tsp cumin

¼ tsp cinnamon

2 or 3 saffron threads, lightly crushed, optional

3 cups Tomato Sauce (page 144)

1. Combine the lamb or beef, grated onion, bread crumbs, parsley, garlic, cumin, paprika, ginger root, cardamom, water, 2 tablespoons cilantro, 1 teaspoon salt, and ¼ teaspoon pepper in a bowl. Mix by hand with a wooden spoon until slightly sticky. Chill at least 1 and up to 8 hours before shaping into oval meatballs about 1 inch in diameter.

2. Heat the olive oil in a deep skillet or Dutch oven over medium-high heat until it shimmers. Add the meatballs to the oil and cook, turning as necessary, until they are browned on all sides, about 8 minutes. Transfer the meatballs to a plate and set aside.

3. Add the chopped onion, harissa, cumin, cinnamon, and saffron, if using, to the pan. Sauté, stirring frequently, until the onion is tender and translucent, 6 to 8 minutes. Add the tomato sauce to the pan, stirring well to dissolve any browned bits in the pan. Bring the sauce to a simmer. Return the meat-

balls to the sauce along with any juices they may have released. Simmer the meatballs over low heat until they are cooked through and the sauce is very flavorful, about 15 minutes. Stir in the remaining cilantro and season to taste with salt and pepper. Serve at once on heated plates.

CLASSIC BOILED LOBSTER

AVAILABLE THROUGHOUT the year, fresh lobsters should be purchased live and stored for only a few hours prior to cooking. It is imperative that lobster be cooked live or killed just prior to cooking. Here a fragrant lemon-herb dipping sauce complements the creamy white meat of the lobster.

MAKES 8 SERVINGS

1 cup butter

2 tbsp lemon juice

4 tsp minced parsley

4 tsp minced tarragon

4 tsp minced watercress

½ tsp salt, or to taste

¼ tsp freshly ground black pepper, or to taste

8 lobsters, 1½ lb each

4 lemons, cut into wedges

1. To make a dipping sauce, melt the butter in a skillet; add the lemon juice, parsley, tarragon, watercress, salt, and pepper. Transfer the sauce to a bowl.

2. Fill an 8-quart stock pot two-thirds full of salted water and bring to a rolling boil. Add the lobsters, cooking in batches if necessary, and boil until they are bright red, 10 to 11 minutes. Replenish the salted water as necessary and be sure to bring the water to a boil in between every batch.

3. Use tongs to place the lobsters on a platter. Serve accompanied by the lemon-herb dipping sauce and lemon wedges.

GRILLED LOBSTER
with Broccoli Raab and
Cannellini Beans with Pancetta

THIS IS an incredible meal. It has a really good ratio of lobster to beans to greens, and the flavor is phenomenal. It is rich and earthy and hearty without being too filling. Peeling all of the lobsters is a little time-consuming for the cook but well worth the effort, since the juices from the lobster work their way into the broccoli raab dish for even more flavor.

MAKES 8 SERVINGS

Water, as needed

Salt, as needed

8 lobsters, about 1½ lb each, prepared for grilling (see note)

2 tbsp olive oil

1 tsp ground black pepper

Broccoli Raab and Cannellini Beans with Pancetta (page 104)

½ cup freshly grated Parmesan cheese

1. Preheat a gas grill to high. If you are using a charcoal grill, build a fire and let it burn down until the coals are glowing red with a light coating of white ash. Spread the coals in an even bed. Clean the cooking grate.

2. Brush the tail and claw meat with the olive oil and season with salt and pepper.

3. Place the prepared lobsters on the grill, shell-side down. Grill the lobsters about 2 to 3 minutes on each side, until the shell turns reddish-orange.

4. Remove the tail and the claw meat from the shells, and cut each tail into ½-inch-thick-slices. Set aside.

5. Divide the broccoli raab and cannelini beans with pancetta among 8 serving plates and sprinkle with the Parmesan cheese. Place the tail and claw meat of each lobster atop the broccoli raab and bean mixture and serve.

Preparing Lobster for the Grill

Purchasing live lobster for cooking guarantees the best flavor and texture. Lay a live lobster belly-side down on a work surface, head pointing toward your cutting hand. Insert the tip of a chef's knife into the base of its head to kill the lobster quickly, and pull the knife all the way down through the shell, splitting the head in half. Turn the lobster 180 degrees. Place the tip of the knife at the same point as your first cut, and then cut completely through the shell of the body and tail.

REMOVING THE MEAT FROM A COOKED LOBSTER

If a recipe calls for only the meat of a cooked lobster, you will need to partially cook the lobster by either grilling, broiling, boiling, or steaming it just until the shell turns a bright color. This firms up the flesh enough so that it will separate from the shell. If you try to pull the flesh from a raw lobster, you will simply pull apart the flesh. Once the lobster is partially cooked, let it cool completely. Twist the tail away from the body. Squeeze the underside of the tail shell to crack it partially and loosen it, then pull the tail meat away in one piece.

Stand the claw on the work surface with its "thumb" edge down. Use the heel of the knife to cut into the outside edge of each claw, without cutting through to the meat, then swivel the knife sharply to the side to crack apart the claw shell. Remove the claw in one piece by wiggling the meat as you pull it out, taking care to slip the "thumb" out slowly. Use a large knife or kitchen shears to cut through the leg knuckles, then pull out the knuckle meat.

Serving Oily-fleshed Fish

Fish like mackerel, tuna, herring, sardines, and salmon have a rich texture, due in large part to the oils they contain. Oily fish is a great source for a beneficial type of oil, known as omega-3s. As long as you keep your servings moderate, most adults can safely enjoy a meal or two each week that features salmon or other oily fish without worry.

When you grill these luscious fish, you have plenty of options when it comes to a good wine to serve. Both white and red wines can be great partners. If you are interested in a white wine, look for wines that are high in acid. Some suggestions include sauvignon blanc, especially those from the Loire Valley in France and from New Zealand. Grüner Veltliner and Rieslings from Austria and Germany are a great match for the rich flavors and textures of these fish. You might also try a white Bordeaux or a crisp rosé from France. The deep flavors from the grill may inspire you to try a red wine with your fish such as Pinot Noir or Beaujolais.

GRILLED SPANISH MACKEREL
with Grilled Asparagus and Sweet Peppers

MACKEREL IS a moderately fatty fish with a distinct flavor. We've kept seasonings simple here to let the fish shine.

MAKES 6 SERVINGS

2 tbsp lemon juice

4 tsp salt

2 tsp ground black pepper

⅓ cup vegetable oil

12 thyme sprigs

6 pan-dressed Spanish mackerel, 14 oz each

1 lemon, cut into wedges

Grilled Asparagus and Sweet Peppers (recipe follows)

1. Preheat a gas grill to medium. If you are using a charcoal grill, build a fire and let it burn down until the coals are glowing red with a moderate coating of white ash. Spread the coals in an even bed. Clean the cooking grate.

2. Combine the lemon juice, salt, pepper, and 1 tablespoon of the oil. Place 2 thyme sprigs in the cavity of each fish. Brush the lemon juice mixture over the inside and outside of each fish. Brush the outside of the fish with some of the remaining oil. (Reserve any excess oil to brush the fish as it grills if needed.)

3. Grill the mackerel over direct heat, turning as necessary, until the fish is cooked through, about 6 to 8 minutes per side.

4. Serve the mackerel at once on a heated platter or individual plates with the lemon wedges and the Grilled Asparagus and Sweet Peppers.

Grilled Asparagus and Sweet Peppers

CHOOSE THICK spears of asparagus for the grill. The flavor is richer. We strongly suggest peeling the stems for the best texture.

MAKES 8 SERVINGS

2 lb asparagus, trimmed

4 red peppers, cored and quartered

4 thyme sprigs

1 rosemary sprig

2 garlic cloves, sliced

½ cup olive oil

Juice of 1 lemon

Zest of 1 lemon

1 tsp salt

1 tsp ground black pepper

½ tsp crushed red pepper

1. Combine all the ingredients in a zip-close bag. Let marinate in the refrigerator for at least 2 and up to 8 hours.

2. Preheat a gas grill to medium heat. If you are using a charcoal grill, build a fire and let it burn down until the coals are glowing red with a moderate coating of white ash. Spread the coals in an even bed. Clean the cooking grate.

3. Remove the asparagus and peppers from the marinade and grill over direct heat until browned on both sides, about 5 to 7 minutes on each side.

MONKFISH STEW
with Wine, Peppers, and Almonds

FOR AN elegant presentation, you can puree the vegetables and broth before you add the ground almonds. This recipe is for a chunky, rustic stew with lots of textures and colors. A flameproof earthenware casserole, or *cazuela*, is perfect for this dish, but be certain that any earthenware cookware is manufactured to stand up to direct heat.

MAKES 6 SERVINGS

⅓ cup olive oil

2½ lb monkfish fillets, cut into 2-inch cubes

Salt as needed

Freshly ground black pepper as needed

2 cups sliced yellow onion

1½ cups thinly sliced carrots

2 tsp thinly sliced garlic

2 cups diced plum tomatoes

2 tbsp all-purpose flour

2½ cups Fish or Vegetable Broth (pages 64–65)

⅔ cup dry white wine

1 bay leaf

⅓ cup whole blanched almonds

8 to 10 saffron threads, lightly crushed

1⅓ cups green peas, blanched if fresh or thawed if frozen

1 cup roasted red bell pepper strips

1. Heat half of the olive oil in a casserole or cazuela over medium-high heat until it shimmers. Season the monkfish with salt and pepper. Sauté in the hot oil until it is colored on both sides, 3 to 4 minutes. Work in batches to avoid overcrowding the pan. Transfer to a plate or dish with a slotted spoon letting the oil drain back into the casserole.

2. Return the casserole to the stove and heat the remaining oil until it shimmers. Add the onion, carrots, and 1 teaspoon garlic and sauté, stirring occasionally, until translucent, about 6 minutes. Add the tomatoes and cook until tender and broken down, then add the flour. Stir well to blend the flour in evenly and cook until pasty, about 5 minutes.

3. Stir in the broth and wine until evenly blended. Use a whisk if necessary to work out any lumps in the stew. Add the bay leaf and bring the mixture to a boil. Immediately reduce the heat until the mixture simmers slowly. Simmer, stirring frequently, until thickened and flavorful, 10 to 12 minutes.

4. Pound the almonds, saffron, and the remaining garlic in a mortar and pestle or chop them together with a chef's knife to a coarse paste. Add the paste to the tomato and broth mixture, stir well, and simmer 2 to 3 minutes.

5. Arrange the monkfish on top of the stew and top with the peas and roasted peppers. Season to taste with salt and pepper. Cover tightly and simmer until the fish is opaque throughout, 10 to 12 minutes. Serve in heated bowls.

MANDARIN PANCAKES

THESE SIMPLE pancakes can be served with the Mu Shu Vegetables on page 177, or used with other fillings in a similar fashion. They can be made ahead of time and frozen.

MAKES ABOUT 18 PANCAKES

2 cups all-purpose flour

¾ to 1 cup boiling water, as needed

3 tbsp sesame oil, or as needed

1. Sift the flour into a large bowl, add ¾ cup boiling water to the flour, and begin stirring it in immediately, adding a little additional water if necessary to make a dough. Knead the warm dough until smooth. Wrap the dough and let it rest at room temperature for 30 minutes.

2. Turn the rested dough out onto a floured surface. Cut the dough in half. Use a lightly floured rolling pin to roll each half out until it is ¼-inch thick. Use a cookie cutter to cut out 3-inch circles of dough.

3. Brush ½ teaspoon of sesame oil over the tops of 2 dough circles. Lay one pancake on top of another, so that the oiled sides are together. (The edges don't have to line up perfectly.) Roll out the pancakes to form a 6-inch circle. Repeat with the remainder of the pancakes. Use a damp towel to cover the prepared pancakes, to keep them from drying out as you work.

4. Heat a skillet over low heat. Add one of the pancake pairs and cook until browned, about 2 minutes. Turn and cook on the second side until browned, another 1 to 2 minutes. Remove the paired pancakes from the pan and pull them apart. Repeat with the remainder of the pancakes. Serve immediately.

Thai Ingredients

Thai cuisine calls for a number of ingredients that once were difficult to find unless you lived near a thriving Asian community.

Galangal is one such ingredient. It looks and tastes a little like fresh ginger, but adds a unique flavor you cannot get from ginger alone.

Thai basil, sometimes known as anise basil or holy basil, has deep green leaves that are smaller and more pointed than Western basil leaves. They grow on purplish stems topped with pretty, reddish-purple flower buds. You can substitute other basils for Thai basil if necessary.

Wild lime leaves add sharpness to dishes. Lemon or lime zest can be substituted if you can't locate fresh wild lime leaves.

Cilantro is stocked in most grocery stores. Select bunches of cilantro that still have the roots attached, if you can find them. Many Southeast Asian dishes call for the root. Once you've thoroughly rinsed the root, chop it very fine with a chef's knife.

Fish sauce, curry pastes, and coconut milk are ubiquitous in curries and stir-fries. Taste several varieties to find the one you like best.

JUNGLE CURRY

GALANGAL IS an essential ingredient in this dish. You can often find this rhizome in some specialty markets, but if you can't find a source for fresh galangal, fresh ginger root would be a better replacement than either powdered or dried galangal root in this recipe. To learn more about some of the ingredients featured in this dish, see the note above.

MAKES 4 SERVINGS

2 tbsp peanut oil

2 tbsp minced garlic

¼ cup Jungle Curry Paste (recipe follows)

1 lb boneless pork shoulder, cubed

2 cups Chicken Broth (page 63)

1 lb Thai eggplant, quartered

½ lb long beans, cut into 1-inch lengths

¼ cup thinly sliced galangal root

4 wild lime leaves, chopped

¼ cup fish sauce

1 cup Thai basil leaves

Salt as needed

1. Heat a wok over high heat. Add the oil and heat until it is nearly smoking. Add the garlic and curry paste and fry until aromatic, about 2 minutes.

2. Add the cubed pork and stir-fry until browned on all sides, about 6 minutes.

3. Add the broth, bring to a simmer, and continue to cook over medium heat until the pork is tender and cooked through, another 10 minutes.

4. Add the eggplant, beans, galangal, lime leaves, and fish sauce. Continue to cook until the eggplant is tender, about 10 minutes.

5. Remove from the heat and stir in basil leaves. Season to taste with salt. Serve with sticky rice, if desired.

Jungle Curry Paste

MAKES ¼ CUP

6 shallots, chopped

1 tbsp chopped garlic

1 tsp salt

2 tbsp minced galangal

1½ tbsp minced lemongrass

8 small dried red chiles, crushed

2 wild lime leaves

2 tsp Thai shrimp paste

Place shallots, garlic, and salt into a mortar, a spice grinder, or a small food processor and grind to a paste. Continue to add the remaining ingredients one at a time, grinding into a smooth paste. The curry paste is ready to use now or it can be stored in a covered jar in the refrigerator for up to 2 days.

GUAVA-GLAZED BABY BACK RIBS

BABY BACK ribs are meatier and less fatty than spareribs. They are sold in racks that may be whole, halved, or quartered when you buy them. Keep an eye on these ribs as they cook, since the danger of overcooking is significant with baby back ribs.

MAKES 8 SERVINGS

2½ cups water

1½ cups red wine vinegar

1½ cups chopped oregano leaves

1¼ cups chopped cilantro leaves

1 cup chopped yellow onion

8 garlic cloves, minced

2 tsp ground cumin

1½ tsp ground black pepper

8 lb pork baby back ribs

4 cups Guava Barbecue Sauce (recipe follows)

1. Make a marinade by puréeing the water, vinegar, oregano, cilantro, onion, garlic, cumin, and pepper in a blender.

2. Place the ribs in a large container and coat with the marinade. Cover and refrigerate for at least 24 and up to 36 hours.

3. Preheat a gas grill to medium; leave one burner off. If you are using a charcoal grill, build a fire and

let it burn down until the coals are glowing red with a moderate coating of white ash. Spread the coals in an even bed on one side of the grill. Clean the cooking grate.

4. Grill the pork ribs over indirect heat, covered, until the ribs are browned on both sides, about 15 minutes per side. (If desired, add wood chips to the grill, either directly onto the hot coals or in a small aluminum pan over one of the burners.)

5. Bring the barbecue sauce to a simmer in a saucepan; reserve 2 cups of the sauce (and keep warm) to pass with the spareribs. Brush the ribs with a light coating of the barbecue sauce and continue to barbecue over indirect heat, turning the ribs every 5 minutes and brushing with sauce after each turn, until the ribs are very tender and a rich glaze has built up on the ribs, another 30 to 35 minutes.

6. Remove the pork ribs from the grill and cut into portions. Serve on a heated platter or plates. Pass the reserved barbecue sauce on the side.

Guava Barbecue Sauce

MAKES 4 CUPS

1½ cups guava marmalade

1 cup water

½ cup dry sherry wine

¼ cup tomato paste

2 tbsp dry mustard

4 tsp molasses

1 habanero chile, minced

5 tsp minced garlic

1 tbsp ground cumin

2 tsp salt

1 tsp ground black pepper

½ cup lime juice

1. Combine all of the ingredients except for the lime juice in a saucepan. Simmer the sauce until slightly thickened, about 30 minutes.

2. Remove from the heat and stir in the lime juice. The sauce is ready to use now, or it can be cooled and stored in a covered container in the refrigerator for up to 1 week.

ALBUQUERQUE GRILLED PORK TENDERLOIN
with Beans and Greens Sauté

PORK TENDERLOIN cooks quickly over a brisk fire, but you can substitute other meats, as well as poultry and even some fish.

MAKES 6 SERVINGS

3 lbs pork tenderloins

Albuquerque Dry Rub, as needed (opposite)

1 cup pomegranate juice

¼ cup molasses

¼ cup sherry vinegar

Olive oil, as needed

Beans and Greens Sauté (page 201)

1. Blot the tenderloins dry with paper towels. Sprinkle all sides of the tenderloins evenly with some of the dry rub. Cover the tenderloins and refrigerate for at least 2 and up to 12 hours.

2. Preheat a gas grill to medium-high. If you are using a charcoal grill, build a fire and let it burn down until the coals are glowing red with a moderate coating of white ash. Spread the coals in an even bed. Clean the cooking grate.

3. While the grill is heating, make the mop: Simmer the pomegranate juice in a small saucepan over high heat until it reduces by half. Add the molasses and sherry vinegar, stir well, and bring to a simmer. Remove the mop from the heat and reserve 3 tablespoons to drizzle on the pork after it is cooked.

4. Brush the tenderloins with a little of the olive oil. Place the tenderloins on the grill and cook until the meat is marked on the first side, about 3 minutes. Turn carefully and brush the upper side of the tenderloins with some of the mop. Turn the tenderloins again when the second side is marked, about 3 minutes, and brush with the mop once again. Grill for another 8 to 9 minutes, covered, then turn once more and brush with mop again. Finish grilling on the second side, covered, until the pork is cooked, another 8 to 9 minutes.

5. Remove the tenderloins from the grill. Allow them to rest for 5 to 10 minutes before slicing. Place slices of the tenderloin on heated plates along with a serving of the Beans and Greens Sauté. Drizzle the reserved mop over the pork slices and serve.

Albuquerque Dry Rub

THIS MAKES enough dry rub to flavor about 3 pounds of meat, fish, or poultry. We suggest starting with whole spices for the best flavor, but you can always substitute ground spices if you prefer.

MAKES ½ CUP DRY RUB

1 tbsp coriander seeds (or 2 tsp ground coriander)

1 tbsp cumin seeds (or 2 tsp ground cumin)

6 tbsp chili powder

1 tbsp onion powder

2 tsp garlic powder

2 tsp dried Mexican oregano

2 tsp salt

½ tsp black peppercorns (or 1 tsp ground pepper)

1. Heat a small sauté pan over medium-high heat. Add the coriander and cumin seeds and toast, swirling the pan constantly, until the seeds give off a rich aroma, about 1 minute. Immediately transfer the seeds to a cool plate and allow to cool for a few minutes before proceeding.

2. Transfer the seeds to a mortar and pestle or a spice grinder. Add the chili powder, onion and garlic powder, oregano, salt, and pepper. Grind the spices to an even texture. The rub is ready to use now, or you can transfer it to a jar, cover it tightly,

 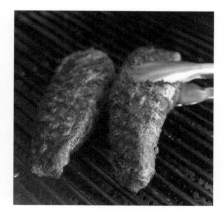

LEFT TO RIGHT Be sure to coat the tenderloins evenly with the dry rub or the flavor will be uneven; you can use gloves if necessary to prevent your hands from getting stained by the dark red rub. Gently turn the pork tenderloins when they are properly marked.

and keep it in a cool, dry cupboard or pantry for up to 1 month.

ROASTED PORK LOIN
with Apricot-Armagnac Compote

Armagnac is a renowned brandy from Gascony, France. Aged in dark oak, the spirit is silky smooth, and when combined with apricot, perfectly compliments the pork loin.

MAKES 8 SERVINGS

3 lb pork loin

1½ tsp freshly ground black pepper, or to taste

2 tsp salt , or to taste

1 tbsp vegetable oil

1 cup onion, diced

¼ cup Armagnac

1 cup dried apricot, diced

1 tsp sage leaves, dried, crumbled

1. Preheat the oven to 350°F. Spray the rack of a roasting pan with nonstick spray and place in pan. Season the pork loins with the salt and 1 teaspoon of the pepper. Heat 2 teaspoons of the oil in a large sauté pan until almost smoking. Add the pork loins and sauté until the meat is golden brown on all sides, about 6 to 8 minutes. Remove the loins and place them in the roasting pan. Roast the loins until they are cooked through, about 30 to 35 minutes, or until an internal temperature of 165°F for well done, and 155°F for slightly pink.

2. Heat the remaining 1 teaspoon oil in a nonstick skillet and add the onion. Sauté, stirring frequently, until the onion is lightly browned, 6 to 7 minutes.

Selecting and Preparing Cuts of Meat for the Grill

You've probably heard that the best meats for grilling are naturally tender. Juicy steaks and chops from the loin or the rib are indeed a good match for the intense dry heat of a grill. The beauty of a grill is that you can control the heat enough to make even tougher cuts a great choice, including veal breast, spareribs, or whole legs of lamb.

SELECT GOOD-QUALITY MEATS

Steaks should be a relatively consistent thickness. Trim any excess fat, but try to leave a thin layer. While you don't want so much fat that it sputters and flares on the grill, a thin, even layer is necessary to prevent the meat from losing moisture and flavor.

ADD A DRY RUB FOR FLAVOR

Rub the mixture evenly over the meat, cover it, and let it sit in the refrigerator for a few hours or even overnight. Shake off the excess before you start to grill it. Otherwise, the rub could scorch and your meat take on an unpleasant, bitter flavor.

TO ADD MOISTURE TO MEATS, USE AN OIL-BASED MARINADE

Put the meat and the marinade in a heavy-duty resealable bag, seal it tightly, and let the meat marinate in the refrigerator. This method keeps the meat evenly coated in marinade without your having to turn it. When you take meats out of the marinade, scrape off the excess. Too much oil on the meat will drip down onto the coals or burner. The smoke from the oil could leave sooty deposits on the food.

3. Deglaze the pan with the Armagnac. Bring the liquid to a simmer and add the apricot and sage, along with the remaining pepper. Allow the mixture to simmer until most of the liquid has evaporated, about 5 to 7 minutes.

4. After removing the roasted pork loin from the oven, allow it to stand 10 minutes before carving. Carve the loin into slices and serve with the warm apricot compote.

SAUTÉED PORK MEDALLIONS
with *Apple Chutney*

C HUTNEY IS a general term that refers to a cooked mixture of fruit, vinegar, sugar, and spices. This recipe combines the delicious seasonal fruits of autumn with walnuts and spices. The result is a bold, slightly spicy condiment that is the perfect accompaniment to the tender pork medallions.

MAKES 8 SERVINGS

¼ cup light brown sugar, lightly packed

¼ onion onion, diced

¼ cup golden raisins

1½ tbsp walnuts, toasted and chopped

1 tbsp cider vinegar

1½ tsp lemon juice

1½ tsp ginger, grated

1 tsp jalapeño, minced

½ tsp lemon zest, grated

½ clove garlic, minced

⅛ tsp ground mace

⅛ tsp ground clove

2½ cups Granny Smith apple, peeled, cored, medium dice

1 tbsp salt, or to taste

½ tsp freshly ground black pepper, or to taste

3 lb pork loin, boneless

¼ cup vegetable oil

1. Combine brown sugar, onion, raisins, walnuts, vinegar, lemon juice, ginger, jalapeño, lemon zest, garlic, mace, and clove in a saucepot, cover, and simmer over low heat for 10 minutes. Add the apples and simmer until the apples are very tender and the juices are reduced and slightly thickened, 10 to 15 minutes. Season with salt and pepper. Hold warm until needed.

2. While the apples are cooking, slice the pork loin into 12 pieces. Season the pork with salt and pepper.

3. Heat one tablespoon of oil in a skillet over medium-high heat. In two batches, sauté the pork medallions until golden brown and cooked throughout, about 3 to 4 minutes each side.

4. To serve, place three medallions on each plate and spoon about 3 tablespoons of the apple chutney over them.

BRAISED RABBIT WITH GARGANELLI
Garganelli con Coniglio in Guazetto

T HE UNUSUAL name of this pasta comes from a Latin word for trachea, *gargala*, whose form the tube-shaped pasta resembles—in part due to the combed indentations running across its width to hold sauce. The traditional way to serve garganelli, which comes from the Romagna region of Italy, is with a rich ragù, such as this braised rabbit dish.

MAKES 4 SERVINGS

½ oz dried porcini mushrooms

3 cups Chicken Broth (page 63) or water, heated

2 tbsp olive oil

2 rabbits, quartered

Salt as needed

Freshly ground black pepper as needed

1 cup small-dice onion

½ cup small-dice carrot

½ cup small-dice celery

1 cup chopped plum tomato

1 tbsp tomato paste

1 cup dry white wine

2 bay leaves

1 sprig rosemary

2 cloves

½ lb garganelli or penne pasta, cooked al dente and drained

2 tbsp minced flat-leaf parsley

Grated Parmesan as needed

1. Preheat the oven to 350°F. Rehydrate the porcini in hot broth or water for 30 minutes. Strain the soaking liquid and set aside. Chop the mushrooms and set aside.

2. Heat the oil in flameproof casserole or Dutch oven over high heat. Dry the rabbit pieces thoroughly, season with salt and pepper, and brown on all sides in the oil, turning as necessary, about 10 minutes. Transfer the rabbit from the casserole to a plate or pan and reserve.

3. Add the onion, carrot, and celery to the casserole and sauté, stirring occasionally, until translucent, about 6 minutes. Add the chopped tomato and tomato paste and sauté, stirring constantly, until the tomato paste darkens in color and smells very sweet, about 2 minutes. Stir in the wine and simmer over low heat until the wine reduces by about half. Season to taste with additional salt and pepper.

4. Return the browned rabbit pieces, along with any juices they may have released, and the chopped

porcinis to the casserole. Add the strained mushroom soaking liquid and enough additional broth or water to cover the rabbit pieces by one-third. Bring the braise to a simmer, add the bay leaves, rosemary sprig, and cloves, then immediately cover the casserole and place in the oven. Braise the rabbit, turning it occasionally, until it is fork-tender, about 45 minutes. Transfer the rabbit to a plate or dish and let it cool until it can be handled. Shred the rabbit meat and reserve.

5. Return the casserole to the medium-high heat, bring the sauce to a rapid simmer, and reduce, uncovered, until the sauce is thickened and flavorful, about 5 minutes. Remove and discard the bay leaves, rosemary sprig, and cloves. Return the shredded rabbit to the sauce and simmer until heated, about 5 minutes. Season to taste with additional salt and pepper. Spoon the rabbit and sauce over the garganelli or penne and serve very hot garnished with parsley and grated Parmesan cheese.

CEDAR-PLANKED SALMON
with Huckleberry-Zinfandel Sauce

THE WOOD adds a lot of flavor to fish as you cook it. For variety, you can use hickory, mesquite, or even fruit tree wood, like apple or cherry. The planks don't last forever, but you should be able to get more than one cooking session from them. You may be able to find smaller, thinner planks that are perfect for individual servings. The sauce we suggest here is a classic brown sauce finished with wild huckleberries. If you want something a little simpler, try one of the compound butters on pages 203 or the Scallion Oil on page 40.

MAKES 8 SERVINGS

3 lb salmon fillet

1 tbsp salt

1 tsp ground black pepper

2 cedar planks, soaked overnight

2 cups Zinfandel Sauce (recipe follows)

1 cup fresh huckleberries (blueberries may be substituted)

1. Preheat a gas grill to medium-high heat. If you are using a charcoal grill, build a fire and let it burn down until the coals are glowing red with a light coating of white ash. Spread the coals in an even bed. Clean the cooking grate.

2. Clean, dry, and trim the salmon to remove any remaining belly bones or pin bones. Cut the salmon into 8 equal pieces and then season with the salt and pepper.

3. Place 4 salmon fillets on each soaked cedar plank, and place the planks on the grill. Grill, covered, until just cooked through, 8 to 10 minutes.

4. Combine the Zinfandel Sauce with the huckleberries. Serve the salmon with ¼ cup of sauce per portion, each portion garnished with some of the huckleberries.

Zinfandel Sauce

THIS IS one instance when making your own broth from rich meaty beef or veal bones that you've roasted beforehand makes a world of difference. Most canned broths are too salty once you've reduced them to a sauce consistency. The quality of the wine is paramount to the flavor of the sauce, too, so don't skimp.

MAKES 2 CUPS

1 tbsp vegetable oil

½ cup medium-dice carrot

½ cup medium-dice yellow onion

¼ cup medium-dice celery

1 tbsp tomato paste

1½ cups Zinfandel wine

8 cups beef broth

1 bay leaf

6 parsley stems

1 thyme sprig

1 garlic clove, peeled and left whole

Salt, to taste

Ground black pepper, to taste

LEFT TO RIGHT Grill the salmon until it is just cooked through; the plank should be slightly charred. Be sure to take the time to reduce the sauce properly; the velvety texture and rich flavor will reward your patience. Opposite, Cedar-Planked Salmon with Huckleberry-Zinfandel Sauce.

1. Heat the oil in a large stockpot over medium-high heat. Add the carrots and onions and sauté until the onions are golden brown, 10 to 12 minutes. Add the celery and continue to sauté until the celery is tender, another 8 minutes.

2. Immediately stir in the tomato paste and cook until the mixture takes on a rust color, about 4 minutes more.

3. Deglaze the pan with the wine, and simmer until reduced by half.

4. Add the broth, bay leaf, parsley stems, thyme, and garlic, and simmer until the sauce is just thick enough to lightly coat the back of a spoon. Add salt and pepper to taste. Keep warm until ready to use.

POACHED SALMON
with *Hollandaise Sauce*

USE A wide, shallow pan to poach the salmon or a skillet with sides high enough to keep the salmon completely submerged as it cooks. To keep the salmon moist and prevent it from separating as it cooks, keep the court bouillon at a bare simmer. You should see tiny bubbles forming around the sides of the pan, but no big bubbles breaking on the surface. Cold poached salmon is delicious with a flavored mayonnaise.

MAKES 8 SERVINGS

2 quarts cold water

1½ cups white wine vinegar

1 medium onion, thinly sliced

1 carrot, thinly sliced

1 celery stalk, thinly sliced

6 parsley stems

1 sprig fresh thyme

1 bay leaf

2 tsp salt, divided use

¼ tsp whole black peppercorns

8 pieces salmon fillet (about 6 oz each)

¼ tsp ground black pepper, or as needed

1½ cups Hollandaise Sauce (recipe follows)

1. To make a court bouillon for poaching the salmon, combine the water, vinegar, onion, carrot, celery, parsley stems, thyme, bay leaf, 1 teaspoon of the salt, and the peppercorns in a large pot. Bring to a simmer over high heat. Reduce the heat and simmer until flavorful, 20 minutes. Strain the court bouillon. (It is ready to use now or it may be properly cooled and stored for later use.)

2. Season the salmon with the remaining salt and ground pepper. Place the strained court bouillon in a wide saucepan or deep skillet and bring to a bare simmer. Add the salmon pieces using a slotted spoon or a poaching rack. Poach until the salmon is cooked through but still very moist, 8 to 10 minutes.

3. Lift the salmon from the court bouillon carefully and let drain briefly. Serve the salmon on heated plates with the warm Hollandaise sauce.

Hollandaise Sauce

YOU CAN use either fresh or pasteurized eggs to make this classic sauce. If you need to make the sauce ahead of time, try holding it in a thermos.

MAKES 2 CUPS

½ tsp cracked peppercorns

¼ cup white-wine or cider vinegar

¼ cup water, or as needed

4 large egg yolks, fresh or pasteurized

1½ cups melted or clarified butter, warm

2 tsp lemon juice, or as needed

2 tsp salt, or as needed

Pinch ground white pepper

Pinch cayenne, optional

1. Combine the peppercorns and the vinegar in a small pan and reduce over medium heat until nearly dry, about 5 minutes. Add the water to the vinegar reduction. Strain this liquid into a stainless-steel bowl.

2. Add the egg yolks to the reduction and set the bowl over a pot of simmering water. Whisking constantly, cook the mixture until the yolks triple in volume and fall in ribbons from the whisk. Remove the bowl from the simmering water and set it on a clean kitchen towel to keep the bowl stationary.

3. Gradually ladle the warm butter into the egg mixture, whisking constantly. As the butter is blended into the yolks, the sauce will thicken. If it becomes too thick and the butter is not blending in easily, add a little water or lemon juice to thin the egg mixture enough to whisk in the remaining butter. Season the hollandaise with lemon juice, salt, pepper, and cayenne if desired.

Filleting a Round Fish

A filleting or boning knife with a flexible blade is ideal for the delicate work of filleting fish. Place the fish on a work surface with its back toward you. Make a cut behind the head and gills down to the bone, angling the knife away from the body, but do not sever the head.

CUTTING THE FIRST FILLET

Without lifting the knife, angle it so that the blade is parallel to the work surface and the cutting edge is pointing toward the fish's tail. Hold the knife handle lower than the blade, to remove as much flesh from the bone as possible. Run the knife down the length of the fish, under the flesh, to cut a fillet. Press the knife against the bones as you slice and do not saw back and forth. Remove the fillet from the bones and place skin-side down.

REMOVING THE BACKBONE

Without turning the fish over, insert the blade just underneath the backbone. Lay your guiding hand flat on top of the bone structure to keep the fish stable. Keeping the knife parallel to the work surface, run the blade down the entire length of the fish underneath the bones. The knife's cutting edge should be angled upward very slightly to cut as much flesh from bone as possible.

TRIMMING THE FILLETS

Remove the belly bones by making smooth strokes against the bones to cut them away cleanly. Trim away excess fat only on the belly edge of the fillets. Cut away the remnants of the backbone by running the blade just underneath the line of the backbone, lifting it up and away from the fillet as you cut.

REMOVING THE PIN BONES

As you look at the fillet, you'll see a midline running its length. To locate the pin bones, run a fingertip down the length of the fillets to one side of the midline. Use tweezers or needle-nose pliers to pull the pin bones out, working with the grain to avoid tearing the flesh.

4. The sauce is ready to serve at this point, or it may be finished as desired. The sauce should be held warm over a hot water bath or it can be held sealed in a thermos.

SEARED SALMON
with a Moroccan Spice Crust

THE IMPACT of this bold spice mixture is a fantastic match for salmon which has its own rich flavor. Easy to prepare, the spices are pressed onto the salmon steaks as a coating before they are seared in a very hot pan. The salmon should be cooked through without overcooking so that the texture is still tender inside and the spicy exterior is browned from the searing.

MAKES 8 SERVINGS

1½ tsp curry powder

1½ tsp coriander seeds

1½ tsp cumin seeds

1½ tsp caraway seeds

1½ tsp anise seeds

1½ tsp black peppercorns

3 lb salmon steaks

1 tsp salt, or to taste

½ tsp freshly ground black pepper, or to taste

4 tbsp olive oil

1. Combine the curry powder, coriander, cumin, caraway, anise, and peppercorns in a small bowl. Coarsely grind the mixture in a spice grinder or mortar and pestle.

2. Season the salmon steaks generously with salt and pepper.

3. Rub both sides of each salmon piece with a generous amount of the spice mixture.

4. Add about 2 tablespoons of olive oil to a preheated pan. The oil should get very hot and shimmer but not smoke.

5. Add half the salmon and cook, turning once, until the fish is browned on the outside and opaque in the center, about 4 minutes per side. Remove to a warm platter, and repeat with the remaining olive oil and salmon. Serve at once.

SWORDFISH WITH A TOMATO-OLIVE RAGÙ
Pesce Spada Siciliana

YOU CAN replace the swordfish in this recipe with any firm, meaty fish you like. Halibut, cod, bass, or tuna are all good substitutes.

MAKES 6 SERVINGS

TOMATO-OLIVE RAGÙ

⅓ cup olive oil

1 cup minced onion

3 garlic cloves, minced to a paste

3 tbsp chopped capers

6 anchovy fillets

3 pints cherry tomatoes, hulled and halved or quartered if necessary

1 cup olives stuffed with chiles

3 tbsp chopped oregano leaves

Salt as needed

Freshly ground black pepper to taste as needed

6 swordfish steaks (about 6 oz each)

Juice of 2 lemons

⅔ cup sliced almonds, toasted

1. Preheat the oven to 400°F.

2. To make the tomato olive ragù: Heat the oil in

an oven-proof skillet over medium heat. Add the onion, garlic, capers, and anchovies to the pan and sauté, stirring frequently, until the onion is a very light golden brown, about 8 to 10 minutes. Add the tomatoes and continue to sauté, stirring or tossing frequently, until the tomatoes are very soft and all of the ingredients are very hot. Add the olives and oregano to the pan and continue to sauté for another 2 to 3 minutes. Season to taste with salt and pepper.

3. Cut 6 squares of foil large enough to hold the swordfish steaks. Place a spoonful of the tomato-olive ragù in the center of each piece of foil, top with a piece of swordfish, and then top with a little lemon juice and sliced almonds. Fold the foil around the fish to make a tight seal (the seams should be on the top of the packet).

4. Place the swordfish steaks in a shallow pan and bake until the fish is cooked through, about 12 minutes. Serve the fish directly from the foil.

GINGER SESAME STIR-FRIED SCALLOPS
with Lo Mein Noodles

SCALLOPS HAVE a sweet flavor that's a perfect foil for the pungent marinade in this stir fry, but other seafood works well, too: shrimp (peeled and deveined first), swordfish cut into chunks, or monkfish cut into rounds.

MAKES 8 SERVINGS

1 lb sea scallops

5 tbsp peanut oil, divided use

1 tbsp rice wine vinegar

1 tbsp soy or tamari sauce

1 tbsp minced ginger

1 tbsp dark sesame oil

1 tbsp fermented black beans, optional

2 tsp minced garlic

1 tsp honey

1 tsp lemon juice

½ tsp salt, or to taste

¼ tsp ground black pepper, or to taste

1½ cups fine julienne carrots

2 cups sliced shiitake mushrooms caps

4 cups finely sliced bok choy or Savoy cabbage

2 packages lo mein noodles

½ cup thinly sliced scallions, cut on the bias

2 tbsp toasted sesame seeds

1. Pull the muscle tabs from the scallops. Blot the scallops dry and set aside.

2. Combine 3 tablespoons of the peanut oil, the rice vinegar, soy sauce, ginger, sesame oil, fermented beans (if using), garlic, honey, lemon juice, salt, and pepper in a bowl and whisk until blended. Add the scallops and toss until evenly coated. Cover and marinate in the refrigerator at least 2 and up to 24 hours.

3. Bring a large pot of salted water to a rolling boil while you stir-fry the vegetables.

4. Heat a large wok or sauté pan over high heat. Add the remaining 2 tablespoons peanut oil. When the oil is very hot, add the carrots and mushrooms and stir-fry for 1 minute.

5. Add the cabbage and stir-fry until the cabbage is wilted, 3 to 4 minutes.

6. Add the scallops and their marinade to the vegetable mixture and stir-fry until the scallops are opaque and just cooked through, 3 to 4 minutes.

7. Add the lo mein noodles to the boiling water at the same time that you add the scallops to the wok. Stir once or twice with a fork or chopsticks to

separate the strands. Boil the noodles until they are fully cooked and tender, about 3 minutes. Drain in a colander and keep hot.

8. To serve, place the noodles on a heated platter or individual plates and top with the scallops and vegetables. Sprinkle with the scallions and toasted sesame seeds.

OSSO BUCO MILANESE

IN MILAN, osso buco is traditionally served on a bed of creamy saffron risotto (see note below) and topped with a pungent, colorful topping of garlic, lemon zest, parsley, and anchovies known as *gremolata*.

MAKES 4 SERVINGS

4 veal shank pieces, about 12 oz each

Salt as needed

Freshly ground black pepper as needed

Flour as needed for dredging veal shanks

3 tbsp olive oil

1 cup diced yellow onion

½ cup diced carrot

4 tsp minced garlic

3 tbsp tomato paste

¾ cup dry white wine

4 cups Beef or Chicken Broth (page 63)

1 tsp finely grated lemon zest

3 tbsp chopped flat-leaf parsley

2 anchovy fillets, chopped

1. Preheat the oven to 350°F.

2. Season the veal shanks generously with salt and pepper. Dredge the shanks in flour and shake away any excess.

3. Heat the oil in an ovenproof casserole or Dutch oven over high heat until it shimmers. Sear the veal shanks in the oil, turning as necessary, until they have a good color on all sides, 10 to 12 minutes. Remove them to a platter and cover loosely with foil.

4. Add the onion, carrot, and 2 teaspoons minced garlic to the hot oil and sauté over medium heat, stirring frequently, until the onion is a deep golden brown, about 10 minutes. Add the tomato paste and sauté, stirring frequently, until the tomato paste turns a rust color, 2 to 3 minutes. Add the wine and stir well to dissolve the tomato paste.

5. Return the veal shanks to the casserole along with any juices they may have released and add enough broth to cover the shanks by about half. Bring the broth to a simmer, cover the casserole, and place it in the oven. Braise the shanks, turning them as necessary to keep them evenly moistened, until they are very tender, about 1½ hours. Transfer the shanks to a serving platter and keep warm while finishing the sauce.

6. Strain the sauce, return it to the casserole, and bring to a boil over high heat, skimming the surface as necessary. Reduce the heat to low simmer until the sauce has a lightly thickened consistency, about 10 minutes. Season to taste with salt and pepper.

7. Combine the remaining garlic, the lemon zest, parsley, and anchovy fillets to form the gremolata. Serve the shanks on heated plates garnished with the gremolata.

Risotto

A creamy risotto can stand alone as a main course, but for this Italian dish of braised veal, it is a traditional side dish. Making risotto is not demanding—you can make it with ease while the veal shanks are braising. Use either beef or chicken broth (or veal stock, if available) to complement the flavors of the veal.

For enough risotto to serve four, heat about 2 tablespoons of butter in a sauce pan. Add 1 cup of a round-grain rice such as Arborio or Carnaroli and stir the rice over medium heat. Add the broth, one cup at a time, until the rice has absorbed 3 cups of liquid. You should stir the risotto frequently as it cooks to get a good creamy texture. (If you like, replace ½ cup of the broth with ½ cup dry white wine.) For a saffron risotto, add a few threads of crushed saffron with the first cup of broth.

Once the rice is tender and creamy, pull it off the heat and add 2 tablespoon butter and ⅓ to ½ cup grated Parmesan cheese. Stir the risotto vigorously until the butter and cheese are blended in. Serve at once on heated plates.

VEAL BRAISED IN ASTI SPUMANTE

ASTI SPUMANTE, or simply Asti, is an effervescent, fruity wine, from the Piedmont region of Italy, made from the Muscat grape. We've included both white and cremini mushrooms in this dish, but feel free to use whatever mushrooms look good at the market—exotic varieties add intriguing flavors and shapes to the dish.

MAKES 6 SERVINGS

3 lb boneless veal shoulder roast or veal breast, rolled and tied

Salt as needed

Freshly ground black pepper as needed

¼ cup olive oil

1 cup chopped onion

2 cups sliced white mushrooms

1 cup sliced cremini mushrooms

1½ cups Asti spumante

2 cups Beef Broth (page 63), as needed

1 cup seedless green grapes, halved

1. Preheat the oven to 350°F.

2. Season the veal roast with salt and pepper. Heat the olive oil in a large Dutch oven over high heat until it shimmers. Sear the veal in the hot oil, turning occasionally, until golden brown on all sides, about 10 minutes. Transfer to a pan and keep warm.

3. Reduce the heat to medium, add the onion to the pan, and cook slowly until tender and golden brown, about 15 minutes. Add the sliced mushrooms and continue to sauté until the moisture they release cooks away, about 10 minutes.

4. Add the Asti spumante and stir well to dissolve the drippings. Simmer over high heat until the Asti spumante reduces by half. Return the veal to the Dutch oven and add enough broth to come about halfway up the sides of the veal.

5. Cover the Dutch oven and braise the veal in the oven, turning as necessary to keep the veal evenly moistened, until it is tender, about 2½ to 3 hours. Add the grapes to the sauce and continue to simmer until the grapes are hot and the veal is fork-tender, about 30 minutes.

6. Transfer the meat to a warm pan or plate, coat with some of the braising liquid, and set aside to stay warm. Return the Dutch oven to medium-high heat and simmer the sauce, skimming as necessary, until it thickens slightly, about 10 minutes. Season to taste with additional salt and pepper. Slice the veal and serve with the sauce.

VEAL SALTIMBOCCA
with Fettuccine

INDULGE YOURSELF in the velvety, rich flavors of veal, butter, white wine, and prosciutto. Pounding the cutlets thin enhances the delicate texture of this dish. If desired, substitute pork cutlets for the veal.

2 lb fettuccine noodles

2 tbsp olive oil

3 lb boneless veal cutlets

4 tsp sage, finely chopped

1 tsp salt, or to taste

1 tsp freshly ground black pepper, or to taste

16 prosciutto slices, paper-thin

2 cups all-purpose flour

½ cup olive oil

1 cup dry white wine

1½ cups butter, chilled and cubed

1/2 tsp salt, or to taste

¼ cup parsley, coarsely chopped

1 lemon, cut into eighths

1. Bring a large pot of salted water to a boil. Cook the pasta in the boiling water for 8 to 10 minutes, or until tender to the bite. Toss with 2 tablespoons olive oil and keep warm.

2. Pound cutlets to an even thickness of about ¼ inch between two pieces of plastic wrap. Season the veal with sage, salt, and pepper. Place 1 slice of prosciutto atop each cutlet.

3. Dredge veal in flour; shake off excess. Heat 2 tablespoons olive oil in heavy, large skillet over medium-high heat. Add 4 pieces of veal and cook until golden, 3 to 4 minutes per side. Transfer veal to a platter and keep warm.Pour off fat from skillet and discard. Add fresh oil as needed until all of the veal is cooked. Pour off excess fat, add the wine to the skillet, and bring to a boil, scraping up any browned bits. Boil until liquid is reduced to ¼ cup, about 3 to 4 minutes. Reduce heat to low.

4. Whisk the chilled butter into the sauce, 2 tablespoons at a time. Season the sauce with salt, pepper

and chopped parsley. Serve the completed veal immediately accompanied by the fettuccine. Pour ¼ cup sauce over the top of each portion and garnish with a lemon wedge.

VEAL SCALOPPINE
with Lemon and Capers

VEAL TOP round is the ideal cut for this dish. Its delicate texture, combined with the lemon and capers, enhance the velvety finish of this favorite.

3 lb boneless veal cutlets

1 tsp salt, or to taste

½ tsp freshly ground black pepper, or to taste

⅔ cup flour, or as needed

2 tbsp olive oil, plus more as needed

1 tbsp butter, plus more as needed

LEMON-CAPER SAUCE

4 tbsp water

6 tbsp capers, rinsed, drained

6 tbsp lemon juice

2 tbsp lemon zest

2 tbsp butter

Salt and pepper, to taste

1. Pound cutlets to an even thickness of about ¼ inch between two pieces of plastic wrap. Season the pounded veal generously with salt and pepper. Dredge the cutlets in flour and shake off excess.

2. Place a large sauté pan over high heat. Add 2 tablespoons of olive oil and 1 tablespoon of butter to the pan.

3. Sauté the veal in batches, adding more butter and oil as needed. Place the veal in the pan and

sauté 1 to 2 minutes, until lightly golden. Flip the veal over, and continue to cook it for an additional minute. Remove and hold warm. Keep the oil/butter in the pan, add the remaining oil and an additional tablespoon of butter. Add the second batch of veal, and sauté in same manner as first batch. Remove and hold warm.

4. Deglaze pan with about 4 tablespoons of water, and add the capers. Gently scrape browned bits from the bottom of the pan. Add the lemon juice, and stir in the remaining 2 tablespoons of butter to emulsify the sauce. Add the lemon zest, and heat for 1 minute, while swirling the sauce in the pan. Adjust the seasoning with salt and pepper. Serve the veal immediately with the lemon-caper sauce.

ROAST TURKEY BREAST
with Pan Gravy and Chestnut Dressing

A GOOD "RULE OF THUMB" for roasting turkey is to allow about 20 minutes per pound; use this to calculate the approximate roasting time for birds larger than the one called for in this recipe.

MAKES 8 SERVINGS

One turkey breast, bone-in, about 7–8 lb

1 bay leaf

1 large sprig fresh thyme

½ bunch fresh flat-leaf parsley

1–2 tbsp fresh lemon juice

Salt and freshly ground pepper

¾ cup diced yellow onion

½ cup diced carrot

½ cup diced celery

5 cups Chicken Broth (page 63), divided use

⅓ cup cornstarch

⅓ cup cold water

6 cups Chestnut Dressing (recipe follows)

1. Preheat the oven to 450°F. Set a roasting rack in a large roasting pan.

2. Rinse the turkey in cool water and pat dry. Stuff the bay leaf, thyme, and parsley under the skin. Rub the lemon juice over the entire bird and season with salt and pepper.

3. Place the turkey skin side up on the rack in the roasting pan, transfer to the oven, and immediately reduce the oven temperature to 350°F. Roast, basting occasionally with the accumulated pan drippings, until an instant-read thermometer inserted in the thickest part of the turkey breast registers 170°F, about 2½ to 3 hours. Add the onion, carrot, and celery to the roasting pan during the final hour of roasting time. Remove the turkey from the oven and transfer it, still on its rack, to a baking sheet. Cover loosely with foil and let the turkey rest while preparing the pan gravy.

4. While the turkey is resting, prepare the pan gravy as follows: combine the pan drippings, onion, carrot, and celery in a saucepan. Add ½ cup of the broth to the roasting pan and stir to deglaze the pan, scraping up any browned bits. Add these drippings to the saucepan along with the remaining broth. Simmer over medium heat, skimming away any fat that rises to the surface, until slightly reduced and flavorful, 20 to 25 minutes.

5. Stir the cornstarch and water together to make a slurry. Gradually add the cornstarch slurry to the simmering broth, whisking constantly, until the gravy has a good consistency. Simmer 2 minutes more, strain, taste, and season with salt and pepper.

6. Carve the turkey into slices and serve with the gravy and the chestnut dressing.

Chestnut Dressing

USING A parchment "lid" as we suggest here keeps the surface of the dressing from drying out too much as it bakes, but still lets it turn a good golden color.

MAKES 8 SERVINGS

8 cups bread cubes

3 bacon strips, minced

2 tbsp water

½ cup minced onion

1 cup chestnuts, roasted and chopped

⅓ cup Chicken Broth (page 63), warmed

1 large egg, lightly beaten

3 tbsp chopped parsley

½ tsp chopped sage

½ tsp ground black pepper, or to taste

1. Preheat the oven to 350°F. Butter a 2-quart baking dish or casserole. Cut a piece of parchment paper to use as a lid and butter it lightly.

2. Spread the bread cubes on baking sheets and place in the oven until dry, about 8 to 10 minutes. Transfer them to a large mixing bowl.

3. Heat a large skillet over medium heat. Add the minced bacon and water and cook slowly until the bacon is crisp. Remove the bacon with a slotted spoon and set aside. Add the onion and sauté, stirring frequently, until tender and translucent, about 5 minutes.

4. Remove from the heat and cool before adding to the bread cubes along with the reserved bacon, chestnuts, chicken broth, egg, parsley, sage, and pepper. Toss the ingredients together until evenly blended and moistened.

5. Place the stuffing in the baking dish and cover with the parchment paper. Bake the stuffing until the top and edges are browned and crisp, about 45 minutes. Serve the dressing very hot.

VEGETABLE STEW
with Herbed Israeli Couscous

PACKED WITH colorful vegetables, this hearty and warming stew is full of slightly sweet and spicy flavors, perfect with the herbed couscous.

MAKES 8 SERVINGS.

1 tbsp olive oil

2 leeks, cleaned, sliced

2 tbsp garlic, minced

1 tsp red curry paste

½ lb butternut squash, peeled, diced

1 lb chickpeas, rinsed, drained

½ cup fava beans, shelled

3 cups Vegetable Broth (page 65)

2 cups zucchini, diced

2½ cups eggplant, peeled, diced

1½ cups carrots, diced

¾ cup celery, diced

⅓ cup currants

3 tbsp tomato puree, canned

2 tsp lemon juice

1½ tsp lemon zest, grated

¼ tsp salt, or to taste

Freshly ground black pepper, to taste

Herbed Israeli Couscous (page 187)

1. Heat the oil in a large pot. Add the leeks and garlic and sauté until translucent, 3 to 5 minutes. Add the curry paste and sauté until fragrant.

2. Stir in the squash, chickpeas, and fava beans. Add enough broth to cover the vegetables and simmer for 10 minutes. Add the remaining broth, the zucchini, eggplant, carrots, celery, currants, and tomato puree. Simmer until the vegetables are tender, about 20 minutes.

3. Add the lemon juice and zest and season the stew with salt and pepper. Serve the stew over the herbed Israeli couscous or rice.

CHICKPEA AND VEGETABLE TAGINE

TAGINE, A gently simmered Moroccan stew, is traditionally cooked in an earthenware vessel of the same name. This tagine of vegetables is redolent with fragrant herbs. Couscous is the traditional accompaniment to a tagine.

MAKES 8 SERVINGS

2 tbsp olive oil

4 cups onions, chopped

3 garlic cloves, chopped

1 tbsp ground cumin

1 tsp freshly ground black pepper, or to taste

Salt, to taste

¼ tsp ground cinnamon

2 cups water

2 lb butternut squash, peeled, seeded, cut into chunks

6 carrots, peeled, cut into chunks

2 lb chickpeas, drained and rinsed

2 lb diced tomatoes in juice (no salt added)

2 sweet potatoes, peeled, cut into chunks

4 parsnips, peeled, cut into chunks

1 bay leaf

¼ cup parsley, chopped

1. Heat the oil in a large saucepan. Add the onions and sauté until softened and translucent, about 5 minutes. Add the garlic and sauté until golden, about 1 minute. Add the cumin, pepper, salt, and cinnamon. Cook, stirring for 1 minute.

2. Stir in the water, squash, carrots, chickpeas, tomatoes, sweet potatoes, parsnips, and the bay leaf; bring to a boil. Reduce the heat and simmer, partially covered, until the vegetables are tender, about 30 minutes. Discard the bay leaf, sprinkle with the parsley, and serve.

MOO SHU VEGETABLES

THESE SWEET and spicy vegetables wrapped in paper-thin pancakes are a healthy and easy alternative to ordering in.

MAKES 8 SERVINGS

3 tbsp peanut oil

1 tbsp garlic, minced

1 tbsp ginger, peeled, minced

1 tbsp scallion, minced

1 red pepper, cut in 1–2 inch strips

4 celery stalks, cut in 1–2 inch strips

4 carrots, cut in 1–2 inch strips

½ head napa cabbage, chiffonade

2 tbsp Hoisin sauce

3 tbsp soy sauce

1 tbsp sesame oil

1 egg, beaten

16 moo shu pancakes (available at Asian markets) or Mandarin Pancakes (page 160)

1. Heat the oil in a wok or large sauté pan over high heat. Add the garlic, ginger, and scallion. Stir-fry until aromatic.

2. Add the red pepper, celery, carrots, and cabbage. Stir-fry until tender, approximately 2 minutes.

3. Stir in the hoisin sauce, the soy sauce, and the sesame oil.

4. Make a well in the middle of the vegetable mixture, pour in the egg and let it set for 30 seconds, then break it up into the vegetables.

5. Serve with moo shu pancakes—the pancakes can be warmed before serving, in a stack with a damp cloth over them, in a 250°F oven for a few minutes or in a microwave for 30 to 45 seconds—or a fresh batch of the easy-to-make Mandarin Pancakes.

SAUTÉED TOFU

with Red Curry Paste, Peas, Scallions, and Cilantro

HERE TOFU is complemented by the bold and exciting flavors of Thai cuisine. Curry pastes come in a broad variety of flavor intensities from mildly spicy to very hot. Prepared Thai red curry paste can be found in jars in the Asian foods section of many supermarkets or in specialty food shops and Asian markets.

MAKES 8 SERVINGS

2 cups brown rice

Grapeseed oil, as needed

1 package tofu, drained, cut into 1-inch cubes (14 oz)

2 tbsp lime juice

1 cup onion, diced

2 tbsp garlic, minced

1 cup coconut milk

2 oz prepared Thai red curry paste

1 tbsp ground turmeric

Salt, to taste

Freshly ground black pepper, to taste

1½ cups peas, blanched

1 cup grape tomatoes, cut in half

⅓ bunch cilantro, chopped

½ bunch scallions, minced

1 cup pea shoots

18 oz brown rice, cooked

¼ cup black sesame seeds

1. Bring 3½ cups of water and the rice to a boil and cover the pot tightly, turn the heat to low and cook for approximately 25 minutes, or until the rice is tender.

2. Heat a small amount of the oil in a medium nonstick sauté pan. Add the tofu and cook until the moisture is evaporated and the tofu is a light golden brown. Remove the tofu from the pan and sprinkle with the lime juice.

3. Heat more oil in the pan, add the onions and cook until translucent, about 5 minutes. Add the garlic and cook for an additional 2 minutes.

4. Add the coconut milk, curry paste, and turmeric. Season with salt and pepper. Reduce the heat and simmer until the sauce has slightly thickened, 10 to 12 minutes.

5. Add the peas, tomatoes, and tofu to the mixture and simmer just to combine. Adjust seasoning if necessary. Toss the mixture with the cilantro and scallions.

6. Serve the tofu mixture with the rice and 2 tablespoons of the peas shoots. Sprinkle the black sesame seeds on top of rice to garnish.

CHAPTER 6

Vegetables and Side Dishes

Grains and Legumes

Nutritionists and chefs alike have been exploring and heralding the importance of grains in any meal. The grains that have the greatest "staying" power and that have the most intriguing flavors and textures are whole or minimally processed grains. You no longer have to seek out specialty stores in order to stock your pantry with exciting and flavorful grains like quinoa or steel-cut oats. Many of our recipes can be prepared with other grains as well. Scotch or pearl barley, oat groats, rye or wheat berries, cracked wheat, colored rices (black, brown, or red), teff, or Job's tears are some potential substitutions.

When purchasing grains keep in mind that grains have a long but not unlimited shelf life. Grains that are older take longer to cook and require more liquid as they cook. Their flavors may turn musty or stale. Whole grains with the bran and germ intact may become rancid if they aren't properly stored since their natural oils are likely to oxidize if they become too warm or if they are exposed to air for too long. Use the following simple guidelines to keep your whole, cracked grains, cereals, and meals fresh and flavorful:

- Look for stores with a good turnover of inventory, and purchase in smaller quantities as needed from bulk bins.
- Keep whole grains in the refrigerator or freezer if you won't be using them within a few weeks of purchase.

PREPARING WHOLE GRAINS

Most grains cook in less than 30 minutes. Some, notably bulgur, cook in 10 minutes or less. Other whole grains like groats or berries may take significantly longer and benefit from soaking prior to cooking.

To cook whole grains by the simmering method, you should bring the recommended amount of liquid and a bit of salt to a boil, then stir in the grain. Stir well to separate the grains and continue to stir from time to time while the grain cooks.

Keep the heat relatively low to avoid scorching the grain. If necessary, add a bit more liquid if the grain looks too dry before it is fully cooked. Properly cooked grains are tender to the bite.

SPECIALTY WHOLE GRAINS

Amaranth To cook 1 cup of grain, you will need 1 cup cooking liquid. Simmer for 12 to 17 minutes. This makes 1½ cups of cooked grain. Add salt after cooking rather than during. Optional: Toast amaranth until it begins to pop or crackle before adding the cooking liquid.

Buckwheat groats (kasha) To cook 1 cup of grain, you will need 1½ to 2 cups cooking liquid. Simmer for 12 to 20 minutes. This makes 2 cups of cooked kasha.

Farro To cook 1 cup of grain, you will need 2 cups of cooking liquid. Simmer for 20 to 25 minutes. This makes 2½ cups of cooked farro.

Job's tears To cook 1 cup of grain, you will need 2 cups cooking liquid. Simmer for 1 hour. This makes 3 cups of cooked Job's tears. Optional: Toast Job's tears until they begin to pop or crackle before adding the liquid and cooking.

Kamut Soak whole kamut overnight in cold water and drain before cooking; use the soaking water as cooking liquid. To cook 1 cup of grain, you will need 1½ cups cooking liquid. Simmer for 1 hour. This makes 2 cups of cooked kamut. Optional: Toast whole kamut until it begins to pop or crackle before adding the liquid and cooking.

Millet To cook 1 cup of grain, you will need 2 cups of cooking liquid. Simmer for 30 to 35 minutes. This makes 3 cups of cooked millet.

Quinoa To cook 1 cup of grain, you will need 1½ to 2 cups cooking liquid. Simmer for 10 to 12 minutes. This makes 3½ to 4 cups of cooked quinoa. To prepare quinoa for cooking, place it in a bowl and cover with cold water. Rub the grain between your palms for several seconds. Drain the water and repeat until the water is nearly clear.

Spelt Soak spelt overnight in cold water and drain before cooking; use the soaking water as cooking liquid. To cook 1 cup of grain, you will need 1½ cups cooking liquid. Simmer for 45 minutes. This makes 2 cups of cooked spelt.

Teff Teff is a dense cereal grain resembling millet but smaller in size. To cook 1 cup of grain, you will need 1 cup cooking liquid. Simmer for 7 minutes. This makes 1½ cups of cooked teff.

Triticale Soak triticale overnight in cold water and drain before cooking; use the soaking water as cooking liquid. Add salt after cooking rather than during. To cook 1 cup of grain, you will need 3 cups cooking liquid. Simmer for 75 minutes. This makes 2½ cups of cooked triticale.

Wild rice To cook 1 cup of wild rice, you will need 3 cups cooking liquid. Simmer for 30 to 45 minutes. This makes 4 cups of cooked wild rice.

PREPARING CEREALS AND MEALS

Oatmeal, polenta, grits, and farina are prepared by simmering and stirring cereal grains and meals in water, broth, or milk. Bring the liquid up to a full boil first, along with any desired seasonings or aromatics. Use one hand to add the measured cereal a little at a time or pour it slowly and gradually into the simmering liquid. Whisk or stir constantly with the other hand as you add the cereal, to keep it from clumping together.

Once you have added all the cereal, continue to cook over medium to low heat, stirring often. The more you stir, the creamier the finished dish will be.

The cereal thickens while it cooks and craterlike bubbles break the surface. When they are fully cooked, some cereals start to pull away from the sides of the pot as you stir. Serve soft and smooth directly from the pot.

ARTICHOKE AND SPINACH RISOTTO

FROZEN ARTICHOKES work nicely in this risotto, but most tinned artichokes have an overly briny, and sometimes slightly metallic taste.

SERVES 8

2 tbsp olive oil

2 tbsp garlic

4 cups chopped cooked artichoke hearts

1½ cups white wine

2 cups small-dice onions

2½ cups Arborio rice

8 cups Vegetable Broth (page 65), heated

Salt and pepper as needed

10 cups baby spinach

2 cups cherry tomatoes, cut in half

1 cup butter, cut into 1-inch pieces

1¼ cups grated Parmesan

1. Heat 1 tablespoon of olive oil in a medium sauté pan over medium-high heat. Add the garlic and sauté until fragrant, about 1 minute, add the artichokes and ½ cup of the wine. Cover the pan and cook until the artichokes are just tender, about 3 minutes. Remove from heat and set aside.

2. Heat the remaining 1 tablespoon of olive oil in a medium sauce pan over medium-high heat, add the onions, and sauté until they are transparent and tender, about 5 minutes. Add the rice and stir to coat well. Continue to sauté until lightly toasted, 2 to 3 minutes. Add the remaining 1 cup of wine and cook until dry, about 5 minutes.

3. Add about one-third of the hot vegetable broth and a generous pinch of salt and cook, stirring gently until dry. Repeat with the remaining stock, add-ing it in thirds, and cook until the risotto has absorbed the broth. Add the spinach and stir to incorporate. Add the reserved artichokes and remove the pan from heat.

4. Stir in the tomatoes, butter, and Parmesan. Season with additional salt and pepper, if needed. Serve immediately in heated bowls or plates.

COCONUT RICE

MAKES 8 SERVINGS

¼ cup butter

1 tbsp minced garlic

2 tbsp minced ginger

3 cups long-grain white rice

2 cups coconut milk

4 cups water

1 tsp salt

½ tsp ground black pepper

1 cup golden raisins

1 cup toasted, sliced almonds

1. Heat the butter in a saucepan. Add the garlic and ginger, and sauté until fragrant, about 2 minutes. Add the rice and sauté until the grains are coated with the butter and give off a toasted aroma.

2. Add the coconut milk, water, salt, and pepper. Bring to a boil, reduce to a light simmer, and cover. Cook until the rice is tender, about 18 minutes.

3. Fluff the rice with a fork, add the raisins and almonds, and toss lightly to mix. Keep warm, covered, until ready to use.

GARLIC CHEESE GRITS

THESE GRITS get a great garlic flavor from just a little bit of garlic, and they are jam-packed with cheese and butter, just the way they should be. The Tabasco and the cayenne give them a little kick. You may opt to leave out the eggs and milk for soft grits that don't have to be baked. Just stir the remaining cheese and seasonings into the hot grits right before serving.

MAKES 8 SERVINGS

2 tsp salt, divided use

1 quart water

1 cup regular grits

¾ cup butter

2½ cups grated sharp cheddar cheese, divided use

1 cup milk

2 large eggs

1½ cloves garlic, minced

½ tsp Worcestershire sauce

¼ tsp Tabasco sauce

⅛ tsp cayenne pepper

¼ tsp freshly ground black pepper, or to taste

1. Preheat the oven to 350°F. Butter a shallow baking dish.

2. Add 1½ teaspoons salt to the water and bring to a rolling boil. Stir the grits into the water and simmer until thick, 10 to 12 minutes. Remove from the heat and stir in butter and 1½ cups cheese until melted and thoroughly combined.

3. Whisk together the milk, eggs, garlic, Worcestershire, Tabasco, and cayenne in a mixing bowl. Stir the egg mixture into grits until well combined. Add the remaining ½ teaspoon salt and the black pepper.

4. Pour the grits into the buttered dish. Bake until firm, about 1 hour. Top with remaining grated cheese and place under the broiler until the cheese has melted and browned slightly, about 3 minutes. Serve the grits very hot on heated plates.

LEFT TO RIGHT Pour the grits into the simmering water while stirring constantly; the mixture should be fairly thin and free of clumps. Cook the mixture until it thickens and the grits have absorbed the liquid; the grits will need to be stirred more frequently as they cook so that they don't stick to the bottom of the pan. Stir in the butter and cheese to provide a smooth and creamy base for the custard mixture. The finished grits should be rich and velvety.

GRILLED HERBED POLENTA

I F YOU prefer, you can cook the polenta in the oven instead of on the stovetop. Once the cornmeal is all moistened, cover the pan and put it in a 350°F oven for about 20 minutes. Give the polenta enough time to firm up and chill before you slice it into pieces for the grill.

MAKES 8 SERVINGS

4 cups Chicken Broth (page 63)

1 tsp salt, or to taste

¼ tsp ground black pepper, or to taste

1⅓ cups coarse yellow cornmeal

⅔ cup grated Parmesan cheese

2 tbsp butter

2 tsp chopped rosemary

1¼ tsp chopped thyme

NOTE: To make soft polenta, decrease the amount of cornmeal to 1 cup.

1. Line the bottom and sides of a half-sheet pan with plastic wrap. You can adjust the dimensions of your pan by adding a temporary wall of aluminum foil placed widthwise.

2. Bring the chicken broth to a boil and season with the salt and pepper. Add the cornmeal in a stream, stirring constantly until it has been all added. Simmer, stirring often, until the polenta starts to pull away slightly from the sides of the pot, about 25 minutes. Remove from the heat and blend in the cheese, butter, rosemary, and thyme. Adjust seasoning with salt and pepper, if desired.

3. Pour the polenta into the prepared pan. Let cool to room temperature, then cover with plastic wrap and refrigerate until cold enough to cut into shapes, at least 1 and up to 24 hours.

4. Preheat a gas grill to high. If you are using a charcoal grill, build a fire and let it burn down until the coals are glowing red with a light coating of white ash. Spread the coals in an even bed. Clean the cooking grate.

LEFT TO RIGHT Make a wall of aluminum foil to adjust the thickness of the finished polenta, if necessary. Cut the polenta into pieces of any shape that will be big enough to hold up on the grill. Give the polenta a quarter turn while it is grilling on the first side to produce crosshatch marks; this will be the presentation side. The Grilled Herbed Polenta can be paired with a simple green salad for a delicious light lunch, or it can be served with a roast chicken breast for an elegant entrée.

5. Cut the polenta into 12 rectangles, 3 inches by 4 inches. Cut each rectangle in half on the diagonal to make 24 triangles. Grill over direct heat until marked and crisp on the first side, about 4 to 5 minutes. (Rotate the polenta a quarter turn after about each minute of grilling time to give the pieces crosshatch marks, if desired.) Turn the polenta once and finish grilling on the second side, about another 4 to 5 minutes. Serve very hot on a platter.

VEGETARIAN REFRIED BEANS

THE BROWN-AND-PINK pinto bean is the standard bean used in frijoles refritos, or refried beans. Refried beans are typically made with lard; this vegetarian version uses corn oil and spices for flavor. As they cook, some of the beans will break down to a puree and some of the beans will remain whole, giving the mixture a creamy, yet slightly chunky texture.

MAKES 8 SERVINGS

1 tbsp corn oil

2 cups onion, diced

2 tbsp garlic, minced

1 cup tomatoes, diced

½ tsp salt, or to taste

Four 15½-oz cans pinto beans, rinsed and drained

1 tsp cumin seeds, toasted, cracked

1 tsp chili powder

Tabasco sauce, to taste

1. Heat the oil in a large sauté pan. Add the onions and garlic and sweat until the onions are translucent, about 5 minutes.

2. Add the tomatoes, salt, and beans. Mash the beans using a potato masher until only some of the beans still remain whole. Cook over low heat, stirring constantly, until the flavor is well developed, about 10 minutes.

3. Season the beans with the cumin, chili powder, and Tabasco.

RICE AND BEANS

IN SOME parts of the Caribbean, pigeon peas are used to replace the kidney beans here.

MAKES 6 SERVINGS

2 slices bacon, diced

1 tbsp minced garlic

1 lb dried red kidney beans, soaked overnight and drained

3 cups Chicken Broth (page 63)

1 cup coconut milk

1 cup long-grain white rice

6 scallions, chopped

1 tbsp chopped thyme

½ tsp salt

¼ tsp ground black pepper

1. Cook the bacon over medium heat in a sauté pan until the fat is rendered. Add the garlic and cook until fragrant, about 30 seconds.

2. Add the beans and chicken broth, bring to a simmer, and cover. Cook until tender, about 50 minutes. (This can be done in advance. Cool the cooked beans quickly and store in their cooking liquid in a covered container in the refrigerator for up to 24 hours.)

3. Add the coconut milk and rice to the beans. Simmer, covered, until the rice is tender to the bite, about 20 minutes.

4. Remove the pan from the heat and fold in the scallions and thyme. Season with the salt and pepper. Serve hot.

BLACK BEAN CAKES

Y OU CAN cook these cakes on squares of aluminum foil instead of in a skillet, if you prefer.

MAKES 8 SERVINGS

1 lb dried black beans

4 cups Chicken Broth (page 63)

1 cup chopped chorizo sausage

⅔ cup medium-dice yellow onion

2 tbsp minced garlic

1 jalapeño, stemmed, seeded, and minced

1 tsp ground cumin

1 tsp chili powder

1 egg, lightly beaten

2 tbsp chopped cilantro

1½ tbsp lime juice

1 tsp salt

½ cup cornmeal

½ cup sour cream

1 cup Chipotle Pico de Gallo (page 20)

1. Soak the beans overnight in enough cold water to cover them by 3 inches.

2. Drain the beans, place in a pot, and add the chicken broth. Bring to a boil, reduce the heat to a simmer, and cook until the beans are tender, about 45 minutes. Drain.

3. Cook the chorizo over medium heat in a sauté pan until the fat is rendered and the chorizo is slightly crispy. Add the onions, garlic, and jalapeño, and sauté until golden, about 8 to 10 minutes.

4. Add the cumin and chili powder, and sauté until fragrant, about 2 minutes. Remove from the heat and allow the mixture to cool.

5. Combine the beans, the chorizo mixture, the egg, cilantro, lime juice, and salt. Mix well, mash-ing some of the beans (this will help keep the cakes together). Form the mixture into 16 cakes about 2 inches in diameter and ½ inch thick. Dust the cakes lightly with the cornmeal.

6. Preheat the griddle to medium heat on the grill. Cook the cakes until heated through, about 4 to 6 minutes per side. Serve immediately with the sour cream and Chipotle Pico de Gallo.

COUSCOUS WITH ALMONDS AND RAISINS

MAKES 6 SERVINGS

1 cup raisins

2 cups boiling water

3 cups Chicken Broth (page 63)

2 tbsp olive oil

1 tbsp salt

1½ tsp ground black pepper

2 cups couscous

1 cup toasted almonds or pine nuts

¼ cup chopped parsley

3 tbsp extra-virgin olive oil

1. Place the raisins in a small bowl and add enough boiling water to cover them. Let the raisins sit in the water until they plump and soften, about 5 to 7 minutes.

2. Bring the chicken broth to a boil in a large saucepan and add the olive oil, salt, and pepper.

3. Stir in the couscous, making sure that all of it is wet. Cover and set the saucepan aside in a warm place until the couscous is tender, 15 to 20 minutes.

4. Stir in the raisins, toasted almonds or pine nuts, and parsley. Drizzle the extra-virgin olive oil over the top.

HERBED ISRAELI COUSCOUS

MANY PEOPLE might not know about Israeli couscous and would be surprised to find out that it is pasta. It can be used in a variety of ways and has even been used as "vegetarian caviar." Here, it is paired beautifully with a variety of savory herbs.

MAKES 8 SERVINGS

2 tbsp olive oil

2 cups Israeli couscous

4 cups Chicken or Vegetable Broth (pages 63, 65)

¼ cup parsley, chopped

1 tbsp tarragon, chopped

1 tbsp rosemary, chopped

¼ cup lemon juice

1 tsp salt, or to taste

½ tsp freshly ground black pepper, or to taste

1. Heat the olive oil in a 2-quart saucepan over medium heat. Add the couscous and sauté, stirring constantly, until well coated and aromatic, about 2 to 3 minutes.

About Potatoes

Potatoes are easy to keep on hand as a pantry staple. They pair well with a wide range of flavors, and the dishes we've suggested here show their versatility.

SELECT THE RIGHT POTATO FOR THE DISH

Baking potatoes, sometimes known as russets or Idahos, are starchy enough to stick together; choose them for pancakes, rösti, and other dishes where you want the potatoes to hold together in a cake. Yukon Golds, red potatoes, and white potatoes hold their shape well after cooking. Try other varieties if they are available in your area, especially fingerlings, banana, and blue potatoes, for something out of the ordinary.

KEEP POTATOES WHITE

When you peel potatoes, they start to discolor if they are left exposed to the air. Before you start peeling, fill your pot about halfway with cold water. Scrub the potatoes well and remove any eyes, green spots, or blemishes with a paring knife. A peeler or a sharp paring knife is the right tool to cut away just the skin. As soon as the potato is peeled, drop it into the cold water. If you know your time is limited, you can peel potatoes ahead of time and keep them in the refrigerator up to 8 hours before you cook them.

SIMMER POTATOES, DON'T BOIL THEM HARD

Potatoes cook more evenly at a gentle simmer, and they'll be less likely to fall apart. Add salt to the water as it comes up to a simmer., enough so that the water has a slightly salty taste. This assures a great potato flavor; you'll most likely be adding additional salt to the dish as you finish it.

BAKE POTATOES PROPERLY FOR A GREAT TEXTURE

Baked potatoes are transformed into a classic potato cake in the Macaire Potatoes (page 189). Scrub potatoes well before you bake them and be sure to pierce them in a few places. This lets the steam escape so you don't end up with potatoes exploding in your oven. Chefs suggest rubbing a little salt on the outside of the potatoes to draw out the moisture and give the baked potatoes a dry, fluffy texture.

2. Add the broth and bring to a boil. Reduce the heat to medium-low and simmer until just tender, about 10 to 12 minutes.

3. Add the herbs and lemon juice. Season with salt and pepper.

Preparing Potatoes for the Grill

Chefs consider the type of potato they have when they choose a cooking technique. Some potatoes are high in moisture and low in starch—new potatoes or red-skinned potatoes for instance. Purple and fingerling varieties are also typically high in moisture. Even though we tend to think of new potatoes as being quite small, new potatoes are actually any potato with a very thin skin that has been freshly dug. You may find either red- or white-skinned varieties. Sweet potatoes, yams, and some squashes are also relatively high in moisture, which means they can be cooked the same way as high-moisture potatoes. All of these potatoes are great on the grill because they hold their shape well even after they are cooked.

Potatoes that are high in starch, like russet and Idaho potatoes, fall apart easily when they are cooked. To prepare them on the grill, wrap them in foil as described in the following recipe.

GRILLED POTATO AND RED ONION FANS

These take a while to cook on the grill—be sure to plan out when your other menu items need to go on the grill accordingly.

MAKES 8 SERVINGS

8 medium russet potatoes

2 cups sliced red onion

2 tbsp olive oil

2 tsp chopped thyme

1½ tsp salt, or to taste

¾ tsp ground black pepper, or to taste

1. Preheat a gas grill to medium-high. If you are using a charcoal grill, build a fire and let it burn down until the coals are glowing red with a light coating of white ash. Spread the coals out in an even bed on one side of the grill. Clean the cooking grate.

2. Peel the potatoes, and keep them submerged in cold water so they do not discolor. Make parallel slices about ¼ inch apart through the potatoes, without cutting all the way through the potato. Insert some of the red onion into each slice in the potato. This will open up the potato a little.

3. Cut a large sheet of foil and brush the dull side lightly with some of the oil. Arrange the potatoes on the foil (they can be quite close to each other but not touching) and drizzle with the remaining oil, the thyme, salt, and pepper. Close the foil around the potatoes.

4. Grill the potatoes over indirect medium heat, turning every 15 to 20 minutes, until the potatoes are very tender, about 1¼ hours. Serve immediately.

To make even cuts without cutting all the way through the potato, try placing two chopsticks on the cutting surface, on either side of the potato; the chopsticks will stop your knife at just the right point, before you cut all the way through the potato. But if you do cut through the potato, don't worry—it will still taste great.

MACAIRE POTATOES

WELL-SEASONED, SIMPLE, and delicious, especially when eaten piping hot. They are crispy on the outside and soft and moist on the inside.

MAKES 8 SERVINGS

8 medium baking potatoes

¼ cup butter

1 large egg, lightly beaten

2 tsp salt, as needed

1/2 tsp ground black pepper, as needed

½ cup canola oil, divided use

1. Preheat the oven to 425°F. Scrub the potatoes well and blot them dry. Pierce the skins in a few places with a paring knife or kitchen fork. Set them on a baking sheet.

2. Bake the potatoes until very tender and cooked through, about 1 hour.

3. Remove the potatoes from the oven. Cut the potatoes in half. Hold the halved potatoes in a clean towel to protect your hands, if needed. Use a serving spoon to scoop the flesh from the potatoes into a heated mixing bowl. It is important to do this while the potatoes are very hot.

4. Add the butter, egg, salt, and pepper to the potatoes. Use a wooden spoon or a table fork to mash them into the potatoes until evenly blended. Shape the potato mixture into 16 equal-sized cakes, about ½ inch thick.

5. Heat 2 tablespoons of the oil in a large sauté pan over medium-high heat. Add the potato cakes to the pan in batches. They should not be touching one another. Sauté until golden and crisp on the first side, 2 to 3 minutes. Turn the cakes carefully and cook until golden and crisp on the second side, another 2 to 3 minutes. Repeat, adding more oil to the pan as necessary, until all of the cakes are sautéed. Serve hot.

GRILLED SWEET POTATOES
with Pecan-Molasses Butter

GRILLING BRINGS out the best in sweet potatoes, giving them a touch of crispness and a more intense flavor. The pecan-molasses butter is a great choice, since it echoes the smoky tastes from the

LEFT TO RIGHT For the Macaire Potatoes, the potatoes should be just cooked through before you cut them and scoop the flesh out; make sure that the first side of the potato cake has a rich golden brown crust before flipping it, otherwise it may fall apart while it is being flipped.

grill and harkens back to the traditional savor of a favorite Thanksgiving side dish, without the mini-marshmallows.

MAKES 8 SERVINGS

1 cup softened butter

¼ cup chopped toasted pecans

1 tbsp molasses

2 tsp salt

1½ tsp ground black pepper

4 large sweet potatoes, peeled and thinly sliced

¼ cup vegetable oil, or as needed

1. To make the pecan-molasses butter: Blend together the butter, pecans, and molasses until smooth. Add ¼ teaspoon of the salt and a pinch of the pepper. Pipe into rosettes or roll into a cylinder (see page 202), and refrigerate until needed.

2. Preheat a gas grill to medium-high; leave one burner off. If you are using a charcoal grill, build a fire and let it burn down until the coals are glowing red with a moderate coating of white ash. Spread the coals in an even bed on one side of the grill. Clean the cooking grate.

3. Brush the sweet potatoes with the oil and season with the remaining salt and pepper.

4. Grill the sweet potatoes over direct heat, turning once, until marked on both sides, about 3 minutes per side. Turn the sweet potatoes over and move to indirect heat. Grill the potatoes, covered and turning as necessary, until tender throughout, about 6 to 8 minutes.

5. Serve the sweet potatoes slices immediately on a heated platter or plates topped with slices or rosettes of the pecan-molasses butter.

POTATO GRATIN

GRUYÈRE. A cow's milk cheese produced in Switzerland and France, has a nutty, rich flavor and melts beautifully, and is the cheese classically used in a potato gratin.

MAKES 6 SERVINGS

1 lb russet potatoes, peeled, cut into 1/4-inch slices

1 cup whole milk

1 cup heavy cream

1 garlic clove, minced

½ tsp salt, or to taste

¼ tsp freshly ground black pepper, or to taste

½ cup Gruyère cheese, grated

3 tbsp breadcrumbs

3 tbsp Parmesan cheese

1. Combine the potatoes, milk, heavy cream, garlic, salt, and pepper in a large saucepan. Simmer until the potatoes are three-quarters cooked, about 8 to 10 minutes.

2. Remove the potatoes from the heat and stir in the Gruyère. Pour the potatoes into a small, shallow pan. Combine the breadcrumbs and Parmesan and scatter evenly over the potatoes. Bake in a 350°F oven until golden brown, about 30 minutes. Allow the potatoes to set for 5 to 7 minutes before slicing.

A Vegetable Primer

Vegetables include a number of foods that botanically are classified as fruits. Tomatoes, peppers, squash, and other seed-bearing foods are really fruits. Because these are often used in savory preparations, their culinary application is the guiding principle for listing them here.

The USDA's Dietary Guidelines divides vegetables into five groups: Dark green vegetables, orange vegetables, legumes, starchy vegetables, and other vegetables. Eating a variety of colors—including red cabbage or red bell peppers, yellow sweet corn, white garlic, and deep green spinach—provides a wide array of vitamins, minerals, and phytochemicals, many of which are found in pigments and fiber. Orange and dark green vegetables are good sources of vitamin C and are high in beta carotene, which the body uses to make vitamin A (the chlorophyll in green vegetables masks the carotenoid pigments). Legumes and dark green vegetables are good sources of folate. Potatoes, avocados, and legumes are also high in potassium.

The Dietary Guidelines recommend 2½ cups of vegetables per day for a 2,000 calorie diet, with the following amounts recommended over the course of a week:

DARK GREEN VEGETABLES: 3 cups/week
(*broccoli, spinach, most greens*)

ORANGE VEGETABLES: 2 cups/week
(*carrots, sweet potatoes, pumpkin, winter squash*)

LEGUMES: 3 cups/week
(*dried beans, chickpeas, tofu*)

STARCHY VEGETABLES: 3 cups/week
(*corn, white potatoes, green peas*)

OTHER VEGETABLES: 6½ cups/week
(*tomatoes, cabbage, celery, cucumber, lettuce, onions, peppers, green beans, cauliflower, summer squash*)

Most Americans do not eat anywhere near these recommended intakes, with the possible exception of starchy vegetables, specifically potatoes.

SELECTING VEGETABLES

The essential point to remember when choosing vegetables is that they are, in general, highly perishable. The more fresh and appealing a vegetable looks when you buy it (or pick it, if you have a garden), the greater its level of nutrients.

As soon as any vegetable is harvested it begins to undergo significant changes. The more delicate the vegetable, the more dramatic the change. Sweet corn and peas, for instance, begin converting sugars into starch, giving over-the-hill corn and peas a telltale sticky texture and pasty taste. When you consider the time that it takes to get foods from the field to the market, you can see why it is best to shop frequently for vegetables, keep them refrigerated, and cook them within a few days. At some times of the year you may find that frozen vegetables, which are typically processed right in the field upon harvesting, are a good alternative to less-than-ripe fresh produce. Peas, spinach, corn, and green beans are good examples of vegetables that might be best frozen.

Root vegetables (sometimes called winter vegetables) are significantly less perishable and generally can be stored without any marked loss of quality for several weeks or, if carefully handled, even months. Hard-skinned squashes, turnips, carrots, parsnips, and cabbages fall into this category of vegetables. The traditional way to store these vegetables is in a root cellar under a good covering of straw or hay, where they benefit from a constant cool temperature and relatively high humidity. Since most of us don't have root cellars, however, it is best to use them within a week or two of purchase.

If vegetables are sold as organic, they must meet specific guidelines regarding the land they are grown on and the types of fertilizers and other cultivating aids that can be used. Look for the "Organic" symbol on the label or posted near the display.

Some markets offer precut vegetables, which can save on preparation time. When inspecting the package, look for fresh, moist surfaces. Even if the produce is labeled "prewashed," you should rinse it in cool water to refresh it.

Vegetable Cooking Primer

Each vegetable has distinct properties when it is properly cooked. Fully cooked green beans, for example, have a very different texture from fully cooked carrots. Different cooking methods also result in different textures in the finished dish. Stir-fried vegetables may be fairly crisp, while stewed and braised vegetables are often cooked until they nearly fall apart. Personal preference and the cuisine your recipe draws from also influence how you judge doneness.

The most reliable doneness tests for vegetables are taste and touch. Bite into a piece of the vegetable when it is raw, and then again at various points as it cooks. Notice the flavor and texture. If tasting the vegetable isn't practical, pierce it with a knife, fork, or skewer and gauge the resistance it gives. Consider the way you will be using the vegetable to determine the right degree of doneness. Will it be served alone or as part of a complex dish?

Most stand-alone vegetable dishes, however they are prepared, turn out best when the vegetables are cooked just until tender. You should be able to bite into the vegetable easily, but it should still offer slight resistance.

Stewed and braised vegetables should be fully cooked. Aim to cook vegetables for these dishes until they are completely tender but retain their shape and color. When you boil or steam vegetables for a purée, cook them until they almost fall apart on their own. At this point, they should be easy to push through a sieve or purée in a blender.

In some recipes, vegetables are blanched, not to cook them through but to set their colors, make them easier to peel, or to improve their flavor. Blanched vegetables are boiled very briefly, just long enough to cook the outermost layer, then submerged in cold water to stop the cooking process. The vegetable retains, for the most part, the texture it had when raw. Similarly, vegetables are sometimes boiled, steamed, or roasted to near doneness, then finished in a second step, sometimes using a different technique, such as grilling or sautéing. Boiling or cooking to near doneness is known as parboiling or parcooking.

Vegetables can be the centerpiece of a meal or can be used to add flavor, eye appeal, and texture to meals featuring meat, fish, or poultry. The recipes in this book offer a wide range of choices for those who want to expand their repertoire of vegetable dishes.

It isn't always easy to determine when a vegetable dish is something to serve "on the side" and when it is the main attraction. Think about a typical Thanksgiving table: At the center, a large, glossy, brown turkey, but ranged all around, a banquet of vegetable sides: Brussels sprouts with chestnuts, green beans flavored with nuts or bacon, creamed corn or spinach, baked squash drizzled with honey. Adding a variety of vegetable dishes to your meals means you have done more than fill up the empty space on your dinner plate, of course. A judicious selection livens up any main dish, even main dishes that feature vegetables.

THE MAIN DISH

The ingredients and cooking technique used for a main dish can help guide you toward the best side dish. Simply prepared foods, whether grilled, roasted, poached, sautéed or baked, can accommodate a more elaborate side dish. Stewed or braised vegetables, or a vegetable served with a sauce or a topping, are possibilities.

The intensity of flavor of the main item also should be taken into consideration. If you are serving a main dish of jerked chicken or a seafood curry, then your side dishes can be simply prepared.

Some main dishes have traditional sides. Apart from Thanksgiving traditions, we have come to expect certain vegetables with specific dishes: lightly steamed new peas with salmon for a New England Fourth of July, corn-on-the-cob with burgers and dogs for a backyard barbecue, glazed carrots with pot roast. It is up to you to decide if you like the tradition or want to turn it on its head by trying something unexpected, like parsnips with roast chicken instead of broc-

OXTAIL STEW IN
RED WINE (PAGE 135)

BEEF IN MUSSAMAN
CURRY SAUCE (PAGE 131)

BRAISED BEEF SHORT RIBS

(PAGE 130)

BEER CAN CHICKEN (PAGE 140)

LEMON-GINGER GRILLED CHICKEN
(PAGE 142)

CHICKEN MOLE
(PAGE 143)

**PAN-SMOKED CHICKEN WITH
APRICOT-ANCHO BARBECUE GLAZE
(PAGE 145)**

**BROILED LAMB CHOPS WITH WHITE BEAN
AND ROSEMARY RAGOUT (PAGE 153)**

LAMB KHORMA (PAGE 152)

CEDAR-PLANKED SALMON WITH
HUCKLEBERRY-ZINFANDEL SAUCE
(PAGE 166)

GINGER SESAME STIR-FRIED SCALLOPS
WITH LO MEIN NOODLES (PAGE 171)

SWORDFISH WITH A TOMATO-OLIVE RAGÙ
(PAGE 170)

SAUTÉED TOFU WITH RED CURRY PASTE,
PEAS, SCALLIONS, AND CILANTRO (PAGE 178)

MOO SHU VEGETABLES
(PAGE 177)

GRILLED HERBED POLENTA
(PAGE 184)

GRILLED ASPARAGUS AND
SWEET PEPPERS (PAGE 158)

BRUSSELS SPROUTS WITH
MUSTARD GLAZE (PAGE 196)

CREAMED SWISS CHARD
WITH PROSCIUTTO (PAGE 200)

SWEET CORN WITH ROASTED GARLIC, SCALLION,
AND LIME-CHILE BUTTERS (PAGE 202)

CHEDDAR CORN FRITTERS
(PAGE 204)

ROASTED CORN SUCCOTASH
(PAGE 204)

MAPLE-GLAZED TURNIPS
(PAGE 209)

**HOISIN-CARAMELIZED
ROOT VEGETABLES (PAGE 210)**

**ZUCCHINI PANCAKES WITH
TZATZIKI SAUCE (PAGE 208)**

coli or green beans, or collard greens with meatloaf instead of creamed spinach or corn.

THE SEASONS

One of the greatest pleasures of shopping at farmstands and local markets is seeing the parade of seasonal vegetables. Whenever something is at its peak, you get more than the best buy. You also get the best flavor and nutrition. Sometimes, you may find it more appealing to let the side dishes you want to make from those fat, juicy asparagus or tender romano beans help you decide what main dish to make, instead of letting the main dish dictate the sides.

FLAVORS

Vegetables have distinct, and in some cases, assertive flavors. Think about how all the flavors will work together on a single plate. Vegetables that are somewhat sweet or starchy may taste too dull or bland if you pair them with a creamy or delicately flavored main dish, but those same vegetable side dishes take on a different character when paired with a more intensely flavored main dish.

COLORS

Too much of any color on a plate can be boring. Vegetables can add vibrant colors—deep greens, soft yellows, reds that range from pink to burgundy, and oranges. A plate of sliced roasted chicken is more attractive when bold colors are added, but less appealing when that same chicken is paired with only white or pale yellow vegetables.

TEXTURES

Just as the texture of a chicken changes depending upon the cooking technique you use, so will the texture of your vegetable side dishes. Zucchini is tender when stewed as part of a ratatouille, but takes on a whole different character when it is turned into crisp pancakes.

ASPARAGUS A LA PARRILLA

THE SPANISH word "parrilla" refers to a grill that is set over an open fire. This dish pairs thick spears of grilled asparagus with a ham, parsley, and olive oil sauce.

MAKES 4 TO 6 SERVINGS

1 lb asparagus

6 tbsp extra-virgin olive oil, or as needed

Salt and pepper, as needed

½ cup fine-dice Serrano ham

1 tbsp minced garlic

¼ cup Chicken Broth (page 63)

¼ cup chopped flat-leaf parsley

1 tbsp lemon juice

2 hard-cooked eggs, chopped

1. Preheat a broiler or grill. Trim and peel the asparagus. Brush liberally with 2 tablespoons olive oil (or as needed) and season with salt and pepper. Broil or grill the asparagus until it is lightly charred and cooked through, turning to cook evenly, about 5 minutes. Transfer to heated plates or a platter.

2. Heat ¼ cup olive oil in a sauté pan over medium heat until it shimmers. Add the ham and garlic and sauté, stirring constantly, until the garlic is aromatic, about 1 minute. Add the broth and parsley and cook an additional minute. Whisk in the lemon juice; the sauce will thicken as the lemon juice is worked into the sauce. Season to taste with salt and pepper.

3. Pour the ham and olive oil sauce over the asparagus. Garnish with chopped, hard-cooked eggs.

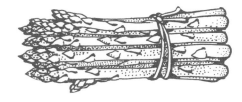

GRILLED LEEKS

LEEKS TEND to trap dirt and sand in their layers, so be sure to rinse them well in cool water.

MAKES 8 SERVINGS

8 leeks

¼ cup olive oil

2 tbsp lemon juice

1 tbsp chopped marjoram

1 tbsp chopped oregano

1 tsp salt

¼ tsp ground black pepper

1. Preheat a gas grill to medium-high; leave one burner off. If you are using a charcoal grill, build a fire and let it burn down until the coals are glowing red with a moderate coating of white ash. Spread the coals in an even bed on one side of the grill. Clean the cooking grate.

2. Trim the leeks to remove the roots and coarse green leaves; rinse thoroughly. (If you are using medium-sized leeks, cut them in half but leave the root end intact.) Let the leeks drain or blot them dry.

3. Combine the olive oil, lemon juice, marjoram, oregano, salt, and pepper to make a marinade.

4. Place the leeks on the grill over indirect heat and brush lightly with some of the marinade. Grill, turning every 5 to 6 minutes and brushing with additional marinade, until the leeks are tender, about 20 to 25 minutes. Move the leeks to the hottest part of

the grill and cook until marked on each side, about 2 minutes per side.

5. Serve the leeks immediately on a heated platter, drizzled with any remaining marinade. For a Greek-style variation, top the grilled leeks with ¼ cup pitted black olives and ⅓ cup crumbled feta cheese.

SAUTÉED BROCCOLI RAAB
with Garlic and Crushed Red Pepper

MAKES 6 SERVINGS

THE FLAVORS in this dish also work beautifully with blanched, chopped spinach, green beans, or cauliflower florets.

3 lb broccoli raab

¼ cup olive oil

3 tbsp thinly sliced garlic

1 or 2 anchovy fillets, optional

¼ to ½ tsp crushed red pepper flakes

Salt and pepper, as needed

1. Bring a large pot of salted water to a boil. Wash the broccoli raab and remove any tough stems and very large leaves. Blanch the broccoli raab in the boiling water until it is bright green, about 3 minutes. Drain and rinse the broccoli raab to stop the cooking. Squeeze dry and chop, if desired.

2. In a sauté pan, heat the oil over low heat. Add the garlic and cook gently, stirring frequently, until the garlic is limp and barely golden, about 2 minutes. (Keep the heat low to avoid scorching the garlic.)

3. Add the anchovy fillets, if using, and smash them into the olive oil with the back of a spoon. Cook until the anchovy is dissolved, about 1 minute. Add the red pepper flakes and stir into the oil. Increase

the heat to high, add the broccoli raab, and sauté quickly until the broccoli raab is very hot, about 3 minutes. Season to taste with salt and pepper. Serve immediately.

About Brussels Sprouts

Brussels sprouts, a member of the cabbage family, are usually available fresh from late summer to late winter. Select small, bright-green sprouts with closed leaves; smaller Brussels sprouts are more tender than the larger ones. Brussel sprouts shine in simple dishes that make the most of their nutty taste. If you can find them sold on the stalk, you may be surprised at the difference in flavor and texture, compared to those sold in small round cartons.

TRIMMING BRUSSELS SPROUTS

Use a paring knife to trim away the end of the Brussels sprout that was attached to the stem. Next, pull away any very small or withered outer leaves. Once the leaves and stem are trimmed, cut into the stem. Hold the sprouts, one at a time, with the stem end facing up. Press the blade of your paring knife into the stem, making a cut about ¼ inch deep. This will help the dense core of the Brussels sprouts to cook quickly. The faster you cook the sprouts, the sweeter they will taste.

FINISHING BRUSSELS SPROUTS

Cook the Brussels sprouts until they have a good color and are nearly tender. For more flavor and a beautiful sheen, heat the ingredients for a glaze— maple syrup, honey, and molasses are all good options. Add the pre-cooked sprouts to the pan and keep them in motion, stirring or rolling them in the glaze, until they are evenly coated. They should be firm enough to hold together when you serve them, but tender enough to slice easily with a table knife.

SAUTÉED BRUSSELS SPROUTS
with Pancetta

THE MAJORITY of the preparation work comes in removing the core and pulling the brussel sprout layers apart. This is well worth the effort, as the tender leaves cook quickly and evenly to a beautiful bright green color, lightly glazed with olive oil and bits of crisp pancetta.

MAKES 8 SERVINGS

6 cups Brussels sprouts, trimmed

2½ oz pancetta, roughly chopped

¼ cup extra-virgin olive oil

½ cup onion, chopped

1 tbsp butter

2 tbsp water

1 tsp salt, or to taste

½ tsp freshly ground black pepper, or to taste

1. Slice each Brussels sprout in half and remove the core. Gently pull the layers of leaves apart.
2. Heat a large sauté pan and add the olive oil and pancetta. Render the fat from the pancetta, until it is lightly crispy. Remove the pancetta and reserve.
3. Add the onions and cook until translucent, about 5 minutes.
4. Add the butter and swirl to melt.
5. Add the Brussels sprouts and 2 tablespoons of water to the pan.
6. Sauté over medium heat, tossing to coat. Cook until leaves are tender and bright green, about 6 to 8 minutes. Season to taste with salt and freshly ground black pepper. Fold in the reserved pancetta and serve immediately.

BRUSSELS SPROUTS
with Mustard Glaze

IF THE Brussels sprouts are to be served with a meat or poultry dish, like pork roast or turkey, you can replace the vegetable broth with a *jus,* or defatted pan juices from the cooking.

MAKES 4 SERVINGS

3 cups Brussels sprouts

¾ cup Vegetable Broth (page 65)

1 tbsp whole-grain mustard

Salt and pepper as needed

1. Rinse the Brussels sprouts, drain, and trim the stem ends by cutting away a thin slice with a paring knife. Cut a shallow X into each stem. Pull away any loose or yellowed leaves.
2. Bring a large pot of salted water to a rolling boil over high heat. Add the Brussels sprouts and cook until the tip of a paring knife goes into the stem end of the largest Brussels sprout easily, 10 to 12 minutes. Drain in a colander and reserve.
3. Return the pot to high heat. Add the vegetable broth and the mustard, whisking until the mustard is evenly blended into the broth. Simmer until the mixture is lightly thickened, about 2 minutes. Return the Brussels sprouts to the pot; stir or toss until evenly coated. Season to taste with salt and pepper. Serve at once in a heated bowl or on heated plates.

BELGIAN ENDIVE
à la Meunière

BELGIAN ENDIVES are deliberately protected from light as they grow to produce pale, satiny heads. Choose tight heads that show no scars or other blemishes. The leaves should be closed into a tight point and should have a pale ivory color, shading to a light yellowish green (or sometimes violet) at the tips.

MAKES 4 SERVINGS

4 heads Belgian endive

2 tsp sugar

Salt and pepper as needed

2 tbsp fresh lemon juice

1 cup whole milk, or as needed

All-purpose flour for dredging

¼ cup vegetable oil

3 tbsp unsalted butter

2 tbsp minced flat-leaf parsley

1. Split each endive in half lengthwise and remove any bruised or damaged outer leaves. Bring a large pot of water to a boil and season with the sugar, 1 teaspoon salt, and 1 teaspoon of the lemon juice. Add the endives and boil, covered, until tender, 3 to 4 minutes. Transfer to a colander and drain, cut side down. When just cool enough to handle, press and drain on absorbent towels.

2. Transfer the endives to a cutting board and flatten each piece slightly by pressing down on it with the palm of your hand. Season the endives with salt and pepper. Put the milk and flour in separate bowls. Dip each endive half in the milk and then dredge in the flour.

3. Heat the oil in a large skillet over medium-high heat. Add the endives, in batches if necessary, and fry on the first side until golden brown, 2 to 3 minutes. Turn and fry on the second side until crisp and brown, 2 minutes more. Transfer the endives to a serving dish and cover to keep warm.

4. Pour off any excess oil from the pan and wipe out the browned flour with a paper towel. Add the butter and cook over medium heat until the butter begins to brown and take on a nutty aroma, about 30 seconds. Add the remaining lemon juice and the parsley and swirl it until the mixture thickens slightly. Pour the sauce over the endives and serve immediately.

SAUTÉED BROCCOLI RAAB
with Toasted Pine Nuts

THE BITTER and pungent flavor of broccoli raab is made more delicate by blanching it first. If a stronger flavor is desired, the trimmed broccoli raab can be added raw to the sauté pan after the shallots have been sweated and cooked in the same pan. Simply add a small amount of water to steam it through.

MAKES 6 SERVINGS

3 lb broccoli raab

¼ cup pine nuts

¼ cup olive oil

1 tsp garlic, chopped

1 tbsp shallots, chopped

1 tsp salt, or to taste

1 tsp freshly ground black pepper, or to taste

1. Bring a large pot of salted water to a boil.

2. Wash the broccoli raab and remove any tough stems and very large leaves.

3. Toast the pine nuts in a small, dry skillet over

medium heat, stirring them frequently, about 3 to 4 minutes.

4. Blanch the broccoli raab in the boiling water until just wilted, about 2 to 4 minutes. Drain.

5. Heat the olive oil in a large sauté pan over medium-high heat. Sweat the garlic and shallots in the oil just until translucent, about 3 to 4 minutes.

6. Add the broccoli raab to the sauté pan. Quickly sauté all the ingredients. Add the pine nuts and adjust the seasoning.

SAUTÉED SWISS CHARD

Swiss chard can be found in the produce aisle near other leafy greens. Look for rainbow chard, which makes this dish truly beautiful.

MAKES 6 SERVINGS

½ cup pine nuts

3 tbsp olive oil

6 tbsp shallots, minced

2 tbsp garlic, minced

2 bunches Swiss chard, torn into pieces

1 tsp salt, or to taste

½ tsp freshly ground black pepper, or to taste

¼ cup white wine

1. Toast the pine nuts in a small dry skillet over medium heat, stirring them frequently, about 3 to 4 minutes.

2. Heat the olive oil in a large sauté pan over medium-high heat. Add the shallots to the pan and sweat until translucent, about 5 minutes. Add the garlic and sweat until aromatic, another 2 minutes.

3. Add the chard to the pan, and season with salt and pepper. Sauté until just barely wilted, about 5 to 7 minutes. Sauté in batches if necessary.

4. Add the white wine to the pan and cover. Steam the chard until the spines are tender and the liquid has almost evaporated, about 5 minutes.

SUMMER SQUASH SAUTÉ

This versatile side adds a refreshing element to almost any dish and using seasonal vegetables eliminates the need for heavy garnishes.

MAKES 8 SERVINGS

1 tbsp olive oil

1 onion, sliced

1 lb zucchini, cut into ¼-inch slices

1 lb yellow squash, cut into ¼-inch slices

2 tomatoes, chopped

Salt, to taste

Freshly ground black pepper, to taste

1. Heat the olive oil in a large sauté pan over medium-high heat.

2. Add the onions, zucchini, and yellow squash, and sauté until light brown and tender, about 5 to 7 minutes.

3. Season with salt and pepper.

4. Stir in the chopped tomato, cook for an additional 2 minutes, and serve.

SWEET AND SOUR GREEN BEANS

These tasty, stir-fried green beans are easy to prepare, and have a refreshing flavor that will complement your favorite Asian-inspired entrées.

MAKES 8 SERVINGS

1 lb green beans, trimmed, cut into 2-inch lengths

2 tbsp soy sauce

2 tbsp hoisin sauce

2 tbsp rice wine vinegar

2 tsp peanut oil

1 tsp (or to taste) hot pepper sauce

1 garlic clove, minced

One 8-oz can water chestnuts, sliced, drained

1 tsp dark sesame oil

1. Place the green beans in a steamer basket and set in a saucepan over 1 inch of boiling water. Cover and steam until just tender, about 5 minutes; drain.

2. Combine the soy sauce, hoisin sauce, vinegar, and the hot pepper sauce in a small bowl.

3. Put 2 teaspoons of peanut oil in a wok or large skillet, and set over high heat. Add the green beans and garlic. Stir-fry the beans for 2 minutes; add the soy sauce mixture and cook, stirring, about 2 minutes. Stir in the water chestnuts and drizzle with the sesame oil. Serve at once.

PAN-STEAMED LEMON ASPARAGUS

S PRING AND early summer is the optimal time for asparagus as delicate, pencil-thin stems are more readily available. This very easy recipe maximizes the unique flavor of fresh asparagus, by using simple seasoning agents for this seasonal favorite.

MAKES 8 SERVINGS

2 bunches asparagus

2 tbsp olive oil

¼ cup shallots, minced

4 tsp garlic, minced

¼ cup lemon juice

¼ cup white wine

1. Trim the bottoms off the asparagus spears so that the asparagus are equal in length.

2. Heat the oil in a large sauté pan over medium heat. Sweat the shallots and garlic until translucent, about 2 minutes. Add the asparagus and cook for 4 to 5 minutes.

3. Add the lemon juice and white wine to the pan and cover. Steam the asparagus for 3 minutes, or until cooked through. Serve immediately.

PAN-STEAMED ZUCCHINI AND YELLOW SQUASH NOODLES

A MANDOLINE IS a manual slicer, with a long rectangular shape and adjustable blade settings, that makes long, narrow, even slicing a snap. It is the ideal tool with which to accomplish the long thin "noodle-like" cuts called for in this dish. Otherwise, use a chef's knife or cleaver to carefully cut the squashes into long, thin julienne strips.

MAKES 8 SERVINGS

1 lb zucchini

1½ lb yellow squash

1 tbsp butter

3 tbsp shallots, minced

1 tbsp garlic, minced

¼ cup Vegetable Broth (page 65)

1 tbsp chives, minced

1 tbsp tarragon, minced

1 tsp lemon juice

½ tsp salt, or to taste

¼ tsp freshly ground black pepper

1. Cut the zucchini and yellow squash lengthwise into ¼-inch thick noodles using a mandoline. Discard the center of the squashes.

2. Heat the butter in a large sauté pan over medium heat. Add the shallots and garlic. Sweat until the shallots are translucent, about 3 to 4 minutes.

3. Add the squash noodles and broth. Cover the pan and steam the squash until tender, about 5 minutes. Drain any excess liquid.

4. Season with the herbs, lemon juice, salt, and pepper. Serve hot.

GRILLED CAULIFLOWER
with Brown Butter Sauce

THIS HAS a very different but delicious flavor that might surprise people. The cauliflower gets crispy on the outside and is still a little creamy on the inside. The brown butter sauce adds a nutty flavor and a rich texture and sheen. Very tasty.

MAKES 8 SERVINGS

2 heads cauliflower

½ cup olive oil

2 tsp salt

1 tsp ground black pepper

½ cup butter

1. Preheat a gas grill to medium. If you are using a charcoal grill, build a fire and let it burn down until the coals are glowing red with a moderate coating of white ash. Spread the coals in an even bed. Clean the cooking grate.

2. Cut each cauliflower into ½-inch-thick slices. Trim the thick part of the stem away, leaving enough of the stem intact that the slices don't fall apart.

3. Bring a large pot of water to a boil. Blanch the cauliflower slices until they are half cooked and you can easily stick a paring knife about halfway into the stem of the cauliflower, about 3 to 4 minutes.

4. Drain the cauliflower and let dry for 5 minutes. Brush the cauliflower with the olive oil and season with the salt and pepper.

5. Grill the cauliflower until there are ample grill marks, about 5 minutes. Turn the cauliflower 90 degrees and grill until there are crosshatch marks on the cauliflower, another 5 minutes. Turn over and grill until the slices are tender in the center and they can be pierced easily with a paring knife, about 10 minutes more.

6. Melt the butter in a small pan over medium heat (about 5 minutes before the cauliflower slices are done cooking). Bring the butter to a light simmer, stirring constantly. Continue to simmer the butter while stirring until it turns a light brown and gives off a nutty aroma, 1 to 2 minutes.

7. Serve the cauliflower immediately with the brown butter sauce drizzled over the top.

CREAMED SWISS CHARD WITH PROSCIUTTO

As THIS dish proves, creamed vegetable dishes don't have to be bland. The assertive taste of chard paired with prosciutto is enhanced, not masked, by the addition of a touch of heavy cream.

MAKES 4 SERVINGS

2 tbsp olive oil

¼ cup diced prosciutto

¼ cup minced yellow onion

1 tbsp minced garlic

8 cups chopped Swiss chard leaves

⅓ cup heavy cream

Salt and pepper as needed

¼ cup grated Parmesan cheese

¼ tsp grated nutmeg

1. Heat the olive oil in a large sauté pan over medium heat. Add the prosciutto and sauté until aromatic, about 1 minute. Increase the heat to high, and add the onion and garlic. Sauté, stirring constantly, until the garlic is aromatic, about 1 minute more.

2. Add the Swiss chard, sautéing just until the leaves wilt, about 5 minutes. Add the heavy cream and bring to a simmer. Cook the Swiss chard until it is tender, about 5 minutes.

3. Season generously with salt and pepper. Remove from the heat, and stir in the Parmesan and nutmeg. Serve immediately in a heated bowl or on heated plates.

BEANS AND GREENS SAUTÉ

PREPARE THIS savory sauté in a cast-iron skillet right on the grill while you grill the pork, or make it ahead of time on the stovetop. If you can't find beet greens, substitute spinach, kale, escarole, collard greens, or turnip greens.

MAKES 6 SERVINGS

2 tbsp olive oil

2 tsp minced garlic

10 cups coarsely chopped beet greens

½ cup Chicken Broth (page 63)

1 tsp salt, or to taste

½ tsp ground black pepper, or to taste

2 cups cooked or canned cannellini beans, drained and rinsed

2 tsp malt vinegar, or to taste

1. Heat a large sauté pan over the hottest part of the fire or a burner set at medium-high heat. Add the olive oil and heat until the oil shimmers. Add the garlic and move the pan or turn down the heat. Sauté the garlic, stirring frequently, until it is tender and aromatic, about 3 minutes.

2. Add the beet greens and cook, stirring and tossing briskly with a wooden spoon to coat the greens evenly with the oil. When the greens have cooked down and are a vivid green color, add the broth. Season with ½ teaspooon of the salt and a pinch of the pepper.

3. Bring the broth to a simmer, then add the beans and cook, stirring frequently, until the greens are fully wilted and the dish is very hot. Season to taste with the malt vinegar, salt, and pepper.

ROASTED CARROTS AND PARSNIPS WITH HERBS

ROOT VEGETABLES like carrots and parsnips develop a mellow, sweet flavor when slowly oven-roasted. By keeping the cuts relatively similar in size, the pieces will all cook in the same amount of time. This side is delicious with roasted meats and poultry, particularly in the fall and winter when root vegetables are more prevalent.

MAKES 6 SERVINGS

4 parsnips

5 carrots

3 tbsp olive oil

1 tsp salt, or to taste

½ tsp freshly ground black pepper, or to taste

2 tsp rosemary, chopped

2 tsp sage, chopped

1. Preheat the oven to 350°F.

2. Peel the parsnips and carrots. Cut them into chunky pieces roughly 2 inches long and I-inch thick. All the pieces should be of uniform size and shape.

3. Toss the parsnips and carrots with the oil, salt, pepper, rosemary, and sage in a large bowl.

4. Spread evenly in a large shallow baking pan. Roast the vegetables in the lower third of the oven until tender, about 30 to 35 minutes.

Flavored Butters

Flavored butters, or compound butters as they are also known, are simple to make. You just blend flavoring ingredients into softened butter. We've suggested some flavoring combinations here, but you can let your imagination run wild. Try adding minced sun-dried tomatoes and pesto to the butter (see page 85 for a pesto recipe), olives, capers, fresh herbs of all descriptions, citrus zest, spices, or horseradish. Choose your flavors with an eye to the food you want to serve the butter with. The flavor should complement but not overwhelm the dish.

After you blend the butter, it can be handled in a number of different ways. Simply pack it into a small crock or bowl to use as a spread for sandwiches or to add as a finish to grilled vegetables. Another option is to pipe the butter into rosettes, about 1 tablespoon each, onto a lined plate or baking sheet, then refrigerate or freeze the rosettes until they are firm.

One efficient option is to shape the mixed butter into a cylinder. Cut a large sheet of plastic wrap. Mound the butter about 3 inches away from one of the long sides of the wrap. Fold the plastic wrap over the mound and then tighten the wrap around the butter. Use a straight edge, like a ruler or the edge of a sheet pan, to tighten up the cylinder to keep the diameter of the log even. Once rolled, twist the ends to press out any remaining air pockets and seal the wrap around the butter. Chill the butter until it is firm enough to slice.

Store flavored butters in the refrigerator for 3 or 4 days. If you plan to hold on to the butter for longer than that, keep it in the freezer for up to 3 weeks.

GRILLED SWEET CORN
with Roasted Garlic, Scallion, and Lime-Chili Butters

THE FLAVORED butters we suggest here are simple to adjust to feature the flavors you like best. It doesn't make sense to try to make less than 1 cup

LEFT TO RIGHT Work the butter with a wooden spoon or using the paddle attachment in a mixer until it is soft enough to incorporate the flavoring ingredients; mix the ingredients until they are evenly incorporated into the butter. Roll the butter into a rough log inside the plastic wrap. Use a ruler or metal spatula to tighten the plastic wrap around the butter and even out the diameter of the cylinder.

of flavored butter, but fortunately, flavored butters keep in the freezer for several weeks.

2 tbsp vegetable oil

8 ears corn, shucked

2 tsp salt

1 tsp ground black pepper

½ cup Roasted Garlic Butter, Scallion Butter, or Lime-Chili Butter (recipes follow)

1. Preheat a gas grill to medium-high. Leave one burner off. If using a charcoal grill, build a fire and let it burn down until the coals are glowing red with a moderate coating of white ash. Push the coals to one side of the grill. Clean the cooking grate.

2. Lightly oil the corn and season with salt and pepper. Grill the corn, covered, over indirect heat, turning as necessary, until the corn kernels are soft and grill marked, about 20 to 25 minutes. Remove the corn from the grill. Serve immediately with your choice of butter.

Roasted Garlic Butter

MAKES 1 CUP

2 heads garlic

2 tsp vegetable oil

½ tsp salt

1 cup softened butter

1. Place each head of garlic on a square of aluminum foil large enough to enclose the entire head. Drizzle with the oil, and season with salt. Wrap the garlic in the foil and seal closed to make pouches.

2. Grill over indirect medium heat (or roast in a 400°F oven) until tender and any juices that escape are deep brown, about 30 to 40 minutes.

3. Let the garlic cool. Squeeze the roasted cloves from the papery skins, and mash to a paste. Blend with the softened butter, then shape the finished butter as described on the facing page.

Scallion Butter

MAKES 1 CUP

1 cup softened butter

⅓ cup minced scallions

¼ tsp minced garlic

1½ tsp chopped parsley

1½ tsp soy sauce

1½ tsp lemon juice

Blend all the ingredients together, then shape the finished butter as described on the facing page.

Lime-Chili Butter

MAKES 1 CUP

1 cup softened butter

3 tbsp lime juice

1½ tsp dried oregano

1½ tsp chili powder

1½ tsp hot chili powder

1½ tsp sweet Hungarian paprika

¼ tsp ground cumin

¼ tsp Worcestershire sauce

2 to 3 dashes Tabasco sauce

Pinch garlic powder

Pinch onion powder

Blend all the ingredients together, then shape the finished butter as described on the facing page.

ROASTED CORN SUCCOTASH

YOU CAN roast or grill the corn for this dish. Dampen the husks before you begin to add a bit of moisture for steam. To check the corn for doneness, pull back some of the husk and look at the kernels. They should be plump and moist, and should "pop" easily when pressed with the tines of a table fork.

MAKES 6 TO 8 SERVINGS

4 ears corn in the husk

1 tbsp extra-virgin olive oil

1 cup diced zucchini

1 cup chopped tomato, peeled and seeded

1 cup cooked lima beans

½ cup scallions, thinly sliced on a diagonal

¾ cup Vegetable Broth (page 65)

1 tbsp chopped parsley

2 tsp chopped tarragon

¼ tsp ground cardamom

Salt and pepper as needed

1. Preheat the oven to 400°F. Dampen the husks with cold water and place the corn directly on the oven rack. Roast until the kernels are tender and cooked through, 10 to 15 minutes. When the corn is cool enough to handle, pull away the husk and the silk. Cut the kernels from the cob and reserve.

2. Heat the olive oil in a large sauté pan over medium-high heat until it shimmers. Add the corn and zucchini and sauté, stirring occasionally, until the zucchini is tender, about 3 minutes. Add the tomato, lima beans, scallions, and broth, and continue to sauté until all of the ingredients are very hot, about 4 minutes. Remove the pan from the heat and stir in the parsley, tarragon, and cardamom. Season to taste with salt and pepper. Serve at once in a heated bowl or on heated plates.

Working with Corn on the Cob

The traditional American way to serve corn is simply boiled, steamed, or roasted on the cob, then swathed in butter. To prepare other corn dishes, such as creamed corn or corncakes, it is necessary to remove the kernels as well as the milk. First, the kernels are scored with a knife to begin to release their juices, or milk, as it is known. Then, the kernels are sliced away and the cob is scraped to express all of the milk.

CORN IN SALADS

Plump, sweet kernels of corn add a refreshing burst of flavor, as well as a flash of color to salads. To prepare corn to serve cold, prepare it as you normally would. We chose to grill the corn in this instance for a subtle, smoky taste. Steaming, boiling, and roasting are also great options.

Pull the husk and silk away from the corn, if you haven't already. Set the broad end of the ear of corn down on a stable work surface. Use a chef's or a utility knife. Cut the kernels away from the cob by making a slice from the tip to the end. The kernels should feel like they are "popping" off the cob. Once you've cut the kernels from the cob, you can break the large pieces up if you wish.

CHEDDAR CORN FRITTERS

CUT THE kernels from the ears of corn and then scrape the cobs with a table knife to release all the milk into a bowl and add it to the batter.

MAKES 6 TO 8 SERVINGS

¾ cup all-purpose flour

2 tsp sugar

1 to 2 tsp chili powder, optional

Salt and pepper as needed

3 ears corn, plus corn milk if available, or 2 cups corn kernels

3 tbsp diced red or green pepper, optional

2 large eggs, lightly beaten

½ cup water

½ cup grated Cheddar

2 tbsp melted butter

Vegetable oil for pan frying

1. Stir together the flour, sugar, chili powder, if using, salt, and pepper in a mixing bowl. Set aside.

2. Combine the corn and corn milk, if available, pepper, if using, eggs, water, and the cheese in a bowl. Add to the flour mixture all at once. Stir just until the batter is evenly moistened. Stir in the melted butter.

3. Pour the oil into a large skillet to a depth of ¼ inch. Heat over medium heat until it registers 350°F on a deep-frying thermometer. Using a serving spoon and working in batches to avoid crowding, drop spoonfuls of batter into the hot oil to make 16 fritters in all. Pan fry on the first side until golden brown and crisp, about 2 minutes. Turn once and fry until golden brown on the second side, 2 minutes more. Drain the fritters on absorbent towels and season with salt. If needed, you can keep the first batches of fritters warm in an oven at 200°F while you finish frying the rest. Serve at once.

RATATOUILLE

THIS CLASSIC Provençal dish hails from the south of France, where it makes the most of the Mediterranean bounty of late summer. On a hot day, it can be served cool for a light supper or lunch dish.

2 tbsp olive oil

3 tbsp minced garlic

2 cups diced yellow onions

1 tbsp tomato paste

¾ cup Chicken Broth (page 63)

4 cups diced eggplant

1⅓ cups sliced zucchini (quartered lengthwise before slicing)

1 cup quartered mushrooms

1 cup diced green pepper

2 cups chopped tomatoes (peeled and seeded)

¼ cup chopped flat-leaf parsley

¼ cup chopped basil

Salt and pepper as needed

1. Heat the olive oil in a sauté pan over medium heat. Add the garlic and sauté until aromatic, about 1 minute. Add the onions and sauté until translucent, 4 to 5 minutes.

2. Add the tomato paste and cook over medium heat until it deepens in color and gives off a sweet aroma, about 1 minute. Add the broth and stir to deglaze the pan, scraping up any browned bits from the pan bottom.

3. Add the eggplant, zucchini, mushrooms, and green pepper and simmer until the vegetables are tender but not falling apart, 10 to 12 minutes. Stir in the tomatoes and continue to simmer until the tomatoes are heated through, 2 to 3 minutes. Add the parsley and basil. Taste, season with salt and pepper, and then serve.

BRAISED KALE

THE ADDITION of white wine to this dish gives it a subtle flavor boost. Another way you can introduce a bit more flavor is to simmer the ham hock in chicken broth while you clean the kale, as we do here.

SERVES 6 TO 8

3 cups Chicken Broth (page 63)

1 ham hock

2 lb kale

2 tbsp olive oil

1 slice bacon, chopped

1 cup chopped onions

½ cup minced garlic

½ cup white wine

Salt and pepper, as needed

1. Preheat the oven to 350°F.

2. Simmer the broth and ham hock together until the broth is very flavorful, about 20 minutes, while you prepare the kale.

3. Bring a large pot of salted water to a rolling boil. Trim the stems from the kale. Thoroughly rinse the leaves and drain well, then tear the leaves into bite-size pieces. Add the torn kale to the boiling water and cook, stirring once or twice, until the kale is bright green, 3 to 4 minutes. Drain in a colander, pressing on the kale to remove as much water as possible.

4. Heat the olive oil in a Dutch oven or casserole over medium heat until it shimmers. Add the bacon and cook, stirring frequently, until the fat is released from the bacon and the bacon bits are crisp, about 2 minutes.

5. Add the onions and garlic and sauté, stirring frequently, until the onions are tender and translucent, 3 to 4 minutes. Add the blanched kale and stir to coat thoroughly with the oil. Add the wine and simmer until the liquid is reduced by half.

6. Add the broth and ham hock, pushing the hock down into the kale. Bring the broth to a simmer, cover the pan, and braise in the oven until tender, 30 to 45 minutes. Using a slotted spoon, lift the kale from the Dutch oven or casserole and keep it warm while finishing the sauce.

7. Return the casserole or Dutch oven to high heat on the stovetop. Simmer the liquid until it is slightly thickened and very flavorful, about 5 minutes. Season to taste with salt and pepper. Return the kale to the casserole or Dutch oven, reheating the kale completely. Serve at once in a in a heated bowl or on heated plates.

OKRA STEWED WITH TOMATOES

OKRA, A member of the hibiscus family, has not been welcomed with open arms in most parts of the country. Its most familiar "home" is in gumbo—the word comes from the Angolan term for okra, *ngombo*. Okra is itself a variant of the term used for it by natives from Ghana, *nkruma*.

MAKES 4 SERVINGS

1 lb fresh small okra pods

2 strips smoked bacon, diced

½ cup Vegetable Broth (page 65) or water

1 cup onion julienne

3 to 4 plum tomatoes, peeled, seeded, and chopped

Salt and freshly ground black pepper to taste

1. Rinse the okra, trim away the caps, and slice about ½ inch thick. Reserve.

2. Combine the diced bacon with ¼ cup of the broth or water in a skillet and set the skillet over

medium-high heat. Cook, stirring from time to time, until the water has cooked away and the bacon has released some of its fat, about 2 minutes.

3. Add the onion to the skillet, and reduce the heat to low. Continue to sauté, stirring frequently, until the onion is a deep golden brown, 12 to 15 minutes.

4. Add the sliced okra, the remaining broth or water, and the tomatoes. Cover the skillet and reduce the heat to low. Cook gently, stirring from time to time and adding a little additional broth or water, if necessary, for about 15 minutes (or longer if you prefer the okra quite soft).

5. Season the mixture generously with pepper. Add salt to taste.

WILD MUSHROOM SAUTÉ

REMEMBER TO cook the mushrooms in batches to achieve a proper golden brown color. Once you add the rest of the ingredients, keep everything moving to prevent burning, or try reducing the fire to moderate heat.

MAKES 8 SERVINGS

¼ cup peanut oil

2 lb assorted mushrooms, large-diced

¼ cup minced shallots

2 tsp minced garlic

3 tbsp chopped parsley

2 tbsp butter

½ tsp salt

¼ tsp pepper

1. Heat the oil in a sauté pan over high heat until smoking. Add the mushrooms to the pan in batches and sauté until golden, about 5 to 7 minutes.

2. Add the shallots, garlic, parsley, and butter to the pan; stir to blend, and sauté until aromatic and very hot, about 2 minutes more. Season to taste with the salt and pepper.

3. The mushroom sauté is ready to use now or it can be cooled and stored in a covered container in the refrigerator for up to 2 days.

About Mushrooms

Mushrooms exist in thousands of varieties, ranging significantly in size, shape, color, and flavor. For a long time, the only widely available mushrooms were white mushrooms (also sold as button mushrooms or Parisian mushrooms). Today, more varieties are being successfully farmed, which means that many so-called "wild" varieties are actually farm-raised.

Europeans, especially those living in the eastern and northern parts of the continent, are inveterate mushroom hunters. It isn't at all unusual to find whole families engaged in a hunt through the woods on a Sunday afternoon. Foraging for wild food used to be common in this country too, but if you aren't familiar with the local flora and fauna, it is probably safest to err on the side of caution. If you aren't sure about a wild mushroom's safety, don't sauté it and serve it for dinner. Contact local agricultural groups or even a community college agricultural program to locate an expert who can help you identify your mushrooms.

• Cultivated mushroom varieties include white mushrooms, as well as portobello, cremini, shiitake, and oyster mushrooms.

• Wild mushroom varieties include cèpes (porcini), chanterelles, morels, truffles, and many other varieties.

• Select mushrooms that are firm, without soft spots, blemishes, or breaks in the cap or stem.

• Keep mushrooms under refrigeration. Cover with lightly dampened paper towels, not plastic wrap, to keep them fresher long.

ZUCCHINI PANCAKES

THESE PANCAKES feature feta cheese and chopped walnuts to punctuate the relatively mild taste of zucchini in these crunchy fritters.

MAKES 6 TO 8 SERVINGS

3 cups coarsely grated zucchini

Salt and pepper as needed

2 cups chopped scallions

4 eggs, lightly beaten

½ cup flour

⅓ cup chopped dill

⅓ cup chopped parsley

2 tbsp chopped tarragon

½ cup crumbled feta cheese

⅔ cup chopped walnuts

Olive oil for pan frying

1 cup Tzatziki Sauce (recipe follows)

1. Place the grated zucchini in colander. Sprinkle with salt and let stand for 30 minutes. Squeeze the zucchini to remove as much liquid as possible. Dry the zucchini by pressing it between several layers of paper towels.

2. In a large bowl, combine the zucchini, scallions, eggs, flour, dill, parsley, tarragon, salt, and pepper until evenly blended. Fold in the feta cheese. (The pancake mixture can be prepared to this point up to 3 hours ahead. Cover tightly and refrigerate. Stir to blend before continuing.) Fold the walnuts into the zucchini mixture.

3. Preheat the oven to 300°F to keep the pancakes warm as you work. Place a baking sheet in the oven.

4. Add enough oil to a skillet to come to a depth of about ⅛ inch, and heat the oil over medium-high heat until the surface of the oil shimmers. Working in batches, drop heaping tablespoons of the zucchini mixture into the hot oil, leaving enough room for the pancakes to spread as they cook. Fry until the pancakes are golden brown and cooked through, about 3 minutes per side. Transfer each batch of pancakes to the baking sheet in the oven to keep warm. Serve immediately with the tzatziki sauce.

Tzatziki Sauce

THIS YOGURT-AND-CUCUMBER sauce cools the heat from fiery curries, and adds richness to Zucchini Pancakes. You also can serve it on its own as a salad.

MAKES 1½ CUPS

½ cup plain yogurt

½ cup sour cream

½ cup grated cucumber, squeezed dry

1 tsp minced garlic

1 tbsp extra-virgin olive oil

1 tbsp minced fresh mint or dill

1 tsp lemon juice, or as needed

½ tsp grated lemon zest

Salt and pepper as needed

Combine the yogurt, sour cream, cucumber, and garlic in a food processor and puree until smooth. Transfer to a bowl and fold in the olive oil, mint or dill, lemon juice, and zest. Stir until combined and season to taste with salt and pepper. Keep refrigerated until ready to serve.

SICILIAN-STYLE SPINACH

THE ADDITION of raisins to this spinach dish reflects the influence of the Ottoman Empire throughout the Mediterranean region. A touch of dry fruit for sweetness highlights the briny taste of the anchovy and the heat of the garlic.

MAKES 4 TO 6 SERVINGS

1 tbsp olive oil

2 tbsp diced pancetta or 1 slice bacon, diced

1 anchovy fillet, chopped

¼ cup minced yellow onion

1 tbsp minced garlic

8 cups spinach leaves

Salt and pepper as needed

2 tbsp dark or golden raisins

1 tbsp toasted pine nuts

1. Heat the olive oil in a large sauté pan over medium heat. Add the pancetta and sauté until the fat renders and the pancetta is translucent, about 1 minute. Raise the heat to high and add the anchovy, onion, and garlic. Sauté until the garlic is aromatic and the anchovy has dissolved into the oil, about 1 minute more. Add the spinach and sauté until deep green, tender, and softened, 3 to 4 minutes more.

2. Drain the mixture, if necessary, and season generously with salt and pepper. Remove the pan from the heat and stir in the raisins and pine nuts. Serve immediately.

RED PEPPER ORZO

IN ITALIAN, *orzo* literally means barley, but most commonly it refers to little pasta that have a rice- or diamond-like shape. This quick-cooking pasta makes for a hearty dish combining red pepper, herbs, fennel, and feta cheese.

MAKES 8 SERVINGS

½ lb orzo

2 tsp salt, or to taste

¼ cup olive oil

1 red onion, diced

1 red pepper, diced

1 green pepper, diced

1 fennel bulb, finely diced

1 tbsp garlic, chopped

1 tbsp thyme, chopped

½ cup tomato juice

¼ cup parsley, chopped

1 tsp freshly ground black pepper, or to taste

1 cup feta cheese, crumbled

1. Boil the orzo in salted water until tender, about 8 to 10 minutes. Drain and rinse under cold water. Toss the orzo with 3 tablespoons of the olive oil, cover, and refrigerate.

2. In a large saucepan, sauté the onions, peppers, and fennel in the remaining 1 tablespoon of olive oil until just tender, about 4 minutes. Add the garlic and thyme and cook an additional 2 minutes.

3. Toss the sautéed vegetables with the reserved orzo. Add the tomato juice. Toss in the parsley, pepper, feta cheese, and remaining 1 teaspoon of salt.

MAPLE-GLAZED TURNIPS

PAN-STEAMING, AN excellent technique for cooking vegetables, uses a small amount of flavorful liquid in a covered pan. There are two benefits: a quick cooking time that helps retain nutrients and color, and a flavorful liquid you can reduce to make a simple sauce.

2 lb purple-top turnips

2 tbsp unsalted butter

3 tbsp maple syrup

¼ tsp ground cinnamon

1 pinch freshly grated nutmeg

Salt and pepper as needed

Water as needed

1 tbsp chopped flat-leaf parsley

2 tsp fresh lemon juice

1. Peel the turnips and cut into even 1-inch cubes. Heat 1 tablespoon of butter in a sauté pan over medium heat. Add the maple syrup, cinnamon, nutmeg, and salt and pepper to taste. Add the turnips and then enough water to reach a depth of ¼ inch. Bring to a boil over high heat. Reduce the heat to a simmer, cover, and pan steam until the turnips are tender, 7 to 8 minutes.

2. Remove the cover from the pan, and continue to cook the turnips until the water has cooked away and the syrup has glazed each piece evenly, about 3 minutes. Add the remaining butter to the pan with the parsley and lemon juice. Shake the pan until the butter is melted and the turnips are evenly coated. Season with additional salt and pepper and serve.

HOISIN-CARAMELIZED ROOT VEGETABLES

T HE HOISIN adds a rich flavor and color to this simple dish of oven roasted vegetables.

MAKES 6 SERVINGS

2 tbsp peanut oil

2 tbsp hoisin

2 cups thickly sliced carrots

2 cups yellow turnip wedges

2 cups thickly sliced parsnips

1 fennel bulb, wedge cut

1 cup pearl onions, peeled, optional

Salt and pepper as needed

¼ cup water

1. Preheat the oven to 350°F. Combine the oil and hoisin and heat in a roasting pan, add the vegetables, and toss until coated evenly. Season generously with salt and pepper. Pour the water over the vegetables.

2. Cover the pan with a lid or aluminum foil and place in the preheated oven. Roast the vegetables until nearly tender, about 30 minutes. Remove the cover and finish roasting, turning the vegetables so that they cook evenly, another 10 to 15 minutes. Season to taste with additional salt and pepper. Serve at once in a heated bowl or on heated plates.

Egg Dishes and Griddle Cakes

Egg Dishes

Eggs are one of the most popular of all breakfast foods and certainly the most versatile. This chapter includes recipes for such familiar favorites as fried and scrambled eggs as well as some contemporary offerings: Tortilla Española (page 219) or Frittata (page 217). The classic brunch dish, Eggs Benedict (page 217), is sure to impress your guests. Eggs baked in a ramekin (page 213) with or without a savory garnish make it easy to prepare brunch or breakfast without a last-minute rush in the kitchen.

SELECTING EGGS

Eggs are graded on the basis of external appearance and freshness. The top grade, AA, indicates that an egg is fresh, with a white that will not spread too much once the egg is broken and a yolk that sits high on the white's surface.

Buy eggs from a refrigerated case. Look at the packaging to be sure it is not dented or ripped. Inspect the eggs. The eggshells should be clean, without cracks, holes, or leaks. To keep eggs wholesome at home, store them in the carton in the coldest part of the refrigerator. As long as the shells remain unbroken, your eggs will keep for 3 to 5 weeks held at 40°F or less. Once eggs are taken out of the shell, store them in clean containers, well covered, and use them within 2 days.

Pasteurized eggs may be used in preparations such as salad dressings, desserts, and eggnog for which the traditional recipe calls for raw eggs. You can buy them in the dairy case, sold in cartons or as pasteurized eggs in the shell. For health reasons, many cooks use egg substitutes that are either entirely egg-free or produced from egg whites with dairy or vegetable products substituted for the yolks. These substitutes are valuable for people who must follow a reduced-cholesterol diet.

SEPARATING EGGS

Eggs separate most easily when they are cold, so keep them in the refrigerator until you are ready. You'll need a clean bowl to break each egg into, as well as bowls to hold the whites and yolks separately, and also a container to hold any eggs that don't separate cleanly.

Crack each egg's shell and carefully pull apart the halves. Gently pour the egg yolk back and forth from one half to the other, allowing the egg white to fall into the empty bowl. Drop the egg yolk into another bowl.

Examine the white in the first bowl to be sure that it contains no bits of yolk. If it is clean, transfer it to the egg white bowl. If you see drops of yolk in the egg white, however, it cannot be used for whipping. Save it for another dish such as scrambled eggs or to use as egg wash for baked goods, and wash out the bowl before separating the next egg.

EGGS EN COCOTTE

ADD GARNISHES to the bottom of the ramekin (about 2 tablespoons per ramekin) before putting in the eggs. Be sure the garnish is hot before you add it. Some options include stewed or braised beans or lentils, diced ham, or sautéed mushrooms.

MAKES 8 SERVINGS

¼ cup butter, room temperature

16 large eggs

1 tsp salt, or to taste

½ tsp freshly ground pepper, or to taste

1. Preheat the oven to 350°F. Bring a kettle or pot of water to a boil.

2. Butter the inside of eight 4-ounce ceramic soufflé dishes or ramekins and set them in a large baking pan. Break 2 eggs into each ramekin, season with salt and pepper, and top with ½ teaspoon butter.

3. Place the pan in the oven and add about ½-inch of boiling water to the pan. Cover loosely with aluminum foil. Cook until the egg whites are opaque and firm and the yolks are set, about 20 minutes. Serve in the ramekins.

FRIED EGGS

YOUR EGGS will look the most attractive if you fry them one serving at a time. If you like the egg yolks set and firm, you can baste the tops with some of the butter or oil or you can sprinkle a few drops of water into the skillet, cover tightly, and "steam" for about 30 seconds.

MAKES 8 SERVINGS

½ cup clarified butter or olive oil

16 large eggs

2 tsp salt, or as needed

1 teaspoon freshly ground black pepper

1. Break 2 eggs per portion into a clean cup or small bowl.

2. To make eggs sunny-side-up, heat 1 tablespoon of butter in a small sauté pan over medium heat and carefully slide the eggs into the pan.

3. When the egg whites are set, after about 2 minutes, tilt the pan, allowing the fat to collect at the side of the pan, and baste the egg whites with the fat as they cook. To make eggs over-easy, -medium, or -hard, turn the eggs near the end of their cooking time with a spatula and cook them on the second side, 20 to 30 seconds for over-easy, 1 minute for over-medium, 2½ minutes for over-hard.

4. Season the eggs with salt and pepper and serve at once on heated plates. Be careful not to break the yolks while sliding the eggs onto the plate.

HUEVOS RANCHEROS
with Salsa Fresca

HUEVOS RANCHEROS are a hearty breakfast of fried eggs over refried beans on a corn tortilla topped with cheese, avocado, and salsa. If you prefer, you can make this dish with Poached Eggs (page 216), instead of frying them.

MAKES 8 SERVINGS

Eight 6-inch corn tortillas

2 cups Refried Beans (page 185)

¼ cup unsalted butter or vegetable oil

16 large eggs

Salt and freshly ground pepper

1 cup grated Monterey Jack cheese

2 avocados

4 tsp fresh lime juice, juice of half a lime

1 cup Salsa Fresca (page 19) or prepared salsa

½ cup sour cream, as needed for garnish

8 cilantro sprigs for garnish

1. Preheat the broiler.

2. Heat the tortillas by toasting them one at a time in a dry cast-iron skillet or directly over a gas flame until lightly toasted. Place on a baking sheet; spread each tortilla with ¼ cup refried beans and cover to keep warm.

3. Working in batches as needed, heat the butter in a large skillet over medium-high heat until it is very hot but not smoking and the foaming has subsided. Crack the eggs directly into the hot butter and reduce the heat to medium-low or low. Fry the eggs, shaking the pan occasionally to keep the eggs from sticking. Season the eggs with salt and pepper. Fry about 2 minutes for "sunny-side up," 3 minutes for medium yolks, and 3½ to 4 minutes for hard yolks.

4. Top each prepared tortilla with 2 fried eggs and 2 tablespoons of the grated cheese. Slide the tortillas under the broiler to melt the cheese.

5. Meanwhile, dice the avocados and toss with the lime juice to prevent the avocados from discoloring. Divide the avocados among the tortillas. Top each serving with 2 tablespoons salsa and 2 tablespoons sour cream. Garnish each serving with a sprig of cilantro and serve.

TOAD IN A HOLE
with Red Pepper Ketchup

THIS IS only as good as the ingredients that go into it. Flavorful artisan bread makes the whole dish taste better. Serve one or two pieces per person, depending on your guests' appetites.

MAKES 8 SERVINGS

16 slices sourdough bread, about ¾ inch thick

1 cup melted butter, or as needed

16 eggs

2 tsp salt, or to taste

1 tsp ground black pepper, or to taste

1 cup Red Pepper Ketchup (recipe follows)

1. Preheat a gas grill to medium-high; leave one burner off. If you are using a charcoal grill, build a fire and let it burn down until the coals are glowing red with a moderate coating of white ash. Spread the coals in an even bed on one side of the grill. Clean the cooking grate.

2. Cut holes in the center of each slice of bread using a 2½-inch biscuit cutter. Be sure not to get too close to the crust of the bread. Brush both sides of each slice of bread with the melted butter.

3. Heat a griddle to medium over direct heat on the grill. Griddle the bread on 1 side until golden brown, about 1 to 2 minutes. Flip each piece of bread over and crack 1 egg into the hole in each piece of bread.

4. Move the pan to indirect heat. Season the eggs with salt and pepper. Fry the eggs for about 2 minutes for sunny-side-up eggs, 3 minutes for medium yolks, and 3½ to 4 minutes for hard yolks. Flip the bread over, being careful not to break the yolk, and cook for 30 seconds more, if desired.

5. Serve immediately with the Red Pepper Ketchup on top or on the side.

Red Pepper Ketchup

MAKES 2 CUPS

¼ cup olive oil

5 red peppers, diced

2 tbsp minced shallots

¾ cup dry white wine

¾ cup Chicken or Vegetable Broth (pages 63, 65)

1 tsp salt

½ tsp ground black pepper

1. Heat the olive oil in a large sauté pan over medium heat. Add the peppers and shallots and sauté until tender, about 5 to 6 minutes.

2. Deglaze the pan with the white wine, making sure to scrape up anything that is stuck to the bottom of the pan.

3. Add the broth and simmer until reduced to half the original volume. Allow the mixture to cool to room temperature.

4. Purée the mixture until smooth. Season the ketchup with the salt and pepper.

Making Scrambled Eggs

Scrambled eggs are perfect to make in large batches. Put cooked eggs into an oven safe dish, cover loosely with aluminum foil, and place in a 200°F oven until ready to serve.

MIXING THE EGGS

For best flavor, you should crack and blend the eggs just before cooking if possible, but if you need to streamline breakfast or brunch, you can crack and blend the eggs up to 12 hours in advance.

Season the eggs well with salt and pepper. If you like, blend them with a small amount of water, broth, milk, or cream for a more tender texture. The eggs should have an even color and consistency after you blend them.

SCRAMBLING EGGS

Since scrambled eggs lose their heat quickly once they come out of the pan, be sure to have heated plates or platters ready to serve them. If the entire crowd isn't on hand and ready to eat, you can make smaller batches rather than one big batch. Use a 4-ounce ladle or a ½-cup measure for each serving you want to prepare.

Heat a nonstick omelet pan or small skillet over high heat and add oil, butter, or a combination of both. Determining when the pan and fat are properly heated is key. Oil should shimmer but not smoke, while butter should melt and foam but not turn brown or black. Water droplets should skitter over the pan but not cook away instantly. Tilt the pan to coat its entire surface.

Add the beaten eggs and use one hand to swirl the pan on the burner and the other to stir the eggs in the opposite direction, using a fork or heat-resistant rubber spatula. Once the eggs set into smooth, small curds and lose their glossy look, they are ready to serve.

SCRAMBLED EGGS

THIS RECIPE is simple to make in smaller amounts. Plan on two or three eggs per person and use enough oil or butter to liberally coat the pan.

MAKES 8 SERVINGS

24 large eggs

½ cup whole milk

2 tsp salt

1 tsp pepper

¼ cup clarified butter or canola oil

1. Whisk eggs and milk in a bowl and season with the salt and pepper.

2. Heat 2 tablespoons butter or oil in a large sauté pan over medium-high heat until almost smoking.

Add half of the eggs to the pan and stir until they are soft and creamy, about 1½ minutes for soft scrambled or 2 minutes for hard scrambled eggs.

3. Remove the eggs from the heat when fully cooked but still moist, and serve at once on heated plates. Repeat with the remaining butter or oil and eggs to make the second batch.

Making Poached Eggs

Eggs should be poached in about 3 inches of water. Adding salt and a small amount of vinegar to the water prevents the whites from spreading too much and helps the egg proteins set faster.

HEAT THE POACHING LIQUID

Bring the seasoned water to a gentle simmer, about 160° to 170°F. The water should appear effervescent, with tiny bubbles collecting on the sides of the pan and breaking evenly over the surface. Adjust the heat to prevent a boil, as larger bubbles would break the egg.

CRACK THE EGGS

Crack the egg first into a small cup or bowl and then gently slide the egg into the poaching liquid. As the egg drops to the bottom of the pot, the whites will set in a teardrop shape around the yolk. Work in small batches without crowding. Too many eggs will cause the temperature of the water to drop, extend the cooking time, and make the eggs more difficult to handle.

DRAIN THE EGGS

After 3 to 4 minutes, lift the eggs out with a slotted spoon and drain on a clean towel to remove excess water. The whites should be set and opaque, while the yolks should be done to your liking. Trim away ragged edges on the egg whites with a paring knife or kitchen shears to form a compact oval shape.

MAKING POACHED EGGS IN ADVANCE

If you are preparing eggs in advance, transfer them to a bowl filled with cold or ice water. Once they are chilled, lift them from the water, blot dry, and store in the refrigerator in a tightly covered container. To reheat the eggs, lower them into gently simmering water for 1 minute.

POACHED EGGS

USE THE freshest eggs possible for poaching, as they will have a more centered yolk, and a more compact white with a cleaner edge. The cooked egg should form a classic teardrop shape. Poached eggs are also the basis, with a few additional components, for the Eggs Benedict recipe that follows.

MAKES 8 SERVINGS

3 quarts water, or as needed

2 tsp salt

4 tsp distilled white vinegar

16 large eggs

1. Combine the water, salt, and vinegar in a deep pan and bring to a bare simmer.

2. Break each egg into a clean cup, reserving any with broken yolks for another use.

3. Carefully slide each egg into the poaching water. Cook for about 3 minutes or until the whites are set and opaque.

4. Remove the eggs from the water with a slotted spoon, blot them on absorbent toweling, and trim the edges if desired. The hot eggs are ready to serve now on heated plates, or the eggs may be properly chilled and held for later service.

EGGS BENEDICT

ALTHOUGH THIS is one of the most complex egg recipes we offer, you can simplify things by poaching your eggs in advance, making the hollandaise sauce ahead of time and keeping it warm over simmering water, and toasting the muffins under the broiler. Serving eggs Benedict on your own freshly made English muffins makes a wonderful difference, but they are still great served on store-bought English muffins.

MAKES 8 SERVINGS

16 slices Canadian bacon

16 Poached Eggs (opposite)

8 English Muffins, split, toasted, and buttered

2 cups Hollandaise Sauce (page 168), warm

1. Heat a sauté pan over medium-low heat. Add the Canadian bacon, working in batches, and sauté on both sides until heated through, about 1 to 2 minutes on each side.

2. If the eggs have been poached in advance, reheat them in simmering water until warmed through. Blot them on paper toweling and shape if necessary. Top each English muffin half with a Canadian bacon slice and a poached egg. Spoon 2 tablespoons warm hollandaise over each egg. Serve immediately.

VARIATIONS:

SALMON EGGS BENEDICT: Substitute slices of smoked salmon for the Canadian bacon.

EGGS FLORENTINE: Substitute 2 tbs drained cooked spinach per serving for the Canadian bacon.

FRITTATA

FRITTATAS ARE traditional Italian open-face omelets perfect for a simple family supper. They are an excellent way to use any leftovers you may have from the night before: cooked pasta or potatoes, cooked vegetables, or a small piece of cheese. If you are adding cooked ingredients, put them in the pan and let them warm over low heat before you add the beaten eggs. Since your leftovers were most likely already seasoned, be sure to take that into account when you season the beaten eggs.

MAKES 8 SERVINGS

12 oz lean bacon, diced

2 cups minced onions

2 cups diced and cooked Yukon Gold potatoes

16 large eggs

½ tsp salt

¼ tsp freshly ground black pepper

1. Preheat the broiler.

2. Cook the bacon in a large skillet over medium heat until crisp, 10 to 15 minutes. Pour off any excess fat, leaving about 1 tablespoon in the skillet. Add the onions and sauté them for 1 minute. Add the potatoes and continue to sauté them until they are lightly brown, 12 to 15 minutes.

3. Beat the eggs and season with the salt and pepper. Pour the egg mixture over the onion-potato mixture in the skillet and stir gently to combine.

4. Reduce the heat to low, cover the skillet, and cook until the eggs are nearly set, about 5 minutes.

5. Remove the cover and place the skillet under a broiler to brown the eggs lightly, 1 to 2 minutes. Cut the frittata into wedges and serve immediately.

ROLLED OMELET

Try the Spicy Mushroom Filling we've included in our crêpe recipe on page 229 as a filling for your omelet. Other filling options include grated cheese, sautéed spinach, roasted peppers, feta cheese, or jelly.

MAKES 8 SERVINGS

24 large eggs

½ cup whole milk, divided use

2 tsp salt, divided use

1 tsp pepper, divided use

½ cup clarified butter or canola oil

1. For each portion, whisk 3 eggs and 1 tablespoon of milk together and season with about ¼ teaspoon salt and ⅛ teaspoon pepper.

2. Heat a nonstick omelet pan over medium-high heat and heat the butter or oil until almost smoking, tilting the pan to coat the entire surface of the pan. Pour the egg mixture into the pan and scramble it with a heatproof rubber spatula or a wooden spoon. Move the pan and utensil at the same time until the egg mixture has coagulated slightly, about 15 to 20 seconds.

3. Smooth out the eggs into an even layer by spreading with a wooden spoon or shaking the pan. Let the egg mixture nearly finish cooking without stirring, 45 seconds to 1 minute. Tilt the pan and slide the spatula around the lip of the pan under the omelet to be sure it is not sticking. Slide the omelet to the front of the pan and use a fork or a wooden spoon to fold it inside to the center.

4. Turn the pan upside down and roll the omelet onto the plate. The finished omelet should be oval shaped. Serve immediately.

NOTE: *For an American-style omelet, fold the eggs in half once they have finished cooking and slide the omelet onto a plate.*

LEFT TO RIGHT Keep the eggs in motion until soft curds begin to form. Smooth out the eggs into an even layer, and add any garnish to the omelet at this point, if desired. If you are using cheese, spread it around the eggs in an even layer to give it a chance to melt; other garnishes, like ham or mushrooms, should be placed in the center of the omelet in a line. Use a spatula to gently lift one side of the omelet and fold it toward the center of the pan. If you are using a garnish, fold over enough egg to enclose the garnish. Use the pan to help roll the omelet onto the plate.

TORTILLA ESPAÑOLA

Spanish-style Potato Omelet

THE SPANISH *tortilla* indicates a flat cake, not the Mexican flour or corn tortillas used to make tacos, burritos, or enchiladas. This version of a tortilla is quite similar to a frittata. At a tapas bar, the tortilla would be cut into pieces and pierced with a wooden toothpick to offer as hors d'oeuvres.

MAKES 8 SERVINGS

¼ cup olive oil, divided use

1½ cups minced onions

¾ cup small-diced green bell peppers

2 cups medium-diced Idaho potatoes

1½ tsp salt

16 large eggs

2 tbsp chopped cilantro

1. In a large nonstick pan, heat 2 tablespoons of the olive oil. Add the onions and bell peppers and cook over medium heat until translucent, 3 to 5 minutes. Stir in the potatoes and mix well. Add salt and cover. Cook over low heat until the potatoes are tender, 12 to 15 minutes. Stir the ingredients every 3 to 4 minutes to prevent sticking. Once the potato mixture is cooked, remove it from the heat and cool for 5 minutes.

2. In a large bowl, whisk the eggs with the cilantro. Add the vegetable mixture and stir until combined.

3. Add the remaining oil to the pan and heat until smoking. Add the egg mixture to the pan, lower the heat, and cook without stirring until the eggs begin to set. When the omelet starts to turn golden brown on the bottom, turn the omelet over. Cook until the second side develops the same color. If necessary, divide the oil and egg mixture between two pans.

4. Serve very hot, warm, or at room temperature.

QUICHE LORRAINE

THIS CLASSIC quiche is rich and delicious. Feel free to substitute different additions to the basic egg and cream mixture to create your own quiche.

MAKES ONE 9-INCH QUICHE

1 tbsp butter

1 cup minced onion

3 large eggs

1½ cups heavy cream

½ tsp salt

¼ tsp freshly ground black pepper

¾ cup grated Gruyère cheese

8 slices bacon, cooked and crumbled

One 9-inch Pie Crust (page 262), prebaked

1. Preheat the oven to 325°F.

2. Heat the butter in a sauté pan over medium heat. Add the onion and sauté until golden, about 8 minutes. Remove from the pan and reserve.

3. Combine the eggs, heavy cream, salt, and pepper in a mixing bowl and whisk until evenly blended. Stir the cheese, bacon, and reserved onion into the egg mixture. Spread the egg mixture evenly over the pie crust.

4. Set the quiche pan on a baking sheet and bake until a knife blade inserted in the center comes out clean, 40 to 45 minutes. If the pie crust begins to overbrown, cover the edges of the crust with strips of aluminum foil or pie shields. Remove the quiche from the oven and cool on a wire rack. Let the quiche rest at least 20 minutes before cutting in pieces.

Pancakes, Waffles, and Crêpes

This chapter introduces a wide range of griddle cakes, from hearty, nubbly buckwheat blinis to tender crêpes to moist and luscious Banana Pancakes. Many other countries have some sort of griddle cake they love, but they don't always serve them for breakfast, the meal at which most Americans have grown to enjoy them.

One of the best things about griddle cakes of all sorts is that you have virtually limitless options when it comes to toppings and garnishes. Hot spiced apples or a honeyed compound butter spiked with citrus zest are just some of the suggestions you'll find in these recipes. Another great thing about griddle cakes and waffles is they can be cooked ahead of time, cooled, and frozen in zip-close bags for a quick alternative to a hot, homemade breakfast. Just pop them in the toaster or toaster oven straight from the freezer. This is a great way to use any leftovers that might linger after breakfast.

Griddle cakes are made from relatively simple batters that blend quickly and can actually be held for a few days in some cases. In fact, crêpes are more tender and delicate when the batter rests overnight. We've included tips and tricks to accompany the recipes throughout this chapter for everything from streamlining your work in the morning to changing a familiar dish from sweet to savory.

THE BEST INGREDIENTS

Pancake, crêpe, and waffle recipes boil down to just four or five basic ingredients: flour, eggs, milk or buttermilk, and butter, shortening, or oil. With so much riding on each individual ingredient, it pays to choose the best raw materials you can find.

FLOURS AND MEALS

The best pancakes and waffles are tender, moist, and delicate. To get that texture you can use all-purpose flour; most brands of all-purpose flour have a moderate protein content. For even more delicate batters, you may wish to try cake or pastry flour. These flours have even less protein.

Many recipes in this chapter include some measure of flours or meals made from other grains, including buckwheat, corn, and oats. When cornmeal is included in a recipe, we have used stone-ground yellow cornmeal. The coarser the cornmeal, the more textured your pancakes and waffles will be.

When a recipe calls for oatmeal, you can use either quick-cooking or rolled oats. (Rolled oats are sometimes labeled "old-fashioned.") Look for oat flour in natural foods shops, or make your own by processing rolled oats in a food processor until a fine meal or powder forms.

Some specialty flours and meals, including buckwheat, oat or wheat bran, or cornmeal, stay fresher and more flavorful if you store them in the freezer. Be sure to use containers or bags that seal tightly and label and date the package.

EGGS AND MILK

Eggs hold pancakes together, give the batter a wonderful golden color, and add flavor and nutritional value. In some recipes the eggs are separated so that the whites can be beaten into a foam. When the beaten whites are folded into the batter, they produce a light, delicate texture.

Buttermilk gives many recipes in this chapter a pleasant tang. In addition, buttermilk reacts with baking soda for exceptionally light pancakes. If you like buttermilk pancakes and waffles but find it hard to keep buttermilk on hand in the refrigerator, look for powdered buttermilk in the baking goods section of most supermarkets.

BUTTER, OIL, AND SWEETENERS

Butter and oil give batters additional tenderness and flavor. Apart from adding butter or oil as an ingredient, you also need oil to keep griddles lubricated. Oil won't burn as readily as butter. If you like to use cooking spray, be sure to take the pan off the heat before you spray it to prevent flare-ups and smoke.

Sugar and other sweeteners are added to batters to provide extra moisture and flavor. In addition, they help pancakes and waffles develop richly colored exteriors. You can usually substitute sweeteners such as honey, molasses, corn syrup, or maple syrup in recipes. Since these ingredients are normally added in relatively small amounts, you can usually substitute using equal amounts.

GRIDDLES, SKILLETS, AND CRÊPE PANS

A gentle touch for mixing pancake batters is one important factor in success. The other is selecting and preparing your pan properly.

Moderate or heavy-gauge pans can hold heat evenly and tend to develop few hot spots. If one part of the pan is significantly hotter than other parts, your pancakes will not cook evenly.

The pan or griddle must have a very flat, smooth surface as well. To keep your pans from becoming warped or buckled, use the following guidelines:

- Preheat pans and griddles completely before adding oil or butter.
- Adjust the heat whenever your sense of smell or touch or sight tells you that the pan is getting too hot or too cold.
- Use a thin layer of oil or butter to lubricate the pan.
- If your pan or griddle has a nonstick surface, use tools designed to prevent scratches when you turn the cakes.

If you like to use cast-iron griddles or skillets, condition them before using them the first time: Get the pan hot, add a liberal amount of oil, and let the oil heat up. Pour out the oil and rub the pan or griddle with paper toweling. (This is the same method you should use to condition unlined crêpe pans.)

Once cast-iron pans are conditioned, maintain their surfaces by wiping out the pan with paper toweling. You can use a little salt as an abrasive if necessary. Do not wash cast-iron pans with soap and water if you can avoid it. Be sure cast-iron pans, skillets, and griddles are completely dry before you put them away, otherwise they can rust.

Soapstone griddles are another classic choice for making griddle cakes. Like cast iron, soapstone has the advantage of being heavy enough to hold and release heat very evenly. Also like cast iron, soapstone griddles require some special maintenance to keep them properly seasoned: Oil the griddle before using it and whenever the surface starts to stick; clean the griddle with a sponge and hot water; avoid abrasives and detergents. (Both cast iron and soapstone can be scrubbed and washed when necessary; you simply need to repeat the seasoning process.) Waffle irons, of course, are a must to make any kind of waffle.

MIXING METHODS

The well method is the most common way to blend a batter, whether you are making pancakes, waffles, or crêpes. The method gets its name from the fact that you literally make a "well" in the center of the dry ingredients. The well lets you blend the dry ingredients into the wet ingredients quickly. Consult your recipe to see if the batter should rest or if it is ready to use directly after mixing.

A few recipes in this chapter (Buckwheat Blinis on page 226 and Buckwheat Flapjacks on page 225) include a small amount of yeast. The yeast needs some time to do its work, so these batters are generally mixed using the same well method as that for a buttermilk pancake. Once blended, the batter is left to "ferment" for several hours or even overnight. If your kitchen is warm, put the batter in the refrigerator to ferment. Let it rest at room temperature while you preheat your griddle or waffle iron.

Making Pancakes

Whether you enjoy silver-dollar pancakes or great big flapjacks that fill up your plate, a few simple steps can ensure that all your griddlecakes are light and tender, with a rich color and flavor.

SIFTING AND BLENDING THE DRY INGREDIENTS

The way you handle the dry ingredients has a direct effect on a griddlecake's texture. The more evenly the dry ingredients are blended, the fewer strokes it takes to blend the batter. Keeping stirring time to a minimum means that your batter won't be overmixed. The less you have to mix the batter, the more tender your pancakes and waffles will be.

We recommend sifting all of the dry ingredients—flour, salt, sugar, baking powder or baking soda—together into a mixing bowl large enough to hold the finished batter.

COMBINING THE WET INGREDIENTS

Blend together the wet ingredients, such as buttermilk or milk, eggs, and oil or melted butter, until they are smooth. This is another way you can be sure your batter is handled gently and mixed quickly.

BLENDING THE BATTER

Use a wooden spoon to blend these batters. Before you actually add the wet ingredients to the dry ones, use your spoon to create a well in the center by pushing the dry ingredients from the center to the sides of the bowl but don't pack them down too much.

Add the wet ingredients all at once and stir the dry ingredients from the edge into the center, mixing just long enough to moisten all of the dry ingredients. You may leave lumps in some batters; others, like crêpes, are strained. See specific recipes for instructions.

CHECKING THE GRIDDLE OR PAN

Set your pan over medium to medium-high heat and let it get very hot while you blend the batter and gather together the syrup, butter, or other toppings. If you use nonstick pans, use slightly lower heat. The pan is hot enough when a few drops of water skitter over the surface and evaporate in a few seconds.

Brush or rub a coating of vegetable oil on the pan once it is hot with a piece of folded paper toweling. Keep the towel and the oil handy to wipe out the pan and re-lubricate it between batches.

ADDING THE BATTER TO THE PAN

More than one pancake can be cooked on the griddle at once. Pancake batter will spread: the thinner the batter, the more it spreads. Be sure to leave enough room between the pancakes to allow them to spread without touching. Leaving some room means that you'll have an easier time of turning the pancakes.

TURNING PANCAKES

You can tell when pancakes are ready to turn by looking for bubbles that break on the surface. Lift the pancake with a spatula or palette knife and check the color. The color should be an even golden brown. Turn the cake and finish on the second side.

BUTTERMILK PANCAKES
with Grand Marnier-Infused Strawberries

IF YOU have a 1-quart measuring cup or a bowl with a spout, use that to mix the batter. You can simply pour the batter out onto a preheated griddle or skillet. If you don't use up all of the batter, you can save it for a day or two. Cover it tightly and stir the batter to blend it again the next morning. The batter may be slightly thinner, but the pancakes will still be tender and delicious. Choose your favorite toppings: butter, syrup, honey, fruit purees, or other toppings as desired.

MAKES 8 SERVINGS

2 cups all-purpose flour

¼ cup sugar

4 tsp baking powder

½ tsp baking soda

½ tsp salt

2¼ cups buttermilk

4 large eggs

¼ cup butter, melted and cooled

Cooking spray or vegetable oil to coat pan, as needed

4 cups Grand Marnier–Infused Strawberries (recipe follows)

1. Sift the flour, sugar, baking powder, baking soda, and salt together into a mixing bowl. Make a well in the center of the flour mixture.

2. In a separate bowl, blend the buttermilk, eggs, and butter. Add to the flour mixture and stir by hand just until the batter is evenly moistened. The batter is ready to use or may be stored covered and refrigerated for up to 12 hours.

3. Heat a large skillet or griddle over medium-high heat. Oil it lightly by brushing or spraying with cooking oil. Drop the pancake batter into the hot pan by large spoonfuls, about ¼ cup. Leave about 2 inches between the pancakes to allow them to spread and to make turning easier.

4. Cook on the first side until small bubbles appear on the upper surface of the pancake and the edges are set, about 2 minutes. Use an offset spatula or a palette knife to turn the pancakes and finish cooking on the second side, another 2 to 3 minutes. Adjust the temperature beneath the skillet or griddle to produce a good brown color.

5. Serve the pancakes at once topped with the strawberries.

Grand Marnier-Infused Strawberries

THIS POTENT strawberry dish is perfect as a topping for ultra-adult pancakes or waffles at Sunday brunch. If you have any left, serve it over ice cream or on its own, topped with whipped cream, for a great dessert dish at night.

MAKES 4 CUPS

2 cups sugar

1¾ cups Grand Marnier, divided use

6 cups hulled and quartered strawberries

1. Mix together the sugar and 1¼ cups Grand Marnier, then add the strawberries and stir together. Cover the strawberries and marinate refrigerated overnight. The strawberries will be submerged in liquid when they are properly marinated.

2. Using a slotted spoon, transfer the strawberries from the marinade to a separate bowl and set aside. Pour the marinade into a saucepan and bring to a boil. Reduce the heat and simmer slowly until reduced to a syrupy consistency, about 30 minutes. It may be necessary to lower the heat while the liquid is reducing.

3. Cool the syrup to room temperature and add the remaining ½ cup Grand Marnier. Pour this syrup over the reserved strawberries.

4. The strawberries are ready to serve now, or they can be stored in a covered container in the refrigerator for up to 5 days.

BANANA PANCAKES
with Blueberry Maple Syrup

A FINE PUREE of sweet ripe bananas gives these pancakes a fine texture, but feel free to leave them a little coarser so that you get nuggets of tender banana in your pancakes.

MAKES 8 SERVINGS

2 cups all-purpose flour

¼ cup sugar

4 tsp baking powder

½ tsp baking soda

½ tsp salt

1¾ cups buttermilk

4 large eggs

¼ cup butter, melted and cooled

Cooking spray or vegetable oil to coat pan, as needed

¾ cup mashed ripe bananas

Powdered sugar for garnish

Blueberries for garnish

2 cups Blueberry Maple Syrup (recipe follows)

1. Sift the flour, sugar, baking powder, baking soda, and salt together into a mixing bowl. Make a well in the center of the flour mixture.

2. In a separate bowl, blend the buttermilk, eggs, and butter. Add to the flour mixture and stir by hand just until the batter is evenly moistened. The batter is ready to use or may be stored covered and refrigerated for up to 12 hours.

3. Heat a large skillet or griddle over medium-high heat. Oil it lightly by brushing or spraying with cooking oil. Just before making the pancakes, fold the bananas into the batter. Drop the pancake batter into the hot pan by large spoonfuls, about ¼ cup. Leave about 2 inches between the pancakes to allow them to spread and to make turning easier.

4. Cook on the first side until small bubbles appear on the upper surface of the pancake and the edges are set, about 2 minutes. Use an offset spatula or a palette knife to turn the pancakes and finish cooking on the second side, another 2 to 3 minutes. Adjust the temperature beneath the skillet or griddle to produce a good brown color.

5. Serve at once, dusted with powdered sugar and garnished with blueberries, accompanied by the blueberry maple syrup.

Blueberry Maple Syrup

YOU MAY prefer to skip the straining step for a more rustic texture, similar to that of a fruit topping. In that case, simply add the maple syrup once the blueberries and their liquid have a soft, jamlike texture.

MAKES 2 CUPS

4 cups blueberries, fresh or frozen

1 tsp lemon zest

1 cup maple syrup

1. Combine the blueberries and lemon zest in a medium-sized saucepan. Bring to a simmer over medium heat and simmer, stirring occasionally, until most of the juice has been released and the mixture develops a saucelike consistency, about 10 minutes.

2. Strain the mixture through a fine-mesh sieve

into a clean saucepan, making sure to press all of the juice out of the blueberry mixture. Return the juice to a simmer and add the maple syrup. Simmer over low heat until the syrup is slightly reduced and thickened, about 10 minutes.

3. The syrup is ready to serve now, or it can be cooled and stored in a container in the refrigerator for up to 10 days. Reheat the syrup over low heat or in the microwave.

Flavored Honeys and Syrups

You might be surprised at how many different flavors and qualities of honey there are. Maple syrup, real maple syrup, has a light body and an intense flavor. But, like anything else, there are ways to "gild the lily" for something special.

To make a flavored honey or syrup, first measure out 2 cups and put it in the top of a double boiler. It is important to use a double boiler to keep honeys and syrups from scorching.

Next, add flavorings. We used hibiscus flowers for the honey paired with our buckwheat flapjacks, but there are other options. Use the following as a guideline, but do taste the syrup or honey as it steeps. Your ingredients may be stronger or weaker in flavor, so let your palate be the ultimate guide. You may want to add more flavoring than suggested below, or perhaps you'll need to shorten or lengthen the steeping time.

- 1 cup hibiscus flowers, steeped for 1 hour
- ¼ cup orange peel, steeped for 45 minutes
- 2 tbsp lemon peel, steeped for 45 minutes
- ½ cup lavender flowers, steeped for 30 minutes
- 2 cinnamon sticks, steeped for 30 minutes
- 1 cup fruit purée (raspberry or blueberry), steeped for 30 minutes
- 2 thick slices ginger, steeped for 30 minutes
- 2 tsp whole cloves, steeped for 15 minutes

Heat the honey or syrup to just below the boiling point (185°F) in a double boiler and keep it at that temperature, stirring constantly, about 10 minutes. Remove the honey or syrup from the double boiler. Add the flavoring of your choice, and let steep according to the times listed. Strain the honey into a clean serving bowl or storage container.

You can keep flavored syrups and honeys on hand in the refrigerator for up to 3 weeks. Serve flavored honeys and syrups slightly warm to really bring out the aroma.

BUCKWHEAT FLAPJACKS
with Hibiscus Honey

HIBISCUS HONEY has a brilliant ruby color from the hibiscus flowers and a slightly tart flavor that tempers honey's natural sweetness. See the note at left for more about adding different flavors to honeys and syrups.

MAKES 8 SERVINGS

2¼ tsp active dry yeast (1 package)

2½ cups milk, warmed to 110°F

2¾ cups all-purpose flour

1¼ cups buckwheat flour

1 tbsp granulated sugar

1½ tsp salt

2 large egg yolks

2 large egg whites

¼ cup canola oil

½ cup Lemon-Cardamom Butter (page 231)

1½ cups Hibiscus Honey (recipe follows)

1. Dissolve the yeast in the warmed milk and set aside until the yeast foams, 5 to 10 minutes.

2. Sift together the flours, sugar, and salt into a large bowl and make a well in the center of the dry ingredients. Add the egg yolks and yeast mixture to the well and stir until smooth. Cover with plastic wrap and let rise in a warm place until doubled, 1 to 1½ hours.

2. Preheat a gas grill to medium. If you are using a charcoal grill, build a fire and let it burn down until the coals are glowing red with a moderate coating of white ash. Spread the coals in an even bed.

3. Once the batter has risen, beat the egg whites to soft peaks and fold into the batter.

4. Preheat a griddle over direct heat on the grill and lightly grease with some of the oil. Ladle ¼ cup of batter for each flapjack onto the griddle. Turn once, when bubbles break on the upper surface and the bottom is golden brown, about 3 minutes. Finish cooking on the second side, about 2 minutes. Repeat with the remaining batter.

5. Serve the flapjacks accompanied by lemon-cardamom butter and hibiscus honey.

Hibiscus Honey

MAKES 2 CUPS

2 cups honey

1 cup hibiscus flowers

1. Heat the honey to just below the boiling point (185°F) in a double boiler and keep it at that temperature, stirring constantly, about 10 minutes.

2. Remove the honey or syrup from the double boiler and add the hibiscus flowers. Let steep for 1 hour and then strain into a serving bowl or storage container. Store any unused honey in a covered container in the refrigerator for up to 3 weeks.

BUCKWHEAT BLINIS
with Apple Butter

THIS BLINI recipe makes breakfast-sized pancakes. Serve them with the apple butter for a hearty breakfast on a cold winter morning. Or you can make smaller blini to top with sour cream and caviar for a classic Russian hors d'oeuvre.

MAKES 8 SERVINGS

2¼ tsp active dry yeast (1 package)

2 cups milk, warmed to 110°F

1½ cups all-purpose flour

1½ cups buckwheat flour

1 tsp sugar

LEFT TO RIGHT Flip the pancakes once the bubbles have risen to the surface and started to break and the flapjack is golden brown on the bottom. Steep the Hibiscus Honey until it has achieved the color and flavor that you like. Warm the strained syrup slightly before serving to make it easier to pour.

½ tsp salt

2 large egg yolks, beaten

3 large egg whites

¼ cup butter or oil

2 cups Apple Butter (recipe follows)

1. Dissolve the yeast in the warmed milk and set aside for 5 to 10 minutes or until yeast blooms.

2. Sift the flours, sugar, and salt together into a large bowl and make a well in the center of the dry ingredients.

3. Add the egg yolks and yeast mixture to the flour and stir until smooth. Cover with plastic and let rise until doubled, 2 to 3 hours.

4. To make the blini, beat egg whites to soft peaks and fold into the batter. Preheat a griddle on medium heat and lightly grease with butter or oil. Ladle ⅓ cup batter for each blini onto the griddle. Turn once, when bubbles break on the upper surface and the bottom is golden brown, about 2 minutes. Finish cooking on the second side, about 1 minute. Repeat until the batter is finished.

5. Serve immediately with the apple butter.

Apple Butter

TART, JUICY apples make a flavorful apple butter that doesn't get too sweet. You can choose a single variety, such as MacIntosh, or mix several varieties. Use a saucepan with a heavy-gauge bottom to prevent the apple butter from scorching as you cook it. A flame diffuser, if you have one, also keeps the heat even and gentle as the apple butter simmers.

MAKES 2 CUPS

12 cups peeled and sliced apples

1½ cups apple cider

1¼ cups sugar

½ cinnamon stick

½ tsp ground cardamom

½ tsp grated lemon zest

¼ tsp salt

1. Combine the apples and apple cider in a saucepan and bring to a slow simmer over medium heat. Reduce the heat, cover the pan, and let simmer, stirring occasionally, until all the apples are soft and pulpy, about 30 minutes.

2. Remove from the heat and puree the apples with a food mill or a sieve into a clean saucepan. Add the sugar, cinnamon, cardamom, zest, and salt to the apple puree and simmer over low heat, stirring frequently, until very thick and deep brown, about 2 hours.

3. Transfer the apple butter to a bowl set in an ice bath and cool, stirring from time to time. Once the apple butter has cooled, it is ready to serve or store in a covered container in the refrigerator for up to 3 weeks.

DUTCH BABY
with Spiced Fruit

FEEL FREE to substitute sour cream or yogurt for the whipped cream, if you prefer. For the spiced fruit, experiment with other fruits or combinations of fruits such as bananas, raspberries, apples, or strawberries.

MAKES 6–8 SERVINGS

½ cup all-purpose flour

½ tsp salt

2 large eggs

½ cup milk

¼ cup butter, melted, divided use

2¾ cups peeled and sliced peaches

1 tsp ground cinnamon

2 tbsp packed brown sugar

1 tbsp lemon juice

Powdered sugar, as needed

¼ cup heavy cream, whipped to soft peaks

1 tsp lemon zest

1. Preheat the oven to 450°F.

2. Sift the flour and salt together into a small bowl. Make a well in the center of the dry ingredients.

3. Put the eggs in a blender and blend at low speed. Add the flour mixture and the milk alternately, in thirds. Scrape down the sides of the blender and continue to blend until smooth. Blend in 2 tablespoons of the melted butter.

4. Pour the batter into a well-greased 10-inch cast-iron skillet or an ovenproof sauté pan. Bake for 20 minutes without opening the oven door. Reduce the heat to 350°F and bake 10 minutes longer.

5. While the Dutch baby is baking, prepare the spiced fruit. Heat the remaining 2 tablespoons melted butter in a medium sauté pan over high heat. Add the peaches, cinnamon, and brown sugar. Continue to cook until the peaches are browned, 5 to 6 minutes.

6. Remove the Dutch baby from the oven. Drizzle with the lemon juice and sprinkle with the powdered sugar. Fill the center of the Dutch baby with the hot fruit mixture. Top with the whipped cream and lemon zest. Serve at once.

CRÊPES

MAKES 12 CRÊPES

1½ cups all-purpose flour

¼ tsp salt

2 cups whole milk

2 large eggs

2 tbsp unsalted butter, melted and cooled

1. Sift the flour and salt together into a bowl. In another bowl, whisk together the milk, eggs, and butter until evenly blended. Add all at once to the dry ingredients. Stir just enough to make a smooth batter. Let the batter rest, refrigerated, for at least 2 hours or up to overnight. If the batter has lumps, strain through a sieve before preparing the crêpes.

2. Heat a crêpe pan or small nonstick skillet over medium-high heat and brush liberally with oil. Ladle about ⅓ cup of the batter into the crêpe pan. Lift the pan from the heat and tilt and swirl to completely coat the pan with a thin layer of batter. Cook on the first side until set and lightly browned, about 1½ minutes. Turn or flip the crêpe and finish cooking on the second side, 30 to 45 seconds more.

3. Flip the crêpe out of the pan onto a plate lined with parchment or waxed paper. Repeat with remaining batter to make 12 crêpes in all.

CRÊPES WITH SPICY MUSHROOM FILLING
and Chile Cream Sauce

W<small>E LIKE</small> the tender texture of crêpes in this dish, but the dish would be equally delicious made with regular or whole wheat flour tortillas.

MAKES 4 SERVINGS

SPICY MUSHROOM FILLING

2 tbsp olive oil

½ cup minced onion

1½ tsp minced garlic

4 cups sliced mushrooms

2 tsp minced serrano chile

2 tbsp lime juice

¾ tsp epazote

Salt and pepper as needed

CHILE CREAM SAUCE

2 cups heavy cream

2 dry poblano chiles, toasted and chopped

1 dry chipotle chile, toasted and chopped

12 Crêpes (opposite)

¾ cup crumbled queso fresco

1. To make the filling, heat the olive oil in a sauté pan over medium-high heat. Add the onion and garlic to the oil and sauté, stirring frequently, until the onions are tender and translucent, 2 to 3 minutes. Increase the heat to high. Add the mushrooms and chile. Sauté the mushrooms without stirring until they are browned on one side, 3 to 4 minutes. Stir the mixture and continue to cook over medium heat until the liquid given off by the mushrooms cooks away, about 5 minutes. Add the lime juice and epazote. Season with salt and pepper. (This filling can be prepared in advance, cooled, and kept in a covered container in the refrigerator for up to 2 days.)

2. To make the chile cream sauce, combine the heavy cream and chiles in a small sauce pan. Simmer over very low heat until the cream is reduced and thickened and the sauce is very flavorful, 20 to 30 minutes. Strain the sauce and season with salt and pepper if needed. The sauce is ready to use now, or it can be stored in a covered container in the re-

LEFT TO RIGHT Tilt and swirl the pan to coat with a thin layer—the crêpe should be thin enough to let some light through. When filling, use your fingertips to pull the edge of the crêpe to the center, trapping the filling and pressing it to make a stuffed cylinder shape.

frigerator for up to 6 days.

3. Preheat the oven to 375°F. Reheat the filling and the chile cream sauce separately over low heat, if needed, stirring occasionally, about 5 minutes.

4. To assemble the crêpes, lay one crêpe flat on a work surface. Place 2 tablespoons of the warm filling in the center of each of the crêpes and top with the crumbled queso fresco. Roll up the crêpe. Place the crêpes seam side down in a baking dish. Ladle the sauce over the crêpes and bake until the crêpes and the sauce are very hot, about 15 minutes. Serve at once on heated plates.

WAFFLES
with Hot Raspberry Syrup

WE MADE these waffles in a round waffle iron. Your yield may be slightly different if your waffle iron makes rectangular or square waffles.

MAKES 8 SERVINGS

3½ cups all-purpose flour

2 tsp salt

½ cup sugar

2 tbsp baking powder

8 large eggs, separated

3 cups milk

1 cup butter, melted

2 cups Hot Raspberry Syrup (recipe follows)

1. Sift together the flour, salt, sugar, and baking powder into a large mixing bowl. Make a well in the center of the dry ingredients.

2. Whisk together the egg yolks, milk, and melted butter in a separate bowl. Pour the wet ingredients into the well of the dry ingredients, stirring until just combined. The batter will be slightly lumpy. Do not overmix.

3. Preheat the waffle iron.

4. Whip the egg whites to soft peaks and fold into the batter in 2 additions. Ladle about ¾ cup batter into the waffle iron. Cook the waffles until they are crisp, golden, and cooked through, 3 to 6 minutes per waffle. Serve at once with the raspberry syrup.

Hot Raspberry Syrup

YOU CAN substitute good-quality vanilla extract for the vanilla bean. Add the extract to the syrup after it has reduced and you've taken it from the heat.

LEFT TO RIGHT Ladle the batter into the center of the waffle iron so that the batter will spread evenly. Remove the waffle using a fork or other utensil; if the waffle iron was greased properly, the waffle should not stick.

7 cups raspberries, fresh or frozen (thaw slightly)

1¾ cups sugar

2¼ cups water

½ vanilla bean, split and scraped or 1 tsp vanilla extract

¾ cup lemon juice

1. Combine the raspberries, sugar, and water in a saucepan and bring to a simmer over medium heat. Simmer until raspberries are soft, about 15 minutes.

2. Strain the raspberry mixture through a fine-mesh sieve, pressing against the solids with the back of a ladle.

3. Discard the seeds and pour the extracted juices into a saucepan; add the vanilla bean, its seeds, and the lemon juice to the saucepan. Simmer until reduced by one-half over medium-low heat or to the consistency of syrup, 20 to 25 minutes.

4. The syrup is ready to serve now, or it can be cooled and stored in a container in the refrigerator for up to 10 days.

THICK-SLICED GRIDDLE TOAST
with Apricot and Lemon-Cardamom Butters

THIS MAKES a great breakfast for the campsite, if you have the cooler space to bring along the already-prepared flavored butters. If you don't have a griddle, you can toast the bread directly on a rack over the fire.

MAKES 8 SERVINGS

1 cup softened Lemon-Cardamom Butter (recipe follows)

16 slices sourdough bread, about 1 inch thick

1 cup Apricot Butter (recipe follows)

1. Preheat a gas grill to medium. If you are using a charcoal grill, build a fire and let it burn down until the coals are glowing red with a moderate coating of white ash. Spread the coals in an even bed.

2. Place a griddle on the grill and preheat to medium-high heat. Spread the Lemon-Cardamom Butter on both sides of all the slices of bread.

3. Griddle the bread until golden brown, about 2 minutes on each side. Serve with the Apricot Butter.

Lemon-Cardamom Butter

MAKES 1 CUP

1 cup softened butter

2 tbsp honey, or as needed

1 tbsp lemon juice

½ tsp ground cardamom

¼ tsp grated lemon zest

Mix together the butter, honey, lemon juice, cardamom, and lemon zest until evenly blended. This can be prepared in advance and stored in the refrigerator for up to 3 days. (For more about flavored butters, see page 202.)

Apricot Butter

THIS BUTTER stores well in the refrigerator, so if apricots are plentiful, double or triple this recipe. Use containers that are perfectly clean and have tight-fitting lids.

MAKES 1½ CUPS

4½ cups sliced fresh apricots

¾ cup apricot nectar

½ cup granulated sugar

½ tsp ground cardamom

¼ tsp ground cinnamon

¼ tsp grated lemon zest

⅛ tsp salt

1. Combine the apricot slices and nectar in a large, heavy-bottomed saucepan; cover and bring the mixture to a simmer over medium heat. Simmer until the apricots are a soft pulp, about 25 minutes.

2. Push the apricots through a food mill or strainer into a clean saucepan. Add the sugar, cardamom, cinnamon, lemon zest, and salt. Simmer over medium-low heat, stirring frequently, until very thick, about 1 hour and 30 minutes.

3. Let cool completely before using. Store any unused butter in the refrigerator for up to 2 weeks.

Strawberry Honey Butter

SHAPE THE butter by piping into rosettes, or roll it into a log to chill and slice. A simple and attractive option is to simply pack it into a pretty cup or crock.

MAKES 1 CUP

¾ cup butter, softened

½ cup minced, hulled strawberries

2 tbsp honey

1 tbsp lemon juice, about ½ lemon

¼ teaspoon orange zest

Combine all of the ingredients and beat together until very smooth, but not soft or oily. The butter is ready to transfer to a pastry bag to pipe into rosettes and serve as a topping or spread now, or cover and store in the refrigerator for up to 2 days. Let the butter soften to room temperature before serving.

LEMON CURD

YOU CAN use a double boiler for this recipe, but it is actually easier to whisk the lemon curd as it cooks if you make a double boiler setup from a stainless-steel bowl set into a saucepan with an inch or

LEFT TO RIGHT Whisk the egg mixture over a hot water bath until it is thick enough to hold a line drawn through it on the back of a wooden spoon; this is called the nappé stage. Stir the butter into the curd a little bit at a time. The curd should pile up on itself slightly after it is strained; this is the proper consistency of the finished curd. Serve the cooled lemon curd as an accompaniment to scones, as shown opposite, or use it to make individual tartlets or a pie.

two of simmering water. For best results, the bottom of the bowl should not sit directly in the water, and the water should be kept below a rolling boil.

MAKES 2 CUPS

9 large egg yolks

⅔ cup lemon juice

¾ cups sugar

4 tsp lemon zest

14 tablespoons butter, cubed, room temperature

1. Bring an inch or two of water to a simmer in a saucepan or the bottom of a double boiler.

2. Combine the egg yolks, lemon juice, sugar, and zest in a stainless mixing bowl or the top of a double boiler and whisk until the sugar is completely dissolved. Set the mixture over the simmering water and continue to whisk until the eggs are thickened and warm, about 12 minutes.

3. Add the butter a few pieces at a time, stirring until each addition is blended into the eggs before adding more. Continue stirring until all of the butter is blended into the curd.

4. Transfer the curd (straining the zest out, if desired) to a bowl set in an ice bath and cool, stirring from time to time. Once the curd has reached room temperature, it is ready to serve or store in a covered container in the refrigerator for up to 3 days.

HAM STEAKS
with Redeye Gravy

I F YOUR ham steaks are large enough, you may want to cut them into portions before you cook them. Spoon the redeye gravy over the cooked steaks, and serve very hot. Traditional accompaniments are scrambled, fried, or poached eggs or grits.

MAKES 8 SERVINGS

3 lb ham steaks (cut into 8 portions, if desired)

⅔ cup very strong coffee

1. Heat a large cast-iron skillet over medium heat. Place the ham steaks in the skillet and cook until they develop a deep brown color, 4 to 5 minutes.

2. Turn the steaks and continue to cook until browned on the second side, another 4 minutes. Adjust the heat as necessary as the steaks cook. Transfer the steaks to a heatproof platter or dish and keep warm. Repeat until all of the steaks have been cooked.

3. Return the skillet to medium heat. Add the coffee, stirring to dissolve the drippings and simmer until very flavorful, about 3 minutes.

4. Serve the steaks at once on a heated platter or plates with the gravy spooned over them.

BUTTERMILK BISCUITS
with Sausage Gravy

B UTTERMILK BISCUITS are a great bread to serve at breakfast or brunch, but you can make them into the main course by adding a substantial gravy.

MAKES 12 BISCUITS

1¼ cups cold buttermilk

1 large egg

2 cups bread flour

1¾ cups all-purpose flour

3 tbsp sugar

2 tbsp baking powder

1¼ tsp salt

¾ cup cold butter, diced

Egg wash of 1 egg yolk whisked with 2 tbsp heavy cream

Sausage Gravy (recipe follows), optional

1. Preheat oven to 425°F. Prepare a baking sheet by spraying it lightly with cooking spray or lining with parchment paper.

2. Combine the buttermilk and egg in a small bowl and blend until evenly mixed. Set aside.

3. Sift the flours, sugar, baking powder, and salt together into a large bowl. Add the butter, cutting it into the dry ingredients until the mixture resembles coarse meal. You should still be able to see small pieces of butter.

4. Add the buttermilk mixture to the flour mixture, stirring until barely combined. The dough will look coarse and shaggy at this point.

5. Transfer the dough to a lightly floured work surface, press into a ball, and knead once or twice. Press or roll the dough out to a thickness of ½ inch. Cut out the biscuits using a 2½-inch cutter. Gather scraps together, reroll, and cut additional biscuits. Place the biscuits on the prepared pan about 1 inch apart and lightly brush the tops with egg wash. Refrigerate uncovered for 15 minutes.

6. Bake the biscuits until they have risen and the tops are golden brown, 18 to 20 minutes. Serve the biscuits very hot, directly from the oven, accompanied by the sausage gravy.

Sausage Gravy

SERVE THIS simple and satisfying gravy over biscuits or use it as a topping for a plain omelet.

MAKES 2 CUPS

8 oz Breakfast Sausage (page 236)

1 tbsp vegetable oil

2 tbsp flour

2 cups milk, plus as needed

1 tsp salt

½ tsp ground black pepper

1. Heat a large skillet over medium heat. Crumble the sausage into the pan and sauté, stirring frequently with a wooden spoon and breaking up the sausage as it cooks, until it is golden brown and thoroughly cooked, about 5 minutes. Transfer the sausage from the pan to a colander set in a bowl and let it drain.

2. Add the vegetable oil and the flour to the same pan used to cook the sausage. Stir to blend and cook over medium heat, stirring well to scrape up any brown bits on the bottom of the pan. Continue to cook, stirring constantly, until the mixture is a pale golden brown, about 3 minutes.

3. Add the milk, whisking constantly to remove any lumps. Simmer over low heat, stirring frequently, until the gravy is thickened, about 20 minutes. Taste the gravy and add salt and pepper to taste. If the gravy is too thick, thin it with a little additional milk; use only enough to get a pourable consistency.

4. Return the cooked sausage to the gravy. Adjust the seasoning with additional salt and pepper, if necessary.

Using a Meat Grinder

You can purchase preground meats to make sausages, but the difference in flavor and texture is dramatic if you make the effort to grind them yourself.

CHILL THE INGREDIENTS AND THE GRINDER PARTS

If you are grinding your own meat, choose meats from the shoulder for their good flavor. Cut the meat into strips or cubes that will fit easily through the feed tube of your grinder.

Add the salt to the meat now, if your recipe calls for it; salt plays a big role in developing a good flavor.

Clean and dry all the grinder parts before you begin and get them very cold. Leaving them in the freezer for about 15 minutes helps keep meats cool as you grind them to preserve freshness and flavor.

PUT THE GRINDER TOGETHER

If you are using the grinder attachment of your stand mixer, be sure that the pieces are tightly secured. Manual meat grinders often attach to the counter top with a clamp. Tighten it down well to keep the grinder stable. Use a medium grinding disk for sausages and hash.

GRIND THE MEAT AND SEASONINGS TOGETHER

Add any additional ingredients or seasonings to the meat now. Put a bowl under the opening of the grinder to catch the ground meat. Drop the meat through the feed tube gradually so that it doesn't get blocked.

CHILL THE GROUND MEAT AGAIN BEFORE MIXING

Sausages are mixed for a while. To counteract the heat that builds up when you mix the meat, chill it for about 15 minutes before you begin. Mix the chilled meat by hand with a wooden spoon or in a stand mixer with the paddle attachment.

MAKE A TEST

You can adjust the seasonings and saltiness of your sausage if necessary, but in order to tell, you need to make a test. Take about 2 tablespoons and shape into a small patty. Sauté over low to medium heat until cooked through and browned. Taste the sausage and adjust the seasonings if needed.

MEXICAN CHORIZO

THIS IS a spicy sausage with just enough heat. Try any dried chiles you enjoy. Thai bird chiles are very hot; dried New Mexican chiles or dried chipotles are less intensely hot. We've given a recipe that makes 2 pounds of chorizo; freeze any of the sausage you don't need right away to enjoy as a topping on pizza or to cook and crumble over a plain cheese quesadilla.

MAKES 2 POUNDS

2 lb ground pork, chilled

2 tbsp ground dried chiles

1 tbsp salt

1 tbsp minced garlic, sautéed and cooled

4½ tsp Spanish paprika

1 tsp ground cinnamon

1 tsp ground oregano

1 tsp ground thyme

1 tsp ground cumin

1 tsp ground black pepper

½ tsp ground cloves

½ tsp ground ginger

½ tsp ground nutmeg

½ tsp ground coriander seed

½ tsp ground bay leaf

2 tablespoons red wine vinegar

1. Mix the ground pork and the seasonings by hand with a wooden spoon or on low speed with the paddle attachment until evenly blended, about 1 minute. Mix for an additional minute, gradually adding the red wine vinegar.

2. Mix on medium speed for 15 to 20 seconds, or until the sausage mixture is sticky to the touch.

3. Make a patty with about 2 tablespoons of the mixture and sauté in a small skillet over low to medium heat until cooked through and browned. Taste and then adjust seasoning and consistency before shaping into patties.

4. The sausage is ready to prepare now or transfer it to storage containers, cover tightly, and refrigerate for up to 3 days or freeze for up to 2 months.

BREAKFAST SAUSAGE

USE THIS simple sausage for any number of dishes—it's wonderful as a pizza topping or made into patties to serve with your morning eggs.

MAKES 2 POUNDS

2 lb ground pork, chilled

1 tbsp salt

1¾ tsp ground white pepper

1½ tsp poultry seasoning

⅓ cup ice-cold water

1. Mix the ground pork, salt, pepper, and poultry seasoning by hand with a wooden spoon or on low speed with the paddle attachment until evenly blended, about 1 minute.

2. Mix for an additional minute, gradually adding the cold water.

3. Mix on medium speed for 15 to 20 seconds, or until the sausage mixture is sticky to the touch.

4. Make a patty with about 2 tablespoons of the mixture and sauté in a small skillet over low to medium heat until cooked through and browned. Taste and then adjust seasoning and consistency before shaping into patties.

5. The sausage is ready to prepare now or transfer it to storage containers, cover tightly, and refrigerate for up to 3 days or freeze for up to 2 months.

Baked Goods and Desserts

Sweet and Savory
Breads and Pastries

Baskets or trays filled with freshly baked pastries, luscious sticky rolls, or buttery brioche are the perfect way to add some elegance and extravagance to breakfast or brunch. We've collected several recipes that give you the option of making your own pastries that feature fresh and dried fruits, nuts, cheeses, and even chocolate.

Classic yeast dough-based breads like Soda Bread (page 243), Sticky Buns with Pecans (page 251), and Raisin Cinnamon Swirl Bread (page 248) give you the opportunity to try your hand at some sweet breads, while the Cottage Cheese Dill Rolls (page 250), Knot Rolls with Poppy Seeds (page 249), Olive Bread (page 247), and Grill-Baked Naan (page 247) have a decidedly savory taste.

Many yeast doughs can be left to rise overnight in the refrigerator. Simply take them from the refrigerator and let them warm to room temperature while you brew the coffee or tea, make juice, or set the table. For breads that are a bit more complex to make, you may prefer to bake them the day before, or try them on the weekend when you have a bit more time to keep track of the dough as it rises.

Feel free to experiment with fillings in pastries that call for them; for example, try substituting the filling for the Mushroom, Leek, and Brie Turnovers (page 32) where a fruit filling is called for, to create a savory pastry that can be a meal on its own.

THE BEST INGREDIENTS

Although any of the recipes in this chapter can be made successfully with all-purpose flour, you'll get the best results if you use the type of flour suggested in the recipe.

FLOURS AND MEALS

Bread flour has a slightly higher protein content than all-purpose flour. That means yeast-raised doughs can rise a little better and will have a satisfyingly chewy texture after they bake.

Cake flour is a soft wheat flour that produces delicate and tender cakes. Because it is softer, it has a tendency to clump. Be sure to sift cake flour to lighten it and break it apart.

Rye flour can be either medium or light. Medium rye has a more noticeable flavor and deeper color than light rye. Compared to white wheat flours, rye flours contain more of the whole grain's germ and bran. You can keep it fresh longer by storing it in a zip-close bag in the freezer.

YEAST

All of the recipes for breads and rolls in this chapter call for active dry yeast, the kind you can find readily in envelopes or jars in your supermarket. If you want to use fresh yeast, then you will need to double the amount of yeast we call for. Instant dry yeast, typically sold in vacuum-sealed pouches, is becoming more widely available. If you want to substitute it for active dry yeast, make your first batch with the same amount as indicated for active dry yeast. Then, if you find it necessary, you can adjust the amount slightly up or down for future batches.

SUGAR

White sugar, brown sugar, and molasses are used in recipes in this chapter to add sweetness and moisture to baked goods.

DAIRY AND EGGS

Butter is at the base of many of the pastries and cakes in this chapter. It is a major component of our basic pastry dough, Blitz Puff Pastry (page 256). If European-style butters are available in your area, try them to see what a difference they can make.

We've featured cream cheese fillings for a few of our pastries; you can substitute reduced-fat versions of cream cheese or Neufchâtel if you prefer. Cottage cheese is an important component of one of our simplest savory breads, the Cottage Cheese Dill Rolls. Our recipes call for full-fat sour cream; you may substitute reduced-fat, but avoid nonfat sour cream.

NUTS AND FRUITS

Cherries, apples, and raisins are some of the fruits used to create sweet fillings for pastries. Feel free to experiment with other fruits when they are in season. Pears, peaches, or plums can usually stand in for apples or cherries, and dried apricots, cranberries, cherries, or blueberries for raisins.

Almonds and pecans add a rich taste to coffee cakes and pastries. Try substituting other nuts you like—hazelnuts, walnuts, or pistachios, for instance. Toasting whole, slivered, or sliced nuts before adding them to a batter boosts their flavor. Almond paste can be purchased in cans or tubes.

EQUIPMENT

The right equipment can make all the difference. A good selection of baking sheets and pans, a sturdy mixer, and assorted hand tools are all you really need.

BAKING SHEETS AND PANS

Baking sheets and cake pans are made in many different sizes and materials. We've used standard sizes, but you may need to make some adjustments to our recipes if you have special bakeware that you like to use.

Dark pans tend to absorb heat. They are great for creating rich, golden crusts. Lighter pans reflect heat and are often suggested for more delicate pastries that should be golden but not brown. If you use glass or ceramic baking dishes, you may need to lower the temperature by 10 or 15 degrees.

Use cooking spray, vegetable shortening, or butter to lightly grease baking pans. If you have parchment paper or a silicone baking mat, they are excellent to use when baking pastries and cookies.

PASTRY BRUSH

A good pastry brush is essential for applying egg wash before baking and a thin coating of apricot glaze after baked goods come out of the oven. Clean the brush in soapy water after you use it and let it dry completely before you put it away.

MIXER

We prepared these recipes using a stand mixer. A dough hook makes quick work of yeast doughs and blitz puff pastry. However, you can also mix batters and doughs with a handheld mixer or by hand. You will need to increase mixing times slightly.

THE OVEN

Preheating the oven properly means that your baked goods come out of the oven with a good texture and color. Most ovens require at least 15 minutes to come fully up to temperature. Position the racks in the middle third of the oven, if possible, to obtain the most even color in your baked goods. Turn pans part way through baking or move them from higher to lower shelves (or vice versa) if your baked goods are starting to develop an uneven color.

The Well Mixing Method

The well mixing method boils down to three basic steps. First, the dry ingredients are measured and sifted together to blend. Second, the wet ingredients, such as milk, cream, or juice, are measured and blended separately from the dry ingredients. Third, the wet ingredients are added to the dry ingredients and stirred just until combined.

COMBINE THE DRY INGREDIENTS AND MAKE A WELL

Measure your ingredients carefully before starting to combine them. Dry ingredients, such as flour, sugar, salt, and baking powder or soda, are blended before they are mixed into a batter by either sifting them together or combining them in a bowl and using a whisk to blend them evenly. Read through the ingredient list and method before you combine the dry ingredients.

You may be asked to reserve a quantity of the flour or sugar to add with a garnish or use as a topping. Some recipes may call for garnish ingredients (dried fruits, grated cheese, minced herbs, and so forth) to be tossed together with the dry ingredients. Make a well by pushing the dry ingredients from the center of the bowl to the sides.

BLEND THE WET INGREDIENTS

Wet ingredients commonly used in quick bread batters include milk, buttermilk, cream, water, fruit juices, oil, and melted butter. Eggs are also considered a liquid. All of these ingredients should be properly measured and, when necessary, warmed enough to blend easily with the rest of the wet ingredients. Batters blend most evenly when the liquid ingredients are all close to room temperature. Use a whisk or a table fork to blend the wet ingredients together until they are smooth.

COMBINE THE WET AND DRY INGREDIENTS

Most quick bread batters made with the well mixing method are best mixed by hand. They are normally not heavy enough to make stirring difficult, and a short mixing time produces the most tender baked goods. Pour the wet ingredients into the well in the dry ingredients. Use a wooden spoon or a rubber spatula to stir and fold together the batter until the dry ingredients are evenly moistened.

Storing and Reheating

For many home bakers, one of the best things about quick breads is their simplicity. You can easily double the recipes in this book, making some to enjoy right away and some to store for later. Most muffins and quick breads can be stored in resealable plastic bags or rigid plastic containers and will last in the freezer for up to 2 months.

To defrost them, simply take them out of the freezer and let them rest at room temperature for an hour or so; a frozen muffin tucked into a bagged lunch in the morning will be perfect by the time you're ready to eat.

CREAM SCONES

B E SURE your cream is very cold for the best texture. Look for coarse sugar along with other baking items in your grocery store, but if it isn't available, you can use regular granulated sugar instead.

MAKES 10 SCONES

3 cups all-purpose flour

½ cup sugar

2 tbsp baking powder

½ tsp salt

2 cups heavy cream, cold

2 tbsp milk

3 tbsp coarse sugar for topping

1. Cut two 10-inch circles of parchment paper. Use one to line a 10-inch round cake pan. Reserve the second piece.

2. Sift the flour, sugar, baking powder, and salt together into a mixing bowl. Make a well in the center of the flour mixture.

3. Add the cream to the flour mixture and stir by hand just until the batter is evenly moistened.

4. Place the dough in the lined cake pan and press into an even layer. Cover the dough with the second parchment paper circle. Freeze the dough until very firm, at least 2 hours.

5. Preheat the oven to 350°F. Prepare a baking sheet by spraying it lightly with cooking spray or lining it with parchment paper.

6. Thaw the dough for 5 minutes at room temperature; turn it out of the cake pan onto a cutting board. Cut the dough into 10 equal wedges and place the individual wedges on the baking sheet about 2 inches apart. Brush the scones with milk and sprinkle with the sugar.

7. Bake the scones until golden brown, 30 to 40 minutes. Cool the scones on the baking sheet for a few minutes, then transfer to cooling racks. Serve the scones warm or at room temperature the day the are baked, or freeze them for up to 4 weeks.

HAM AND CHEDDAR SCONES

THE CHEESE gets nice and brown and bubbly on the outside, and the ham adds a lot of flavor. The green onions provide a nice counterpoint to the ham and cheese and give these moist scones a fantastic fresh flavor.

MAKES 10 SCONES

3 cups all-purpose flour

½ cup sugar

2 tbsp baking powder

½ tsp salt

1 cup medium-diced ham

½ cup medium-diced cheddar cheese

½ cup sliced scallions

2 cups heavy cream

1. Cut two 10-inch circles of parchment paper. Use one to line a 10-inch round cake pan. Reserve the second piece.

2. Sift the flour, sugar, baking powder, and salt together into a mixing bowl. Add the ham, cheese, and scallions and toss together with the dry ingredients until evenly distributed. Make a well in the center of the flour mixture.

3. Add the cream to the flour mixture and stir by hand just until the batter is evenly moistened.

4. Place the dough in the lined cake pan and press into an even layer. Cover the dough with the second parchment paper circle. Freeze the dough until very firm, at least 2 hours.

5. Preheat the oven to 350° F. Prepare a baking sheet by spraying it lightly with cooking spray or lining with parchment paper.

6. Thaw the dough for 5 minutes at room temperature; turn it out of the cake pan onto a cutting board. Cut the dough into 10 equal wedges and place the individual wedges on the baking sheet about 2 inches apart.

7. Bake the scones until golden brown, 30 to 40 minutes. Cool the scones on the baking sheet for a few minutes, then transfer to cooling racks. Serve

LEFT TO RIGHT Mix the cream with the dry ingredients until it is just combined. This is known as the shaggy mass stage. Cut the dough into 10 equal pieces so that each scone will bake evenly..

the scones warm or at room temperature the day the are baked, or freeze them for up to 4 weeks.

DRIED CHERRY SCONES

A TOUCH OF salt in the dough is the perfect counterpoint to the sweetness of the dried fruit. As the scones bake, the cherries plump up and take on a great jammy texture. Try dried currants or apricots instead of cherries.

MAKES 10 SCONES

3 cups all-purpose flour

½ cup sugar

2 tbsp baking powder

1½ tsp salt

1 cup dried cherries

2 cups heavy cream

SUGAR GLAZE (OPTIONAL)

2 tbsp milk

1 cup confectioners' sugar, sifted

1. Cut two 10-inch circles of parchment paper. Use one to line a 10-inch round cake pan. Reserve the second piece.

2. Sift the flour, sugar, baking powder, and salt together into a mixing bowl. Add the dried cherries and toss them together with the dry ingredients until evenly distributed. Make a well in the center of the flour mixture.

3. Add the cream to the flour mixture and stir by hand just until the batter is evenly moistened.

4. Place the dough in the lined cake pan and press into an even layer. Cover the dough with the second parchment paper circle. Freeze the dough until very firm, at least 2 hours.

5. Preheat the oven to 350° F. Prepare a baking sheet by spraying it lightly with cooking spray or lining it with parchment paper.

6. Thaw the dough for 5 minutes at room temperature; turn it out of the cake pan onto a cutting board. Cut the dough into 10 equal wedges and place the individual wedges on the baking sheet about 2 inches apart.

7. Bake the scones until golden brown, 30 to 40 minutes. Cool the scones on the baking sheet for a few minutes, then transfer to cooling racks.

8. Mix the milk and confectioners' sugar together to make a glaze, if desired, and spoon over the scones while they are still warm. Serve the scones warm or at room temperature the day the are baked, or freeze them for up to 4 weeks.

Making Biscuits, Scones, and Soda Bread

The technique used to make biscuits, as well as scones and soda bread, is known as a rubbed dough method. Instead of soft batters that drop easily from a spoon, biscuits, scones, and soda bread are made from a stiff dough that can be rolled and cut.

KEEP INGREDIENTS COOL

Any liquids or fats that you add to these doughs should be kept very cold. Cold ingredients are important if you want a light flaky texture.

CUT THE FAT INTO THE FLOUR

Instead of blending the ingredients to make a smooth batter, as you do for muffins and cakes made with the straight or creaming mixing methods, you should cut the butter into the flour with a pastry knife or two table knives, just long enough to produce a mealy texture. You should still be able to see small pieces of butter.

ADD THE LIQUID INGREDIENTS AND BLEND BRIEFLY

Although the mixing method for biscuits and soda bread is similar to that for pie crust (page 262) and blitz puff pastry (page 256), these doughs contain enough liquid to make a soft dough. Chill the liquid (and eggs, if called for) and add them to the fat and flour mixture. Work quickly and instead of stirring, use a fork to pull the flour into the liquid. The dough is properly blended when it looks very rough, a condition bakers sometimes refer to as a "shaggy mass."

KNEAD THE DOUGH BRIEFLY

The purpose of kneading these doughs is simply to gather them together into a smooth ball. Turn the dough out onto a lightly floured surface and press it together. Knead the dough two or three times. It is ready to shape by either rolling and cutting or molding into a loaf.

If making biscuits, pat or roll out the dough. Keep the dough very lightly dusted, just enough so that it doesn't stick. Your biscuit cutter should have sharp, clean edges. Press the cutter into the dough and twist it slightly to lift the biscuit up. Make your cuts as close together as possible. Once you've cut out all you can, gather the scraps together, pressing them enough so that you can roll out the dough. Then cut additional biscuits.

COOL THE DOUGH ONCE MORE BEFORE BAKING THE BISCUITS

This final cooling lets the dough relax and counteracts the potential toughness that might result from blending flour and liquid. It also gives the oven time to come up to the right temperature. You'll notice that the suggested baking temperature for biscuits and soda bread is usually 400° to 425° F. They need to bake quickly in a hot oven for a good rise and a great color. If your recipe recommends it, apply a thin layer of egg wash or cold milk for a rich color and a slight sheen.

Rolling Garnishes into Biscuits

When you pat out the biscuit dough the first time, add a garnish such as chopped herbs, grated cheese, or bacon bits by scattering it in an even layer over the dough. Fold the dough in thirds, like a letter.

Turn the dough so that the long side is now parallel to the edge of the work surface and use a rolling pin to make a larger square. Fold the dough in thirds once more and roll out for the final time.

SODA BREAD

TRADITIONAL RECIPES for soda bread suggest wrapping the freshly baked loaves in a clean tea towel. This keeps the soda bread moist and preserves its unique texture.

MAKES 2 LOAVES OR 16 ROLLS

4 cups cake flour

2 tsp baking soda

½ cup sugar

¼ tsp salt

¼ cup vegetable shortening

1 cup dark raisins

1 tbsp caraway seeds

2 cups cold buttermilk

1. Preheat the oven to 400°F. Prepare a baking sheet by spraying it lightly with cooking spray or lining it with parchment paper.

2. Sift the flour, baking soda, sugar, and salt together into a large bowl. Using a pastry cutter or 2 knives, cut the shortening into the dry ingredients until it resembles coarse meal.

3. Add the raisins, caraway seeds, and buttermilk. Mix the dough just until it forms a shaggy mass.

4. Turn the dough out onto a lightly floured surface. Press the dough into a ball. Form the dough into 2 equal loaves, or cut into 16 equal pieces to

make rolls. Dust with flour and lightly score a cross into the top of each roll or loaf with a sharp knife.

5. Bake the soda bread until it is lightly browned and sounds hollow when tapped on the bottom, about 8 to 10 minutes for rolls and 25 minutes for loaves. Wrap the bread in a tea towel directly out of the oven.

6. Cool the soda bread in the tea towel on a wire rack before serving. It can be held at room temperature for up to 2 days or frozen for up to 4 weeks.

BANANA NUT LOAF

IF YOUR bananas are ready to make into banana bread before you are ready to use them, freeze them (in their peels) until your next baking day. They'll keep for up to 2 months.

MAKES 2 LOAVES

6 bananas, very ripe

1 tsp lemon juice

3¼ cups all-purpose flour

½ tsp baking powder

1¼ tsp baking soda

½ tsp salt

2 cups sugar

2 large eggs

½ cup vegetable oil

¾ cup chopped toasted pecans

1. Preheat the oven to 350°F. Prepare two 8-inch loaf pans by spraying lightly with cooking spray or rubbing with softened butter.

2. Puree the bananas and lemon juice together using a blender or by hand. You should have about 2 cups mashed bananas.

3. Sift together the flour, baking powder, baking soda, and salt. Set aside.

4. Combine the banana puree, sugar, eggs, and oil and mix on medium speed with a paddle attachment until blended, about 3 minutes. Scrape the bowl as needed. Add the sifted dry ingredients and mix until just combined. Mix in the pecans.

5. Divide the batter evenly between the loaf pans. Gently tap the filled pans to burst any air bubbles. Bake until the bread springs back when pressed and a tester inserted near the center comes out clean, about 55 minutes.

6. Cool the loaves in the pans for a few minutes, then remove the bread from the pans, transfer to cooling racks, and cool completely before slicing and serving or wrapping. They can be held at room temperature for up to 3 days or frozen for up to 6 weeks.

CORNBREAD

TO GET a crisp crust on the bottom and sides of your cornbread, use a cast-iron skillet. (A 10-inch pan is perfect for this recipe.) Alternately, this batter can be used to make corn sticks. Most of these pans bake 7 corn sticks at a time. Put the skillet or corn stick pan into the oven while you mix the batter so that it gets very hot. Brush the hot pan liberally with oil just before pouring in the batter.

MAKES 12 SERVINGS

1¼ cups all-purpose flour

½ cup yellow cornmeal

½ cup sugar

⅓ cup powdered milk

2 tbsp baking powder

½ tsp salt

2 large eggs

½ cup water

⅓ cup corn oil

¼ tsp vanilla extract

1. Preheat the oven to 350°F. Spray an 8-inch square baking pan with cooking spray, or prepare a cast-iron skillet or corn stick pan as directed.

2. Combine the flour, cornmeal, sugar, powdered milk, baking powder, and salt in a bowl and mix thoroughly. Make a well in the center of the flour mixture.

3. Combine the eggs, water, oil, and vanilla in a separate bowl and mix thoroughly. Add the egg mixture to the flour mixture and stir by hand just until the batter is moistened.

4. Pour the batter into the pan and bake until a knife inserted in the center comes out clean and the top of the cornbread springs back lightly to the touch, 25 to 30 minutes.

5. Allow the cornbread to cool slightly before cutting. Serve warm or at room temperature.

JALAPEÑO JACK AND CHEDDAR CORNBREAD

MAKES 8 SERVINGS

THE ADDITION of the two cheeses makes this cornbread extremely moist. Look for a good aged cheddar, which will have a sharp bite and pronounced flavor.

1½ cups yellow cornmeal

1½ cups all-purpose flour

¼ cup sugar

1 tsp baking powder

½ tsp baking soda

¼ tsp salt

1 cup buttermilk

3 large eggs

¼ cup butter, melted

⅓ cup shredded sharp cheddar cheese

⅓ cup shredded jalapeño Jack cheese

1 tbsp minced jalapeños

1. Preheat the oven to 375°F. Lightly grease a 9 × 12-inch baking pan.

2. Sift the cornmeal, flour, sugar, baking powder, baking soda, and salt together into a mixing bowl. Make a well in the center of the cornmeal mixture.

3. In a separate bowl, blend the buttermilk, eggs, and butter. Add the buttermilk mixture to the cornmeal mixture and stir by hand just until the batter is evenly moistened. Add the cheeses and jalapeños and blend just until evenly distributed throughout the batter.

4. Spread the batter evenly in the prepared pan. Bake until a skewer inserted into center of the cornbread comes out clean and the top is golden brown, 30 minutes.

5. Cool the cornbread in the pan before cutting into individual servings. Serve warm or at room temperature.

Making Yeast Doughs

Use the guidelines given here to make any of the yeast dough recipes included in this chapter.

REHYDRATE THE YEAST

Dried yeast needs to soften in some liquid. To be sure that your yeast is still active, our bread recipes call for blending the yeast with some or all of the liquid before adding the remaining ingredients. This step is sometimes referred to as "proofing" the yeast. If a foam develops on the top of the liquid after the yeast has rested for a few minutes, then it is still alive.

ADD THE DRY INGREDIENTS AND MIX

If you are mixing a yeast dough in a stand mixer, use the dough hook to blend in most of the flour. Reserve about 1 cup to add at the end. If your mixer is struggling with a heavy dough, turn it out onto a lightly floured surface and knead the rest of the flour into the dough, adding it just a bit at a time and using the least amount possible to keep the dough from sticking to your hands or the work surface.

KNEADING

Kneading dough stretches the gluten in the flour, making it strong, flexible, and elastic. To knead by machine, simply increase the speed of the machine. (The mixing times in our recipes are for machine kneading.) To knead by hand, turn the dough out of the bowl onto a floured work surface. Press the heels of your hands into the dough and use them to push the dough away from you.

Give the ball of dough a quarter turn with your fingertips to fold the far edge back over onto the dough. As you continue to push and pull the dough, stretching all sides evenly, dust the dough, the work surface, and your hands with flour to keep the dough from sticking. Kneading a dough by hand can take anywhere from 10 to 15 minutes or more. The dough should feel smooth, satiny, and springy when it is fully kneaded.

THE FIRST RISE

Bakers call this stage of bread-making "bulk fermentation." Put the kneaded dough into a lightly greased bowl, cover it with a cloth or plastic wrap, and let it rise in a warm place, away from any drafts. As the dough rises, it will double in volume. Some doughs rise enough in 20 or 30 minutes, others require longer rising times. Consult the recipe for guidance.

FOLDING OVER THE DOUGH

You may have heard or read the instruction to "punch down" yeast doughs after the first rise. Actually, you should treat the dough with a gentle touch. Press down on the dough in three or four places to deflate the dough.

Some doughs call for a second rise; replace the cover and let it rise once more. The second rise usually takes less time than the first. After completing the appropriate number of rises, fold the dough over on itself and turn it out onto a lightly floured work surface. It is ready now to shape into rolls or loaves as directed in the recipe

OLIVE BREAD

OLIVE BREAD makes an excellent accompaniment to many of the soups in this book. Dry-cured olives (as opposed to brine-cured) are ideal for this bread, because they are packed in salt, which removes much of their moisture. Many supermarkets now feature olive bars from which you can select a combination of dry-cured olives, which you can identify by their slightly wrinkled skin. Some varieties may be coated in olive oil or packed with herbs. If you are making olive bread on a very hot day, use cool water (60 to 70°F) or the dough may rise too quickly. This bread is best eaten the day it is made.

MAKES ONE 1-POUND LOAF

1½ tsp active dry yeast

½ tsp sugar

3 tbsp plus ¼ cup tepid water (95 to 100°F)

½ lb bread flour (1⅔ cups)

¼ tsp salt

2 tbsp extra-virgin olive oil

½ cup pitted, dry-cured olives, chopped (about 2½ oz)

1. Line a baking sheet with parchment paper.
2. Mix the yeast and sugar with 3 tablespoons water. Let the yeast develop, 15 minutes, in a warm (not hot) place.
3. Combine the flour and salt in the bowl of an electric mixer or a large mixing bowl, if working by hand. Add the remaining ¼ cup water, yeast mixture, and 1½ tablespoons of the olive oil. Mix and knead the dough with a dough hook (about 8 to 10 minutes) or by hand (12 to 15 minutes) until elastic. Add the olives and mix well.
4. If using an electric mixer, transfer the dough to a large mixing bowl. Rub the remaining ½ tablespoon oil on the dough to prevent a skin from forming. Cover the dough and let it rise in a warm place, 30 minutes.
5. Punch down the dough, cover, and let rise until the dough has doubled in volume, about 30 minutes more.
6. Punch down the dough and shape into a loaf. Place on the baking sheet. Cover and let rise until doubled, about 1 hour. Preheat the oven to 475°F.
7. Bake until the loaf sounds hollow when tapped on the bottom, about 30 minutes. (If the loaf gets too dark on the bottom during baking but does not yet sound hollow, lower the oven temperature to 400°F and continue to bake.) Cool on a wire rack.

GRILL-BAKED NAAN

NAAN IS a perfect bread for the grill. The rising and shaping time for the dough is less than 2 hours, and it cooks in less than 10 minutes.

MAKES 8 SERVINGS

2½ tsp active dry yeast

¾ cup water

3 cups all-purpose flour

⅓ cup plain yogurt

¼ cup vegetable oil

1 egg, lightly beaten

2 tbsp granulated sugar

1½ tsp salt

¼ cup melted butter

2 tbsp poppy seeds

1. Combine the yeast and water in a bowl and stir to dissolve. Let the mixture sit until a thick foam begins to form.

2. Add the flour, yogurt, oil, egg, sugar, and salt, and stir by hand, or mix on low speed in an electric mixer using the dough hook attachment, until very smooth and elastic but still soft and slightly sticky.

3. Transfer the dough to a second bowl that has been lightly oiled. Cover the dough with a clean kitchen towel and let rest at room temperature until nearly doubled in size, about 1 hour.

4. Gently press down the dough to release any trapped gas. Divide the dough into 8 pieces. Shape the pieces into rounds and then flatten into disks about 4 inches in diameter. Set them on a lightly floured board and cover with a clean towel. Let the dough rest for 15 to 20 minutes.

5. Preheat a gas grill to medium-high; leave one burner off. If you are using a charcoal grill, build a fire and let it burn down until the coals are glowing red with a moderate coating of white ash. Spread the coals in an even bed on one side of the grill. Clean the cooking grate. Spray 2 baking sheets with cooking spray.

6. Gently stretch each piece of dough into a 7-inch disk. The center should be about ¼ inch thick and the outside edge should be closer to ½ inch thick. Pull 1 edge out to elongate it and make a teardrop shape. Place the naans on the baking sheets, brush the tops with the melted butter, and sprinkle the poppy seeds on top.

7. Transfer the dough from the baking sheet to the grill and cook over direct heat, poppy-seed-side down, until stiffened and golden brown, about 2 minutes. Turn the bread over and grill over indirect heat until baked through, about 8 minutes more. Lower the heat or move the breads to keep them from browning too much before they finish grilling. Repeat until all the naan is cooked. Serve immediately.

RAISIN CINNAMON SWIRL BREAD

THIS WONDERFUL bread develops a deep brown and very shiny crust as it bakes, giving it an almost lacquered look. If you have any leftover bread, it is great for toasting to enjoy the next morning. Or, you can use it in place of brioche or challah to make delicious French toast.

MAKES 2 LOAVES

1½ tsp active dry yeast

1½ cups whole milk, warmed to 110°F

4½ cups bread flour

¼ cup butter, softened

¼ cup sugar

1 large egg, lightly beaten

2 tsp salt

⅔ cup packed raisins

4 tsp ground cinnamon, divided use

Egg wash of 1 egg whisked with 2 tbsp cold milk or water

¼ cup brown sugar, packed

1. Place the yeast and warm milk in the bowl of a mixer and stir to completely dissolve. Let the yeast proof until foamy, about 5 minutes. Add the flour, butter, sugar, egg, and salt. Mix the ingredients together on low speed using the dough hook just until the dough begins to come together (it will look rather rough), about 2 minutes.

2. Increase the speed to medium-high and mix until the dough is smooth, an additional 4 minutes. Transfer the dough to a lightly floured work surface; add the raisins and 2 teaspoons of the cinnamon. Knead just long enough to swirl them through the dough, about five or six times.

3. Shape the dough into a ball and place it in a

lightly greased bowl. Cover with plastic wrap and let the dough rise in a warm place until doubled in size, about 2 hours.

4. Fold the dough gently over on itself in three or four places, turn the dough out onto a lightly floured work surface, and cut it into 2 equal pieces. Cover the dough and let it rest until relaxed, about 15 minutes.

5. Lightly grease two 9-inch loaf pans.

6. Working with one piece of dough at a time, roll the dough into a rectangle 8 × 12 inches and ½ inch thick. Dust the dough and rolling pin lightly with flour if needed to prevent the dough from sticking.

7. Brush lightly with egg wash. Mix the brown sugar with the remaining 2 teaspoons cinnamon and sprinkle half of this mixture evenly over the dough. Roll the dough into a cylinder, starting with the long side of the dough. Pinch the dough together to seal the seams and tuck the ends under. Place the loaf seam side down in a loaf pan. Brush lightly with egg wash. Repeat with the second piece of dough to make the second loaf.

8. Cover the loaves and let rise in a warm place until they nearly fill the pans and spring back slowly to the touch without collapsing, about 1½ to 2 hours.

9. Preheat the oven to 375°F.

10. Gently brush the bread again with egg wash. Bake the loaves until the crust is brown and the sides spring back when pressed, about 25 to 30 minutes. Remove the bread from the pans and cool completely on a rack before slicing and serving.

KNOT ROLLS
with Poppy Seeds

THESE BUTTERY rolls are best served warm. Enjoy them with big cups of frothy cappuccino or hot chocolate for breakfast. You can let the dough rise very slowly in a cool spot or overnight in the refrigerator. Let the dough return to room temperature before final shaping and baking.

MAKES 24 ROLLS

¾ cup milk

½ cup water, warmed to 110°F

2 tsp active dry yeast

2 tbsp sugar

3 tbsp butter, room temperature

2 large eggs, lightly beaten

2½ to 3 cups bread flour, divided use, plus extra as needed

1 tsp salt

Egg wash of 1 large egg whisked with 2 tbsp milk

2 tbsp poppy seeds

1. Scald the milk by bringing it just to a boil over medium heat, then allow it to cool to room temperature.

2. Combine the water, yeast, and sugar in a large bowl and stir well. Let sit for 2 to 3 minutes or until it is quite frothy.

3. Add the cooled milk, butter, eggs, 1½ cups of the flour, and the salt. Stir well for several minutes until the dough begins to form long elastic strands. Gradually add more flour until the dough is too heavy to stir.

4. Turn the dough onto a lightly floured work surface and knead for about 10 minutes, adding only enough flour to prevent the dough from sticking. The dough should be moist, smooth, and springy when it is properly kneaded.

5. Transfer the dough to a lightly oiled bowl, turn to coat, cover with a clean cloth, and place in a warm, draft-free spot to rise until doubled in volume, 1 to 2 hours.

6. Fold the dough over and let it rest for 10 minutes. While the dough is resting, spray two 9 × 11-inch baking pans with cooking spray.

7. Turn the dough out onto a lightly floured surface. With your fingertips, press the dough down and flatten to about ¼-inch thickness. Cut rectangles of dough about 1 inch long by 2 inches wide. Roll each piece into a long cylinder, about 6 inches long. Wrap the cylinder around the index and middle fingers of one hand to make a circle of dough. Bring one end up and through the circle to make the knot and pinch the two ends together. Place the rolls in the prepared pans, leaving at least 3 inches between the rolls. Cover the rolls and let them rise until nearly doubled in size.

8. Preheat the oven to 350°F.

9. Brush the rolls lightly with egg wash and sprinkle with poppy seeds. Bake until golden brown and baked through, 15 to 20 minutes. Let the rolls cool slightly before serving.

COTTAGE CHEESE DILL ROLLS

COTTAGE CHEESE gives these rolls a slightly tart flavor and a tender texture. Dill is a perfect counterpoint flavor. You can also add a bit of dill seed or substitute other fresh herbs for the dill—chives, scallions, or oregano would all be good choices.

MAKES 24 ROLLS

4½ tsp active dry yeast

⅓ cup water, warmed to 110°F

4¼ cups bread flour

1½ cups small-curd cottage cheese

¼ cup minced yellow onions

2 large eggs

1 tbsp butter, softened

3 tbsp chopped fresh dill

2 tsp prepared horseradish

2 tbsp sugar

1½ tsp salt

2¼ tsp baking soda

⅓ cup butter, melted, divided use

3 tbsp coarse salt for sprinkling

1. Place the yeast and warm water in the bowl of the mixer and stir to completely dissolve. Let the yeast proof until foamy, about 5 minutes. Add the flour, cottage cheese, onions, eggs, 1 tablespoon softened butter, dill, horseradish, sugar, salt, and baking soda to the yeast mixture. Mix the ingredients together on low speed using the dough hook just until the dough begins to come together (it will look rather rough), about 2 minutes. Increase the speed to medium-high and mix until the dough is smooth, an additional 5 minutes.

2. Turn the dough out onto a lightly floured surface, knead once or twice, and gather it into a smooth ball. Place in a lightly greased bowl, cover with plastic wrap, and let the dough rise in a warm place until doubled in size, about 2 hours.

3. Fold the dough gently over on itself in three or four places. Cover once more and let the dough rise a second time until doubled in size, about 1 hour.

4. Preheat the oven to 400°F. Line 2 baking sheets with parchment paper or grease lightly.

5. Fold the dough gently over on itself in three or four places, turn the dough out onto a lightly floured work surface and cut it into 16 equal pieces (about 2 ounces each). Cover the pieces and let them rest until relaxed, about 15 minutes. Round each piece into a smooth ball and place in even rows on the prepared baking sheets. Cover and let rise until the

dough springs back when lightly touched but does not collapse, 20 to 30 minutes.

6. Brush the top of each roll with a little of the melted butter. Bake until golden brown, about 20 to 30 minutes. As soon as the rolls are removed from the oven, brush lightly with the remaining melted butter and sprinkle lightly with salt.

7. Transfer to wire racks to cool completely before serving.

Making Sweet Rolls and Sticky Buns

After the dough is risen and folded over, roll it into an even layer with regular dimensions. Brush one of the long edges with a little egg wash. The egg wash will help hold the seams together and keep the buns from unrolling as they bake.

A light coating of melted butter holds the cinnamon sugar for cinnamon rolls in place and gives them a richer flavor. The cinnamon smear for the Sticky Buns recipe that follows has some butter in it. Be sure it is at room temperature as you spread it so you won't tear the dough.

Starting with the edge that was not brushed with egg wash, begin to roll the dough up into a cylinder. Try to keep the tightness of the roll even from one end to the other for a smooth, regularly shaped roll. Continue to roll up, and press gently to seal the seam. Slice the roll into pieces to make buns of the desired size and set them in a baking pan that has been coated with a pan smear.

STICKY BUNS WITH PECANS

IF YOU and your family love sticky buns, you can double or even triple the recipes for the cinnamon smear and pan smear and store them for later use. Keep them in airtight containers in the refrigerator for up to 2 weeks. Our recipe produces oversized buns with plenty of sticky caramel, but you can make smaller versions if you prefer. You will need to reduce the overall baking time somewhat.

MAKES 12 STICKY BUNS

2¼ tsp active dry yeast

¾ cup milk, warmed to 110°F

LEFT TO RIGHT Roll up the sticky bun dough with your fingertips, using light, even pressure to make sure that the log is of an even thickness. Place the sticky buns in the pan on top of the smear; they should be evenly spaced and just touch each other slightly. Notice the size of the sticky buns now that they have proofed properly; they should nearly fill the pan.

4 cups bread flour, as needed

¼ cup sugar

¼ cup butter, softened

2 large eggs, lightly beaten

1 tsp salt

Egg wash of 1 egg whisked with 2 tbsp cream or milk

2 cups Pan Smear (recipe follows)

1 cup Cinnamon Smear (recipe follows)

1. Place the yeast and warm milk in the bowl of a mixer and stir to completely dissolve. Let the yeast proof until foamy, about 5 minutes. Add 3½ cups flour (more if needed), the sugar, butter, eggs, and salt. Mix the ingredients together on low speed using the dough hook just until the dough begins to come together (it will look rather rough), about 2 minutes.

2. Increase the speed to medium-high and mix until the dough is smooth, an additional 5 minutes.

3. Shape the dough into a ball and place it in a lightly greased bowl. Cover with plastic wrap and let the dough rise in a warm place until doubled in size, about 2 hours. Fold the dough gently over on itself in three or four places. Cover again and let rise until doubled a second time, about 1 hour.

4. Preheat the oven to 400°F. Prepare two 9-inch square baking pans by pouring 1 cup of the pan smear into each of them.

5. Roll the dough into a rectangle that is 8 × 14 inches and about ¼ inch thick. Dust the dough and rolling pin lightly with flour if necessary to prevent the dough from sticking. Lightly brush a 1-inch wide strip of egg-wash along the long side of the dough closest to you. Spread the cinnamon smear evenly over the remaining dough. Roll the dough up to form a log, starting with the edge opposite the egg washed strip. Pinch the dough together to seal the seam. Slice into 12 equal pieces. Place 6 rolls in each of the prepared pans. Cover the rolls and let them rise until they have nearly doubled, about 30 minutes. Brush lightly with egg wash.

6. Bake the rolls until they are baked through and the crust is golden brown, about 25 to 30 minutes. As soon as you remove the pans from the oven, turn each pan over onto a plate. Lift the pan away and let the rolls cool before serving them. If the sticky buns cool down and are hard to get out of the pan, you can warm the bottom of the pan to loosen them.

Pan Smear

IF YOU prepare the pan smear in advance, be sure to recombine it by stirring it with a wooden spoon before adding it to your baking pan.

MAKES 2 CUPS

1 cup light brown sugar

¾ cup dark corn syrup

1 cup heavy cream

Combine all of the ingredients together in a saucepan and heat to thread stage (220°F), stirring frequently to prevent scorching. Cool to room temperature before using.

Cinnamon Smear

MAKES 1 CUP

½ cup bread flour

⅓ cup sugar

2 tsp ground cinnamon

3 tbsp butter

3 large egg whites

½ cup pecans, toasted and chopped

1. Mix together the flour, sugar, and cinnamon in the bowl of a mixer. Add the butter to the flour mixture. Using the paddle attachment, mix on medium speed for 1 minute, or until it looks like coarse meal and there are no visible chunks of butter.

2. With the mixer on medium speed, add the egg whites one at a time. Continue to mix until fully combined, scraping down the bowl as necessary. Stir in the nuts and mix just until combined.

SOUR CREAM STREUSEL COFFEE CAKE

A s an alternative to the Bundt pan, you could bake this in a loaf pan, or even bake the batter and streusel in muffin tins.

MAKES 1 BUNDT CAKE

STREUSEL MIXTURE

¼ cup plus 2 tbsp packed light brown sugar

⅓ cup finely chopped toasted walnuts

¼ cup chocolate chips

½ tsp ground cinnamon

½ tsp cocoa powder

SOUR CREAM BATTER

2¼ cups all-purpose or cake flour

1 tsp baking powder

½ tsp baking soda

½ tsp salt

3 large eggs

¾ cup sour cream

1 tsp vanilla extract

¾ cup unsalted butter, room temperature

¾ cup sugar

1. Preheat the oven to 350°F. Prepare a Bundt pan by spraying it lightly with cooking spray or rubbing with softened butter.

2. To prepare the streusel, toss together the brown sugar, walnuts, chocolate chips, cinnamon, and cocoa until evenly blended. Set aside.

3. Sift the flour, baking powder, baking soda, and salt together. Set aside.

4. In a separate bowl, blend the eggs, sour cream, and vanilla. Set aside.

5. Cream the butter and sugar together until very smooth and light by hand with a wooden spoon or with an electric mixer using the paddle attachment, about 3 minutes.

6. Add the egg mixture in three additions, alternating with the flour mixture. Mix the batter until it is evenly blended after each addition, scraping down the bowl as needed. After the final addition, continue to mix the batter until smooth, 2 to 3 minutes.

7. Spoon half of the batter into the Bundt pan. Scatter the streusel mixture evenly over the batter and swirl with a skewer to blend the streusel in slightly. Add the remaining batter over the streusel.

8. Gently tap the filled pan to release any air bubbles. Bake until a skewer inserted into center of the cake comes out clean and the top is golden brown, 45 to 50 minutes.

9. Cool the cake in the pan for about 10 minutes before removing from the pan. Transfer to a cooling rack to finish cooling before slicing and serving or wrapping to store. This cake can be held at room temperature for up to 3 days or frozen for up to 2 months.

CHEDDAR AND THYME MUFFINS

ADD THESE muffins to your repertoire as a savory alternative for breakfast or brunch.

MAKES 12 MUFFINS

2 cups all-purpose flour

2 tbsp dry mustard

1 tbsp baking powder

1 tsp salt

¼ tsp freshly ground black pepper

Pinch cayenne pepper

1 cup grated sharp cheddar cheese

1 tbsp chopped thyme

1½ cups milk

1 large egg

¼ cup butter, melted

¼ tsp hot sauce such as Tabasco, or to taste

1. Preheat the oven to 350°F. Prepare the muffin tins by spraying them lightly with cooking spray or lining them with muffin liners.

2. Sift the flour, mustard, baking powder, salt, and peppers together into a mixing bowl. Add the grated cheddar and thyme; toss together until evenly distributed. Make a well in the center of the flour mixture.

3. In a separate bowl, blend the milk, egg, butter, and hot sauce. Add the milk mixture to the flour mixture and stir by hand just until the batter is evenly moistened.

4. Fill the prepared muffin tins about three-quarters full. Gently tap the filled tins to release any air bubbles. Bake until a skewer inserted into the center of a muffin comes out clean, 20 to 25 minutes.

5. Cool the muffins in the pan for about 10 minutes before removing them from the pan. The muffins can be served warm, or transfer them to a cooling rack to finish cooling before storing in an airtight container. Muffins can be frozen for up to 6 weeks.

MORNING GLORY MUFFINS

THESE SWEET, rich muffins are a perfect choice for breakfast on the road or at your desk.

MAKES 12 MUFFINS

⅔ cup pastry flour

⅔ cup all-purpose flour

⅔ cup sugar

¾ tsp baking soda

½ tsp cinnamon

½ tsp salt

⅔ cup grated carrots

½ cup shredded coconut

½ cup dark raisins

½ cup peeled and shredded apple

⅓ cup crushed and drained pineapple

⅓ cup chopped toasted walnuts

2 large eggs

½ cup canola oil

½ tsp vanilla

¼ cup rolled oats for topping

1. Preheat oven to 375°F. Prepare the muffin tins by spraying them lightly with cooking spray or lining with muffin liners.

2. Sift the flours, sugar, baking soda, cinnamon, and salt together into a mixing bowl. Add the carrots, coconut, raisins, apple, pineapple, and walnuts, tossing together until evenly distributed. Make a well in the center of the flour mixture.

3. In a separate bowl, blend the eggs, oil, and vanilla. Add to the flour mixture and stir by hand just until the batter is evenly moistened.

4. Fill the prepared muffin tins about three-quarters full. Gently tap the filled tins to release any air bubbles. Scatter a little of the rolled oats over each muffin. Bake until a skewer inserted into the center of a muffin comes out clean, 20 to 25 minutes.

5. Cool the muffins in the pan for about 10 minutes before removing them from the pan. The muffins can be served warm, or transfer them to a cooling rack to finish cooling before storing in an airtight container. Muffins can be frozen for up to 6 weeks.

RASPBERRY MUFFINS
with Pecan Streusel

R ASPBERRIES MAKE a great change from the ever popular blueberry muffin, and works well with either fresh or frozen berries.

MAKES 12 MUFFINS

1½ cups all-purpose flour

½ cup sugar

2 tsp baking powder

½ tsp salt

½ cup milk

½ cup butter, melted and cooled

1 large egg, beaten

1 cup raspberries, fresh or frozen, divided use

¾ cup Pecan Streusel (recipe follows)

1. Preheat the oven to 375°F. Prepare the muffin tins by spraying them lightly with cooking spray or lining with muffin liners.

2. Sift the flour, sugar, baking powder, and salt together into a mixing bowl. Make a well in the center of the flour mixture. In a separate bowl, blend the milk, butter, and egg. Add the milk mixture to the flour mixture and stir by hand just until the batter is evenly moistened. Fold in ½ cup of the raspberries.

LEFT TO RIGHT Make a well in the center of the dry ingredients and add the wet ingredients; fold the wet ingredients into the dry ingredients and mix until thoroughly combined. Gently fold the raspberries into the batter by lifting and folding the batter over the raspberries; if you simply stir the raspberries into the thick batter, the raspberries will break and color the batter. Use scoops or measuring cups to divide the batter evenly among the prepared muffin cups

3. Fill the prepared muffin tins about three-quarters full. Gently tap the filled tins to release any air bubbles. Divide the remaining raspberries among the muffins and sprinkle the tops with the streusel. Bake until a skewer inserted into the center of a muffin comes out clean, 25 to 30 minutes.

4. Cool the muffins in the pan for about 10 minutes before removing them from the pan. The muffins can be served warm, or transfer them to a cooling rack to finish cooling before storing in an airtight container. Muffins can be frozen for up to 6 weeks.

Pecan Streusel

SUBSTITUTE OTHER nuts for the pecans, such as walnuts or hazelnuts. Try this streusel instead of the walnut streusel on the Sour Cream Streusel Coffee Cake (page 253).

MAKES 2 CUPS

⅔ cup chopped toasted pecans

⅔ cup packed brown sugar

⅔ cup all-purpose flour

5 tbsp butter, melted

Combine the pecans, brown sugar, and flour in a small bowl. Stir in the melted butter with a table fork until the mixture resembles moist crumbs. Use as directed in the recipe.

Toasting and Chopping Nuts

Nuts will hold better if they are purchased raw. Once they are roasted, their oils are drawn to the surface, making it easier for them to turn rancid. Toasting nuts right before you want to use them heightens their flavor and improves their texture. You can toast small amounts of nuts in a dry skillet as follows:

Heat a small dry skillet over high heat (cast iron is ideal). Add the nuts and swirl the pan over the heat to keep them from scorching. Continue until the nuts begin to give off a rich, toasted aroma and are just starting to brown, usually about 2 minutes. Immediately transfer them to a bowl to keep them from burning.

Once the nuts are cool, chop them by hand using a chef's knife, or place them in a mini to food processor and pulse it on and off just until the nuts are coarsely chopped.

BLITZ PUFF PASTRY

BLITZ PUFF pastry lives up to its name. It is as flaky and buttery as the classic puff pastry, but you can put it together quickly. The rolling and folding process may appear lengthy, but most of that time is taken up by letting the dough chill enough to handle easily. Double or even triple the recipe if you like. For larger batches, you can use a stand mixer with a dough hook to blend the dough. Divide the dough into smaller pieces before wrapping and freezing to have your own pastry on hand to make sweet and savory pastries.

MAKES 2½ POUNDS OF DOUGH

2 cups butter

3½ cups all-purpose flour

1¾ tsp salt

1 cup cold water

1. Cut the butter into ¼-inch cubes. Refrigerate until the cubes are chilled and firm.

2. Combine the flour and salt in a large mixing bowl. Add the butter and toss with your fingertips until the butter is coated with flour. Add all but about 2 tablespoons of the cold water. Mix with a pastry blender or a table fork until an evenly moist but still

rough dough forms. Add additional water if necessary as you mix the dough if it is not moist enough to hold together when pressed into a ball.

3. Cover the dough tightly with plastic wrap. Cool in the refrigerator until the butter is firm but not brittle, about 20 minutes.

4. Turn the dough out onto a lightly floured work surface. Roll it into a rectangle approximately 12 × 30 inches; the dough should be about ½ inch thick.

5. Fold the dough in thirds like a letter (this is the first of four 3-folds). Turn the dough 90 degrees. Roll the dough out again to a rectangle as described above and fold once more (this is the second of four 3-folds). Wrap the dough tightly in plastic wrap and chill for 30 minutes in the refrigerator. Remove the dough from the refrigerator, and working quickly, continue rolling and folding the dough for the third

and fourth 3-folds as described above, chilling the dough in between each of these folds for 30 minutes at a time.

APPLE-FILLED TURNOVERS

THIS RECIPE provides the basic instructions for filling and folding turnovers. Once assembled, you can keep the pastries in the freezer for up to 3 months. These turnovers are full-sized pastries, but you may want to make miniature versions instead. Resist the temptation to overfill the pastry though, or the filling can ooze out as the pastries bake. To dress these turnovers up, make a thin icing of confectioners' sugar and milk (see the glaze used for the Dried Cherry Scones, page 242).

Shaping Breakfast Pastries

We've replaced Danish dough in our breakfast pastries with our Blitz Puff Pastry. You can substitute frozen prepared puff pastry sheets if you prefer.

KEEP BLITZ OR PREPARED PUFF PASTRY DOUGH VERY COOL

Keeping the pastry dough chilled preserves the layers of fat. These layers are responsible for the flaky texture and dramatic rise of breakfast pastries like turnovers, cheese pockets, bear claws, and elephant ears.

USE THE LEAST POSSIBLE AMOUNT OF FLOUR
WHEN ROLLING THE DOUGH

Dust the work surface and the rolling pin lightly with flour as you work. Use enough pressure to roll the dough to the appro-

priate thickness, but don't press down too hard in any one place. Stop rolling just short of the edges of the dough. If the pin runs over the edge of the dough, the layers there will be pressed together and your pastries may not have the best possible texture or height. If the dough starts to soften too much as you work, put it back in the refrigerator for 10 or 12 minutes to firm up before you go on to cut out the shapes for your pastries. (The dough should feel cool to the touch.)

CUT SHAPES WITH A SHARP KNIFE

If the dough is cool, it won't stretch out as you cut it into squares or rectangles. Use a very sharp knife to cut the dough so that the dough is not torn or pulled out of shape as you work

1½ lb Blitz Puff Pastry (page 256)

Egg wash of 1 egg whisked with 2 tbsp cream or milk

1½ cups Apple Filling (recipe follows)

1 cup Apricot Glaze, warm (recipe follows)

1. Line a baking sheet with parchment paper.

2. Roll the puff dough into a rectangle 12 × 16 inches. Dust the dough and rolling pin lightly with flour if necessary to prevent the dough from sticking. Cut the dough into twelve 4-inch squares. Place the squares on the prepared baking sheet and let them chill in the refrigerator until firm, about 10 minutes.

3. To assemble the turnovers, take the puff pastry from the refrigerator. Brush the squares lightly with egg wash. Place 2 tablespoons of the filling in the center of each square. Fold one corner of the dough over the filling and line it up with the opposite corner of the dough to make a triangle. Press the edges firmly together to seal in the filling. Chill the turnovers for 10 minutes before baking.

4. Preheat the oven to 425°F.

5. Brush the turnovers lightly with egg wash. Cut a small opening in the center of each turnover with a sharp knife to allow steam to vent.

5. Bake the turnovers until golden brown, about 20 minutes. Transfer to cooling racks and brush with apricot glaze while they are still hot. Cool the turnovers completely before serving.

Apple Filling

YOU CAN use this filling for turnovers, or as a filling for Crêpes (page 228), or try substituting it for other fruit fillings called for in your favorite breakfast pastry recipe.

¼ cup applejack or apple-flavored brandy

¼ cup apple juice

3 tbsp canola oil, divided use

4 cups Granny Smith apples, peeled, cored, and sliced

6 tbsp granulated sugar

3 tbsp currants

¾ tsp orange zest

½ tsp vanilla extract

¼ tsp ground cinnamon

⅛ tsp ground nutmeg

1. Combine the applejack or brandy and the apple juice in a small bowl and set aside.

2. Heat a sauté pan over medium-high heat and add 1 tablespoon of the oil. Toss the sliced apples with the sugar.

3. Add about one-third of the sugared apples (they should be in a single layer) and sauté the apples until golden on both sides, about 4 minutes. Transfer the apples to a bowl. Add one-third of the apple juice mixture to the pan, stirring to release the sugar from the pan, and simmer until slightly reduced and thickened, 30 seconds. Pour the apple juice mixture over the sautéed apples.

4. Sauté the remaining apples in two more batches as directed above. When you add the final third of the applejack mixture to the pan, stir in the currants, orange zest, vanilla, cinnamon, and nutmeg. Add the mixture to the bowl and stir the filling gently until the currants are evenly distributed throughout.

5. Place the filling in a bowl set in an ice bath and cool, stirring from time to time. Once the filling has cooled, it is ready to use or store in a covered container in the refrigerator for up to 5 days. Warm the filling over low heat or in the microwave if necessary.

Apricot Glaze

THIS GLAZE adds sheen and flavor to a number of different baked goods. It holds well, so you can make a double batch and keep it on hand. Try apple jelly instead of apricot jam for a glaze with a subtle flavor. If you use apple jelly, there is no need to strain the glaze. Brush a thin, even coating of warm glaze on cooled baked goods with a pastry brush, wiping away any pools that develop on the surface.

MAKES 2 CUPS

¾ cup apricot jam

¾ cup water

¾ cup corn syrup

⅓ cup brandy

1. Combine the jam, water, corn syrup, and brandy in a saucepan; bring to a boil over high heat, stirring until the jam is completely melted. Strain the glaze through a wire-mesh sieve into a bowl.

2. The glaze is ready to use once it has cooled to room temperature or store it in a covered container in the refrigerator for up to 3 weeks. Warm the glaze over low heat or in the microwave until it is thin enough to brush easily.

CHEESE POCKETS

THESE POCKETS are simple to shape, once you've rolled out the blitz puff pastry.

MAKES 12 PASTRIES

1½ lb Blitz Puff Pastry (page 256)

1½ cups Cheese Filling (page 260)

¼ cup sliced almonds, as needed

¾ cup Apricot Glaze (above), warmed

1. Line a baking sheet with parchment paper.

2. Roll the puff dough into a rectangle 12 × 16 inches. Dust the dough and rolling pin lightly with flour if necessary to prevent the dough from sticking. Cut the dough into twelve, 4-inch squares. Place the squares on a baking sheet and let them chill in the refrigerator until firm, about 10 minutes.

3. Spoon or pipe 2 tablespoons of the cheese filling into the center of each pastry square. Fold each corner into the center, overlapping them. Press the overlapped corners gently to seal them, and pierce each one with some almond slices to keep the pocket closed as it bakes. Transfer to the prepared baking sheet and chill for several minutes while you preheat the oven.

4. Preheat the oven to 425°F.

5. Bake the pockets until golden brown, about 20 minutes. Transfer to cooling racks and brush with apricot glaze while they are still hot. Cool completely before serving.

CHERRY CHEESE BASKETS

BAKE THESE flaky pastries with the cheese filling, then add the cherry filling after they bake for a wonderful, fresh look and flavor.

MAKES 12 BASKETS

1½ lb Blitz Puff Pastry (page 256)

¾ cup Cheese Filling (recipe follows)

¾ cup Apricot Glaze (left), warmed

¾ cup Cherry Filling (recipe follows), warmed

1. Line a baking sheet with parchment paper.

2. Roll the puff dough into a rectangle 12 × 16 inches. Dust the dough and rolling pin lightly with flour if necessary to prevent the dough from stick-

ing. Cut the dough into twelve 4-inch squares. Place the squares on a baking sheet and let them chill in the refrigerator until firm, about 10 minutes.

3. To make a basket, fold squares of dough in half to make a triangle. Position the triangle so the closed point of the triangle is away from you. Use a sharp knife to make a cut parallel to the two shorter sides of the triangle. These cuts should come to within ¼ inch of the point but should not cut entirely through the point. These two cuts make the rim for the basket.

4. Open out the triangle and brush very lightly with egg wash. Fold one basket rim over to line up with the opposite side. Repeat with the second rim. Add 1 tablespoon of the cheese filling to each basket. Transfer to the baking sheet and chill for several minutes while you preheat the oven.

5. Preheat the oven to 425°F.

6. Bake the baskets until golden brown, about 20 minutes. Transfer to cooling racks and brush with apricot glaze while they are still hot. Spoon 1 tablespoon of the cherry filling into each basket. Cool completely before serving.

Cheese Filling

THE CORNSTARCH in this filling helps it hold together as it bakes. You can store the filling in a zip-close plastic bag. When you are ready to fill your pastries, simply cut away one corner and use the bag as a disposable pastry bag.

MAKES 2 CUPS

12 oz cream cheese

6 tbsp granulated sugar

⅓ cup sifted cornstarch

¾ tsp lemon zest

¾ tsp orange zest

1 tsp vanilla extract

2 eggs

1. Cream the cheese, sugar, cornstarch, lemon zest, orange zest, and vanilla extract together until very smooth and light by hand with a wooden spoon or with an electric mixer using the paddle attachment. Add the eggs one at a time, mixing until smooth and scraping down the bowl between each addition. Scrape down the bowl to blend evenly.

2. The filling is ready to use now or store in a covered container in the refrigerator for up to 2 days.

Cherry Filling

YOU CAN find bottled cherry juice in the produce section and in some specialty shops. If you are using frozen cherries, let them thaw in a colander set in a bowl. Use the juices the cherries release to replace some of the cherry juice.

MAKES 2 CUPS

2 tbsp cornstarch

½ cup cherry juice or water, divided use

½ cup sugar, plus as needed

¾ tsp lemon juice

¼ tsp ground cinnamon

⅛ tsp ground nutmeg

⅛ tsp salt

3 cups pitted sour cherries, fresh, frozen, or jarred

1 tbsp butter

1. Combine the cornstarch with ¼ cup of the cherry juice or water in a small bowl and stir until the cornstarch is completely dissolved.

2. Combine the remaining cherry juice or water,

the sugar, the lemon juice, cinnamon, nutmeg, and salt in a saucepan; bring to a boil over high heat, stirring until the sugar is dissolved. Add the dissolved cornstarch and return the mixture to a boil, stirring constantly, until thickened and smooth, about 3 minutes.

3. Add the cherries to the mixture and simmer until the cherries are very tender and the liquid is very flavorful, 5 to 6 minutes. Taste the filling as it simmers and add more sugar, if desired.

4. Remove the filling from the heat and stir in the butter until it melts and is evenly blended. Transfer to a bowl set in an ice bath and cool, stirring from time to time. Once the filling has reached room temperature, it is ready to use or store in a covered container in the refrigerator for up to 10 days.

Working with Pie Dough

ROLLING OUT DOUGH

Working with one piece of the dough at a time, unwrap the dough and place it on a lightly floured work surface and scatter a little flour over the top. Use the least possible amount of flour to prevent the dough from sticking as you work.

Lightly flour your rolling pin. Use a back-and-forth motion to roll the dough and give the dough a quarter turn periodically to maintain a round shape.

Lift the dough periodically and dust the work surface if necessary to keep the dough from sticking. The dough should be between ⅛ and 1⁄16 inch thick, depending upon your recipe.

LINING THE PAN WITH DOUGH

Pie dough can be used to line pans of various sizes. The pie dough should remain cool to the touch while you are working with it. If it begins to get too warm, refrigerate it briefly until it firms up again.

For large crusts, roll the pastry loosely around the rolling pin to lift it to the pan. Let the pastry roll off the pin and into the pan. Smaller pieces can be carefully lifted and set into the tartlet pan. Ease the dough into the pan, making sure that the sides and the rim are evenly covered. Press the dough gently against the sides and bottom.

Trim the overhanging dough to ¼ to ½ inch for pie pans, depending upon the size of the pan. In general, the larger your pan, the more overhang you should have. Tuck the dough overhang under itself and flute the edges for a raised edge, such as that for a quiche. For tartlet pans (see the recipe for Bananas Foster Tartlets, page 266), trim the dough even with the edge of the pan. Return the pastry to the refrigerator to firm up before baking blind, about 15 minutes.

STORING DOUGH TO USE LATER

To store any leftover dough, pat the dough into flat disks or blocks and put them in a zip-close bag, pressing out as much air as possible before sealing the bag. It will hold 3–4 days in the refrigerator or up to 2 months in the freezer.

Another option for freezing the dough is to roll it out and fit it into a disposable aluminum pie pan. Crimp the edges as you would normally, then freeze the dough directly in the pie pan, well wrapped. To keep the crust well covered, line it with a piece of plastic wrap or waxed paper. Set a second pie plate inside the shell, and then wrap well with plastic wrap, using freezer tape or a zip-close bag to keep the wrap from coming loose.

PIE CRUST

If the filling for your pie crust is very moist or wet, you need the relatively sturdy crust made by the technique described in this recipe. For a flakier crust that you can use with fruit filling, cut the butter in only until the pieces are about the size of a lentil.

MAKES ENOUGH FOR 1 DOUBLE-CRUST
OR 2 SINGLE-CRUST PIES (9-INCH PANS)

2¾ cups all-purpose flour, plus extra as needed

1 tsp salt

1 cup diced cold butter (or ½ cup diced cold butter and ½ cup diced cold shortening)

½ cup ice cold water

1. Combine the flour and salt in a bowl and stir with a fork to blend the salt evenly with the flour.

2. Cut the butter into the flour using a food processor, pastry cutter, or 2 knives until the mixture looks like coarse meal. Drizzle a few tablespoons of the cold water over the flour mixture and quickly rub the water into the flour.

3. Continue to add the water a few tablespoons at a time until the dough is evenly moist although not wet and shaggy or rough in appearance. It should just hold together when you press a handful of it into a ball.

4. Turn the dough out onto a lightly floured work surface. Gather and press the dough into a ball. Divide the dough into 2 equal pieces for 1 double-crust or 2 single-crust pies, pat them into even disks, wrap well, and let chill in the refrigerator for 20 minutes before rolling and baking.

5. To prebake a pie crust, preheat the oven to 400°F. Prick the dough evenly over the bottom and sides with the tines of a table fork. Line the dough with a piece of parchment or waxed paper and fill about half-full with pie weights, dried beans, or rice. Bake until the crust is set and dry, 12 to 15 minutes.

6. Remove the pan from the oven and remove the paper and pie weights. Return the crust to the oven and bake until the crust is completely dry and a light golden brown, another 5 to 6 minutes. Let cool to room temperature before adding a filling.

TART DOUGH

For a delicious variation on the regular tart dough, add 1 tablespoon of finely grated lemon zest when creaming the butter.

MAKES 1½ POUNDS

1 cup butter, softened

½ cup sugar

1 tsp vanilla extract

1 egg

3 cups cake flour, sifted

1. Cream together the butter, sugar, and vanilla extract in an electric mixer on medium speed using a paddle attachment, scraping down the bowl periodically, until smooth and light in color.

2. Add the egg and blend until smooth. Add the flour all at once and mix on low speed until just blended.

3. Turn the dough out onto a lightly floured work surface. Wrap tightly and refrigerate for at least 30 minutes before rolling.

CLAFOUTI

Clafouti originated in the Limousin region in central France, a simple country dessert of fresh fruit baked in a custard-like batter. Though traditionally made with cherries, other fruits, such as apples or pears, may be easily substituted. If you replace the cherries with apples or pears, replace the kirsch with Calvados or pear brandy, respectively.

1 pint milk

1 vanilla bean, split

¼ tsp salt

¾ cup sugar

4 eggs

½ cup all-purpose flour

3 cups cherries, tart, pitted

1. Preheat the oven to 350°F.

2. Combine the milk, vanilla bean, salt, and half of the sugar in a saucepan. Bring to a boil.

3. Combine the eggs, flour, and the remaining half of the sugar in a stainless steel bowl. Fully whisk the mixture together. Add half of the hot milk to the egg mixture and whisk thoroughly to temper.

4. Add the egg mixture to the remaining hot milk and mix well.

5. Strain the mixture and skim any impurities off of the top.

6. Divide the cherries equally between 8 buttered and sugared shallow ramekins.

7. Pour the custard evenly over the cherries and bake at 350°F for approximately 16 to 18 minutes or until custard is firm.

FRESH FRUIT GALETTE

ELEGANTLY RUSTIC, these tantalizing fruit tarts are simple to prepare. Use fresh seasonal fruits at their peak of sweetness.

MAKES 8 SERVINGS

1 quart fruit, firm-fleshed (pears, apples, peaches, apricots, cherries, etc.)

1 package puff pastry dough, thawed

6 tbsp apricot jam, strained, warm

1 egg

1 tsp water

½ cup coarse sugar

1. Preheat the oven to 350°F.

2. Wash, peel, trim, core, and slice or otherwise prepare the fruit as needed.

3. Let the dough relax just a few minutes, but work quickly enough that it does not get too soft and pliable.

4. Roll the dough slightly until it is 12-inches square and of a uniform thickness.

5. Cut four 6-inch round circles out of each sheet of dough.

6. Lay the pastry circles onto baking sheets that have been lined with parchment.

7. Refrigerate the dough for 5 to 10 minutes if it is too soft.

8. Spread ½ teaspoon of the apricot jam in the center of the circle, leaving a ¼-inch border around the edge of the dough. Place ½ cup of prepared fruit on top of the jam, leaving a 1-inch border around the edge of the dough.

9. Fold a ½-inch section of dough up onto the fruit, pressing gently so that it adheres slightly. Crimp another ½-inch section of dough over the fruit and lightly press the dough that overlaps together. Crimp the remaining dough around the fruit. The fruit should be barely encased inside the dough. Repeat with the remaining galettes.

10. Mix the egg with the water to make an egg wash.

11. Lightly brush the dough and the crimped seams with the egg wash. Sprinkle coarse sugar on the egg wash. Bake at 350°F for about 30 minutes or until golden brown and baked through.

CHOCOLATE MOUSSE

CHOOSE A good bittersweet chocolate for this luscious dessert.

MAKES 6 SERVINGS

2 egg whites

6 tbsp sugar

1 cup heavy cream, plus extra for garnish

4 egg yolks

3 tbsp brandy

1 cup bittersweet chocolate chips, melted

1 recipe Espresso-Hazelnut Brittle (recipe follows)

1. Beat the egg whites and 2 tablespoons sugar in the bowl of an electric mixer until the meringue forms medium peaks, about 8 to 10 minutes. Reserve under refrigeration until needed.

2. Whip the heavy cream with 2 tablespoons sugar until the mixture forms soft peaks. Reserve under refrigeration until needed.

3. Combine the egg yolks with the brandy and the remaining sugar. Whisk over a hot water bath until mixture reaches 110°F, about 6 to 8 minutes. Add the melted chocolate and blend together over the hot water bath. Whip the mixture to room temperature in the bowl of an electric mixer, about 5 minutes.

4. Fold the meringue into the chocolate mixture in two additions. Fold in the whipped cream. Spoon into serving dishes and refrigerate until needed. Garnish with whipped cream and pieces of espresso-hazelnut brittle.

NOTE: This recipe calls for raw egg whites; if you are concerned about possible health risks associated with raw eggs, substitute pasteurized egg whites.

Espresso-Hazelnut Brittle

MAKES 1 HALF-SHEET TRAY

1 cup hazelnuts, coarsely chopped

1 cup plus 2 tbsp sugar

½ tsp brandy

¼ cup heavy cream

3 tbsp espresso roast coffee beans, coarsely ground

2½ fluid oz water

2 tbsp light corn syrup

1. Coat the hazelnuts in ½ tablespoon of the sugar and the brandy. Toast in a 350°F oven until golden brown, about 7 to 8 minutes. Remove from the oven and reserve.

2. Bring the cream and the espresso to a simmer. Remove from the heat, cover and allow to steep for 10 minutes. Strain the mixture and keep warm.

3. Prepare an ice bath. Combine the remaining sugar, water and corn syrup, and bring to a boil, stirring constantly. Skim off any scum that floats to the top. Continue to boil the sugar syrup, brushing the sides of the pan occasionally with water, until it turns a light golden brown. Shock the caramel in the ice bath for about 10 seconds.

5. Carefully stir in the cream and the chopped hazelnuts. Pour the brittle onto a lightly greased piece of parchment paper or a silicone baking mat and spread as thin as possible.

6. Allow the brittle to cool to room temperature. Break into medium-sized pieces for use as garnish or into smaller pieces to use as a topping.

FRIED EGGS (PAGE 213) AND HAM STEAK
WITH REDEYE GRAVY (PAGE 233)

HUEVOS RANCHEROS WITH
SALSA FRESCA (PAGE 213)

TOAD IN A HOLE WITH RED PEPPER KETCHUP
(PAGE 214)

FRITTATA (PAGE 217)

EGGS BENEDICT
(PAGE 217)

BANANA PANCAKES WITH
BLUEBERRY MAPLE SYRUP (PAGE 224)

WAFFLES WITH HOT RASPBERRY SYRUP
(PAGE 230)

**BUCKWHEAT FLAPJACKS WITH
HIBISCUS HONEY (PAGE 225)**

CRÊPES WITH SPICY MUSHROOM FILLING
AND CHILE CREAM SAUCE (PAGE 229)

DUTCH BABY WITH SPICED FRUIT
(PAGE 228)

BUTTERMILK BISCUITS WITH
SAUSAGE GRAVY (PAGE 233)

LEMON CURD (PAGE 232)

CREAM SCONES
(PAGE 240)

DRIED CHERRY
SCONES (PAGE 242)

HAM AND CHEDDAR
SCONES (PAGE 241)

SODA BREAD (PAGE 243)

BANANA NUT LOAF
(PAGE 244)

KNOT ROLLS WITH POPPY SEEDS (PAGE 249)
AND COTTAGE CHEESE DILL ROLLS (PAGE 250)

STICKY BUNS WITH PECANS (PAGE 251)

FRESH FRUIT GALETTE
(PAGE 263)

BANANAS FOSTER TARTLETS (PAGE 266)

GRILLED PEPPERED PINEAPPLE
WITH TEQUILA-ORANGE SAUCE AND
CANDIED KUMQUATS (PAGE 273)

GRILLED BANANA SPLIT WITH
HOMEMADE ICE CREAM (PAGE 276)

**GRILLED PEACHES WITH VANILLA ICE CREAM
AND RASPBERRY COULIS (PAGE 280)**

TIRAMISU (PAGE 273)

CHOCOLATE CHUNK COOKIES (PAGE 281)
AND SAND COOKIES (PAGE 282)

FRESH FRUIT SABAYON

THIS DELICATE, frothy dessert sauce of egg yolks, whisked and cooked with sugar and a bit of wine or liqueur, should be made just before serving, as it does not hold well.

MAKES 8 SERVINGS

10 egg yolks

1 cup sugar

½ cup dessert wine or liqueur

3 lb fruit, ripe, trimmed, and cleaned, (seasonal stone fruit or berries)

1. Combine the egg yolks, sugar and wine in a mixing bowl. Whisk over a pot of barely simmering water until the eggs become frothy and begin to thicken. Continue to whisk vigorously until the eggs reach the "ribbon stage" or approximately 165°F.

2. Portion about 1 cup of fruit per serving into dessert bowls or parfait glasses. Top with about ¼ cup of the sabayon. Serve immediately.

RICE PUDDING

MAKES 8 SERVINGS

1 quart milk

½ cup long-grain white rice, rinsed

½ cup sugar

1 tsp ground cinnamon

2 tsp cornstarch

2 eggs

1. Combine 3½ cups of the milk along with the rice, sugar, and cinnamon in a medium saucepan. Cover and simmer until the rice is tender, about 25 minutes.

2. Combine the remaining milk with the cornstarch and eggs. Remove the simmering milk mixture from the heat and add approximately 2 cups of the hot liquid to the cornstarch mixture, whisking constantly. Add the warmed cornstarch mixture to the remaining milk mixture in the pan. Return the pan to the heat and while stirring constantly, bring the pudding to a boil and cook for 1 minute.

3. Portion the pudding into dessert dishes. The pudding can be served warm at this point, or cooled completely and refrigerated, covered with plastic wrap to keep a skin from forming.

BROWNIES

MAKES 16 BARS

1⅔ cup butter

2 cups chopped unsweetened chocolate

6 large eggs

3⅔ cups granulated sugar

2 tsp vanilla extract

¼ tsp salt

⅓ cup cake flour, sifted

2 cups coarse-chopped toasted pecans

1. Preheat oven to 350°F. Line a baking pan (13 × 9 × 2 inches) with parchment paper, making sure the paper comes up the sides of the pan.

2. Melt the butter and chocolate in a metal bowl over a pan of simmering water, blending gently (or use a double boiler). Remove from heat.

3. Whip the eggs, sugar, vanilla, and salt on high speed until thick and light in color, about 8 minutes. Blend ⅓ of the egg mixture into the melted chocolate. Return it to the remaining egg mixture and blend on medium seed, scraping the bowl as needed.

4. Mix in the flour and nuts on low speed until just blended. The batter will be very wet. Pour the batter into the prepared pan and spread out evenly.

5. Bake the brownies until a crust forms but they are still moist in the center, about 45 to 50 minutes. Let cool completely in the pan. Cut into 16 bars.

BANANAS FOSTER TARTLETS

Bananas foster is a classic, and dramatic, table-side dessert. Here we've grilled the bananas instead of flambéing them, and present them over pastry cream in tartlet shells rather than ice cream.

MAKES 8 SERVINGS

1-2-3 Dough (recipe follows)

½ cup Pastry Cream (recipe follows)

¼ cup heavy cream

6 tbsp butter

¼ cup granulated sugar

1 tsp lemon juice

6 tbsp dark or light rum

2 tbsp banana liqueur

3 bananas

¼ cup chopped toasted macadamia nuts

1. On a lightly floured surface, roll the dough out to ⅛-inch thickness. Cut eight 4-inch rounds out of the dough, and line 8 greased 3-inch tartlet pans with the dough. (If you cannot get 8 rounds after rolling out the dough the first time, gather up the scraps, re-roll the dough to ⅛-inch thickness, and cut out the needed rounds.) Trim any excess dough from the tartlet pans.

2. Line the dough with 4-inch squares of parchment paper and fill the bottom of the tartlet pans with dried beans or pie weights. Chill the dough for 10 minutes in the refrigerator before baking.

3. Preheat oven to 350°F.

4. Bake the tartlets for 12 minutes, or until par baked. Remove the beans and the parchment paper and return the tartlet shells to the oven for 5 minutes, or until the shells are golden brown. Allow the shells to cool to room temperature.

5. Whip the pastry cream until smooth if it has been refrigerated. Whip the heavy cream to soft peaks. Combine the pastry cream with the whipped cream, and spoon the mixture into the tartlet

LEFT TO RIGHT Carefully shingle the bananas on top of the pastry cream; it may be necessary to use a palette knife or small butter knife to place the bananas, as they will be soft. Spoon the sauce over the tartlets while they are still on the parchment paper just in case it drips.

shells, filling each ¾ full. Refrigerate the shells, covered, until ready to use.

6. Heat the butter in a medium-sized skillet over medium-high heat. Add the sugar and cook until the sugar has started to darken slightly. Add the lemon juice and swirl it into the butter mixture.

7. Remove the pan from the heat, and pour in the rum and the banana liqueur. Return the pan to the heat and bring to a simmer. (If desired, you can "flame" the rum with a match.) Keep warm.

8. Preheat a gas grill to high. If you are using a charcoal grill, build a fire and let it burn down until the coals are glowing red with a light coating of white ash. Spread the coals in an even bed.

9. Peel the bananas and cut into rounds or on the diagonal about ½ inch thick.

10. Grill the bananas until just softened, about 1 to 2 minutes, basting with the sauce once.

11. Divide the bananas evenly among the tartlet shells, shingling the bananas, if desired. Drizzle the remaining sauce over the bananas. Garnish with toasted macadamia nuts and serve immediately.

1-2-3 *Dough*

MAKES ENOUGH FOR 8 TARTLETS

1 cup softened butter

½ cup granulated sugar

¾ tsp vanilla extract

1 egg

½ tsp grated lemon zest

3 cups all-purpose flour

1. Cream together the butter, sugar, and vanilla extract by hand or on medium speed using the paddle attachment of an electric mixer until very light and fluffy, about 5 minutes.

2. Add the egg and beat until fully incorporated, scraping down the sides as necessary.

3. Add the lemon zest and flour, and mix until just incorporated.

4. Shape the dough into a disk and chill in the refrigerator for 1 hour before using.

Pastry Cream

YOU'LL HAVE better control over this pastry cream as it cooks, with less danger of scorching, if you make the full batch. Any pastry cream you don't use can be kept in the refrigerator for up to 5 days. You can make it into a quick dessert by folding in some whipped cream and serving it as a mousse or pudding.

MAKES 4 CUPS

4 cups milk

1 cup granulated sugar

⅔ cup cornstarch

6 eggs

1 tbsp vanilla extract

6 tbsp butter

1. Combine the milk with half the sugar in a saucepan and bring to a boil.

2. Combine the remaining sugar with the cornstarch, add the eggs, and mix until smooth.

3. Temper the egg mixture (see note on page 278) into the hot milk and bring to a full boil, stirring constantly.

4. Remove from the heat and stir in the vanilla and butter. Transfer to a clean container, place a piece of plastic wrap directly on top the pastry cream, and let cool. Store any unused cream in a covered container in the refrigerator; cool thoroughly before storing.

MARBLEIZED POUND CAKE

Marbling two batters by gently folding them together results in a beautiful baked cake.

MAKES 2 LOAVES

¾ cup chopped bittersweet chocolate

3½ cups all-purpose flour

1 tsp baking powder

1 tsp salt

2 cups butter

2¼ cups sugar

9 large eggs, beaten

1 tsp vanilla extract

1. Preheat the oven to 375°F. Prepare two 9-inch loaf pans by spraying lightly with cooking spray or rubbing with softened butter. Dust them lightly with flour, shaking out any excess.

2. Melt the chocolate over very low heat or in the microwave. Transfer to a mixing bowl and let the chocolate cool to room temperature.

3. Sift together the flour, baking powder, and salt. Set aside.

4. Cream the butter and sugar together until very smooth and light by hand with a wooden spoon or with an electric mixer using the paddle attachment, about 3 minutes.

5. Add the eggs in three to four additions, mixing until smooth and scraping down the bowl between each addition. Scrape down the bowl to blend evenly. Blend in the vanilla.

6. Stir the flour mixture into the creamed butter mixture until it is evenly blended, scraping down the bowl as needed.

7. Add half of the batter to the melted chocolate and mix thoroughly. Gently fold the chocolate mix-ture into the remaining batter just until the choco-late batter is swirled throughout.

8. Divide the batter evenly between the prepared loaf pans, filling them about three-quarters full. Gently tap the filled pans to release any air bubbles. Bake the cakes until a skin has formed on the cakes, about 15 minutes. Use a sharp paring knife to cut a slit down the center of each loaf. Continue to bake until a skewer inserted into center of the loaf comes out clean and the tops are golden brown, another 40 to 45 minutes.

9. Cool the cakes in the pans for about 10 min-utes before removing from the pan. Transfer them to a cooling rack to finish cooling before slicing and serving or wrapping to store. They can be held at room temperature for up to 3 days or frozen for up to 6 weeks.

MOLTEN CHOCOLATE CAKE

Decadent and delicious, these individual cakes are irresistible for true chocolate lovers. Serve the cakes directly from the oven, so that the molten center remains liquid as you take your first bite.

MAKES 6 SERVINGS

GANACHE FILLING

¼ cup heavy cream

2 tsp light corn syrup

⅓ cup semi-sweet chocolate, chopped finely

CAKE BATTER

½ cup butter, softened

¼ cup semi-sweet chocolate, melted

1½ tbsp unsweetened chocolate, melted

2 eggs

2 egg yolks

6 tbsp all-purpose flour

½ cup confectioners' sugar

1. Preheat the oven to 375°F.

2. To make the ganache, bring the cream and the corn syrup to a simmer and pour over the chopped chocolate. Let sit for 5 minutes and mix until smooth. Place in the freezer until just firm enough to scoop, about 20 minutes. Stir the ganache occasionally while it is in the freezer.

3. While the ganache is cooling, lightly beat the egg yolks; whisk the butter and the two chocolates together and add to the eggs.

4. Sift the flour and sugar together and fold into the chocolate mixture.

5. Butter and flour six 4-fluid-ounce ramekins. Fill the ramekins with 3 tablespoons batter and

The Creaming Mixing Method

Creamed batters, often used to make cakes as well as quick breads, result in rich baked goods with an exceptionally smooth, light, and even texture. Warm the butter to room temperature so you can beat it easily to a smooth consistency together with the sugar, usually white granulated or brown sugar. As the butter and sugar are beaten, or "creamed," small pockets of air are trapped in the butter and distributed evenly throughout the batter. Eventually, these tiny air pockets expand in the oven's heat. This action, along with any other leavener you use, produces a very fine texture and a soft, moist crumb. Adding eggs to the creamed butter and sugar adds moisture; this moisture eventually turns to steam, further leavening the cake.

CREAMING BUTTER AND SUGAR

Take the butter from the refrigerator 15 to 20 minutes (slightly longer in colder kitchens, less time on warm days) before you begin to let it soften slightly so it is easier to whip. Cream the butter on its own to soften it enough to make it easier to blend in the sugar. To do this, beat it with the paddle attachment of a stand mixer on low speed for about 2 minutes. You can also soften the butter by hand; use a wooden spoon and stir vigorously. When the butter is light in texture, add the sugar and mix until blended. The sharp edges of the sugar crystals trap some air and create small pockets in the batter that give the finished baked good a light texture.

ADDING THE EGGS

Any eggs and other wet ingredients you add to the creamed butter-and-sugar mixture should be at room temperature. If they are very cold, they may cause the butter to harden into little flecks; if this happens, keep mixing until the flecks disappear before adding more ingredients. Eggs are usually added to the creamed butter-and-sugar mixture before any other liquid ingredients so that they can mix evenly into the butter.

ADDING THE DRY INGREDIENTS

Add the sifted dry ingredients as directed in your recipe. Some call for the dry ingredients to be added all at once, while others indicate to add them in two or three additions, alternating with the liquid ingredients.

ADDING OTHER INGREDIENTS

Hot ingredients like melted chocolate should be cooled to room temperature before they are added to the batter and will combine with it most readily if they are blended with a small amount of the batter first make a small well in the center by pushing the batter up slightly on the sides. However, the bottom of the ramekin should not be visible.

6. Scoop 1 tablespoon of the ganache and place it in the center of each ramekin.

7. Spoon another 2 tablespoons of cake batter on top of the ganache, making sure to seal it between the two layers of batter. The batter should come up to ¼-inch from the top of the ramekin.

8. Bake the cakes in a 375°F oven for 15 to 20 minutes or until the top of the cake springs back lightly to the touch.

9. Loosen the edges of the cakes before unmolding, and place on a small dessert plate. Serve with a dollop of whipped cream and Vanilla Sauce (opposite) or Raspberry Coulis (page 280).

Baking Angel Food Cake

Angel food cake is baked in an ungreased pan so that the batter can cling to the sides as the cake bakes. Then, to protect the fragile structure of the cake just as it comes from the oven, turn the pan upside down and set it on top of a wine bottle. Let it cool completely before you try to get the cake out of the pan.

To release the cake from the pan, run a thin blade around the edges of the pan. Work carefully to avoid cutting into the cake. Gently remove the angel food cake from the pan and hold on a plate until needed.

GRILLED ANGEL FOOD CAKE
with *Fresh Berries and Chantilly Cream*

A NGEL FOOD cake, though light and delicate to the bite, has enough resilience to go on the grill. The sugar in the cake takes on a deep caramel taste for an intriguing take on strawberry short-

cake. Try flavoring the Chantilly cream with a liqueur or other flavor to add another dimension of flavor to this dish.

MAKES 12 SERVINGS

¾ cup cake flour

1 cup granulated sugar

Pinch salt

6 egg whites

1 tsp vanilla extract

Pinch cream of tartar

2 cups Chantilly cream (recipe follows)

4 cups strawberries, hulled and halved

1. Preheat oven to 350°F.

2. Sift together the flour, ½ cup of the sugar, and the salt. Set aside.

3. Combine the egg whites, vanilla, and cream of tartar in a large bowl and whip with a whisk or beat on medium speed using the whip attachment of an electric mixer until frothy. Gradually add the remaining ½ cup sugar and beat to medium-stiff peaks.

4. Gently fold the sifted dry ingredients into the beaten egg whites just until evenly blended. Immediately pour the batter into an ungreased tube cake pan.

5. Bake until the cake springs back when lightly touched, 35 to 40 minutes. Allow the cake to completely cool upside down on a cooling rack before removing it from the pan.

6. Preheat a gas grill to medium-high. If you are using a charcoal grill, build a fire and let it burn down until the coals are glowing red with a light coating of white ash. Spread the coals in an even bed. Clean the cooking grate.

7. Cut the cake into 12 wedges. Grill the wedges

until well marked on both sides and warmed through, about 3 to 4 minutes on each side.

8. Serve the grilled cake topped with the strawberries and the Chantilly cream.

Chantilly Cream

CHANTILLY CREAM gets it name from the region of France where it was famously served to King Louis XIV. To make a Chantilly cream, whip well-chilled heavy cream until it thickens and add a bit of sugar (superfine or powdered sugar dissolves most easily). Continue to whip the cream until it is thick enough to spoon or pipe onto your dessert. If you can find cream that is not stabilized and hasn't been ultra-pasteurized, your reward is a slightly stiffer, denser, richer cream.

VANILLA SAUCE

THIS BASIC vanilla custard sauce is very versatile, excellent with bread pudding, fruit tarts, or chocolate desserts.

MAKES 2 CUPS

1 cup heavy cream

1 cup whole milk

½ vanilla bean

½ cup sugar

9 egg yolks

1. Bring the milk, vanilla bean, and half of the sugar to a boil. Be sure to watch for scorching.

2. Combine the egg yolks with the remaining sugar and pour ¼ cup of the hot milk into the egg mixture to temper it. Whisk to combine.

3. Add the tempered egg mixture back into the hot milk, whisk to combine, and return to a low heat.

4. Stirring constantly with a wooden spoon, heat the mixture to 165°F. Remove immediately from the stove. Strain through a fine-mesh sieve into a container that is set into an ice bath.

5. The sauce may be stored under refrigeration for 5 to 8 days

FRESH BERRY NAPOLEON

THIS ELEGANT French dessert is usually made with puff pastry; however, this version uses phyllo dough. Napoleons should be assembled just prior to serving so that the phyllo layers remain crispy.

MAKES 8 SERVINGS

8 sheets phyllo dough, thawed

¼ cup breadcrumbs, plain

¼ cup butter, melted

¼ cup sugar

1 egg white

½ cup sour cream

1 tbsp light brown sugar, packed

½ tsp vanilla extract

¼ cup heavy cream, whipped to medium peaks

2 cups fresh berries (sliced strawberries, blueberries, raspberries, etc.)

2 tbsp confectioners' sugar

1. Preheat the oven to 350°F. Spray a nonstick baking sheet with nonstick spray, or line with parchment paper.

2. As you work, keep the sheets of phyllo covered with plastic wrap to keep them from drying out. Place one phyllo sheet on a clean, dry cutting board;

lightly brush the dough with a little of the melted butter and sprinkle with 2 teaspoons of breadcrumbs. Continue layering the remaining sheets, brushing with butter and sprinkling with the crumbs in between each layer. With a pizza wheel or sharp knife, cut the phyllo into twenty-four 3-inch squares. Transfer to the baking sheet. Sprinkle each of the rectangles with sugar (use about 1 to 2 tablespoons for all of the pieces) and bake until crisp and golden brown, about 6 to 8 minutes. Transfer to a wire rack and cool completely.

3. With an electric mixer (or a hand-held mixer) beat the egg white until thick and foamy. Gradually add the remaining sugar while beating the white. Beat on high speed to stiff peaks.

4. Combine the sour cream, brown sugar and vanilla extract. Fold in the whipped cream, followed by the beaten egg white.

5. To assemble the napoleons, place a small dollop of the filling mixture on the plate to secure the napoleon. Top with a phyllo square. Add 2 tablespoons of the filling mixture and 2 tablespoons of the fruit. Add another phyllo square and top with another 2 tablespoons of filling and fruit. Add the final layer of phyllo and dust lightly with confectioner's sugar. Repeat to complete all of the remaining napoleons.

CRÊPES SUZETTE

Crêpes suzette is a classic dessert, one often prepared at the table so that you can enjoy the dramatic flaming presentation. Warm the Grand Marnier and brandy to make them easier to ignite. And, if pyrotechnics in the morning seems a little too dramatic, you can simply let the sauce simmer without setting it aflame.

MAKES 8 SERVINGS

3 tbsp sugar

1 cup butter, cubed

3 tbsp orange zest

¼ cup orange juice

24 Crêpes (page 228)

3 tbsp Grand Marnier

3 tbsp brandy or cognac

Orange zest for garnish

1. Preheat a small sauté pan over medium heat. Sprinkle the sugar evenly over the bottom of the pan. As the sugar begins to caramelize, 2 to 3 minutes, add the butter to the outside edges of the pan and gently shake the pan to evenly blend with the sugar.

2. Add the orange zest and shake the pan gently to thoroughly blend all the ingredients and let the sauce become a light orange caramel color, 1 to 2 minutes. Pour the orange juice on the outside edges of the pan slowly, allowing it to blend with the sugar. Shake the pan gently, incorporating all the ingredients and simmer until the sauce thickens.

3. Place one crêpe at a time in the sauce, coating both sides, and remove. Repeat with the remaining crêpes, moving quickly so the sauce does not become too thick.

4. Remove the pan from the heat and add the Grand Marnier, being careful not to allow the liquor to flame. Return the pan to the heat and stir gently until sauce is hot.

5. Remove the pan, add the brandy, and tip the pan slightly to collect the liquid on one side. Use a lit match to set the brandy on fire. Shake the pan until the flame dies.

6. Fold each crêpe into fourths; place 3 on each plate, slightly overlapping, and coat with sauce. Garnish with orange zest.

TIRAMISU

IN ITALIAN, tiramisu literally means "pick me up." After one bite of the espresso-and-Kahlua-soaked ladyfingers, creamy mascarpone cheese, and grated chocolate, you will understand why this dessert is a classic. For a contemporary twist on the original, make the tiramisu in individual glasses.

MAKES 8 SERVINGS

1 egg

6 egg yolks

1½ cups sugar

1 tsp vanilla extract

3¼ cups mascarpone cheese

3 egg whites

1 cup espresso

½ cup Kahlua

48 ladyfingers

¼ cup cocoa powder

2 tbsp powdered sugar

1. Whip the egg, egg yolks, 1 cup of the sugar, and the vanilla together in a large stainless steel bowl over simmering water for about 3 to 4 minutes, or until the volume nearly doubles and the mixture becomes a light lemon yellow.

2. Transfer the egg and sugar mixture to the bowl of an electric mixer and beat on high speed until the mixture has cooled to room temperature, about 8 to 10 minutes. Add the mascarpone and blend on low speed until very smooth, about 2 to 3 minutes. Scrape the sides and bottom of the bowl to blend evenly.

3. Beat the egg whites with the remaining sugar in a clean bowl to medium-stiff peaks, about 5 to 6 minutes. Fold the beaten egg whites into the mascarpone mixture in two additions. Refrigerate until needed.

4. Combine the espresso and Kahlua to make a syrup. Place a layer of ladyfingers in a 2½-quart bowl. Moisten the ladyfingers well with the syrup and dust evenly with cocoa powder. Top with a 1-inch thick layer of the mascarpone filling. Repeat layering in this sequence until the bowl is full, ending with a layer of filling.

5. Dust the entire surface of the cake with cocoa power and powdered sugar. Chill thoroughly before serving.

GRILLED PEPPERED PINEAPPLE
with *Tequila to Orange Sauce and Candied Kumquats*

IF YOU can't find kumquats in the store, cut the peel of two oranges into thin strips and use that in place of the halved kumquats called for in the Candied Kumquat recipe.

MAKES 8 SERVINGS

3 cups orange juice

1 cup silver tequila

½ cup honey

1 large pineapple, cut into ½-inch-thick rings

1 tbsp brine-packed green peppercorns, rinsed well

2 cups French Vanilla Ice Cream (see page 278)

¾ cup Candied Kumquats (recipe follows)

1. Combine the orange juice, tequila, and honey in a small, heavy saucepan. Simmer over medium heat until reduced to about 1 cup, about 45 to 50 minutes. The sauce will appear slightly thick and syrupy. Keep warm. (If made in advance, cool the sauce and store in a covered container in the refrigerator for up to 5 days. Warm the sauce before serving.)

2. Preheat a gas grill to high. If you are using a charcoal grill, build a fire and let it burn down until the coals are glowing red with a light coating of white ash. Spread the coals in an even bed. Clean the cooking grate.

3. Rub both sides of the pineapple rings with the peppercorns. Grill over direct heat, turning as necessary, until both sides are well caramelized, about 6 to 8 minutes.

4. Serve the grilled pineapple on dessert plates, drizzled with the tequila-orange sauce and topped with a ¼-cup scoop of vanilla ice cream. Garnish with the Candied Kumquats and serve immediately.

Candied Kumquats

KUMQUATS LOOK like miniature oranges. They look wonderful in arrangements of flowers and fruit, but it would be a shame to miss their fragrant aroma and intriguing texture: you can eat fresh kumquats whole, skin and all. They are seasonal items, so when you see them, grab a few containers and make these candied kumquats to enjoy for weeks to come.

MAKES 1¼ CUPS

Water, as needed

1¼ cups halved and seeded kumquats

2¼ cups granulated sugar

⅓ cup corn syrup

1. Bring a large pot of water to a boil and add the kumquats. Boil for 1 minute, then drain. Repeat twice more, using fresh water each time. Set aside.

2. Combine 1½ cups water, the sugar, and corn syrup in a saucepan and bring to a bare simmer. Add the blanched kumquats and let poach until all traces of bitterness are gone and the kumquat peel is very soft, about 1 hour and 45 minutes. (There should be only very slight action on the surface of the poaching liquid with few if any bubbles breaking the surface. Some steam should billow from the surface.)

3. Remove the pan from the heat and let the kumquats cool to room temperature in the cooking syrup. Store the kumquats in the syrup in covered containers in the refrigerator for up to 4 weeks.

S'MORES

S'MORES ARE a classic campfire dessert. Although they are traditionally made by toasting the marshmallows on a stick over an open fire, you can use your grill. Everyone has their own technique—and preferences—about toasting marshmallows, so let everyone (except small children) toast their own. For a deep golden brown and fewer flames, turn the marshmallow slowly over the flame or glowing coals, and if it starts to cook too quickly in certain spots, move the marshmallow a little farther away from the flame.

MAKES 8 SERVINGS

Eight 1-oz pieces dark, semisweet, or milk chocolate

16 Graham Cracker Cookies (recipe follows)

8 Cinnamon Marshmallows (recipe follows)

1. If you don't have a campfire burning, preheat a gas grill to high. If you are using a charcoal grill, build a fire and let it burn down until the coals are glowing red with a light coating of white ash.

2. Place 1 piece of chocolate on each of 8 graham cracker cookies.

3. Place the marshmallows on metal skewers and

hold the skewers over the grill until gooey or to the desired doneness.

4. Top each chocolate-covered graham cracker with a marshmallow, then top each with one of the remaining graham cracker cookies. Serve at once.

Graham Cracker Cookies

GRAHAM CRACKERS were actually introduced in the nineteenth century as a health food, by a minister and nutritional advocate named Sylvester Graham. Crumbs from these honey-sweetened, whole-wheat crackers are used as the basis for this delicious cookie.

MAKES 16 COOKIES

1 cup softened butter

½ cup granulated sugar

1 large egg, lightly beaten

¾ tsp vanilla extract

2½ cups cake flour

½ cup graham cracker crumbs

1. Cream together the butter and sugar by hand or with an electric mixer on medium speed, scraping down the bowl periodically, until smooth and light in color, about 5 minutes.

3. Mix in the egg and vanilla, scraping down the bowl and blending until smooth.

4. Add the flour and graham cracker crumbs all at once, mixing on low speed until just blended.

5. Turn the dough onto a floured work surface. Shape it into a flat disk, wrap tightly, and refrigerate for at least 1 hour.

6. Preheat oven to 350°F. Grease a baking sheet or line with parchment paper.

7. Roll the dough to ⅛-inch thickness. Cut six-teen 3-inch squares or rounds out of the dough, and place them on the prepared baking sheet. (Gather up the scraps and re-roll the dough as necessary.) Chill the dough in the refrigerator for 10 minutes before baking.

8. Bake the graham cracker cookies until golden brown, about 12 to 15 minutes. Let the cookies cool to room temperature on a wire rack.

9. Serve the graham cracker cookies now, or store in an airtight container at room temperature for up to 5 days.

Cinnamon Marshmallows

MAKING YOUR own marshmallows is a fascinating process. These treats are softer and more flavorful than the kind you buy at the store, plus you can customize them by adding your own favorite flavor, like the powdered cinnamon we've used here, or by cutting them into a variety of shapes. The number of marshmallows you get from this recipe will vary, depending upon how you choose to cut them out. Regardless of the shape and size you like, remember that any extras can be packed up and stored in the freezer to enjoy another day. They thaw in just a few minutes at room temperature.

MAKES 1 JELLY-ROLL PAN

Vegetable oil, as needed

2 tbsp powdered gelatin

1 cup cold water

1½ cups granulated sugar

½ cup honey

½ cup corn syrup

1½ tsp vanilla extract

1½ tsp ground cinnamon

¼ cup cornstarch

1. Line a jelly-roll pan with parchment paper and lightly grease the parchment paper with the oil. Cut a second piece of parchment paper of the same size, oil it lightly, and set aside.

2. Sprinkle the gelatin over ½ cup of the cold water and briefly stir to completely moisten it and break up any clumps. Let the gelatin sit in the cold water until it swells and softens, 10 to 15 minutes.

3. Combine the sugar, honey, and corn syrup with the remaining ½ cup of water in a heavy-bottomed saucepan and stir to moisten the sugar. Cook over high heat, stirring constantly, until the mixture comes to a boil. Immediately stop stirring and skim the surface to remove any scum that has risen to the top. Continue to cook over high heat, occasionally brushing down the side of the pan using a pastry brush and water, until the mixture registers 242°F on a candy thermometer.

4. Remove the mixture from the heat and let cool to approximately 210°F.

5. Place the gelatin in a heatproof bowl over a pan of simmering water. Stir constantly until the mixture is clear and liquid. Mix the vanilla into the dissolved gelatin.

6. Mix the gelatin into the cooked sugar mixture and transfer to a mixing bowl. Stir in the cinnamon. Whip the mixture with an electric mixer on high speed until medium peaks form, about 8 to 10 minutes.

7. Spread the mixture in the lined pan. Top the mixture with the prepared parchment paper and use a rolling pin to spread the mixture into an even slab. Place in the freezer for at least 8 and up to 24 hours before taking the slab out of the pan.

8. Gently peel off the paper from 1 side. Lightly dust the marshmallow slab with some of the cornstarch. Flip the slab over and gently peel off the parchment paper from the other side. Dust the sec-ond side of the marshmallow slab lightly with more of the cornstarch.

9. Use a 2½-inch biscuit cutter, dipped into the cornstarch, to cut rounds out of the marshmallow, or simply cut into pieces with a sharp knife. If the cutter or knife begins to stick, dip it in additional cornstarch or dust the marshmallows lightly with a little more cornstarch.

10. Serve the marshmallows now, or store in an airtight covered container in the freezer for up to 4 months.

GRILLED BANANA SPLIT
with Homemade Ice Cream

CHOOSE FIRM-RIPE bananas for this dish. The heat of the grill will intensify the bananas' natural sweetness. Fully ripe and soft bananas won't hold up to the intense heat of the grill.

MAKES 6 SERVINGS

6 bananas, peeled and cut in half

2 tbsp melted butter

3 cups ice cream: French Vanilla, Dark or White Chocolate, Cherry Vanilla, and/or Praline Ice Cream (pages 278, 279)

2 cups sauce: Chocolate, Cherry, and/or Butterscotch Sauce (recipes follow)

½ cup coarsely chopped toasted almonds

1 cup whipped cream

6 brandied or maraschino cherries

1. Preheat a gas grill to low. If you are using a charcoal grill, build a fire and let it burn down until the coals have a heavy coating of white ash. Spread the coals in an even bed. Clean the cooking grate.

2. Brush the bananas with the melted butter and place on the grill. Grill the bananas until lightly

marked on the first side, about 1 minute. Turn the bananas carefully and grill on the second side until lightly marked and hot, 1 minute more.

3. Place 2 banana halves on each serving plate. Top each serving with 3 small scoops of the ice cream and spoon the sauces over the ice cream. Garnish with the whipped cream, toasted almonds, and cherries.

Hot Chocolate Sauce

MAKES 2 CUPS

2 cups fine-chopped bittersweet chocolate

1 cup heavy cream

2 tsp vanilla extract

1. Place the chocolate in a stainless-steel bowl.
2. Bring the cream just to a simmer and pour it over the chocolate. Add the vanilla and whisk until smooth.
3. Serve the sauce now, or let cool and store in a covered container in the refrigerator for up to 10 days. Reheat in a microwave on low power or in a double boiler.

Cherry Sauce

MAKES 2 CUPS

1¼ lb pitted Bing cherries (about 3¾ cups)

2½ cups granulated sugar

¾ cup water

¼ tsp almond extract

1½ tsp lemon juice, or to taste

1. Combine the cherries, sugar, and water in a saucepan, crushing the cherries slightly with the back of a wooden spoon to release some of their juices. Bring to a simmer over medium heat. Remove from the heat, cover, and let the cherries steep for 1 hour.

2. Add the water and almond extract. Return the pan to medium heat and bring to a simmer. Reduce the heat to low and continue to simmer the sauce until the juices thicken, about 30 minutes.

3. Add the lemon juice. (Optional: Let the sauce cool slightly and then purée the sauce in a blender for a smooth sauce.)

4. Serve the sauce now, or let cool and store in a covered container in the refrigerator for up to 10 days. Reheat in a microwave on low power or in a double boiler.

Butterscotch Sauce

MAKES 2 CUPS

1⅓ cups packed dark brown sugar

¾ cup light corn syrup

½ cup butter

2 tbsp water

Pinch salt

½ cup heavy cream

1. Combine the brown sugar, syrup, butter, water and salt in a heavy saucepan and bring to a boil over medium heat, stirring constantly. Boil for 2 minutes.

2. Remove the pan from the heat, let cool slightly, and stir in the cream.

3. Serve the sauce now, or let cool and store in a covered container in the refrigerator for up to 10 days. Reheat in a microwave on low power or in a double boiler.

FRENCH VANILLA ICE CREAM

T HIS BASIC ice cream can be flavored to suit your mood or the bounty of the farmer's market. See the suggestions following this recipe, but don't limit yourself to what we've included here. Try peaches, pistachios, caramel sauce, chocolate chunks, or crushed cookies to create your own specialty of the house.

MAKES 4 CUPS

2 cups heavy cream

½ cup granulated sugar

⅛ tsp salt

1 vanilla bean, split, or 2 tsp vanilla extract

6 large egg yolks

1. Combine the cream, ¼ cup of the sugar, and the salt in a heavy-gauge pan over medium heat and bring to a simmer. If you are using a split vanilla bean, add it to the milk and cream as it comes to a simmer. Remove the pan from the heat as soon as it reaches a simmer.

2. Blend the egg yolks with the remaining ¼ cup sugar until smooth and light. Ladle about half of the hot cream mixture into the blended yolks, adding it a little at a time and whisking constantly as you work. (See tempering note below.)

3. Pour the yolk mixture into the cream and return the pan to low heat. Cook, stirring constantly with a wooden spoon, until thickened enough to cling to the back of the spoon. (Do not bring to a full boil.)

4. Strain the mixture through a fine-mesh sieve into a clean container set in a bowl of ice water. If you are using vanilla extract, stir it into the mixture now. Continue to stir until the ice cream base has cooled to 70°F. Cover the container, refrigerate for at least 12 hours.

Tempering

Pastry cream and the custard base for ice creams rely upon a specific technique, known as tempering. These recipes include a significant amount of eggs. *Tempering* means that you slowly increase the heat of the eggs before adding them to the hot milk or cream. Then, they can be added without scrambling or curdling in the pan. To temper eggs into a hot liquid, follow these steps:

1. Bring the liquid (milk, cream, or a mixture of both) to a simmer, along with any flavorings you want to include (see page 200 for more about flavoring ice creams), and some of the sugar.

2. Meanwhile, blend the eggs and remaining sugar until smooth. Pastry cream always includes a thickener; our recipe calls for cornstarch. To break up the cornstarch, stir it together with the sugar before you add the sugar to the eggs. Blend until smooth.

3. Once the milk or cream reaches a simmer, remove the pan from the heat. Ladle a small amount of the hot milk into the egg mixture, stirring as you add it. Continue adding the hot milk or cream until you've blended about ⅓ of it into the egg mixture. The eggs are tempered at this point.

4. Now, pour the egg mixture back into the pan with the rest of the hot milk or cream and stir.

5. Return the pan to low heat and carefully heat the pastry cream or custard sauce, stirring the mixture constantly with a wooden spoon as it heats.

5. Set up your ice cream freezer according to the manufacturer's directions, add the ice cream base, and freeze until it is very thick but still soft enough to stir.

6. Transfer the ice cream to a freezer container and place in the freezer to firm and ripen for at least 4 hours before serving.

Dark or White Chocolate Ice Cream

Add 1 cup of milk to the cream before bringing it to a simmer. Strain the ice cream base over ⅔ cup finely chopped dark or white chocolate, and stir the mixture until the chocolate has melted and is well blended. Place the bowl over an ice bath and stir until cooled properly.

Cherry Vanilla Ice Cream

Omit the vanilla bean. Add 1½ teaspoons almond extract to the ice cream before you put it in the ice cream freezer. Fold 1 cup pitted sweet or sour cherries into the ice cream when you take it out of the ice cream freezer, before putting it into the freezer to firm and ripen.

Praline Ice Cream

Substitute brown sugar for the granulated sugar. Add 2 tablespoons praline paste (available in specialty shops or through mail-order sources) to the milk and cream as the mixture comes to a simmer. Fold 1 cup coarse-chopped toasted hazelnuts into the ice cream when you take it out of the ice cream freezer, before putting it into the freezer to firm and ripen.

BUTTERMILK ICE MILK

AN ICE MILK is lower in fat than a traditional custard-based ice cream, but adding a bit of heavy cream along with the buttermilk gives this ice milk a noticeable richness.

MAKES 8 SERVINGS

3 cups milk

1 cup heavy cream

1 cup plus 2 tbsp granulated sugar

¼ tsp salt

1¼ cups egg yolks

1 tbsp vanilla extract

1 cup buttermilk

1. Heat the milk, heavy cream, ½ cup of the sugar, and the salt in a saucepan over medium heat until the mixture just reaches a boil. Remove from the heat.

2. Whisk together the egg yolks and the remaining sugar. Temper the egg mixture (see tempering note on opposite page) by gradually adding about one-half of the hot milk mixture into the egg mixture, whipping constantly. Add the tempered egg mixture to the remaining hot milk in the saucepan and whisk to combine.

3. Return the saucepan to the heat and cook, stirring constantly, until the mixture thickens enough to evenly coat the back of a spoon (180°F), about 2 to 3 minutes.

4. Stir in the vanilla extract. Strain the mixture into a metal container and immediately transfer to an ice bath. Cool to below 40°F. Cover and refrigerate the mixture for at least 8 and up to 12 hours.

5. Stir the buttermilk into the chilled base. Process the mixture in an ice cream machine according to the manufacturer's instructions. Transfer the ice milk from the machine to storage containers, and pack it tightly. Cover and freeze for several hours or overnight before serving.

GRAND MARNIER-HONEY CHOCOLATE FONDUE

Fondue is a concept that originated in Switzerland, though its popularity has spread throughout the world. Originally intended as a savory preparation of melted cheeses, the concept of a sweet preparation, using chocolate, has become equally as popular. Grand Marnier, a brandy-based liqueur flavored with orange peel, adds a distinctive flavor.

MAKES 6 SERVINGS

1 cup bittersweet chocolate, melted

1 cup semi-sweet chocolate, melted

½ cup heavy cream

2 tsp orange zest

Pinch salt

2 tbsp honey

¼ cup Grand Marnier

Assorted fresh fruit, cut into bite-sized pieces, as needed

Ladyfingers or pound cake, cut into bite-sized pieces, as needed

1. Combine the melted chocolates together and keep warm.

2. Bring the heavy cream, orange zest, salt, and honey to a simmer. Remove from heat and allow the zest to steep for 5 minutes. Strain the mixture into the chocolate and whisk together.

3. Add the Grand Marnier and mix thoroughly. Serve warm in a fondue pot with a variety of foods to dip (e.g. strawberries with the stems on, pitted cherries, sponge cake pieces, apricots, ladyfingers, orange segments, etc.).

NOTE: If you prefer, omit the Grand Marnier and substitute an additional ¼ cup of heavy cream.

VARIATION: For white chocolate fondue, substitute 2 cups melted white chocolate for the bitterweet and semi-sweet chocolate.

GRILLED PEACHES
with Vanilla Ice Cream and Raspberry Coulis

This dessert echoes the flavors of a classic dessert, peach Melba.

MAKES 8 SERVINGS

4 peaches, pitted and cut into ½-inch-thick slices

¼ cup granulated sugar

2 tbsp lemon juice

4 cups French Vanilla Ice Cream (page 278)

1 cup Raspberry Coulis (recipe follows)

8 Citrus Crisps (recipe follows)

1. Preheat a gas grill to high. If you are using a charcoal grill, build a fire and let it burn down until the coals are glowing red with a light coating of white ash. Spread the coals in an even bed. Clean the cooking grate.

2. Toss the peaches with the sugar and lemon juice. Grill the peaches over direct heat until tender in the middle and well marked, 2 to 3 minutes per side.

4. Serve the peaches over the ice cream, topped with the raspberry coulis and garnished with the citrus crisps.

Raspberry Coulis

A coulis is simply a term used to refer to a thick puree or sauce. It is easy to create variations of this sauce by substituting fresh or frozen strawberries, kiwi puree, or chopped mango for the raspberries.

1 cup raspberries, fresh or frozen

½ cup granulated sugar, or more to taste

1 tbsp lemon juice, or more to taste

1. Combine the raspberries, sugar, and lemon juice in a saucepan over medium heat. Simmer, stirring, until the sugar has dissolved, about 10 minutes.

2. Strain the sauce through a fine-mesh sieve. Add additional sugar and/or lemon juice to taste, if desired. Serve now, or store in a covered container in the refrigerator for up to 7 days.

Citrus Crisps

MAKES 24 COOKIES

1 cup softened butter

½ cup granulated sugar

½ tsp salt

½ tsp vanilla extract

1½ cups quick-cooking rolled oats

1 cup all-purpose flour, sifted

½ cup grated lemon zest

1. Preheat oven to 350°F. Line 2 baking sheets with parchment paper or silicone baking mats.

2. Cream together the butter, sugar, salt, and vanilla extract by hand or using the paddle attachment of an electric mixer until very smooth and light, about 3 minutes.

3. Add the oats, flour, and lemon zest, and mix on low speed until just combined, scraping down the bowl as necessary to blend evenly.

4. Form the dough into 1-inch balls (about 1 tablespoon of dough per ball) and place in even rows approximately 2 inches apart on the prepared sheet pans.

Flatten slightly with the palm of your hand. Bake until the edges are light golden brown, about 12 to 15 minutes. Transfer to wire racks and let cool completely before serving or storing in airtight containers.

CHOCOLATE CHUNK COOKIES

FOR A delicious twist on a classic, add 1 cup chopped dried cherries to the dough along with the chocolate chunks.

MAKES 16 COOKIES

1½ cups all-purpose flour

½ tsp baking soda

¾ tsp salt

½ cup butter, softened

½ cup sugar

⅓ cup light brown sugar

1 egg

½ tbsp vanilla extract

1 cup semi-sweet chocolate chunks

1. Preheat the oven to 375°F.

2. Line 2 cookie sheets with parchment paper.

3. Sift together the flour, baking soda, and salt.

4. Cream the butter and sugars on medium speed with the paddle attachment, scraping down the bowl periodically, until the mixture is smooth and light in color, about 5 minutes.

5. Combine the eggs and vanilla. Add to the butter-sugar mixture and mix until fully incorporated, scraping down the bowl as needed. On low speed, mix in the sifted dry ingredients and the chocolate chunks until just incorporated.

6. Scale the dough into 2-tablespoon portions and place onto prepared cookie sheets. Alternately,

the dough may be shaped into a 16-inch long log, rolled tightly in plastic wrap, and refrigerated until firm enough to slice. The chilled log may be sliced into 16 pieces and arranged on the prepared cookie sheets in even rows.

7. Bake at 375°F until golden brown around the edges, about 12 to 14 minutes. Cool completely on cookie sheets.

SAND COOKIES

Named for the slightly "gritty" texture that coarse sugar lends to this short dough, these cookies are perfect with coffee or tea, and are sure to satisfy your sweet tooth.

MAKES 42 COOKIES

½ cup confectioners' sugar, sifted

½ cup butter, softened

½ tsp vanilla extract

2 tbsp lemon zest, grated

2 cups cake flour

¼ cup milk

½ cup coarse sugar

1. Using an electric mixer with the paddle attachment, cream together the sugar, butter, vanilla extract, and lemon zest on high speed until smooth and light, about 3 minutes.

2. Add the flour all at once and mix on low speed until combined.

3. Divide the dough in half and roll into 6-inch long cylinders (they should be 1¼-inch in diameter). At this point the cookies may be tightly wrapped in plastic wrap and frozen or refrigerated for later use or they may be prepared for baking.

4. To bake the cookies, preheat the oven to 350° F. Brush the cylinders of cookie dough with milk and roll them in the coarse sugar.

5. Cut the logs into ¼-inch thick slices and place them on parchment-lined cookie sheets.

6. Bake for 12 minutes or until light golden brown.

SWEDISH OATMEAL COOKIES

These delicate oatmeal cookies are made with cake flour and without eggs. Though the cookie looks the same as the traditional, its texture will amaze you.

MAKES 36 COOKIES

1¾ cups cake flour

1 tsp baking soda

1¼ cups butter, room temperature

¾ cup, plus 2 tbsp sugar

1¾ cups rolled oats

½ cup raisins

½ cup golden raisins

1. Preheat the oven to 375°F.

2. Line 4 cookie sheets with parchment paper.

3. Sift together the cake flour and the baking soda.

4. Cream the butter and sugar together on medium speed with the paddle attachment, scraping down the bowl periodically, until the mixture is smooth and light in color, about 5 minutes.

5. On low speed, mix in the sifted dry ingredients and oats until they are just combined. Mix in the raisins until they are just incorporated.

6. Drop rounded tablespoons of the dough onto the parchment-lined sheets and bake at 375°F for 10 to 12 minutes or until golden brown.

APPENDIX: Charts and Tables

Volume Measures Conversion

U.S. and Metric. Values have been rounded.

1 teaspoon	5 milliliters
1 tablespoon	15 milliliters
1 fluid ounce (2 tbsp)	30 milliliters
2 fluid ounces (¼ cup)	60 milliliters
8 fluid ounces (1 cup)	240 milliliters
16 fluid ounces (1 pint)	480 milliliters
32 fluid ounces (1 quart)	950 milliliters

Weight Measures Conversion

U.S. and Metric. Values have been rounded.

¼ ounce	8 grams
½ ounce	15 grams
1 ounce	30 grams
8 ounces (½ pound)	225 grams
16 ounces (1 pound)	450 grams
32 ounces (2 pounds)	900 grams
40 ounces (2¼ pounds)	1 kilogram

Temperature Conversion

Degrees Farenheit and Celcius; values have been rounded.

32°F	0°C
40°F	4°C
140°F	60°C
150°F	65°C
160°F	70°C
170°F	75°C
212°F	100°C
275°F	135°C
300°F	150°C
325°F	165°C
350°F	175°C
375°F	190°C
400°F	205°C
425°F	220°C
450°F	230°C
475°F	245°C
500°F	260°C

Cooking Meat

Certain cuts of meat, such as tenderloin of beef, suggest time and effort in the kitchen. However, with just a few pieces of basic information, you'll be able to select several cuts of meat that will work interchangeably in your recipes, resulting in delicious dishes that are both quick and easy. These tables provide information on the best cuts of meat for quick cooking and the ideal cooking methods for each.

TRIMMING MEAT

Trimming meat before cooking results in a finished dish with better texture. Remember to always use a clean cutting board and knife when cutting meat, and then wash all equipment and your working surface thoroughly before preparing any other ingredients. Purchase meat from a reputable market, avoid storing it for more than one day, and cook it to the proper temperature (see the table on page 286). Since heating meat to specific temperatures will kill bacteria, be sure to check for doneness with a thermometer.

If you buy larger cuts of meat, you may find gristle and excess fat that need to be removed. Although a small amount of fat adds flavor and helps keep meat tender, too much will make meat look and taste unpleasant. Feel the meat for gristle or hard spots and cut them away carefully. Some cuts, such as rack of lamb, have an even layer of fat that can often be removed by gripping a corner of the fat layer and peeling it back firmly. For thicker fat cov-

Best Quick Cooking Methods for Meat

	CUT	QUICK COOKING METHODS
BEEF	Ribeye Steak (bone-in or boneless)	Grilling, broiling, sautéing
	Porterhouse or T-bone Steak	Grilling, broiling, sautéing
	Tenderloin Steak (filet mignon)	Grilling, broiling, sautéing
	Strip Loin/Shell/Top Loin Steak (bone-in or boneless)	Grilling, broiling, sautéing
	Tri-tip Steak	Grilling, broiling, sautéing, stir-frying
	Top Sirloin Steak (bone-in or boneless)	Grilling, broiling, sautéing, stir-frying
	Flank Steak	Grilling, broiling, sautéing, stir-frying
	Skirt Steak	Grilling, broiling, sautéing
	Hanger Steak	Grilling, broiling, sautéing
	Flat Iron/Top Blade Steak	Grilling, broiling, sautéing, stir-frying
	Shoulder London Broil	Grilling, broiling
	Top Round London Broil	Grilling, broiling

	CUT	QUICK COOKING METHODS
VEAL	Loin chops	Grilling, broiling, sautéing
	Cutlets	Grilling, broiling, sautéing, pan frying
	Rib/Rack Chops	Grilling, broiling, sautéing
	Tenderloin	Grilling, sautéing
PORK	Loin Roast (boneless)	Roasting
	Loin Chops, center-cut or end (bone-in or boneless)	Grilling, broiling, sautéing, roasting
	Rib/Rack Chops	Grilling, broiling, sautéing, roasting
	Tenderloin	Grilling, roasting
	Cutlets	Sautéing, pan frying, stir-frying
	Blade Steak	Grilling, broiling
LAMB	Rack	Roasting
	Rib/Rack Chops (single or double)	Grilling, broiling, sautéing, roasting
	Shoulder Chops	Grilling, broiling, sautéing
	Loin chops (bone-in or boneless)	Grilling, broiling, sautéing
	Leg, butterflied (boneless)	Grilling
	Top Round	Broiling, roasting

erings, use a sharp knife and cut slowly with small movements to be sure that only fat is removed and not the meat itself. Pull away the fat as you cut it, holding it to reveal the line of separation between the fat and the meat. You may also choose to leave a thin layer of fat over a roast, to allow for self-basting as it cooks. In this case, use a sharp knife to shave all but a ½-inch-thick layer of fat.

Be sure to remove the silverskin completely before cooking a piece of meat. This tough membrane, named for its silvery translucent appearance, tends to shrink when exposed to heat, causing uneven heating as well as an unpleasant texture and appearance. It is most likely to appear on the tenderloin of beef, pork, veal, and lamb; top round of beef and veal; and venison loin. Work the tip of a boning knife under the silverskin membrane. Grip the end of the silverskin, holding it taut at a low angle over the meat, and glide the knife blade just underneath the membrane. Angle the blade upward slightly to cut away only the silverskin. If the silverskin is wide or if it wraps around the contours of a rounded piece of meat, you may need to remove the membrane in several narrow strips.

Testing Meat for Doneness

Combine temperature and touch to test meat while it cooks. Generally, cuts of meats that are more tender, like a beef tenderloin, require less cooking time; while tougher meats, like a beef shank, require longer cooking time.

Temperature is the most accurate method for judging the doneness of meat. You can use either an instant-read thermometer or a meat thermometer with a probe that stays in the meat while it cooks. It is important to remember that meat retains heat and continues to cook after it is taken off the grill or out of the oven. This "carry-over cooking" can account for an increase of up to 10°F, so it is essential to take meat out of the oven before it reaches its desired doneness. For example, if you like your beef tenderloin medium rare (145°F), take it out of the oven at 135°F, so that it will carry over to a perfect medium rare, rosy pink and juicy. See the table below for helpful guidelines.

Touching meat to judge its firmness offers another useful guideline to gauge the progression of cooking. With the tip of one finger, press the meat in the center to judge its resistance. The less done a piece of meat is, the softer and more yielding it will feel. Practice recognizing the feel of meat cooked to various stages of doneness by using your own hand as a guide. Hold one hand open, palm up, with your fingers relaxed and slightly curled. Touch the flesh at the base of your thumb. It will feel soft and yielding; this is how rare meat will feel. As you gradually spread your fingers open and flat, the flesh will become increasingly firm and unyielding, just as meat will feel as it cooks to well done.

Doneness Temperatures and Tests for Meat

DESIRED DONENESS:	REMOVE FROM HEAT AT:	CARRY-OVER TO:	MEAT SHOULD LOOK:
Beef, Veal, and Lamb			
Rare	125°F	135°F	Red and shiny interior.
Medium rare	135°F	145°F	Rosy pink interior, juicy.
Medium	150°F	160°F	Pink only at center, pale pink juices.
Well done	160°F	170°F	Evenly brown throughout, no traces of red or pink, moist but no juices
Pork			
Medium	150°F	160°F	Opaque throughout, slight give, juices with faint blush
Well done	160°F	170°F	Slight give, juices clear

Grilling Temperatures and Times for Meats

Times listed are for medium doneness; cook slightly less for rare, slightly more for medium-well.

Beef steaks (porterhouse, T-bone, sirloin, New York, tenderloin)	¾ inch thick	4 to 5 minutes per side, medium direct heat
	1 inch thick	5 to 6 minutes per side, medium direct heat
	1½ inches thick	8 to 9 minutes per side, start over high direct heat (2 minutes per side), finish with medium indirect heat (6 to 7 minutes more per side)
Beef roasts (loin, sirloin, rib)	5 pounds	1½ to 2 hours total, indirect medium heat
Beef flank steak	¾ inch thick	7 to 8 minutes per side, high direct heat
Beef skirt or hanger steak	½ inch thick	3 to 4 minutes per side, high direct heat
Pork chops from rib, loin, or shoulder	¾ to 1 inch thick	5 to 6 minutes per side, medium direct heat
	1½ inches thick	7 to 8 minutes per side, start over high direct heat (2 minutes per side), finish with medium indirect heat (5 to 6 minutes more per side)
Lamb chops from rib, loin, or shoulder	¾ to 1 inch thick	4 to 6 minutes per side, medium direct heat
Pork tenderloin (whole)		10 to 12 minutes per side, indirect medium heat
Pork ribs (country-style, baby back, spareribs)	3 pounds	1½ to 2 hours total, indirect medium heat
Pork or veal roasts (loin, sirloin, rib)	4 pounds	1¼ to 1½ hours total, indirect medium heat
Ground meat patties	¾ inch thick	4 to 5 minutes per side, direct medium heat
	1 inch thick	5 to 6 minutes per side, direct medium heat

Cooking Poultry

The famous seventeenth-century French gastronome Jean Anthelme Brillat-Savarin wrote: "Poultry is for the cook what canvas is to the painter." Sold fresh and frozen, available throughout the year, bred to be leaner, more tender, and less expensive than ever, poultry continues to rise in popularity, and it has been projected that the average American will consume 113.3 pounds per person in the year 2009.

While roasting a whole turkey requires substantial cooking time, poultry is available in various sizes and forms, making it swift and effortless to prepare. Dark meat, such as chicken thighs or duck breast, stays moist longer than white meat and generally requires longer cooking time. White meat, by contrast, requires shorter cooking times and a more careful eye, as it may become tough and dry if overcooked. One of the great challenges when cooking whole poultry is to get leg (dark) meat fully cooked without overcooking breast (white) meat. By cooking a cut-up chicken or a combination of leg and breast portions you can eliminate this problem. Start the leg portions first, then add the breast portions to the pan or grill several minutes later. Then, the dark and white portions are done at the same time, perfectly cooked and moist.

Safety

When working with any type of poultry, keep all tools and work surfaces clean to avoid cross-contamination of other foods with bacteria commonly

Best Quick Cooking Methods for Poultry

BIRD	QUICK COOKING METHODS
Cornish Game Hen	Grilling, broiling, roasting
Chicken Pieces:	
White meat	
Bone-in breast, with skin	Grilling, broiling, pan frying, roasting
Boneless, skinless breast	Grilling, sautéing, deep-frying
Dark meat	
Bone-in leg, thigh, wing	Suitable for all cooking techniques
Duckling:	
Boneless breast	Grilling, sautéing, pan searing

Doneness Temperatures and Tests for Poultry

DESIRED DONENESS:	REMOVE FROM HEAT AT:	CARRY-OVER TO:	MEAT SHOULD LOOK:
Whole birds	170°F	180°F	Legs move easily in sockets and when pierced in the thigh, juices run clear. Juices in an unstuffed bird's cavity no longer have a red or pink hue.
Breasts	160°F	170°F	Meat becomes opaque and firm throughout.
Legs, thighs, and wings	170°F	180°F	Meat releases easily from the bone.
Stuffing	155°F	165°F	For stuffing cooked separately or inside a whole bird.
Ground poultry	155°F	165°F	Even opaque color throughout, no hint of pink.

TO CHECK POULTRY FOR DONENESS:

- *Be sure your thermometer is accurate. If you aren't sure, stick the stem of your thermometer into a glass of ice water. The temperature should read 32°F.*

- *Insert the tip of the thermometer's stem at least 1 inch into the meat, avoiding any bones, to get an accurate reading.*

Allow the thermometer to remain in place about 1 minute to come up to temperature.

- *If your meat is too thin to take an accurate reading with an instant-read thermometer, use the touch test (meats will feel firm to the touch) or cut into a piece.*

- *Clean the thermometer properly after every use to avoid cross contamination.*

found in poultry. Wash cutting boards and knives thoroughly with hot, soapy water before and after you use them to cut poultry. Rinse poultry with cold water and pat dry with absorbent paper towels before cooking. Store uncooked birds in leak-proof containers in the refrigerator. Never place raw poultry directly above cooked meat or fresh vegetables.

This will prevent raw juices from dripping onto these other ingredients.

Testing Poultry for Doneness

A reliable way to determine doneness in poultry is to use a thermometer. Use the table and guidelines above as a reference. Remember, as with any meat, poultry will continue to cook after it is removed from its cooking medium.

Butterflying Boneless Cuts

By carefully cutting a boneless chicken breast nearly in half and then opening it like a book (or a butterfly), you create a cut that is thin enough for cooking rapidly with high heat or for rolling around a filling. Place the breast flat on a work surface. Put your guiding hand flat on the breast; this will keep breast stable and also help you keep the blade parallel to work surface. With a sharp knife, make long but shallow cuts into the curved side of the breast. Keep your knife's blade paral-

Grilling Temperatures and Times for Poultry

Times listed are for fully cooked birds, with an internal temperature of 165°F. Cook duck slightly longer if you prefer medium-rare.

Chicken, whole	3 to 3½ pounds	1 hour, indirect medium heat
Chicken, halved	1 to 1½ pounds	1 to 1½ hours, indirect medium heat
Chicken leg pieces, bone-in	6 ounces	10 to 12 minutes, direct medium heat
Chicken thighs, boneless, skinless	4 ounces	12 to 15 minutes, direct medium heat
Chicken breast pieces, bone-in	9 ounces	12 to 15 minutes, direct medium heat
Chicken breasts, boneless, skinless	6 ounces	10 to 12 minutes, direct medium heat
Cornish game hens, whole	1¼ to 1½ pounds	1 hour, indirect medium heat
Cornish game hens, halved	10 to 12 ounces	35 to 40 minutes, indirect medium heat
Turkey, whole	10 pounds	2 to 2½ hours, indirect medium heat
	12 pounds	2½ to 3 hours, indirect medium heat
	15 pounds	3 hours, indirect medium heat
	18 pounds	3½ hours, indirect medium heat
Turkey breast, bone-in	5 pounds	1½ hours, indirect medium heat
Turkey drumstick, bone-in	12 to 14 ounces	45 minutes to 1 hour, indirect medium heat
Duck, whole	5 pounds	1½ to 2 hours, indirect medium heat

lel to the work surface and cut almost through to the other side, stopping ½ to 1 inch short. This intact portion creates the "hinge" that allows you to open the breast into a flat, thin piece. If desired or directed in a recipe, after butterflying the breast, place it between 2 sheets of plastic or parchment paper and pound it lightly with a mallet or meat pounder to an even thickness.

Best Quick Cooking Methods for Fish

ITEM	CHARACTERISTICS	QUICK COOKING METHODS
Bass	Moderately fatty, fairly firm, smooth	Excellent steamed or *en papillote*, also grilled, but suitable for all techniques
Bluefish	Oily, flaky, soft, strong taste	Roasting, broiling, grilling
Catfish	Moderately fatty, firm, sweet	Excellent pan-fried, but suitable for all techniques
Cod	Lean, firm, mild taste	Poaching, braising, stewing, steaming
Flounder	Lean, flaky, mild taste	Shallow-poaching, steaming, deep-frying
Grouper	Lean, firm, mild taste	Sautéing, pan frying, steaming, shallow-poaching
Halibut	Lean, fine texture, flaky, mild taste	Pan frying, braising, poaching
Perch	Lean, delicate, sweet flavor	Steaming, poaching, deep-frying
Pompano	Moderately fatty, firm, full flavor	Broiling and *en papillote*
Salmon	Moderately fatty, firm, rich flavor	Excellent poached, baked, and grilled, but suitable for all techniques
Shad	Lean, flaky, sweet	Sautéing, pan frying
Snapper	Lean, firm	Excellent *en papillote* or baked, suitable for all techniques
Sole	Lean, flaky, delicate flavor	Shallow-poaching, pan frying, braising
Swordfish	Lean, very firm	Grilling, broiling, roasting
Trout	Moderately oily, flaky	Pan frying, roasting, poaching
Tuna	Moderately oily, firm	Roasting, broiling, grilling

Cooking Fish and Shellfish

Versatile, flavorful, healthy, and fast-cooking, seafood makes a perfect centerpiece for quick meals. Great seafood dishes highlight the fish's absolute freshness and natural tenderness. Generally, fish and shellfish don't require excess preparation or a long cooking time, making it easy to get a seafood meal on the table in minutes.

Shopping for Seafood

To enjoy great fish consistently, you need a great fish market, whether it is a shop specializing in fish, or a section of a larger store. All great fish markets have certain characteristics. First off, a fish market should smell of the seashore, without any unpleasant or "fishy" odors. Also, when shopping for fish check to make sure that the fish looks fresh, with moist flesh and skin, that all the fish and shellfish are iced or cooled, and the entire display is clean and orderly. The staff should handle the fish safely by keeping all work surfaces and scales clean and sanitized.

Select from familiar varieties of fish, but don't be afraid to try new varieties with confidence. See the tables on pages 291–292 for tips on cooking different types of fish. Don't be afraid to ask questions at the fish counter. If you're uncomfortable portioning fish yourself, ask the person behind the counter to do so for you. Make your stop at the fish shop, counter, or freezer case the last one you make before heading home, to keep your purchase as cold as possible. Once home, keep fresh fish in the coldest part of your refrigerator and remember to put a plate or dish underneath any packages that might drip or leak.

Many fish are now frozen right on the fishing ships using blast freezers. The fish freezes very quickly without the large ice crystals that form when you try the same thing in your home freezer. When you examine the packaging, check that it is intact and that there aren't a lot of ice crystals in the package (that's a sign the fish may have thawed at some point during its trip from the ship to your store).

As long as the fish or seafood is properly thawed, there is relatively little difference between the flavor, moisture, and texture of a frozen fish and a fresh one. Keep frozen fish or seafood in the freezer until you are ready to thaw it. Most fish thaws evenly and safely overnight in the refrigerator.

Best Quick Cooking Methods for Shellfish

ITEM	QUICK COOKING METHODS
Clams	Steaming, grilling, deep-frying
Oysters	Broiling, stewing, pan frying
Lobster	Boiling, steaming, roasting, broiling, grilling
Mussels	Steaming, roasting, stewing
Scallops	Sautéing, baking, roasting, broiling, grilling
Shrimp	Suitable for all techniques

Grilling Temperatures and Times for Fish and Seafood

Times listed are for medium doneness, or 145°F; cook slightly less for meatier fish, like tuna or swordfish, if you prefer medium-rare.

Fish fillets or steaks	½ inch thick	2 to 3 minutes per side, direct high heat
Fish fillets or steaks	1 inch thick	4 to 5 minutes per side, direct high heat
Fish fillets or steaks	1½ inches thick	5 to 6 minutes per side, direct high heat
Whole fish, pan-dressed	1 pound	8 to 10 minutes per side, indirect medium heat
Whole fish, pan-dressed	2 pounds	10 to 12 minutes per side, indirect medium heat
Whole fish, pan-dressed	3 pounds	15 to 18 minutes per side, indirect medium heat
Clams		About 10 minutes over direct high heat, or until clam shells open
Mussels		About 5 minutes over direct high heat, or until mussel shells open
Oysters		About 4 minutes over direct high heat, or until oyster shells open
Lobster	1½ to 2 pounds	10 to 12 minutes per side, indirect medium heat
Scallops		1 to 2 minutes per side, direct high heat
Shrimp		2 to 3 minutes per side, direct high heat

Market Forms of Fish and Shellfish

Seafood is available at the market in a variety of forms. Whole or pan-dressed fish are usually big enough for a single portion. They are typically gutted and scaled. The head, tail, and fins are sometimes removed. Steaks are cut from large fish such as tuna, salmon, or halibut. They normally contain some of the backbone; the skin may be removed or not. Although scales are generally removed before the fish is cut into steaks, it's a good idea to check your steaks for any stray scales before cooking.

Fillets are boneless cuts. Salmon or halibut fillets are often cut into individual portions, but you may prefer to buy the intact fillet to cut yourself; since there aren't any bones, it is very simple if you have a good sharp knife. Fish with relatively tough skin such as catfish or perch are skinned before they are sold as fillets. For some fish, however, you might

Best Cooking Methods for Vegetables

VEGETABLE/FAMILY	REPRESENTATIVE MEMBERS	WHAT TO LOOK FOR	BEST COOKING METHODS
Cabbage family	Broccoli, broccoli raab, Brussels sprouts, cauliflower, cabbage	Firm, heavy heads; good color; florets, if any, tightly closed	Boiling, steaming, stir-frying, grilling, braising, stewing
Corn	Yellow, white, and bi-color	Husk firmly attached, kernels plump	Boiling, steaming, roasting, grilling, stewing
Eggplant	Globe, Japanese	Skin firm and glossy, leaves unwilted	Grilling, broiling, roasting, stewing, pan-frying, deep-frying
Greens (leafy)	Arugula, chard, collards, dandelion, kale, mustard, spinach	No wilting or yellowing in leaves, heads heavy for size	Sautéing, stir-frying, steaming, boiling, stewing, braising
Legume family	Green beans, haricots verts, fava beans, garden peas, snow peas	Beans and pea pods that are plump, crisp, and evenly colored	Steaming, boiling, sautéing, stir-frying, stewing, braising
Mushroom family	Chanterelle, porcini, morel, white, portobello, oyster, shiitake	Caps plump; earthy smell; gills intact; stems firmly attached	Sautéing, stir-frying, stewing, braising, grilling, roasting, baking, pan-frying, deep-frying
Onion family (fresh)	Leeks, green onions	Green portions intact and unwilted; bulb firm	Sautéing, grilling, broiling, stewing, braising
Onion family (dried)	Cipollini, red onions, shallots, white onions, yellow onions	Firm and heavy for size, outer layers tight with good color	Sautéing, grilling, broiling, stewing, braising roasting, baking, pan-frying, deep-frying
Pepper family	Bell, chile	Fruit plump, skin glossy and taut	Roasting, grilling, broiling, sautéing, stir-frying, stewing, deep-frying
Roots and tubers	Beets, carrots, parsnips, potatoes, rutabagas, salsify, turnips	Firm and heavy for size, no withering; greens unwilted	Boiling, steaming, roasting, baking, sautéing, stir-frying, grilling, broiling, stewing, braising
Squash family (soft-skinned)	Chayote, crookneck, pattypan, yellow, zucchini	Good color, firm, no bruises or soft spots	Sautéing, stir-frying, pan-frying, deep-frying, grilling, broiling, roasting, stewing, braising
Squash family (hard-skinned)	Acorn, butternut, Hubbard, spaghetti, pumpkin	Firm; heavy for size; stem, if any, firmly attached	Boiling, steaming, roasting, baking, sautéing, stewing, braising
Tomatoes	Beefsteak, cherry, currant, pear, plum (Roma)	Good color, skin glossy and intact, slightly yielding when ripe	Sautéing, stir-frying, roasting, grilling, broiling, stewing, braising, simmering

prefer to leave the skin on for a crisp, flavorful contrast to the flesh, especially if you are grilling or pan searing the fish.

Oysters, clams, and mussels are sold live by the dozen or by weight. Lobsters and crab are sold live by the pound, as well as frozen in the shell or as cooked meat, pasteurized and tinned or frozen. Shrimp is sold according to a system known as "count" that identifies the size by counting the number of shrimp in a pound; it is generally frozen before sale. Many larger markets also offer live lobster or crab which they will cook to order.

Cooking Vegetables

The chart at left shows the best cooking methods for different types of vegetables, along with guidelines when shopping for produce. Vegetables can be the centerpiece of a meal or can be used to complement meals featuring meat, fish, or poultry.

As soon as any vegetable is harvested it begins to undergo significant changes. The more delicate the vegetable, the more dramatic the change. Sweet corn and peas, for instance, begin converting sugars into starch, giving over-the-hill corn and peas a telltale sticky texture and pasty taste. When you consider the time that it takes to get foods from the field to the market, you can see why it is best to shop frequently for vegetables, keep them refrigerated, and cook them within a few days. At some times of the year you may find that frozen vegetables—typically processed right in the field upon harvesting—are a better alternative to less-than-ripe fresh produce. Peas, spinach, and corn are good examples.

Each vegetable has distinct properties when it is properly cooked. The most reliable doneness tests for vegetables are taste and touch. Bite into a piece of the vegetable when it is raw, and then again at various points as it cooks. Notice the flavor and texture. If tasting the vegetable isn't practical, pierce it with a knife, fork, or skewer and gauge the resistance it gives. Consider the way you will be using the vegetable to determine the right degree of doneness. Most stand-alone vegetable dishes, regardless of cooking technique, turn out best when the vegetables are cooked just until tender. You should be able to bite into the vegetable easily, but it should still offer a slight resistance.

Stewed and braised vegetables should be fully cooked. Aim to cook vegetables for these dishes until they are completely tender but retain their shape and color. When you boil or steam vegetables for a purée, cook them until they almost fall apart on their own. At this point, they should be easy to push through a sieve or purée in a blender.

In some recipes, vegetables are blanched, not to cook them through but to set their colors, make them easier to peel, or to improve their flavor. Blanched vegetables are boiled very briefly, just long enough to cook the outermost layer, then submerged in cold water to stop the cooking process. The vegetable retains, for the most part, the texture it had when raw. Similarly, vegetables are sometimes boiled, steamed, or roasted to near doneness, then finished in a second step, sometimes using a different technique, such as grilling or sautéing. Boiling or cooking to near doneness is known as parboiling or parcooking.

Index

A Note on the Type

This book was set in the OpenType version of Adobe Warnock.
Begun as a personal typeface for the co-founder of Adobe Systems, John
Warnock, by noted type designer Robert Slimbach, the project gradually grew
to include an italic and multiple weights, and it was decided to release the
typeface to the general public. A full-featured modern composition family
designed for versatility in a variety of mediums and printing situations,
Warnock synergizes classically derived letterforms of old style types
with elements of transitional and modern type design.

Art direction and design by Kevin Hanek

Composition by Kevin Hanek and E.C. Graham

Printed in Singapore by Imago Worldwide Printing